*participating*
*all ways = listen vs*

# Models of the Eucharist *respond*

*listening / reflecting*
*vs.*
*actively participating*
*and getting BOC*

*3 + 6*

# Models of the Eucharist

*Kevin W. Irwin*

PAULIST PRESS
New York/Mahwah, N.J.

Cover design by Cynthia Dunne

Book design by Celine Allen

Library of Congress Cataloging-in-Publication Data

Irwin, Kevin W.
  Models of the Eucharist / Kevin W. Irwin.
    p.  cm.
  Includes bibliographical references and index.
  ISBN 0-8091-4332-1 (alk. paper)
  1. Mass.  2. Catholic Church—Doctrines.  I. Title

  BX2230.3.I79 2005
  234'.163—dc22

                                          2004027313

Published by Paulist Press
997 Macarthur Boulevard
Mahwah, New Jersey, 07430

www.paulistpress.com

Printed and bound in the United States of America

*To the Memory of Walter J. Schmitz, S.S.*

# CONTENTS

## PART THREE

# PREFACE

I first met Kevin Irwin in the sacristy, prior to a Mass of Christian Burial for the father of a seminary classmate of mine. He was directing my confrere's dissertation at the time at The Catholic University of America and had driven to Philadelphia from Washington that morning. I remember being very impressed by this professor's dedication to and support for his doctoral student. Talk about "modeling the Eucharist"! Little did I realize then that not only would our paths cross again at CUA but also that, a little over ten years to the day of our initial meeting, I would be writing the preface to his book. Life takes us in mysterious directions, to be sure.

In a sense, Monsignor Irwin's latest book, *Models of the Eucharist*, is precisely about several mysterious paths to life, ten to be exact. Although each one of these "models" reveals something different in our theological approach to "the source and summit of the Christian life" (*Lumen Gentium*, n. 11), there is an intrinsic pastoral connection each to the other that serves to create a unifying dynamism that draws us ever deeper into the mystery of Christ's life and love for us and that, through the Eucharist we celebrate, moves us to live for and love others in that same mysterious, sacrificial way, "Do this in memory of me."

On the one hand, as Irwin writes, the Eucharist is complete in itself, a "real, living actualization of all that Christ accomplished" for us. On the other hand, the Eucharist is unfinished, promising what

Christ "will accomplish for us and our salvation." In that sense, the
Eucharist embodies the "already but not yet" tension that is the kingdom of God in our midst, both the "end" and the "means" that
change and transform human life.

Irwin's work is particularly timely, following on the heels of Pope
John Paul II's April 17, 2003 encyclical *Ecclesia de Eucharistia*. His
writing responds to the Holy Father's hope expressed so clearly at the
beginning of his letter, "that the Eucharist will continue to shine
forth in all its radiant mystery" (*Introduction*, n. 9). That radiance is
reflected in each of the ten models that attempt to grasp the breadth
of eucharistic theology, in itself a timeless spiritual enterprise.

As we progress through the chapters of this book, the author's
methodology introduces us to "aspects of what the Eucharistic liturgy
*says* and *does*." Monsignor Irwin explains that "in saying words, the
liturgy does something; in doing something the liturgy also says something." He begins each chapter with a familiar phrase drawn from
some liturgical text that frames his description of each model, identified for the purpose of helping us "to put nothing less than life into
perspective"—human life, spiritual life, Christian life—transformed
and redeemed by "the perspective of Christ's dying and rising." There
is no one preference among these models of the Eucharist that Irwin
advocates above the others. The true test of the efficacy of one, he
insists, indeed, the credibility and efficacy of all ten, is the way in which
the Eucharist changes and shapes the lives of those who celebrate.
Praying (*lex orandi*) and believing (*lex credendi*) find their ultimate
authentication in truly Christian living (*lex vivendi*). "The Eucharist,"
he observes, "is integral to and integrating of the Christian life." When
that process occurs in and through the Eucharist, an internal logic and
a deeper truth are revealed in terms of a "spirituality" that takes
"responsibility for belonging to others in the church, sharing their concerns, bearing others' burdens and washing each other's feet."

What first impressed me about Kevin Irwin in that Philadelphia
sacristy ten years ago was his willingness to do just that. I am quite
sure that this accomplished theologian had myriad other commitments and plans that could have understandably excused him from
being present at a funeral for his student's father that late May morning in 1993. He chose to celebrate the Eucharist and, in so doing, to
bear witness to the dying and rising of the Lord at a time when his

grieving student needed more than intricate theological analysis. His writing communicates clearly and convincingly because Irwin is a man, a priest, and a scholar who prays, believes, and lives his subject matter in the church, with the church, and for the church.

Monsignor Irwin holds an endowed Chair in Liturgical Studies in the School of Theology and Religious Studies of The Catholic University of America, named for another accomplished CUA professor, the late Monsignor Walter J. Schmitz, S.S. Their teaching and writings have done much over the years to distinguish this venerable academic institution, established by the American hierarchy in 1887 to be the place where the church in our country does its thinking. As president of CUA, I want to express my gratitude to Monsignor Irwin and to all who continue make this "community of scholars" a vibrant center of learning, faithful to Christ and the church, through what they teach and write and, most especially, through the way in which they celebrate and live their lives "in memory of Him."

> Very Reverend David M. O'Connell, C.M.
> President
> The Catholic University of America
> Washington, DC

# INTRODUCTION

The purpose of this book is to reflect on the jewel in the crown of Catholicism—the celebration of the Eucharist. Simply put, my concern is to help to explore and explain (as much as is humanly possible!) what happens when Mass is celebrated and what our central act of worship means in terms of Catholic belief and in living the Christian life. This book is meant to be theological, pastoral, and current. In essence it is concerned with issues about the Eucharist that face us today, some four decades after the truly historic and unprecedented revisions that took place in our liturgy after the Second Vatican Council. Some of these concerns are the result of unforeseen developments about the Eucharist resulting from other factors, for example the decline in numbers of clergy, which has led in some places (in our country as well as in others) to Sunday celebrations without the Mass. Other concerns arise from a lack of proper catechesis about the Mass (e.g., doctrine of the real presence and eucharistic sacrifice) and (more generally) a keen desire to understand why and how the Eucharist is at the center of Catholic life.

In addition to being expressly theological, this book is also expressly pastoral in that it is a reflection on the lived life by the church as it enacts the Eucharist and seeks to live out what the Eucharist celebrates. The book is aimed at the audience of educated Catholics who seek a deeper appreciation of what the Eucharist is and who want to appropriate that understanding in the way they live their lives. It is

my hope that this book will be of particular interest to pastoral ministers, both those present and those in training, and the communities of
faith whom they serve.

Today Catholics are confronted with all kinds of statistics about the
Eucharist and engage in a number of practices regarding it. Often
enough, however, the terminology we use in surveys and conversations about the Eucharist may not be as precise as it could be. While
we often use them interchangeably, the terms "Eucharist," "Mass,"
"blessed sacrament," "holy communion," and "body and blood of
Christ" (among others) carry very precise meanings and should not be
used interchangeably—at least without making some distinctions
among them. Put somewhat differently, this is to say that the words
and phrases we use should be chosen as precisely as possible to reflect
the many facets of what this "mystery of faith" is all about. In Catholic theology, precision in words matters. This book is about using
words, names, and terms as precisely as possible simply because different terms reflect different emphases and shades of meaning about
the same reality. If in fact the Eucharist is the *jewel* in the crown of
Catholicism, trying to appreciate the different aspects, facets, and
contours of this jewel is well worth all the effort. Like any jewel with
many facets, it is best appreciated when light is shed upon it from various directions and then it is viewed from various angles. Such a
view—or *re*view—of the Eucharist is what this book is all about.

Throughout this book, *the dynamic character of the Eucharist* as
*event*, *action*, and *enactment* is at the heart of our considerations. This
means that throughout this book I will presume and use the actual
liturgy of the Mass as the primary point of reference, because this is
how and where the Eucharist *happens*. The dynamism of celebrating
the liturgy of the Eucharist is the heart of Catholicism.

The structure of the book requires a word of explanation. It is
obviously divided into three unequal parts. The first part deals with
some of the studies about what (American) Catholics believe about
the Eucharist, some contemporary practices, and the methodological
principles for understanding the Eucharist that undergird the rest of
the book. In essence, this first part concerns the way I will use *liturgical theology* as the theological heart of the book. Part 2 of the book is
its heart. It articulates ten intrinsically interrelated, complementary,
and mutually enriching models for understanding the Eucharist. What

is presented in these models is regarded as truly interdependent and not a buffet of ideas from which one can "pick and choose." The variety of models is meant to offer rich fare when taken together as an ensemble of insights and ideas. Throughout, my concern is not primarily with the protocols we follow to celebrate the Mass—that is, "how to." Instead, my main concern will always be what these rites and prayers have to "say" about the Eucharist—namely, "what does it mean?" in terms of belief in the Eucharist and our leading eucharistic lives. Therefore it will be no surprise that Part 3 of the book draws together the themes that come from articulating these ten models for the Eucharist as these relate to our spiritual lives.

The discussion questions and recommendations for reading at the end of each chapter may be used in a variety of settings (for example, adult education, mystagogy for the newly initiated, First Eucharist preparation classes, pastoral formation courses, etc.) or they may help to summarize what is contained in the chapter for personal reflection and appropriation. It would be helpful if readers could have the texts of the eucharistic liturgy close at hand. I will refer to them again and again. But these texts are not meant to be exhaustive in any way. To immerse ourselves in (all of) the prayers and actions of the Mass is *the most important way* of appreciating what the Eucharist is.

This book began as a lecture given at The Catholic University of America in spring 2001 (which lecture was subsequently published in *Origins* 31:3, May 31, 2001). The occasion for delivering the lecture was the establishment of the Walter J. Schmitz S.S. Chair in Liturgical Studies. I am honored to be the first holder of this endowed chair.

A native of Madison, Wisconsin, Msgr. Walter J. Schmitz served in various capacities at both Theological College (the seminary located at The Catholic University of America) and in the School of Theology at the University from 1935 until his retirement in 1986. During that time he also served as Master of Ceremonies for the archdioceses of Baltimore and Washington. He defended his doctoral dissertation in 1956 on the then recently revised rites of Holy Week. The thesis was popularized in two books: *Holy Week Manual for Priests* and *Sermon Instructions for Holy Week*. His compendium on the pre–Vatican II liturgy entitled *Liturgikon* served generations of clergy in guiding their celebration of the liturgical rites of the church. I was privileged to have known "Wally," since his last year of teaching was my first on the faculty at The Catholic University of America. He was a congenial, encouraging colleague to many during his tenure on the faculty. He remained so for me until his death in 1994.

Among his many friends in the Washington area are Ralph and Joan Wells of Potomac, Maryland. It was largely through their hard work and assistance that the Walter J. Schmitz Scholarship Fund was established in 1984. It was that same hard work as well as wise counsel given both to Msgr. Schmitz and to officials at The Catholic University of America that made it possible to establish an endowed chair in his honor. Therefore I wish to thank Ralph and Joan for all of this important work, past and continuing in the present, as well as their unfailing support and personal interest in my professional development.

Among the matters that were central to Msgr. Schmitz's appreciation of the sacred liturgy were his concern that we take seriously what we say and do in the celebration of the Mass, that we understand what is at stake as we do it, and that we live our lives in conformity with what we celebrate. Both prayer and belief shape how we look at and live the Christian life. For Msgr. Schmitz, a key to all of this was found in the celebration of the Eucharist. It is therefore both an honor and a privilege to dedicate this book to his memory.

I

# THE QUESTIONS:
## Eucharistic Polls, Practices, and Polarization

*"Taking part in the eucharistic sacrifice, the source and summit of the Christian life, [the priestly community] offer[s] the divine victim to God and themselves along with it."*
—Second Vatican Council, Constitution on the Church, n. 11

It probably seems strange to begin a book on ways of understanding the Eucharist by treating polls concerning Catholic belief about the Eucharist and contemporary eucharistic practices relating to "the mystery of faith." But I do so simply because all of these help to establish the contemporary context for this book. The purpose of this section is to sketch out the terrain that I judge indicates the need for a book such as this at this time. American Catholics have been polled about the Eucharist at least nine times in the last decade.[1]

While we can (and do) quibble about polls, there is some value in summarizing what certain of them reveal about what American Catholics think and say about the Eucharist. Hence, I shall begin this chapter by referring to a few representative polls, in particular the one conducted by *The New York Times*/CBS in May 1994, and to offer a summary of their results and some insights about what they mean.

With regard specifically to practices, I want to contextualize what I will say in this chapter about them (and some possible areas of tension regarding them) by recalling what I said in the Introduction, namely that my main focus in this book will be on the *celebration* of the Eucharist. However, from fairly early on in our tradition there have been quite legitimate uses of the eucharistic species outside of Mass—for example, to take communion to those unable to be present for the celebration of Mass. Because the species was reserved for distribution outside of Mass, it was logical that devotional practices would spring up whereby Christians could pray before the reserved sacrament.[2] As time evolved, one of these devotions to the consecrated bread was called exposition and benediction—taking the consecrated bread out of the place of reservation and placing it on the altar in either the ciborium (the vessel used to distribute the Eucharist) or the monstrance (a decorated metal vessel sometimes made of gold and containing a large consecrated host in the center). These practices are now termed the "worship of the Eucharist outside of Mass,"[3] a ritual given to us as part of the liturgical reforms of the Second Vatican Council. A recent addition to these devotions in many parishes, however, is "perpetual adoration of the Eucharist," the popularity of which in certain parts of the country is indisputable. In addition, because there are not sufficient priests to celebrate the Eucharist in all American parishes on Sundays, we have a rite presently called *Sunday Celebrations in the Absence of a Priest*[4] that contains the option of distributing communion without the celebration of Mass. These practices deserve discussion.

Regarding polarization, one need only recall the opening chapter in the recent book by Thomas Rausch, *Reconciling Faith and Reason*, entitled "A Divided Church," which begins with describing the way adjustments in liturgical language and practices have polarized and continue to polarize some communities in the American church today.[5] For Rausch, what ought to unite us—the liturgy—is apparently what more readily divides (at least some of) us. Then there is the question of polarizing rhetoric about the Eucharist, heard today, for example in the question "Is it a sacrifice or a meal?" Both of these helpful and traditional terms—sacrifice and meal—among others, deserve better than to be placed over against each other.

For me, polls about the Eucharist and contemporary eucharistic practices and polarizations reflect the urgency of this project. Hence the words in the subtitle of this chapter, "polls, practices, and polarization."

## POLLS

Certainly the results of the 1994 *The New York Times*/CBS News Poll
have taken hold among many in the Catholic Church in America as a
clarion call to do something about Catholic belief in the Eucharist.[6]
Respondents were given two choices to the question about what happens at Mass: that the bread and wine "are changed into the body and
blood of Christ" or that they are "symbolic reminders of Christ."
Respondents were divided into age groups. Fifty one percent of those
over 65 chose the first option ("changed into the body and blood").
This option was chosen by 37 percent of those between 45 and 64, by
28 percent of those between 30 and 44, and by 29 percent of those
between 18 and 29. Not surprisingly, this data was greeted with consternation by many leaders in the American church. And obviously,
on the face of it, work had to be done.

However, in a letter to the editor of the *Times*, Dr. Peter Casarella of The Catholic University of America questioned the adequacy
of the wording of the poll's proposed responses about the Eucharist.
He asked: "[C]ould an informed Catholic really choose between these?
Real symbolic presence and the memorial meal are standard features of
traditional Catholic theology. Conversely, even the post-Reformation
doctrine of transubstantiated real presence does not state that the
outward form of the material elements is transformed into the physical body of Christ."[7] Much more will be said throughout the rest of
this book about a number of the phrases in Dr. Casarella's letter.
However, what is crucial to realize at this point is that the phrase
"changed into the body and blood of Christ" could easily be understood by respondents to mean that the Eucharist is equivalent to the
physical body of Christ—an assertion that has never been made in
orthodox Catholic magisterial teaching,[8] which has consistently preferred such terms as "real," "true," "substantial," and "corporeal."

The problem with asserting *physical* presence is that it is simply
too localized to the historical past when Jesus walked this earth and
too limited to the physical features of the God-Man historical Jesus.
Rather, theologians and those who drafted the church's magisterial
teachings were concerned to use words that would reflect the breadth
and depth of Christ's true, real, corporeal presence in the manner

proper to sacraments. When such terms as "true," "real," and "corporeal" modify Christ's *presence* in the Eucharist (admitting that "presence" itself needs to be supplemented by other terms, e.g., "sacrifice," to describe the Eucharist), then there is the opportunity to reflect on how in the Eucharist we are drawn into the fullness of the mystery that is Christ—preexistent with the Father, incarnated on this earth as the Word made flesh, whose paschal mystery is the unique source and cause of our salvation and whose second coming will take place at the end of time to bring time to an end and unite us with the Father for all eternity.

The fullness of the mystery of Christ is so enormous as to confound our minds and hearts. And yet, it is precisely through the celebration of the Eucharist that we are drawn into and made sharers in the fullness of the life of God through Christ. Hence the importance of using language that transcends the parameters of any particular time and space to describe the Eucharist. The Eucharist draws our minds, our hearts, and all our lives into a real, living actualization of all that Christ accomplished and will accomplish for us and our salvation.

All this comes to bear on the words we use about the Eucharist and the precise meanings that individual terms carry. The point I wish to make about the *Times* poll is that the phrasing of both the questions and the proposed answers deserves attention, evaluation, and critique.

The data from a more recent poll about eucharistic belief among those between the ages of twenty and thirty-nine is summarized in the book *Young Adult Catholics*.[9] It reveals a particularly strong fascination in this age group with sacramentality as an appreciable characteristic of Roman Catholicism. The poll asserts that the chief characteristics of Catholicism are not diminished among these young adults, even though the ability to articulate what the characteristics (e.g., the doctrine of the real presence) mean is sometimes unclear or unfocused. The authors observe that "regarding the distinctive Catholic understanding of the Mass, our sample [of respondents] have a stronger belief in the real presence than indicated in other polls." In fact 87 percent of the non-Latinos and 96 percent of the Latinos surveyed agreed with the statement "in the Mass the bread and wine actually become the body and blood of Christ." In addition, what is of interest is that what was positive about their experience of liturgy was homilies, music, and a vibrant sense of community. They rated the liturgy negatively when it was "boring," "mechanical," or "unwelcoming."

Clearly what is important is the way polls are worded.[10] In his evaluation of the polls conducted about the Eucharist in the past decade, James Davidson argues that results are better (that is more able to be interpreted as an accurate reflection of what people actually believe) when respondents are provided with succinct responses in terms that are theologically precise and accurate. He offers two hypotheses: (1) that there has been some decline in belief in the real presence of Christ in the Eucharist—"Steps [to be taken to address this] might include changes in the way priests, religious, and lay leaders present the Real Presence to the laity"[11] and (2) that most recent research shows that a majority of Catholics still agree with the church's teaching that the bread and wine actually become the body and blood of Christ. A majority also believe that the real presence is closer to the core of the Catholic faith than many other church teachings.

For our purposes it is interesting to note that in these polls terms and phrases such as "real presence," "the body and blood of Christ," "Eucharist" and "Mass" are all used, but that they are used largely interchangeably. In fact, however, each deserves its own (more) precise definition, description, and elaboration. That each carries its own unique emphasis and nuance is important to realize and to underscore, especially in a book such as this. Part of our intention throughout this book will be to make such distinctions as we elaborate on the many facets of what the Eucharist is and does. And this will be done with an eye toward seeing all of these ways of looking at the Eucharist in relation to each other.

## PRACTICES

*Mass Attendance.* The first glaring issue about practices concerns attendance at Sunday Mass. While exact numbers are hard to determine, recent figures from the National Opinion Research Center (as of this writing in 2004) indicate that 30 percent of American Catholic respondents said that they attend Mass weekly and that 40 percent responded that they attend (at least) once a month. The survey *Young Adult Catholics* (published in 2001) reports that for those between the

ages of twenty and thirty-nine weekly attendance in the United States
is 31 percent. Statistics for other countries also vary, but almost all
indicate a decline in Sunday Mass attendance. Clearly among some
ethnic groups here in the United States the practice of attending
Mass on Sundays has not been a high priority; conversely, among
other groups (e.g., the Irish) it traditionally has been. It was observed
that one of the reasons why Pope John Paul II issued *Dies Domini*
("On the Day of the Lord") in 1998 on the theology of Sunday and
the celebration of Eucharist on Sunday was to address the contemporary decline in Mass attendance.

The central—not to say pivotal—theological point to be made
here is that if the celebration of the Eucharist is at the heart of church
life then we need to face the fact that many who regard themselves as
Catholics choose not to celebrate Sunday Mass. In doing so they are
really choosing to distance themselves from the Catholic faith. One
of the major dilemmas pastoral ministers face is that of nonpracticing
Catholics who present themselves or their children for sacraments.
Often enough in preparation programs for sacraments these same
ministers find themselves dealing with issues of church belonging, literacy about the faith, and (lack of) knowledge of church teaching and
the liturgy. Theoretically one should be able to presume commitment
to church belonging and a rudimentary knowledge of the faith and its
practice among those who approach the church for sacraments. Para-
doxically, for at least some who present themselves for sacraments,
these are absent. Thus preparation programs for sacraments become
instances of evangelization and basic catechesis.

***Eucharistic Devotions.*** I noted above that devotion to the eucharistic
species has marked much of Catholicism's devotional practice. Whether
or not exposition and adoration were regarded as "liturgical" before the
contemporary liturgical reforms from Vatican II was matter for some
debate, with most arguing that they were not. After Vatican II this
answer is less clear, since we now have an official ritual for the "worship
of the Eucharist outside of Mass."[12]

This rite repeatedly asserts theologically and liturgically that eucharistic devotion derives from and directly relates to the celebration of the
Eucharist. That these devotions should (now) contain scripture readings, psalms, and prayers is clear. In this way the (new) ritual follows the

structure of all post–Vatican II liturgical rites—particularly in its inclusion of the Liturgy of the Word. In addition, the first option noted for the way one exposes the species for adoration is the ciborium, which is the vessel that is used for communion distribution at Mass.[13] This seemingly minor rubrical suggestion in fact contains rich theology. The vessels we use for the Mass can be the same vessels we use for devotion to the Eucharist outside of its celebration. This is what happens on Holy Thursday night after the Evening Mass of the Lord's Supper. The Eucharist that is carried in procession and placed in the repository is contained in a vessel used for communion distribution, not in a monstrance. This is an example of how the way in which one carries out the liturgy of the Roman rite bears important theological meanings. Using the same vessel underscores the intrinsic relationship between the celebration of Mass and eucharistic adoration. Using this practice for eucharistic adoration would highlight the liturgical principle that undergirds the worship of the Eucharist outside of Mass—namely that "the celebration of the eucharist in the sacrifice of the Mass . . . is truly the origin and goal of the worship which is shown to the eucharist outside Mass."[14]

What is fascinating today, however, is that some participants deliberately opt for a rite that goes against these prescriptions, choosing only to be silent before the monstrance—the very practice the present rite was intended to redirect. In addition, the phenomenon of "perpetual adoration of the Eucharist" has often enough evolved in ways not envisioned by such liturgical norms.

The theological point to be made here is that for some people devotions are (or at least seem to be) more important for their personal (individual) prayer life than the celebration of the Eucharist is. There are even some for whom such devotions are a mark of true Catholic belief and practice. The liturgical issue here concerns the normativity of the post–Vatican II liturgical rites (including the norms for eucharistic worship outside of Mass), confidence in them, and a spirituality derived from them.

One would have hoped for a greater serenity and acceptance of the liturgical reforms overall. If in fact the celebration of the Eucharist is attended to with reverence and obvious care, then any devotions that derive from that kind of celebration of Mass (which is really presumed in the revised Order of Mass) can certainly be understood to draw out fuller and richer dimensions of what the celebration of Mass is and does. Observing the post–Vatican II prescribed rites for the worship of the Eucharist outside of Mass can go a long way toward ensuring that the celebration of the Eucharist and such devotions are intrinsically connected. In addition, one's individual visiting of the reserved sacrament can certainly continue to be enhanced by praying over the wealth and variety of the scripture readings and prayers contained in this rite.

One happy result from praying over these readings (for one's own *lectio divina*) and the prayers in these rites would be to ensure that the theological balance and depth of the church's prayer tradition would be reflected in one's own individual, personal prayer. (For example, there would be a clear balance between praise and petition, between thanksgiving and intercession.) When left to one's own devices it is possible that less than theologically accurate and precise notions could flood one's mind and heart. To allow one's imagination to be shaped by the scripture readings and prayer forms can help to allow the formative nature of such prayer to be truly effective. (This is an offshoot of the thesis I will offer more fully in the next section of Part 1, "A Proposal.") If the church's liturgical prayer shapes the church's belief, then using the church's liturgical prayer as fully and as often as possible in one's personal prayer and *lectio divina* cannot but help to shape a proper theology and spirituality derived from both the enactment of the Eucharist and from eucharistic devotion.

This would also match the intention of Vatican II's Constitution on the Sacred Liturgy, which asserts that "popular devotions... are to be highly endorsed, provided they accord with the laws and norms of the Church... But these devotions should be so fashioned that they harmonize with the liturgical seasons, accord with the sacred liturgy, are in some way derived from it, and lead the people to it, since, in fact, the liturgy, by its very nature, far surpasses any of them" (n. 13).[15]

***Sunday Celebrations in the Absence of a Priest.*** In the last decade the churches in North America (both Canada and the United States) have seen the proliferation of Sunday worship services in places where no priests are available to celebrate the Eucharist. The Vatican Directory about this phenomenon (published in 1988 with the title *Directory for Sunday Celebrations in the Absence of a Priest*) was followed in Canada by the publication of *Sunday Celebration of the Word and Hours*. In the United States the ritual's title *Sunday Celebrations in the Absence of a Priest* obviously follows the Vatican lead and emphasizes that what is normative is the enactment of the eucharistic liturgy ("the sacrifice of the Mass") on Sundays presided over by a priest or bishop. In the absence of a priest, the Sunday assembly is led in a service of the word (i.e., the regular Liturgy of the Word for that Sunday) or a celebration of morning or evening prayer (from the Liturgy of the Hours) with the scripture readings of that Sunday. Most often this is followed by the distribution of communion. However this is not required and in some places communion is not distributed, simply because it would then "look like" Sunday Mass. That this kind of service is meant to be a stopgap and to be used rarely is clearly asserted in the accompanying introductory documentation. In his encyclical *On the Eucharist in Its Relationship to the Church* (n. 32) Pope John Paul II speaks about "the sacramental incompleteness of these celebrations." At the same time, in many areas (e.g., in the Pacific Northwest), it is clear that these Sunday celebrations have become the regular practice of many parishes in some dioceses. Whether or not the "incompleteness" of these celebrations is understood or appreciated by those who participate in them regularly is an open question.

Several issues are raised by this practice and by using these specific rituals. One issue concerns the distribution of communion from the reserved sacrament. Classically the rationale for reserving the eucharistic species is for communion to the sick (including viaticum) and (then) adoration. Presently in pastoral practice a third motive exists for reservation—Sunday distribution in the absence of a priest. Among others, the leadership of the Federation of Diocesan Liturgical Commissions (FDLC) has raised the issue of the extent to which this Sunday celebration in the absence of a priest (SCAP) ritual is perceived to be any different from the ritual for the celebration of the Mass itself. That there is even a question about perception is confounding. Clearly the action of the church in the celebration of the Eucharist is qualitatively different from SCAP. Yet, when the eucharistic prayer is not missed and distribution of hosts from the tabernacle is normative for both the celebration of Mass and the SCAP ritual, then the very heart of what Eucharist is and means is in jeopardy. Apparently there is no little confusion about distinguishing this rite from the Mass.

Furthermore, the practice of communion distribution with hosts taken only from the tabernacle also causes concern. If people do not perceive any difference between receiving from the species consecrated at Mass and receiving from hosts taken from the tabernacle then there is a theological problem that goes back to the eighteenth century. It was in 1742 when Pope Benedict XIV asked priests to distribute communion from hosts consecrated at the Mass being celebrated, not from hosts in the tabernacle. His rationale was as follows. At the Council of Trent the magisterium defended and elaborated on the presence of Christ in the Eucharist and the sacrificial nature of the Eucharist (more on this below in Part 2, Models Eight and Nine specifically). These two assertions became the twin poles of orthodox Catholic belief after the Reformation. However, the pope argued, if only the priest received communion at the enactment of the sacrifice of the Mass and the laity received only from the reserved sacrament, then laypeople might come to separate in their minds what should not be separated—namely sacrifice from sacrament. Receiving communion from the species consecrated at that very Mass would help to avoid such a separation. (This admonition has been in the papal and other aspects of the magisterium since.)

As of this writing, the U.S. Bishops' Committee on the Liturgy is addressing the issue of the structure of SCAP celebrations. It is likely that at least some aspects of the ritual will change. What is unlikely to change in the near term, however, is the phenomenon that many parishes will use such accommodated rituals because of the absence of ordained priests as pastors to preside at Sunday Eucharist.

## POLARIZATION

*Use of the Tridentine Mass.* While the Mass as promulgated by Pope Paul VI in 1970 remains the norm for liturgical practice in the whole church, there are some places where Mass today is celebrated according to the ritual that was approved for use after the Council of Trent. Sometimes this can cause confusion. Not surprisingly, people wonder which Mass is right in terms of language, texts, and gestures (both for the priest and the assembly). In fact, while the new "Order of Mass" decreed by Pope Paul VI is normally celebrated in the vernacular, it can be celebrated in Latin. This means that the distinguishing characteristic of the Tridentine Mass is not that it is in Latin, but rather its rites and prayers.[16] For our purposes in this book, the Mass approved by Pope Paul VI will be the basis for our theological description of the Eucharist. Some prayers and rites have been changed from those of the Tridentine Mass, often with a view to make clear(er) the theological meaning of those prayers and rites.

For example, Pope John Paul II notes in his encyclical on the Eucharist (n. 12) that in the Mass we repeat the words of Jesus, who "did not merely say 'this is my body,' 'this is my blood,' but went on to add 'which is given for you,' [and] 'which is poured out for you,'" words that expressed the "sacrificial meaning of the Eucharist." Here the pope does two things. First he underscores that there was a change from the Tridentine Mass in which the priest said "this is my body" (*hoc est enim corpus meum*) and he indicates that, despite the criticisms of some that the "new Mass" eliminates the sacrificial element of the Eucharist, in point of fact it is the new Order of Mass from Paul VI that contains this more explicit reference to sacrifice. Second, what the pope does here is to make a theological argument from the text of the new Order of Mass, not the Tridentine wording. This follows the presumption that from 1970 on the new Order of Mass approved by Paul VI is liturgically and theologically normative for the Catholic Church. In discussing all the models that follow, I will use the same new Order of Mass as the base and benchmark for arguing the value of many ways of looking at the Eucharist.

But there is a deeper issue as to why certain groups in the church have been allowed to celebrate the Tridentine Mass. It concerns the theology of the church, specifically the theology of church unity. Part of the issue has to do with those who found themselves unable to adjust to the celebration of the Mass of Paul VI. Another part has to do with the followers of Archbishop Lefevbre who were excommunicated from the Catholic Church. In both cases Pope John Paul II has been very concerned about the unity of the whole church, and the disunity caused by some insisting (without permission) on celebrating the Tridentine Mass. For these ecclesial reasons, both in 1984 and

1988 documents were published to accommodate such disaffected people. The first (1984) was from the Congregation for Divine Worship.[17] It indicated that the diocesan bishop may allow the use of the Tridentine Mass for those who had remained attached to it. But in allowing this, the Congregation asserted that the priest and people involved in such celebrations must "have no ties with those who impugn the lawfulness and doctrinal soundness of the Roman Missal promulgated in 1970 by Pope Paul VI."

The second document (in 1988) is from the pope himself. Its very title—*Ecclesia Dei*, "The Church of God"—indicates that the main concern is indeed church unity, not the rite for the Mass. The pope addresses "those Catholic faithful who feel attached to some previous liturgical and disciplinary forms of the Latin tradition," and he indicates his "will to facilitate their ecclesial communion by means of the necessary measures to guarantee respect for their rightful aspirations."[18]

The pope ordered the establishment of a commission tasked with finding ways to reconcile anyone "until now linked in various ways to the society founded by Archbishop Lefebvre who may wish to remain united to the successor of Peter in the Catholic Church while preserving their spiritual and liturgical traditions..." He called for "a wide and generous application of the directives already issued some time ago [1984] by the Apostolic See for the use of the Roman Missal according to the typical edition of 1962."[19]

Again, what is paramount for the pope and the Vatican in these texts is the unity of the church. What is also clear in these texts is that the Missal as approved by Pope Paul VI should not be regarded as being in any way not orthodox. Therefore, any rhetoric that the two ways of celebrating Mass are equal or that it makes no difference which rite for Mass is followed is simply not true. Pastoral concessions are made to help certain specific groups of people.

A pastoral difficulty arises, however, when younger people (who were never attached to the Tridentine Mass and could have had no problem "adjusting" to the Mass of Pope Paul VI because in fact they had not been alive when the Tridentine Mass was celebrated) seek out the Tridentine Mass for Sunday worship. This is where a pastoral accommodation for a certain group can be abused in favor of what some feel is better for them. As will be clear throughout this book, the celebration of the church's liturgy is less about what individuals "feel" than it is about celebrating the Eucharist correctly according to the words and rites that the church judges to be theologically normative and precise. It is about thinking and acting in accord with what we say and do in celebrating the Mass.

As we become accustomed to what liturgical texts "say" and become more familiar with hearing them in ever new ways, since they are proclaimed and sung aloud in the vernacular, we are in a very advantageous position today that allows the liturgy to shape how we understand what we believe simply because what we pray liturgically shapes that belief. Our catechetical programs, catechumenal structures, and experiences of mystagogy can only be the richer because of the vernacular and because of the theological precision found in the Missal of Pope Paul VI. We hope that what we say and do liturgically will have an impact on the beliefs and faith lives of all Catholics.

***Strained Rhetoric.*** At times in the contemporary climate there is a "sound bite" mentality that often looks for theological truth in succinct phrases or terms that at the same time caricatures other terms. I call this the "either...or" mentality. With regard to the Eucharist, we hear terms placed in opposition where they should be placed in juxtaposition. Examples include "table or altar," "sacrament or sacrifice," "holy meal or most blessed sacrament," etc. My own sense is that it is far better to use rhetoric that is more truly inclusive and Catholic, that is, a rhetoric that is "both...and."

Examples of the use of such rhetoric in the contemporary context can be found in the *Catechism of the Catholic Church*, which employs a large number and wide variety of categories to describe the Eucharist. These include assembly *(synaxis)*, action of thanksgiving, breaking of bread, memorial, holy sacrifice, holy and divine liturgy, holy communion and holy Mass.[20] Other categories for understanding the Eucharist drawn from the liturgy and our tradition include food for the journey (viaticum), holy gifts for holy people, holy banquet, eschatological meal, and the body of Christ. As will become clear, variations on a number of these will be used in this book. The intention is to offer a number of complementary terms in order to sustain a "both...and" "Catholic" vision of the Eucharist. (By "Catholic" here and throughout this book I mean a theology that reflects the theological and liturgical premises that can be shared by other Christian churches, especially those with a decided "liturgical" tradition.)

At the same time, I would not want this to be perceived as implying that "any and every" term is useful. The very fact that Catholicism is a theological tradition (as opposed to a fundamentalist religious tradition) and that it espouses a body of magisterial teaching that corrects errors indicates the continued need for refining terminology and for offering clarification of the tenets and practices of our faith. In the end we must realize that we are dealing with what is ultimately incomprehensible—the reality of God and the mystery of the Eucharist. In the Catholic Church we should always strive to be as expansive as possible in our rhetoric and theology when it comes to as confounding and expansive a mystery as the Eucharist. At the same time, we also (obviously) need to be as correct as possible in terms of what we say about and do in the Eucharist. That it will ever be totally adequate or completely correct is hard to imagine. That it can (and should) always be less inadequate is a very legitimate theological goal.

By its very nature and as reflected in its history, the Catholic faith tradition places great value on theology. As noted above, Catholicism is a theological—not a fundamentalist, literalist, or romanticist— tradition. In a real sense, to assert things this way makes the word "development" redundant. By its nature Catholic theology develops. The basis for any contemporary articulation of beliefs is scripture, liturgy, and the work of theologians and teachers as well as the magisterium. This is to suggest that Catholicism is a "traditional" religion (is there a religion that is not?) in which we must hand over to the present and the next generation what we ourselves have derived from those who have preceded us in the faith (as biblical authors, theologians, and the church's official teachers). At the same time the challenge to the church in any and every age is to articulate what it believes based on these foundations in such ways that what we believe is reflected in appropriate language, idiom, and system to suit the needs for contemporary believers.

Catholicism always strives to rephrase and reframe beliefs derived from the sources of our tradition in ever fresh and new ways. Simply to repeat the words, phrases, and theological systems of a former age could in fact mar the integrity and depth of the very faith we wish to preserve and pass on because over time words and language evolve, sometimes to the point of changing their meanings. One thinks here of the rich, substantial meaning originally conveyed for much of Catholicism's existence by the term "symbol" and the way "symbol" or "symbolic" is used today to refer to that which is not real or merely an empty gesture. Nothing could be further from the way "symbol" was classically used in our tradition to refer to the fact that signs and symbols in liturgy contain and reflect what is really the most "real" thing imaginable—God working among us through Christ dead, risen, and to come again.

Therefore, simply to repeat the words of the magisterium derived from one period in the church's history is no guarantee of doctrinal orthodoxy in another. The histories of the christological and trinitarian doctrines are classic examples of ways in which the church responded to new contexts as language and philosophies changed and as words canonized in one era or context took on new meanings in another. We see this also in the development of the church's teaching on sacraments.[21]

In the next section I will turn to the task of sketching out the principles that will guide the articulation of Catholic belief in the Eucharist throughout the rest of this book. It makes no claim to completeness. However it does claim to be traditional, classical, and probing from within Catholic tradition. And its chief source is the celebration of the eucharistic liturgy.

# A PROPOSAL:

## Principles for a Liturgical Theology of the Eucharist

*"The law of prayer establishes the law of belief."*
—*Prosper of Aquitaine*

The basic premise for the models of the Eucharist to be developed in this book is that the enactment of the Eucharist is theologically, liturgically, and spiritually normative for the life of the church and for our understanding of what the Eucharist is, does, and means. Two main principles govern what follows. The first is that I want to develop a theology derived from the liturgy (both rites and prayers) that respects the breadth of the Catholic tradition's teaching about the Eucharist and its experience of the Eucharist, especially as it is expressed in the rites and prayers of the present reformed liturgy in the Catholic Church. The second is that offering a number of "models" is the best way to grasp the breadth of eucharistic teaching and practice.

### LITURGICAL-SACRAMENTAL THEOLOGY

Among other ways of looking at it, in my estimation sacramental theology may be understood to be the systematic study of the sacraments

based on reflection on the liturgical celebration of these rites throughout history, on the insights of theologians and other teachers about
them in light of the magisterium, throughout the breadth and length of
what is the Catholic tradition.[1] At given historical periods certain theological points came to be emphasized (sometimes for polemical reasons) and assertions of the magisterium clarified issues of conflict.
Conventional theological understanding of the sacraments did not
always see the celebration of the liturgy and the theology of the sacraments as intrinsically interrelated. In fact, it was common that the study
of liturgy was separated from the study of sacramental theology (especially from the medieval period through the modern era). When this
was the custom, *liturgy* concerned the celebration of the sacraments
(texts and rubrics); *sacramental theology* concerned the theological understanding of what sacraments are. This separation between "liturgy" and
"sacramental theology" was reflected in the post-Tridentine liturgical
rituals and manuals of theology; the former were rubrically and textu-
ally precise (requiring strict conformity) while the latter were most
often neo-Scholastic treatises largely devoted to issues that were con-
troversial at the time of the Reformation and Trent (such as proving
the number of seven sacraments from scripture, the nature of causality,
the right intention of the minister, etc.).

However, in the present several factors have converged so that
we can reunite these fields and view sacramental theology as a craft
that should reflect on the liturgical rites of the church as an anchor
for elaborating on, exploring, and trying to describe what sacraments
are and do (for our purposes here specifically, what the Eucharist is
and does). The fact that today sacraments are commonly celebrated
in the vernacular and that therefore their texts are readily compre-
hended offers the liturgical assembly a common set of texts to shape
and form their understanding of what sacraments are and do. Furthermore, we now use liturgical rites that were revised after Vatican
II on the basis of serious historical scholarship as well as prudent
pastoral judgments about what rites would serve the church's liturgical prayer. This is to say that in what follows we presume the present
revised liturgy to contain a wealth of theological insight that may
well not have been as readily found in the pre–Vatican II liturgical
books and rites. When I use the term "normative" to refer to the
present post–Vatican II rites, what I mean is that what is contained in

the post–Vatican II liturgical rituals is to be presumed to be what the whole church uses to celebrate the mysteries of faith and that what is contained in these rituals can be relied upon to be theologically orthodox and to provide the protocols about what to follow when enacting them.

At issue is the theological meaning of what we say and do—what is spoken and enacted—in the liturgy. Theological shorthand often calls this the *lex orandi*, the "law of prayer," which influences the *lex credendi*, "the law of belief," meaning what the church believes (in general, although our concern here is obviously with the Eucharist). While some elements of the Eucharist have remained constant throughout history and have not changed (for example, the proclamation of the eucharistic prayer), the postconciliar liturgical reform often offers us more than one text to use when celebrating the liturgy. In the case of the Eucharist this means that we have a number of eucharistic prayers to choose from in celebrating the liturgy, not just the single Roman Canon that has been in use from the time of St. Ambrose on. Hence a theology derived from the liturgy needs to respect both the structure and content of this part of the Mass (often from a number of prayers), taking into consideration the different assertions that different eucharistic prayers make about the Eucharist, God, Christ, the church, salvation, etc. Another important issue that needs to be underscored in the present liturgical reform is the emphasis given to greater communal involvement in symbol, gesture, texts, and music as constitutive of sacramental liturgy. Hence a theology derived from the liturgy requires that we appreciate these liturgical, ritual actions as reflecting theological meanings.

Many of the present (post–Vatican II) liturgical rites have been revised on the basis of both historical models (e.g., from the patristic era) and the perceived need to incorporate into the revised rites one or another aspect of Catholic belief and practice which was not found in previous rites. For example, as will be described in Model Ten, one of the most important additions to the post–Vatican II eucharistic liturgy is the specific and explicit emphasis on the role of the Holy Spirit in the enactment of the liturgy as specified by certain parts of the eucharistic prayers, i.e., the *epicleses* (meaning prayers of invocation). This is an example of the way that the church's belief—the *lex credendi* (the church's "law of belief")—has influenced and clearly changed what is contained in the liturgical rites, or *lex orandi* ("law of prayer"). Obviously there is a clear relationship between *lex orandi* and *lex credendi*—between liturgy and theology. What is crucial in developing a *liturgical theology* of the Eucharist (or any sacrament, for that matter) is to appreciate the breadth and depth of what the revised liturgical rites say, do, and mean—especially theologically. For our purposes in this book, what is of central importance is respecting the liturgy in all its richness and deriving from it as integral and complete a theology of the Eucharist as possible.[2]

This confluence of factors relating to the reformed liturgy has influenced many contemporary sacramental theologians to favor the collapse of the division between liturgy and sacramental theology, with the liturgy thus recognized as a foundation for the theology of individual sacraments and for an appreciation of the dynamism of sacraments in general. Along with the revival of interest in liturgy as a theological source has been the revival of interest in certain of its component elements, among which are the word, prayers, symbol, ritual, and the arts.[3]

*Word.* Recent interest in the dynamism of the scriptural word concerns the way the proclamation of the scriptures functions in sacramental liturgy. When communities gather for sacraments, they gather to engage in acts of memory of the mighty deeds God has done in history and which God continues to do through the liturgy here and now for us and for our salvation. These liturgical acts specify how, when, and where God acted to save the chosen people in the past in saving history and acts in the present for us and for our salvation. The ritual of the liturgy composed of the proclamation of the scriptures, the proclamation of blessing prayers, and engagement with the symbols and gestures comprises the act of sacramental liturgy which is the event of our salvation and sanctification. Thus the restoration of the proclamation of the Liturgy of the Word to all sacramental rituals can help us to develop an understanding of any sacraments based in some way on these biblical proclamations. In effect, the God who acted in those original acts and stories of salvation acts now through that very proclamation to save, redeem, and sanctify us anew. Hence in what follows particular attention will be paid to scriptural texts that are used in the *Lectionary for Mass* to help to explain the scriptural background for the Eucharist. At times the way the Lectionary structures the scripture readings will be used to illustrate the theological points being made. (For example, the Old Testament readings from the Lenten Sunday Lectionary will be used in Model Five to describe the biblical foundations for the Eucharist as "Covenant Renewal.")

Seen from this perspective, the restoration of a Liturgy of the Word for each sacrament makes both a liturgical and a theological statement about the primacy of the word and the nature of sacramental engagement as requiring that the word be seen as foundational to all liturgical-sacramental activity. In addition, such an appreciation of the operation of the word in sacraments sustains how preaching can serve to apply that proclamation to today's congregations, with all our strengths and weaknesses. It also serves as an important link joining word and sacrament; otherwise, the two parts of one sacramental act can seem to be two separated entities. Thus an essential component of the *lex orandi* in sacramental liturgy is the proclamation of the scriptures.

**Prayers.** Closely allied with this understanding of scripture in the liturgy is an appreciation of how language in general functions in sacraments, and especially of how the language of prayers functions in the liturgy. Among other things, liturgical prayers are *evocative* in that they both engage and fascinate the imagination. They are also *effective* in the sense that when they are spoken something happens (consecration of things and persons). However, not all of the liturgy's prayers have the same use liturgically nor do they bear the same weight theologically. Hence it is important to distinguish centrally important prayers, such as prefaces, eucharistic prayers, and other "presidential" prayers such as the opening prayer, the prayer over the gifts, and the prayer after communion, from comments and instructions during the Mass (for example, at the introductory rite) or greetings ("The Lord be with you") and the dismissal admonitions ("The Mass is ended. Go in peace"). In what follows it will become clear that there is a certain hierarchy of liturgical texts. That hierarchy should be respected. In this book, greater weight will be given to those prayers that are regarded as more important and central than others for the liturgy, and thus more important theologically in order to understand what the Eucharist means.

According to the *General Instruction of the Roman Missal*[4] (GIRM, n. 78) "the center and summit of the entire celebration" of Mass is "the Eucharistic Prayer." Therefore, the contents of the eucharistic prayer will be given more weight theologically than what is said in other prayers of the Mass.

***Symbol.*** One of the more demonstrable characteristics of the present revised liturgy is the emphasis it places on the signs and symbols of the liturgy destined for symbolic engagement (that is, our participation in those symbols—our "taking part" in them and, through them, in God's mighty deeds of salvation). That this emphasis finds its way into contemporary theologies of the sacraments should therefore be most welcomed. What is of supreme importance theologically in this recovery is the characteristically Catholic view of creation that sees the mediation of the divine through created matter and human interaction. Symbolic actions in the liturgy involve and evoke many meanings and many levels of meaning. To engage in symbolic activity is to unleash a power that cannot be reduced to a single meaning.

The use of water, for example, evokes images of washing, cleansing, refreshment, purification, and an end of thirst (hence the continuance of life), as well as images of the uncontrollable force of storms, torrents, the realm of demons, and the place of drowning (hence the loss of life). Even though the sacramental use of water is accompanied by a blessing prayer recalling scriptural (mostly positive) images of water in salvation history, which are all brought to bear at this sacramental moment, nonetheless contradictory meanings will also be disclosed when water is used in the liturgy simply because such meanings are inherent in the use of this symbol.[5] What is crucial in any contemporary liturgical theology of the Eucharist is to respect the many meanings reflected in our taking and communicating in the consecrated bread and wine—dining, communion, participation, reconciliation, forgiveness, church unity, foretaste of future glory, mission, etc. By its nature, liturgical theology should reflect many concepts and ideas. It should be polyvalent, having many meanings. Hence the value, from our point of view, in a "models" approach to the Eucharist to reflect the manifold reality that is the Eucharist.

*Ritual.* Recent studies on ritual have produced a growing body of literature that emphasizes the nature of ritual as a stylized, repetitious, and familiar communal activity. In this perspective, Christian sacraments are appreciated as rituals that are essential for the Christian life because they mediate Christian identity in different (and some will argue in more traditional) ways than does intellectual assent to theological truths only. The effect of involvement in Christian sacramental ritual is communal and social cohesion and a reaffirmation of personal and communal identification with the Trinity, particularly through Christ in the church.

Sociological studies of initiation rituals, for example, demonstrate the enduring power of religious ritual and the importance of tactility in the use of symbols in ritual. Such studies also show the deep impact that certain rituals can have and continue to have on participants at events such as marriages and funerals. Just like symbols used in worship, the ritual actions that structure our Catholic eucharistic liturgy have many meanings and many nuances that need to be respected as intrinsic to a eucharistic theology to be derived from the liturgy.

Christian ritual is the means of perpetuating or actualizing (but not redoing or repeating) the saving event of Christ's paschal mystery (more on this in Model Four). As such it takes an event of the definitive past and makes it operative in a way that involves and incorporates people in the present. Sacraments do this specifically in ways that help to articulate times of the liturgical year and transition times in human life such as birth, marriage, and death. Here studies on rites of passage have been influential (at least to some degree) on sacramental theologians, chiefly in their appreciating the social and cross-cultural foundation of Catholic sacramental ritual. Particularly helpful has been the drawing of important parallels between rites of passage and adult initiation.

All of this is to suggest that in developing a liturgical theology of the Eucharist from the word, prayers, symbols, and rituals used in the liturgy we are presenting what is at once a traditional approach to this theology and a method for sacramental theology that takes liturgical rites so seriously as to make them the basis for what we say and believe about the Eucharist.

## LITURGICAL THEOLOGY OF THE EUCHARIST

To reflect on the liturgy of the Eucharist as a primary source for our theology of the Eucharist is to engage in a craft that is often called "liturgical theology." The classic adage in theological and liturgical circles is that "the rule of prayer establishes the rule of belief" *(lex orandi, lex credendi)*.[6] This theological adage is ascribed to a fifth-century document from Prosper of Aquitaine. In writing about those coming into the church through the rites of initiation at Easter, he noted that on Good Friday the whole church prayed for them in the general intercessions and asked that God's grace would come upon them. He argued that what this liturgical prayer said, namely that we need grace from God, was a proof that we do not "earn" salvation, we "receive" it from God through grace. Then he asserted that what we pray is what we believe—"the rule of prayer establishes the rule of belief." Theologically, he was concerned with fighting the heresy of Pelagianism (part of which is that we can work to earn our salvation). For Prosper, the fact that we pray for God's grace for those coming into the church is thus a demonstration of a decidedly anti-Pelagian appreciation of the way the Christian life works.

This insight about the rule of prayer and belief has come to be revived by a number of contemporary theologians and popes (e.g., Pius XI, Pius XII, and John Paul II) who have sought to emphasize that the liturgy—with its rites and prayers—contains important and rich theological insight.[7] In addition, one advantage of the post–Vatican II liturgical rites is that each of them contains an introduction,[8] the contents of which also deserve attention. These introductions or, in the case of the Mass, the GIRM, contain important theological information about the liturgy being celebrated and they describe the protocols to be followed. This is a complementary "source" for the kind of liturgical theology of the Eucharist we can develop today from the enacted liturgical rites themselves.

That the liturgy of the Eucharist can and should be approached
from a theological point of view is articulated in the GIRM 2002
when it says: "In this new Missal, then, the Church's prayer (*lex
orandi*) corresponds to her perennial rule of belief (*lex credendi*) by
which namely we are taught the Sacrifice of the Cross and its sacramental renewal in the Mass . . . are one and the same, differing only in
the manner of offering and that consequently the Mass is at once a
sacrifice of praise and thanksgiving, of propitiation and satisfaction"
(n. 2). Similarly, in referring to liturgical inculturation it adds that
when adapting the Roman liturgy to various cultures it is important
that "the faith may be passed on in its integrity, since the Church's
rule of prayer (*lex orandi*) corresponds to her rule of belief (*lex credendi*)" (n. 397).

Pastorally the truth articulated here was expressed in the PBS tele-
vision series (of a decade and a half ago) on Vatican II. Again and again
those interviewed stated that it was when the changes in the liturgy
took place that they realized that the decrees from the Second Vatican
Council had brought about real, concrete changes in the church—
among which was the way we pray the Eucharist together. In a real
sense there is no such thing as "just" a liturgical change. Among other
things, to change a rite is at once to change or adjust our notions of
God, of ourselves, of each other, of grace, of redemption, of the
church etc. For example, when the funeral rites were first changed in
pastoral practice in America, obvious ritual adjustments included
white, not black vestments, communal singing, not listening to a
soloist or an organist, and a much more hope-filled tone to the
preaching rather than an emphasis on judgment and the possibility of
condemnation. In hindsight, we may well say today that perhaps this
was too quick and simplistic a change. (One does wonder whether
what is said and done in some contemporary funeral liturgies do not
leave the impression that the deceased is not being prayed for but that
he or she is being canonized!) But what is clear is that, in post–Vatican
II funeral liturgies, images of a compassionate and benevolent God
and of a participating, caring community have come to be expected,
and legitimately so. At the same time, however, a careful comparison
of many of the liturgical texts formerly used at funerals and those that
are in the present Order for Christian Funerals shows that they are

remarkably similar. This is to say that certain practices (color of ves-
ture, choice of music to be sung) convey meanings that may not be so
precisely sustained in what the texts of the liturgical ritual have to say.
But ritual changes (of almost any kind) affect people on many levels—
emotional, psychological, spiritual, and, yes, theological. Similarly,
there is no such thing as "just" a ritual change.

In what follows I will be concerned with underscoring the normativity and value—theological, liturgical, and spiritual—of the liturgical reforms of Vatican II. But at the same time my main interest will
not be the external reforms themselves. My main interest will be what
these reformed texts and rites *say* and *mean theologically.* Principally I
am concerned with how these *reforms* serve church *renewal.* This is to
suggest that liturgical reforms are *means,* not *ends* in themselves. They
are important for the building up of the church, the body of Christ
on earth, so that the church can witness to and live the values of the
(paradoxical) kingdom of God on this earth.

Sometimes I wonder whether some of the rhetoric about and preoccupation with the externals of the contemporary liturgy is really
not misguided from the start. It is almost as though what happens in
our solemn assemblies is all that matters (that we get the "rite" right).
What we do in our solemn assemblies does matter, and conducting
rites carefully and reverently does indeed matter. But more emphasis
on the way liturgy shapes our view of reality, how it challenges us to
look at life from the perspective of Christ's dying and rising and our
dying and rising through, with, and in him is really the heart of the
matter. If this becomes our focus, then the liturgy can be put in
proper perspective, because one of its purposes is to enable us to put
nothing less than life into perspective. Liturgy is a means to the ever
elusive goal of church renewal, of communal self-transcendence, and
of becoming ever more committed witnesses to God's rule and kingdom in our world.

Because what our rituals say and do is very important—liturgically,
theologically, and spiritually—part of the post–Vatican II liturgical
revolution about the Mass has been to implement changes in the
Order of Mass that help bring out things that were judged as needing
reemphasis. Liturgical theology has to do with how the liturgy shapes
our understanding of what the liturgy itself is and does. This is not to

suggest, however, that liturgical theology is divorced from the rest of
Catholic theology and the magisterium. Rather, I see liturgical theol-
ogy as an essential part of the common teaching of the Catholic
Church.

Both Catholic liturgy and theology evolved over centuries. A
proper way to understand both the liturgical rites and the theological
assertions of any time and place is to locate those statements within
their original historical and cultural contexts. With regard to Catholic
theology about the Eucharist, what is very clear is that when certain
aspects of the Eucharist were doubted, or eclipsed, or ignored, it was
the role of theologians (such as St. Thomas Aquinas) and of the
church's official magisterium from church councils (such as the
Council of Trent and Vatican II) to shore up what was lacking and to
assert more clearly what had become ambiguous or even, in fact,
erroneous in common liturgical practice and church teaching.[9] In a
sense one can say that the church always refocuses and reshapes its
magisterial teaching about the Eucharist on the basis of contemporary challenges to orthodox belief. Further, one can also say that at
some particular periods of its life the church has reshaped and refo-
cused parts of the liturgical rite of the Mass in order to express more
clearly what it is we engage in at Mass. This is what happened after
Vatican II. Trying to draw out the theology derived from those shifts
remains a "work in progress."

When it comes to developing a theology of the Eucharist, it is
best to see magisterial statements

- in their historical context, in order to determine why certain
  things were emphasized at certain times and places

- in relation each other, in order to provide a "both...and" appreciation of church teachings in their totality rather than a "pick
  and choose" selective use of one teaching over another

- and in relation to the liturgy that was celebrated at the time in
  the church's life when those statements were crafted and defined,
  in order to see the extent to which liturgy and the magisterium
  reflected each other.

An appreciation of church teaching requires a synthesis so that
the fullness of the church's teaching can be understood and appropri-

ated. Magisterial teachings are crucial signposts and guides for correct belief. In the liturgical theology articulated in the rest of this book, the liturgy is viewed in relation to other sources of church teaching, especially the magisterium. Thus, in what follows, liturgical theology is not fundamentalistic in the sense that it excludes other sources of teaching. Rather, giving primacy to the liturgy allows other sources of teaching—for example, theologians and the magisterium—to be companions and dialogue partners in this enterprise.

In addition, in my own thinking I have always made an addition to the adage *lex orandi, lex credendi*—namely *lex vivendi*, that is, the law of (Christian) living.[10] This last aspect capsulizes another strong suit of Catholicism—namely *spirituality*. The contemporary interest in "spirituality" in America can only be enhanced by this kind of study of what the eucharistic liturgy says and means because it puts forth a truly Catholic vision of reality, of God, of liturgy, of the Eucharist, and of how we live our lives in "communion" with God and each other. One of my suspicions is that a lot of what passes for "spirituality" today is really too self-concerned and self-preoccupied to be real Christian spirituality. Much more of this will become obvious in the rest of the book. (In particular, the Conclusion will contain explicit application of these "models" of the Eucharist to Christian spirituality.)

One of the chief characteristics of Catholicism (in particular) is its emphasis on living the spiritual life. Especially notable is the variety of ways in which Catholic Christians have come to live out their spiritual lives with the guidance of a number of "schools" of spirituality. Among others, these include the monastic, the mendicant, and those inspired by apostolic communities (such as the Jesuits). What is clear in each of these "schools" is that the forms of prayer that characterize them always include the celebration of the liturgy, especially the Eucharist. And, in each of them, the prayer that is fostered must be reflected in the way one lives out one's Christianity in all of life. In what follows, "spirituality" is not to be identified with prayer or even the celebration of the liturgy. What characterizes Catholic spirituality in particular is that it concerns the way we view and live out our lives of faith with and among each other. The conversion that prayer and liturgy foster and sustain is meant to be lived in the way we live converted lives.

There are always consequences to prayer and to celebrating the Eucharist. One consequence is nothing less than living according to the gospel as the norm of faith and living out the paschal mystery we have enacted in the Eucharist. For our specific purposes in this book, the key Catholic insight is that the object of liturgy is not the liturgy; the object of liturgy is experiencing the paschal victory of Christ, enacted through the power of the Holy Spirit in and through the liturgy (of the Eucharist), and then living out that paschal mystery in the mystery of our own lives. The liturgy of the Eucharist is an essential and central part of our faith. But it is a means to an end. It is not an end in itself. Hence the importance of the essential third part of our premise, not just *lex orandi, lex credendi,* but also *lex vivendi.*

At the heart of developing a liturgical theology of the Eucharist is the *enactment* of the Eucharist in the Mass. This places the emphasis on the dynamic, event character of what occurs when Mass is celebrated. At the same time, I want to underscore the fact that the enactment of Eucharist is not the same as other "special events," or that it is an action of our own doing. As I will underscore throughout this book, the Mass is a ritual whose structure invites familiarity and participation. It is also an action both human and divine. For me, the Latin term *actio* captures this in a subtle way—it is about the doing of something, not the objectification of it. Liturgy is always about our doing something at God's gracious invitation and through God's continuing sustaining grace.

In what follows I will presume and underscore the role of liturgy as central, formative, and transformative. My concern is to help us look at the way we pray at the Eucharist, what the liturgy means and what it does (uniquely so). From my perspective, this places emphasis on the liturgy as a theological source, not to say norm for a Catholic theology of liturgy and sacraments. It is also to assert that reflection on the tradition and the present reformed liturgy opens important, sometimes quite new vistas for theological reflection, especially today, given the care that was involved in reforming the Tridentine liturgy and the normativity of the present liturgical reforms.

Just after the approval of the Constitution on the Sacred Liturgy at Vatican II, the French theologian-liturgist Louis Bouyer wrote the masterful study entitled *Eucharist* on the theology and spirituality of the eucharistic prayer.[11] The aim of the book was to uncover the meaning of the Eucharist from the structure and contents of the eucharistic prayer—prayers both from the past and in the present, from the East and from the West. Bouyer argued for the necessity of his study because he judged that from the Council of Trent onwards Catholics had been concerned with articulating a theology *about* the Eucharist, not a theology *of* the Eucharist. For Bouyer, what we pray in the eucharistic prayer is crucial for the theology of what the Eucharist is and means. Thus, a study of these prayers from liturgical tradition would yield a rich harvest of theological bounty. In Bouyer's language, a theology "about" Eucharist (principally after the Council of Trent) concerned real presence and sacrifice. A theology "of" the Eucharist, rather, would begin with the biblical and liturgical tradition of the theology of "blessing" God (from the Hebrew *berakah*) and of unpacking what terms such as "bless," "praise," "glorify," and "thank" mean when placed in their native context of a lyrical prayer derived from both the Jewish synagogue service and Jewish table prayers. This move in understanding the Eucharist, a move enunciated by Bouyer and others, was to have a great impact on the way contemporary theologians and pastors articulate a theology of the Eucharist today.

Some three decades later it is understandable that some scholars have criticized and amplified some of Bouyer's points. From my own perspective, I would want both to appropriate and to go beyond Bouyer's thesis about the eucharistic prayer to include a theology derived from the whole of the eucharistic rite. This is to say that I want to argue a liturgical theology from the whole eucharistic rite, specifically emphasizing all the other rites of the Mass, e.g., proclamation of the word, presenting gifts, their transformation, communion, etc., including the eucharistic prayer itself. In effect, what I aim to articulate is a theology *from* both the whole of the *lex orandi* of the liturgy and the insights provided by the church's magisterium on the Eucharist.[12]

I would argue that there is a great need for a clear exposition of what Catholics hold and teach about the Eucharist and that it is best met from a perspective that is *integral* (and thus truly "catholic"), that is *traditional* (and respects the historical evolution of the Catholic faith from the apostles, therefore "apostolic"), and that is *ever new* in the sense that the perennial challenge of the church in our—and in fact every—age is to articulate its beliefs in ever new "systems" that speak to the idioms, language, and mindset of different times and places. This is to say that a true Catholic understanding of the Eucharist must draw on the strength of the breadth and depth of our liturgical and theological tradition.

Such a theology does not seek merely to repeat what Catholics have said and held about the Eucharist. Rather, it seeks to articulate what Catholics hold and believe about the Eucharist in this day and age based on the living tradition of our faith expressed in a privileged and unique way in the liturgy of the Eucharist. For me this is what a liturgical theology of the Eucharist is all about. That this approach offers a plurality of ideas is to be presumed and encouraged. How this multiplicity evolves into something of a "system" with order and logic requires some methodological parameters. One particularly useful way to describe this is to locate these insights in a "models" approach to the Eucharist.

## MODELS OF THE EUCHARIST

In 1974, (Cardinal) Avery Dulles published his best selling book *Models of the Church*. I rely on his fundamental and foundational insight as I venture to articulate various "models" as ways to understand what the Eucharist is and does. In the Introduction to his book Dulles states: "The method of models is applicable to the whole of theology, and not simply to ecclesiology... The method of models, or types, I believe, can have great value in helping people to get beyond the limitations of their own particular outlook, and to enter into fruitful conversation with others having a fundamentally different mentality."[13] He also asserts (citing Paul Minear) that the "profuse mixing of metaphors... reflects not logical confusion but theological vitality."[14]

In endorsing this understanding of the way a "models" approach to theology should be used with regard to the Eucharist, I specifically want to go beyond the rhetoric of an "either... or" approach to church teaching that can characterize, not to say caricature, another approach to Catholic truth that might be equally valuable and valid. When "traditional" "Catholic" concepts about the Eucharist, such as real presence and sacrifice, are juxtaposed with equally traditional concepts about the Eucharist, such as sacrificial meal and foretaste of the totally "real" presence of Christ in the kingdom of heaven (among others), then a clarity of vision and an integral understanding of what the Eucharist is and means can result. My overriding concern here is that what can be regarded as truly Catholic components of eucharistic theology need to be placed in dynamic and mutually enriching relationships. A "models" approach is not meant to leave one with a "pick and choose" option. It is intended to offer a series of concepts which when taken together offer rich insight into the reality that is the Eucharist. The result is the kind of integral theology of the Eucharist I judge to be needed in the church today.

The image here is of a mosaic. No one color or shape of one kind of glass makes up a mosaic. It takes the juxtaposition of each and every piece to make a work of art. Different colors, shapes, and sizes of varied pieces are necessary for a mosaic to be a true and integral work of art. The same is true for sacramental theology derived from the liturgy. It is not monolithic. It is multivalent. It contains and reflects a number of mutually enriching meanings. This is especially true of eucharistic theology. When juxtaposed and assessed together, the models articulated in what follows are intended to explore (but never to explain fully!) what the Eucharist is and does as well as what it means in terms of how we view the Christian life and how we live out what we celebrate in our Christian lives. Often the very terms we use to describe the Eucharist were coined at a time and place in the church's life that were very different from our own. Merely to repeat the terms does not guarantee doctrinal orthodoxy. What we need to do is to appropriate what they meant then and mean today. But, in addition, we need to view the terms in relation to other terms and emphases that have come down to us and been regarded as important to use in order to preserve the integrity of orthodox belief in the Eucharist.

My thesis here is simple: sustaining a number of mutually enriching models drawn from the church's liturgy and in the light of our magisterial tradition that can provide a useful way of advancing a truly Catholic eucharistic theology and practice.

The task that lies ahead is to articulate complementary aspects of Catholic thought about the Eucharist. The ten "models" to be articulated here are derived largely from the prayers we say when we celebrate the eucharistic liturgy, from the gestures and actions that accompany those prayers, from the doctrines that have come down to us within Catholicism in the magisterium, and from the concepts articulated in the Eucharist section of the *Catechism of the Catholic Church*. In essence, the models *of* the Eucharist described here derive *from* the models of the Eucharist contained in the eucharistic liturgy we celebrate.

The Greek term *perichoresis* means a dance. What I should like to adopt here is a "perichoretic" approach, one that includes a number of factors and approaches understood as mutually enriching and as presuming on each other to be adequate (or at least less inadequate) in describing the Eucharist. However, one of the problems with such an approach is deciding which "model" to treat first, precisely because this can signal priority and emphasis. None such is intended. All of the models are important, even though not all are on the same footing theologically, liturgically, or historically. This is to say that a model on eucharistic presence will be a crucial aspect of the Roman Catholic doctrine of the Eucharist simply because of the controversies surrounding how to describe the Eucharist from the ninth century on. At the same time, a model about the proclamation of the word of God will be particularly timely today because of the restoration of the Liturgy of the Word to a place of greater prominence than it had in the Tridentine Mass.

The models to be delineated are: Cosmic Mass, The Church's Eucharist, The Effective Word of God, Memorial of the Paschal Mystery, Covenant Renewal, The Lord's Supper, Food for the Journey, Sacramental Sacrifice, Active Presence, and Work of the Spirit. The book's conclusion offers something of a summary of the main issues presented throughout the book aimed toward outlining what might be called a spirituality of the Eucharist as derived from the liturgy. Each model is to be seen in relation to all the others.

In addition to delineating a liturgical theology of the Eucharist, our use of the liturgy's rites, signs, symbols, texts, and prayers throughout this book will enable people to "hear" them at Mass in fresh and new ways.

In the words of T. S. Eliot

With the drawing of this Love, and the voice of this Calling
    We shall not cease from exploration
    And the end of all our exploring
    Will be to arrive where we started
    And know the place for the first time.
       —"Little Gidding," *The Four Quartets*

The "place" in this book is at the Eucharist, at the event of the Mass, the jewel in the crown of Catholicism. Our aim is to enable us to know it more fully and deeply—and always to discover it anew, as if "for the first time."

## MODEL ONE
# Cosmic Mass

*"Blessed are you, Lord God of all creation."*
*—Jewish Table Prayer*

This model, on "Cosmic Mass," and the book's conclusion, on "A Liturgical Eucharistic Spirituality," should be seen as setting both the framework and (to a large extent) the contents for the rest of the book. This is to say that all sacramental liturgy takes place within the context of our human lives lived on this good earth where God is revealed in many ways, including through the world itself and the things on it and that inhabit it. In a real sense, the term "cosmic Mass" reminds us of something we already know—that God is revealed, disclosed, and discovered in all of life. Our purpose in discussing cosmic Mass first is simply to set the framework in the world and in human life in which the Eucharist (and in fact all sacramental liturgy) is celebrated. The purpose of concluding the book with a chapter on a liturgical eucharistic spirituality is its logical complement —namely that we find God and are discovered by God before, during, and after the celebration of the liturgy in the world in which we live.

The "earthiness" of every act of liturgy will be emphasized in this model (and noted in several others) and the life relation of every act of liturgy will be emphasized in the Conclusion (as well as in several of the models to be delineated). I have deliberately chosen the phrase *cosmic Mass* in order to underscore what may have been lacking in some modern descriptions of the liturgy.[1] That is, every act of liturgy affects the cosmos, which to my way of thinking means both the world in which we live and the history of our salvation as worked out on this earth. If the (not illegitimate) distinction between the *sacred* and the *profane* is taken to an extreme, then liturgy can come to be viewed as an escape from the secular in favor of the sacred. In point of fact, I will argue in this chapter that the liturgy is the unique place where any such distinctions collapse and where we worship the God of creation and redemption by using creation itself. And I will argue that liturgy itself makes statements about the reunification of all things in heaven and on earth, through, with, and in the redeeming Christ. Hence "cosmic" is not meant to imply any sort of New Age star (or navel) gazing or "reading" crystals in order to determine one's life path or to foretell the future! Rather the use of "cosmic" is meant to be a continual reminder that every act of liturgy—especially that of the Eucharist—is an expression and experience of that which is most sacred (God, redemption, forgiveness, etc.) through that which is most available to us (the things on and of this good earth). And it is to say that every act of liturgy has its effects on the whole cosmic sweep of the world's salvation and on the personal sanctification of those who participate in it or who are remembered through it.

These assertions are nothing new. But that they need to be reemphasized is on the minds of some contemporary liturgical theologians. My sense is that placing a cosmic lens on the liturgy helps us to situate the role of human beings in proper context. And it allows us to see the things we "use" in liturgy as truly revelatory of God, not as utensils to be discarded or props that have no meaning except when they are used in the liturgy. In fact, the opposite is the case in (classical) Christian theology and spirituality.

This is reflected in St. Benedict's Rule for monks where he asserts that the monastery cellerer (the monk charged with caring for the goods of the monastery) "will regard all utensils and goods of the monastery as sacred vessels of the altar..."[2] More recently it is reflected in some of the writings of Aidan Kavanagh (himself a Benedictine) where he writes compellingly that "world frames Church, and cosmology is the foundation on which ecclesiology rests."[3] That a section on "the visible world as a prerequisite for liturgy" is part of Michael Kunzler's recent text on liturgy is a step in the right direction of reasserting this premise in general,[4] and it is one of the important cautions (and critiques) named by Cardinal Ratzinger, specifically any separation between the cult of so called "natural religions" based on the cosmos and Christianity's cult as based on history. To argue in any way that would "oppose" cosmos and history is false, especially when it comes to the celebration of liturgy.[5]

It is commonplace to assert that the Eucharist derives from the *context* of human life and daily living. The Eucharist also returns participants back to that life lived on earth with their vision of the Christian life sharpened and the challenge of living that vision the more clear. My concern here is to draw this out more sharply by emphasizing how our lives are lived on this earth and that the whole world—nothing less than the *cosmos*—is the primary context for all sacramental liturgy. This model of the Eucharist relies on, and at times will articulate, aspects of what can be termed a truly Catholic sacramental vision of life (understanding, of course, that this vision is not particular to Roman Catholicism). Such a "Catholic" vision is always integral and integrating. It is *integral* in the sense that it is essentially holistic and comprised of a number of factors including teaching, liturgy, and prayer. It is also *integrating* in that it articulates our relationship with all of humanity and with all that lives and moves on this earth, and with the earth itself. This integral vision of life and the integrating function of the Catholic vision of life are presumed and celebrated in liturgy. One of the purposes of sacramental liturgy is to articulate and enact this vision. That the rest of our life still needs to achieve the harmony expressed and experienced in liturgy is among the more precise tasks of (what I term) *spirituality*.[6]

In this chapter we shall be concerned with relating sacraments with the foundational notion for all sacramental liturgy—namely *sacramentality*—and then with applying this understanding to the nature of Eucharist as a sacred, sacramental, and sacrificial meal with special foods, protocols, and challenges.

## SACRAMENTALITY

What makes this section a challenge is perhaps the overuse of the very term we have and will repeatedly use throughout this book—*sacrament*. Certainly from Peter Lombard in the thirteenth century on, the Western church has been accustomed to numbering the sacraments as seven and to describing them as *causing* grace (to use Lombard's term) or as *conferring* grace (as defined at Trent).[7] That the post-Tridentine church catechized on the number "seven" and what they "do" is clearly shown in the kind of precise catechetical instruction contained in the catechisms published after Trent. Clearly, from the Council of Trent to the modern era these central tenets of Catholic teaching and practice about sacraments continued to take deep root in Catholic consciousness.

In fact, the use of the term "sacrament" itself as well as the adjective "sacramental" to describe teaching and practice about the seven sacraments were so familiar to Catholics after Trent that a major revolution occurred in the mid twentieth century when contemporary Roman Catholic theologians capitalized on the seminal insights of Edward Schillebeeckx, Karl Rahner, and Otto Semmelroth (among others) who had focused attention on Jesus and the church as primordial sacraments.[8] Spurred on by the teaching in the Constitution on the Church from Vatican II that the church is "a kind of sacrament or sign of intimate union with God, and of the unity of all humankind,"[9] much subsequent postconciliar writing on sacraments has referred to Christ and the church as "fundamental" or "ground sacraments," foundations for the celebration of all liturgy (including the sacraments themselves). Thus the ritual celebration of liturgy and sacraments has commonly been placed within a "foundational framework"[10] (to use Kenan Osborne's term) that emphasizes the role and action of Jesus and the church in the celebration of the liturgy of sacraments.

More recently, however, some theologians have taken to nuancing these assertions, not to ignore or diminish them, but rather to make them more precise, to get behind them and to explore their core meaning more fully. Significant voices here include Edward Kilmartin,[11] Louis Marie Chauvet[12] and Kenan Osborne himself.[13]

On the one hand it is clear that emphasizing Jesus and the church as intrinsic to ritual sacramental actions has been all to the good. After all, this returns us to the Augustinian premise that Christ and the church are the "great sacrament or mystery" *(magnum sacramentum-mysterium)*. However, I wonder whether our use of the phrases "Jesus as sacrament" and "the church as sacrament" have been overused since the council.[14] The issue for me is that calling such realities as Christ and the church "sacraments" or "sacramental" can be a rhetorical or theological stretch. In effect what can happen is that the Tridentine teaching that (necessarily and legitimately) emphasized seven sacraments as chief means of experiencing God's grace becomes the rhetorical and theological basis for talking about Jesus and the church. This is legitimate insofar as it capitalizes on the use of a language that respected and reflected how the seven sacraments had been so highly prized in Catholicism as unique ways of experiencing God in the here and now. To say that Jesus and the church were "sacraments" in the literature leading up to the Second Vatican Council (especially) was to capitalize on conventional theological language about privileged signs and symbols of God's action among us in our world and in our human lives.

However, one possible difficulty with such terminology is that it can appear to emphasize (only) the sacral character of seven sacraments as the means to transmit God's grace and life. The framework implied by such language would be that in the mundane world in which we live we need the sacraments to transmit that which is sacred and divine. What may be missed in this linguistic usage about sacraments is perhaps an unwitting lack of respect paid to the principle of *sacramentality*—that is, naming and using things from this world and discovered in human life that reveal and disclose the presence and action of God among us. The principle of sacramentality means that things matter and that matter is not just a thing. Things in this world reveal God with us; matter is never divorced or separated from the God who made all things.

Put somewhat differently, what I am suggesting is that perhaps the Tridentine and post-Reformation emphasis on the number, origin, and efficaciousness of the seven sacraments may well have eclipsed the principle of sacramentality on which they were based. That is to say that the broad meaning of sacramentality—that God is disclosed and discovered here and now on earth and in human life even as we yearn for life eternal and complete union with God—is the theological ground and liturgical foundation on which all liturgy and the celebration of seven sacraments (sacramental liturgy) is based. This means that a broad appreciation of sacramentality is a better framework to use when describing the foundation for celebrating liturgy and sacraments. Prior to God's blessings sending us forth from sacraments to do God's work on earth is the theological substratum of sacramentality. In fact, it is the God we experience and discover in all of life— especially in creation and in human relationships—before and after the celebration of liturgy who gives shape to sacramental liturgy and gives it its purpose and meaning.

It is the principle of sacramentality that reminds us of the fact that God, Father, Son, and Spirit and all that they reveal and contain, can be experienced in all of life. This means that there is a deep and rich continuity between who we are, how we look at the world, and how we understand what we do in human life before and after engaging in sacraments. And it is this continuity which grounds both the sacramental rituals themselves and how we name these rituals as "sacraments." The principle of sacramentality underscores the continuity between the celebration of sacraments and all of life; it is also meant to highlight the intrinsic and essential role that sacramental celebration plays in ensuring that we experience this Catholic vision of reality in and through the liturgy.

One way of expressing this is to say that all reality "is potentially or in fact the bearer of God's presence and the instrument of God's saving activity... This principle is rooted in the nature of a sacrament as such, i.e., a visible sign of the invisible presence and activity of God. Together with the principles of mediation (God works through secondary agents to achieve divine ends) and communion (the end of all of God's activity is the union of humanity), the principle of sacramentality constitutes one of the central theological characteristics of Catholicism."[15] In light of this premise, my argument is that Jesus, the church, and the seven sacraments are best appreciated as *particular and privileged* expressions of the God who has revealed and continues to reveal the divine—yes, God's very self—through the material of human existence and in the community of human relationships, all placed within a world that is itself regarded as sacramental. My use of the term *sacramental* is meant to underscore a premise that is fundamental to a Catholic world view that sustains the unity of both the divine and human and the sacred and the secular. By *sacramental* I also mean that God is both revealed and yet also remains hidden in this world and that any particular revelation of God in this world can never be totally complete or completely full. The *sacramental world* is the foundation for any and all celebrations of the sacraments. Sacramentality itself emphasizes how God is discoverable here and now; it also leads us to yearn for the fullness of our experience of God in eternity,[16] an eternal experience that is expressed and revealed in a partial way in the here and now in the celebration of liturgy, especially the sacraments.

Edward Kilmartin effectively argues that this kind of fundamental outlook corresponds to the more general comprehensive view of the theological value of all created reality, a view that prevailed throughout the patristic era and in the early Middle Ages. This is a world view in which salvation history began with creation. All creation—especially humanity, the crown of creation—bears the mark of God's love. The systematic theologians of the twelfth and thirteenth centuries had the same basic outlook, namely, that the Word Incarnate, who created the world, came in the flesh and established the sacraments to draw humanity into union with the Incarnate Word himself. At the same time they affirmed that created reality when used in sacraments attains its full meaning. "It does not merely manifest the mystery of God's love but is employed by God to communicate himself to believers in the special way signified by each sacrament. Hence, they [described] the sacraments as a means of a holy exchange, a *sacrum commercium*."[17] While one can legitimately assert that from the middle of the twelfth century on theologians became concerned about points that individual sacraments shared in common with other sacraments and began to develop treatises on what came to be called "on sacraments in general" (*de sacramentis in genere*[18]) and to number the sacraments as "seven," it is equally true that at the same time a Catholic world view respecting sacramentality in general was also presumed and sustained.

One key challenge today therefore is to retrieve the principle of sacramentality that has been operative and presumed in our understanding and appreciation of sacramental liturgy and that is a chief characteristic of Catholic sacramental practice and theology. When it is eclipsed (and I would argue that recently in some sacramental writing it has indeed been eclipsed in favor of naming Jesus and the church as "sacraments") then the very premise that it is through materiality—the human, the fragile, and the things of this earth— that we experience the divine, is itself eclipsed. It is not a giant step from this rhetorical move of naming Jesus and the church as "sacraments" to dichotomizing what ought to be unified, namely to separate the sacred from the secular, rather than to see this world as graced in Christ yet also as an imperfect realization of God's life and love among us. The rhetoric of sacramentality is always "both...and" rather than "either...or." In a sacramental world, all is both graced and in need of complete redemption. In an "either...or" framework, sacraments offer escapes from the world and send us back to it charged to work more adequately in it for the cause of God's kingdom. This insight is not illegitimate. But it is limited and limiting in the face of an alternate (and more traditional) premise that in a sacramental world, it is the world itself that is, in the familiar words of Gerard Manley Hopkins,

> charged with the grandeur of God...
> Because the Holy Ghost over the bent
>     World broods with warm breast and with ah! Bright wings.

The celebration of sacraments is thus the church's unique and focused way of penetrating how God can be and is experienced in all human life lived on this good earth.

My thesis here is as traditional as the Catholic principle of sacramentality and the sacramental economy;[19] it is as challenging as is the demand to discover God in "worldly worship" that draws on the world for its symbolism and that is at home in the world and among all who dwell in it. This world is where the incarnate God is experienced. It is in the here and now that, because of Christ, our lives are supremely human and profoundly divine at the same time. My thesis is about a truly "Catholic" way of looking at life, not just a Catholic way of doing liturgical ritual. And in the end this way of understanding things is one fundamental key to sacramentality and to sacraments —namely a sacramental world view.[20]

Liturgy and life are correlatives, intrinsically interconnected and mutually enriching. Liturgy and the sacraments bear a heavy burden to be what they are—that is, signs of the way the divine is manifested in the human, of the sacred in our secular world, of how all that is of God is incarnated among us through Jesus Christ as we await "a new heaven and a new earth" (Rev 21:1). We do not live in "two different worlds," the sacred and the secular, with liturgy and the sacraments offering an escape from the mundane to the eternal. Rather, we live in one world, called "good" in Genesis (1:4) and graced through Christ whose becoming human is the means whereby we humans become God (to paraphrase St. Augustine). But we also live in an imperfect world marred by the sin we call "original," the effects of which are obvious all around us.

It is this world with all its flaws and problems that is the stage for the enactment of liturgy and the sacraments. And liturgy and the sacraments themselves are the privileged means for us to experience the Triune God alive and dwelling among us here and now on this good earth even as we also yearn for this world to pass away. In a sacramental world view, the world in which we live is interdependent —all that dwell in it are part of God's plan for us all. It is also a locus where God is revealed, disclosed, and experienced. This means that the world, humans, and all creatures great and small, are signs of God among us.

*[handwritten: what it was created for    all the potential there]*

## EUCHARIST AND SACRAMENTALITY

Sacramentality is a centrally important key that unlocks and unleashes the depth and value of any liturgy and all sacramental celebration. In Catholicism (all kinds of) things matter. In liturgy and the sacraments we use "daily and domestic things"[21] from human life to reveal and experience the life of God. The phrase "daily and domestic things" capsulizes what it means to live in a sacramental world because in the liturgy we use the things of this world in order to experience particularly "strong moments" of God's self-disclosure this side of eternity. In human life humans communicate by words and gestures; we bathe and we dine. These are examples of what we "use" from the ordinary and everyday in order to experience the extraordinary breadth and depth of God's life and love. Liturgy uses words and gestures to communicate. In baptism we bathe in water those to be initiated. At the Eucharist we dine on "the bread of life and the cup of eternal salvation."

The unfathomable depth and profound meaning of the liturgy as understood here is that it draws on our experiences of God in all of life and puts these experiences together in an integrated way. Liturgy ritualizes a particular and privileged experience of God so that through these ritual actions we can evaluate life's flaws and problems, put them into perspective, and in joy and hope transcend them. We do this in and through the liturgy. Such actions do not offer an escape from this world; rather, they deepen our experience of God in this world, in the midst of all its flaws and of our own human weaknesses.

That this fundamental principle needs to be refurbished in our own day is exemplified in the intervention made by Cardinal Godfried Daneels (of Mechelen-Brussels) at the special consistory in Rome in May 2001. He stated that "the Western churches of established Christianity are passing through a profound crisis of sacramentality... [L]iturgy risks being dominated largely by an excess of words or of being merely a way to recharge one's batteries for *diakonia* and social action."[22] What is needed, he argues, is reclamation of the historical and christological dimensions of the sacraments—the unique and particular elements that are constitutive of the celebration of Christian sacraments.

Liturgy and the sacraments presume a sacramental world view. Yet I would assert that sacramentality is in need of retrieval for the very survival not only of liturgy and the sacraments but also for the identity of core values in Catholic Christianity itself. In an American context the phenomenon of the "mega-churches" reflects something of the phenomenon to which Cardinal Daneels refers. It amounts to nothing less than a severe crisis for the very celebration of liturgy and sacraments. The "mega-church" emphasis on contemporary music (tangential at best to the gospel), on skits depicting contemporary life, on "participation" by observation, and on the emotional aspects of faith contributes to nothing less than a crisis for the survival of Christian churches that celebrate and value liturgy and sacraments. The sacramental and the symbolic are here jettisoned for the immediate, the emotional, and the ephemeral. Ongoing conversion to the gospel as mediated by liturgical rites and symbols is replaced by the quick fix of "self-help" and "problem-solving." What is severely diminished is the very premise of sacramentality and the value of the ritual enactment of liturgy itself. What is needed, therefore, is a retrieval of the sacramental value of meal taking and dining which set the stage for developing a theology about the Eucharist *from* the Eucharist.

## MEALS AND FOODS

Much of the eucharistic doctrine debated and taught in the Western church has focused on the eucharistic species and tried to answer the question: "What are bread and wine after the consecration?" Given our history, this is legitimate and most understandable. However, it seems to me that today, without the polemics of the past (e.g., the Reformation) and in line with the eucharistic teaching and practice that come to us from Vatican II's Constitution on the Sacred Liturgy through the revised Order of Mass and Missal, we not only can but need to articulate a eucharistic theology that is broader and (in fact) more traditional.

This is to say that if we take the liturgical action as our starting point we can frame our understanding of Eucharist today within a series of contexts that can perhaps best be envisioned in concentric circles. In the innermost circle the eucharistic species are placed within the context of a holy, sacrificial meal during which they are consumed in communion. This act of sharing consecrated foods is set within the context of a meal during which specially prepared foods are brought forth and over which blessings and prayers are proclaimed. These gifts are blessed by those who gather as a community for the shared meal—those who are our sisters and brothers in the faith. The act of blessing and sharing the sacred food of the Eucharist is done by and for the church. But this act of blessing foods is itself also a way of declaring that what we have to offer at Mass is from the world—the cosmos—in which we live. The act of blessing foods is really a way of acknowledging God as present and active among us in our world. The very taking of food and drink and using them for the enactment of the Eucharist make the theological statement that at Mass we rely on and acclaim the God of the covenant—who is so often named in our liturgical prayers as the God of creation and redemption (at the same time). These acts of blessing foods are set within the context of a people who come together to share stories from the scriptures of our forebears in faith, especially of the way God (particularly in Christ) acted in redeeming, liberating, and sanctifying them (in the past) and now us (in the present). It is in the telling of these stories (in the proclamation of the scriptures) and in the sharing of sacred meals here and now that we experience the salvation that God first worked for our forebears in the faith through, with, and in Christ. That same salvation is worked for us here and now in the Eucharist.

Notice the context and framework of what we have just described as the eucharistic action (in the liturgy)—that it occurs in an act of dining together and taking meals, not just ingesting food. This is where what we do in human life, the "daily and domestic thing" of dining, is presumed as the locus where God is experienced. This is the human-life context for what Judaism experiences to this day in sabbath and Passsover meals. It is the human-life context for our sharing in the food of the Eucharist—the Lord's body and blood.

But before we go any further, we need to raise a question about dining and meal-taking in our contemporary American culture (and other "Westernized" cultures as well). It is succinctly summarized in the provocative title (of an equally provocative article by Margaret Mackenzie) "Is the Family Meal Disappearing?"[23] The author's thesis is that in fact studies show that the practice of families dining together cannot be presumed. A glance at the proliferation of stores that provide "fast food" and "take home" meals evidences this for many in modern America. Although Mackenzie's research nuances her findings and prevents our making generalizations across the board in terms of urban, suburban, and rural America, her assertion that most of the food consumed during the week in American families is either prepared on the weekend or brought in from outside the home is very telling (and rings true for many Americans). This means that there is at least a diminishment in the presumption that foods are prepared daily in American homes. Her research also suggests that many Americans dine without others—or at least not in family units. The fact that work hours exceed the nine-to-five timeframe and that evenings are for meetings, sports, and other (sometimes largely individual) activities needs to be acknowledged.

In line with our argument thus far in this chapter—that sacramentality grounds sacraments—what we need to look at is the phenomenon of what has traditionally been presumed to be the experience in human life of sacramentality to ground the celebration of the Eucharist —namely, food preparation and coming together for a meal. This can no longer be presumed, at least on a daily basis. For Americans, Thanksgiving Day is probably the single commonly shared example of this sacramental presumption (specifically work expended to prepare and relationships deepened because the food is taken together in a ritual way). But that kind of experience may itself be understood as unique because it occurs once a year and is not a "daily and domestic thing."

The challenge, therefore, is to name the issue and invite families to address how and when they can in fact not just take food, but share meals with each other, in effect, "dine." By "dining" I mean the decision to sit down together at table for whatever is prepared—from the simple to the sumptuous—to share conversation about ideas, values, and life experiences as the food is eaten and beverages are drunk. This is the reality on which eucharistic sharing is based. The retrieval of some semblance of family dining can go a long way toward underscoring family relationships and the unity that comes (simply?) from dining together as a family. It also would evidence the sacramentality of dining itself.

Another aspect of the sacramentality that grounds the Eucharist is the use of the goods of this earth that at Mass become the food of everlasting life. A premise of the celebration of sacramental liturgy is that we use the good things of this earth to worship God.[24] Some of these are "natural," meaning that they are found in nature. Others are "manufactured"—"the work of human hands."

We use water for baptism. Water is the only primal element on this earth without which we cannot live. Is it any wonder that it is used for sacramental initiation? The element that sustains human life is the element we use to initiate us into the very life of God.

In the Eucharist we use a different kind of gift—bread and wine. These are not "natural" in the sense that they derive directly from nature itself. Rather, they are gifts that are clearly derived from this good earth but that require human ingenuity and productivity to allow them to become what they are destined to be—the food of everlasting life.

Cardinal Basil Hume (former archbishop of Westminster, London) once remarked: "No work, no Mass." This phrase summarizes part of the premise of sacramentality, namely, that human work goes into making and manufacturing all the things we will use for the Eucharist. One of the contributions that humans make to enact the liturgy is what human ingenuity, creativity, and productivity have accomplished prior to the liturgy. We manufacture ("make with the work of human hands") what we use to worship God. In that sense, the worship and honor paid to God begin long before the liturgy in church begins. They begin in the liturgy of human life as blessed by God when humans work to produce the bread and wine for the Eucharist—from planting to harvesting to baking and delivering these gifts to the church for the Eucharist. The talents we humans have for thought and work are brought to bear on the manufacturing of what we need to celebrate the Eucharist. Again the sacramental principle is at work. What we are and use outside of the liturgy is brought into the act of liturgy to be transformed.

While the texts of the blessings said over the bread and wine at the presentation of the gifts are somewhat debatable as to nature and content,[25] the theology of sacramentality as reflected in the phrases: "Lord God of all creation... this bread to offer, which earth has given and human hands have made," as well as "fruit of the vine and work of human hands" is truly important. What lies behind the theology of these prayers and the manufacture of these foods is that they are *paschal processes*. There is a dying and rising in planting, harvesting, baking/fermenting—all of which form the foundation for the celebration of the paschal mystery in the Eucharist.

Clearly at the heart of the Eucharist is paschal dying and rising—both of Christ and of us through, with, and in him. When viewed through the lens of (Catholic) sacramentality, the very elements we use to enact and share in the event and experience of paschal dying and rising make a theological statement about our place in the cosmos and how we understand the cosmos from an incarnational perspective. This is to say that "the work of human hands" before and after the eucharistic action needs to be respected and taken seriously as an intrinsic part of what the Eucharist means. At the same time, preparations for the act of the liturgy of the Eucharist presume that we take the good things of this earth and make them into fitting symbols for the body and blood of Christ. These actions—planting, harvesting, baking bread, and producing wine—are intrinsic to the eucharistic action. Why?

Theologically they demonstrate graphically what all liturgy is—the unique ritual enactment of our faith in the paschal dying and rising of Christ. What better way to do this than to take things of this earth and human life that we use to satisfy human hunger and thirst—bread and wine—and use them in the Eucharist to worship the God of the covenant, the God of creation and of redemption? What better way to demonstrate our belief in the paschal mystery of dying and rising than to present gifts—bread and wine—which themselves are the results of dying and rising? What, after all, is planting, harvesting, milling grain, and crushing grapes if not a paschal process? At the Eucharist we take these good gifts and then bless, break, and share them as reflections of both our life and work outside the Eucharist and of our life in and through Christ, especially his paschal dying and rising. How appropriate, then, is the theology derived from the eucharistic prayer (and also in the tradition of numberless other eucharistic prayers of both East and West in history and today), which always articulates our place in the world and our role as offering thanks and praise to God for all good gifts. There is a theology of creation and of human work underlying any theology of the Eucharist. In particular, when the Eucharist is understood to be the perpetuation of the paschal mystery of Christ for and in the church, what better way to demonstrate this than by emphasizing the paschal theology that is involved and presumed in the preparation of bread and wine?

Certainly one of the major themes of the internationally acclaimed film *Babette's Feast* is that the preparation of foods and the largesse she

expended on that famous meal makes an important theological statement about what the Eucharist really is. Underlying themes from the
film that apply to the Eucharist are certainly fulfillment in human
work as well as joy, festivity, and thanksgiving (among others). Dining
at the Lord's table in and through the Eucharist is possible only
because of human work and God's graciousness to us in ways that are
nothing short of amazing and confounding.

In a parallel way, we can say that there is a spirituality derived
from every act of the Eucharist in that what we do at Mass shapes
how we live our lives. But lest this seem too energetic—not to say
Pelagian—I would argue that a chief aspect of all eucharistic participation is to allow the paschal dying and rising enacted through what
occurs at the altar table to be the real measure of anything that is of
real value in life. The challenge is twofold. First, it is to allow what
we enact in the Eucharist to be the measure of our lives. In effect we
are to view life through the lens of the paschal mystery, a mystery that
helps us evaluate what is really important in life. It is this lens that
allows us to took at apparent defeats—sickness, suffering, and setbacks in life, even death itself—and to evaluate them against the
paschal mystery. Similarly, a requisite consequence of eucharistic
enactment is to share the goods of this earth with the poor and the
needy. This evidences one of the important life-dimensions of the
Eucharist. It is a key building block in developing a spirituality of the
Eucharist derived from the liturgy.

Today most dioceses in the United States have programs for the
diaconate. One of the contributions of the (permanent) diaconate is
evident in the relationship between the deacon's service at the altar
and his life of service outside of Mass, especially to the poor, the
imprisoned, the homebound, the marginalized, the alienated, the dis-
enfranchised. What the deacon does in the liturgy is derived from
and leads to what he does outside the liturgy. This very ministry
images for the whole church, especially all who participate in the
Eucharist, the kind of ministerial life presumed by eucharistic participation. The Eucharist, understood as the body of Christ to be shared
for the unity of the church, should challenge us to overturn some of
the selfishness in our lives through self-giving and surrender of the
self so that others may eat and be cared for by the same Lord. Christ's

paschal victory began with his humble acceptance of suffering and death. The deacon's ministry reflects the Lord when it is humble service at the altar and in all of life as a consequence of what occurs at the altar table. Like all good church ministry, the deacon's ministry is meant to be a mirror for all of us of the ways we should live our lives in service, both in the liturgy celebrated in church and in the living out of that liturgy in the liturgy of life.

One of the less emphasized rubrics contained in the liturgy of the Evening Mass of the Lord's Supper is that gifts for the poor may be collected at the time of the presentation of the eucharistic gifts. This custom is actually ancient and reflects the liturgical tradition of the Roman liturgy. In fact, many commentators on the text of the Roman Canon indicate that the phrase toward its end "[through] him you give us all these gifts, you fill them with life and goodness, you bless them and make them holy" refers not only to the (already consecrated) eucharistic species but also to the gifts brought up in the collection for the poor. This means that the very end of the eucharistc payer always contains a reference to sharing gifts of food and nourishment outside the liturgy from the goods brought to the liturgy for this purpose.[26]

The taking and collecting of gifts for the Eucharist always implies the sharing of some of those gifts with the poor and needy. The symbolism of the deacon as one who ministers both at the altar and to the poor outside the liturgy personifies and exemplifies this ritual. The sharing of one's talents and offerings at the Eucharist reflects the generous sharing of one's talents with others outside the celebration of the Eucharist. From the perspective of "sacramentality" as articulated here, we can say that there is a direct relationship between preparing and sharing food at the Eucharist and sharing food in everyday life— especially at the daily and domestic "ritual" of taking meals together.

## CREATION MOTIF IN THE EUCHARISTIC LITURGY

One of the contributions of emphasizing the *lex orandi* in our theology and spirituality is that what the liturgy of the Eucharist says and does about creation and the Creator are most significant. It is to these aspects of the *lex orandi* that we now turn.

## Prayers

I have repeatedly used a cluster of terms and attributes to describe God—the God "of the covenant," "of creation," and "of redemption." This is deliberate because it underscores the terms used in the prayers of the liturgy of the Eucharist and the concepts that stand behind those terms. In essence, it is at and through the liturgy that we pray to the God who acts and who is a God of relatedness to the people chosen to be his special possession in both testaments, a bondedness signified in the ratification and renewal of the covenant.

True to the church's *lex orandi–lex credendi* equation, it is worth pondering what we say to God and about our belief in the God of creation. That the title "Lord God of all creation" from the Jewish tradition of table prayers is used at the presentation of the gifts in our eucharistic liturgy is telling. To praise God for creation—at the beginning as well as here and now—becomes a motive we use in each and every eucharistic prayer to praise and thank this God. Certainly among the eucharistic prayers presently in use in the Roman rite, the fourth contains the most explicit statements about praise for the God of creation:

Source of life and goodness, you have created all things,
  to fill your creatures with every blessing
  and to lead all [men] to the joyful vision of your light.[27]

The most concise is in the second eucharistic prayer:

He is the Word through whom you made the universe.

The subtitle for one of the Sunday prefaces for Ordinary Time (Sunday Preface V) is simply "Creation" and it contains the phrase:

All things are of your making,
  all times and seasons obey your laws,
  but you chose to create [man] in your own image,
  setting [him] over the whole world in all its wonder.
  You made [man] the steward of creation,

> to praise you day by day for the marvels of your wisdom and
>     power...

Another very explicit example is found in the prayer over the gifts for
the Eighth Sunday in Ordinary Time:

> God our Creator,
> may this bread and wine we offer
> as a sign of our love and worship
> lead us to salvation.

The message in these examples is that we need to be attentive to what
such texts say, even when the references are brief (and sometimes
oblique). That there is a creation theme to every eucharistic prayer is
a strong and continual reminder that this is a required motivation for
our prayer at the Eucharist. The creation theme is most often enunciated in the preface section of the eucharistic prayer.

*[handwritten marginal note: God the creator]*

The fact that such assertions are followed by the "Holy, holy,
holy" acclamation is deliberate. The first part of the "Holy, holy,
holy" acclamation is taken from Isaiah 6:3, "Holy, holy, holy is the
Lord of hosts," and refers to the holiness of God and the holiness of
God's temple. That it leads to the assertion "heaven and earth are
filled with your glory..." is significant because it transcends "finding" God only in the temple and in temple worship. It directs our
sights to finding God in all that is around us, not only in the heavens
but on this good earth. The use of the term "God, Lord, Sabaoth" (a
term currently translated as "Lord God of power and might") with the
phrase "heaven and earth are filled with your glory" helpfully combines a naming of God's attributes and strength with a statement about
where we experience the fruit of that "power and might"—both in
heaven and here on earth. "God Sabaoth" translates the biblical name
that means "the God of all gods," which presumes a "council" of gods
and states that the God we name and adore is above them all and the
highest of all. In effect, we here acclaim the God whose power and
might are higher than anything we could ever imagine. This name for
God is taken from the Pentateuch and emphasizes majesty, splendor,
and glory.

Used at every Mass at the end of the preface, this "Holy, holy, holy" acclamation offers a reference back to the text of the preface where God's act of creation is (almost always) noted; it also challenges us to find God and to see God at work on this good earth, the place where we work out our salvation here and now.

It is also helpful to "unpack" the classic clusters of terms that are used together to "name" God in the Roman rite at the beginning of the eucharistic prayer: "Father, all powerful and ever living God" (which translates *Domine, sancte Pater, omnipotens aeternae Deus*). Behind these words is a wealth of meaning about who God is in terms of power and sovereignty as well as how some of the images refer to table partnership in the scriptures. In succinct yet poignant words Gail Ramshaw states that:

> at the beginning of the Great Thanksgiving we pray along with Abraham, who obeyed the call (Gen. 12:4), with Moses, who received the Torah (Ex. 19:20), and with Jesus, who was the Word (John 1:1). As we eat the bread and wine, we recall Abraham, who shared his food with three mysterious visitors (Gen. 18:8), Moses, who ate and drank with God on Sinai and did not die (Ex. 24:11), and Jesus, who breaking bread on Sunday evening, showed forth his wounds (Lk. 24:31).[28]

Among the lessons to be learned from this brief exposition is that the names we use for God and the terms we use to describe his almighty power are most significant. One of the values of the ritual of liturgy and sacraments is that we hear these names again and again, a repetition that can invite us to reflect again and again on the variety of images articulated here.

The Latin term *commercium* ("exchange," "interchange") has been classically used in the Roman liturgy in a number of ways, principally in prayers at Mass, as referring to the gifts of bread and wine to become the body and blood of Christ and in the Liturgy of the Hours during the Christmas season referring to Christ's incarnation and our humanity being graced and forever changed by our share in his divinity. In the present Roman Missal it is found a dozen and a half times, almost always in the text of the prayers over the gifts. (The others are in the prayer after communion.[29]) When used at the eucharistic liturgy,

the term *commercium* carries with it the meaning of "exchange," namely
that we who present gifts of bread and wine look to their transformation into the holy gifts of the food and drink of Christ's body and
blood. And, as already noted, at other times in the Roman liturgy *commercium* is used to refer to the wondrous exchange at the incarnation
when Christ assumed our humanity so that we humans could become
like God. Take for example the prayer we pray during the Christmas
season:

> Lord,
> receive our gifts in this wonderful exchange:
> from all you have given us
> we bring you these gifts,
> and in return, you give us yourself.[30]

For me this rather terse prayer reflects a number of theological
meanings that are intrinsically related to the Eucharist as sketched in
this chapter. Concretely, we prepare bread and wine which become the
means of the church's sharing here and now in who Christ is and what
Christ came to accomplish in his incarnation and paschal dying and
rising. Thus there are clear theological points to be made "just" by
presenting gifts for their transformation during the eucharistic prayer.
The holy exchange that is articulated in (some) prayers over the gifts
and prayers after communion really give words to what is always
expressed, namely, that the gifts of this earth are gifts of God for sustenance in life and for strengthening us on our journey to the hereafter.
These phrases are understood to be both demonstrative and proleptic.
This means that they state what the gifts are now ("demonstrative") as
we present them (the "work of human hands" from what the "earth
has given" and the "fruit of the vine"). And they also say what the gifts
will become ("proleptic") through eucharistic transformation (the
body and blood of the Lord). Thus they are always reminders of the
paschal mystery on two levels. One is that they are the result of the
cycle of planting, harvesting, and baking/fermenting—all because of
human ingenuity and care. The other is what results when we receive
them in communion. We become sharers in the paschal mystery of
Christ's dying and rising by the very act of taking, blessing, sharing,
and receiving these gifts.

In sum, what the Roman liturgy of the Eucharist reveals, sometimes by the most subtle terms and turns of phrase, should be noted and taken to heart. When we take gifts from creation and use them in the liturgy we are making a number of theological statements, both by these actions themselves and by the words that accompany them. It is not coincidental that all but three uses of *commercium* in the Missal occur in either the Christmas or Easter seasons. Just when the church's liturgy emphasizes the incarnation and paschal mysteries, these prayers underscore the way these theologies are joined in any and every act of Eucharist.

### General Instruction of the Roman Missal

One of the more helpful emphases in the GIRM 2002 is its description of the bread and wine to be used in the celebration of Mass. Under requisites for celebrating Mass it asserts that "the bread for celebrating the Eucharist must be made only from wheat, must be recently baked, and, according to the ancient practice of the Latin church, be unleavened" (n. 320). In its most expressive paragraph about bread and the breaking of bread, the GIRM underscores how sacramental liturgy is enacted through the use of signs and symbols. It states:

> The meaning of the sign demands that the material for eucharistic celebration truly have the appearance of food. It is therefore expedient that the Eucharistic bread, even though unleavened and baked in the traditional shape, be made in such a way that the priest...is able in practice to break it into parts for distribution to at least some of the faithful...The action of the fraction or breaking of bread, which gave its name to the Eucharist in apostolic times, will bring out more clearly the force and importance of the sign of unity of all in the one bread and of the sign of charity by the fact that the one bread is distributed among the brothers and sisters. (n. 321)

> The wine for eucharistic celebration must be from the fruit of the grapevine (cf. Luke 22:18), natural, and unadulterated, that is, without admixture of extraneous substance. (n. 322)

These statements about the bread and wine help to explain what is said earlier in the GIRM about the act of preparing the eucharistic gifts. In relation to the sacrifice of Christ the text asserts:

At the Last Supper Christ instituted the Paschal Sacrifice and banquet, by which the Sacrifice of the Cross is continuously made present in the Church, whenever the priest, representing Christ the Lord, carries out what the Lord himself did and handed over to his disciples to be done in his memory.

For Christ took the bread and the chalice and gave thanks; he broke the bread and gave it to his disciples saying: "Take, eat, and drink: this is my Body; this is the cup of my Blood. Do this in memory of me." Accordingly, the Church has arranged the entire celebration of the Liturgy of the Eucharist in parts corresponding to precisely these words and actions of Christ. (n. 72)

The words of the *Didache* (the early church document describing the Christian way of living) contains the following text which illuminates the close relationship between the natural symbolism of bread and wine, the unity of the church, and the hope of God's kingdom derived from eucharistic participation. "As this broken bread was scattered over the mountains, and when brought together became one, so let your Church be brought together from the ends of the earth into your kingdom..."[31] The cosmic context for the eucharistic bread is thus underscored; it is specified in an agrarian setting and involves the domestic action of baking bread. These meanings are presumed in every celebration of the Mass. They should never be far from our consciousness when we celebrate the Eucharist.

## IMPORT OF THE CELEBRATION OF THE EUCHARIST

The principle of sacramentality presumes and needs the celebration of liturgy because the very doing of the liturgy makes a number of theological statements, one of which concerns sacramentality itself. That we always celebrate the Eucharist by using gifts from human life and human productivity makes a clear theological statement about the sacramentality of all of life. Then, on a deeper level, we can say that we need the perpetuation of Christ's paschal victory through sacramental liturgy in order to put the world into proper perspective as both graced-filled and flawed, as reflective of God's grace but also as standing in need of complete redemption. That we do this in the celebration of the eucharistic liturgy is to suggest that regular engagement in sacramental liturgy prevents us from becoming too optimistic about the world—a temptation not always overcome in some contemporary approaches to what we have come to call "creation theology" and "creation spirituality." But when liturgy and sacraments are celebrated regularly and are regarded as essential to Catholic doctrine and practice, then theologies and spiritualities of creation achieve proper theological balance even as they receive proper theological emphasis in the very fact of doing the liturgy.

The celebration of sacramental liturgy also does a number of other things, among which are the following.

1.  It substantiates the contemporary emphasis on the theology of creation and places it on a truly theological ground in that it always stresses that the things of this earth used in liturgy are from God's goodness. This is to say they are both natural symbols from God's providence (water) or the results of human manufacture from what the earth has produced (bread, wine). These are not only objects, they are the means we humans need to use in order to articulate our faith in the Triune God. Sacramental liturgy regularly places on our eyes a prism through which to view creation and the world, a prism that is biblical and paschal. It is biblical in the sense that it makes us "see" the world as created and sustained by the God of the covenant—God the creator and redeemer. It is paschal in the sense that we "see" all things not through rose-colored glasses but through lenses that enable us to evaluate everything in life from the perspective of Christ's paschal mystery. Especially in an incarnational world view, to see the world as sacramental means that even as we name its flaws we are confident in its final perfection as a result of Christ's paschal victory.

2.  Sacramental liturgy prevents us from being pessimistic about the
    world and world events. By its very shape and structure, sacra-
    mental liturgy is a ritual experience that reflects an optimistic
    approach to human life. In the end "all will be well." In the
    meantime, we need sacramental liturgy to put the world into
    focus and perspective. Opportunities for experiences of hope
    abound in the celebration of sacraments—hope in the act of
    liturgy and hope derived from the act of liturgy which enables us
    to face and deal with human life. Among other examples in the
    eucharistic liturgy, the singing of the "Holy, holy, holy" acclama-
    tion is insightful and instructive. Every time we celebrate the
    Mass we acclaim "heaven and earth are full of your glory..." The
    earth itself is a locus where God's glory is seen and experienced.

3.  Sacramental liturgy articulates our belief that we worship God by
    using the things of this world. This means that sacramental
    liturgy is always both anthropological and cosmic; it articulates
    what we believe about the human person and the cosmos. Or,
    better, through sacramental liturgy human persons put their lives
    and the world itself into proper perspective. We use "daily and
    domestic things" in liturgy, things that are both from creation
    and the result of human productivity and that reflect back on the
    goodness, generosity, and largesse of the God we worship. We use
    them to put order into (what is sometimes) the chaos of human
    life and to set us in proper relation with the world and all who
    dwell in it.

To my mind, among the things which the enactment of the Eucharist
accomplishes is that bread and wine, taken and shared, are the regular
ritual reminders of what it means to share in God's very life and grace
in all of human life. It is the liturgical taking of food and drink, the
liturgical act of blessing food and drink and of sharing the Eucharist
as food and drink that puts human dining into perspective and gives it
its depth. This is to say that the very manufacturing of these foods,
the ritual proclamation of the eucharistic prayer, and the sharing of
these gifts in eucharistic communion do more than simply articulate
what the sacrament of the Eucharist means. They also derive from

the prior experience of sacramentality in human life when we use words and actions to communicate with each other and to sustain life. In both God is at work. The sacrament of the Eucharist expresses and specifies for believers that here and now God is operative in all of their lives. Sacramental liturgy thus provides the lens we need in order to view all of reality—a reality that is always integrative of the sacred and secular and of what is both fully divine and fully human.

Our task is to make sure we view liturgy as a deep and strong ritual expression of the fact that God lives among us prior to, in a unique way within, and following upon sacramental engagement. The function of sacramental liturgy in its uniqueness is less about bringing to the world what we have experienced in the liturgy (as important as that truly is) than it is to underscore how what we do in liturgy derives from the world and everyday life, the liturgical ritualization of which helps us order our lives and our world once more in God's image and likeness. From the perspective of sacramentality, one can say that sacraments are less doors to the sacred than they are the experience of the sacred in and through human life, an experience shaped by the liturgical action of the Eucharist.

Every time we take bread and wine in the act of doing the Eucharist we articulate the theology of the goodness of creation and our need for food to sustain us as the "pilgrim church on earth" until we are fed at the "Supper of the Lamb." In the meantime, the very taking, blessing, and sharing of bread and wine make the central theological statement about our place in the cosmos. All sacramental liturgy makes sense in the first place because the use of goods from the earth reminds us of our place in this world even as we yearn for it to pass away.

Part of our thesis about a "Cosmic Mass" concerns the way we truly look at life. Having a wide-angle lens on as much of life as possible is true to the Catholic principle of sacramentality. Sacramental liturgy can help us reflect back on the world in which we live and ponder our care for it as well as our concern for those who dwell on it. It can help us take seriously our obligation of stewardship for the world. We are never to presume that we are its masters or that we are its lords. We are its stewards, responsible to succeeding generations for our care of and for it.

My intention here has been a modest one, namely to review and perhaps to revive a truly fundamental principle of all liturgical and sacramental activity as well as a central Catholic trait. Among other things, sacramentality holds in tension what is and what is not, that the human and the divine are inseparable in Christ and that both of these apparent polar opposites are totally intertwined in both the sacramental world and sacramental liturgy. Sacramentality should shape our vision of the *sacrum commercium*. This perspective of "marvelous exchange" should ground our appreciation of what it means to share meals both in family settings at home and at the Lord's table in the eucharistic liturgy. When this regularly occurs, then the sacramentality that grounds sacraments is placed in proper order and perspective. It also means that the cosmos is always reflected in liturgy, because liturgy needs the cosmos for there ever to be "daily and domestic things" that can then be transformed into the holiest of gifts, bread and wine, transformed and shared. In the end, because of the principle of sacramentality, every Mass is *cosmic*.

*Discussion/Reflection Questions*

1. Do I realize the value of dining as opposed to eating food? What does dining imply in terms of hospitality and revering Christ as he comes to us in others?

2. How does an appreciation of the work that goes into the liturgy of the Mass help me appreciate the phrase that the Mass is "the work of our redemption"?

3. What is it about bread and wine that reveals the mystery of Christ's incarnation and paschal dying and rising?

*Further Reading*

Kevin W. Irwin, "The Sacramentality of Creation and the Role of Creation in Liturgy and Sacraments," in *Preserving the Creation:*

*Environmental Theology and Ethics*, ed. Kevin W. Irwin and Edward J. Pellegrino (Washington, DC: Georgetown University Press, 1994) 67–111.

Philippe Rouillard, "From Human Meal to Christian Eucharist," in *Living Bread, Saving Cup*, ed. R. Kevin Seasoltz (Collegeville: The Liturgical Press, 1987) 126–57.

# The Church's Eucharist

*"Strengthen in faith and love your pilgrim church on earth."*
—*Eucharistic Prayer III*

Because we are delineating a liturgical theology of the Eucharist, some aspects of this theology are particular to the Eucharist itself (e.g., how in it a sacrifice is offered, a topic that will occupy us in Model Eight). At other times we will articulate what the Eucharist has in common with other aspects of sacramental liturgy. More specifically, this is to say that we will discuss what the Eucharist shares liturgically and theologically with other aspects of sacramental liturgy. What I want to argue in this model about the church can and should be argued about the liturgy in general, namely that every act of liturgy is done by, for, and in the name of the church. Thus it is appropriate to begin our consideration of "the church's Eucharist" with a consideration of how liturgy—by its very nature—is always about the church and church life is always concerned with the liturgy.

## THE "WORK" OF THE PEOPLE

Among other things, the word "liturgy" means the "work of the people." It always refers to a work, an event, an action undertaken by the
whole church—that is, all those assembled including all liturgical
ministers—for the sake of the whole church—that is, the local assembly, the diocese of which it is a part, and the church universal. According to what many regard as a classic text for a description of the
liturgy, every time we celebrate the eucharistic liturgy "the work of
our redemption is accomplished" (prayer over the gifts, Evening Mass
of the Lord's Supper).[1] The "work of the people" (one of the literal
meanings of the Greek term for liturgy, *leiturgia*) undertaken at the
liturgy is for the sake of experiencing again and again "the work of
our redemption." Notice the text does not say that "the work of the
*liturgy* is accomplished." What is accomplished by God and hopefully
what is appropriated by the church *in and through* the liturgy is nothing less than the work of our being redeemed by God. Synonyms for
the redemption "worked" at liturgy are initiating us into the very life
of God at baptism, deepening the salvation first experienced at baptism in other sacraments, sanctifying us by allowing us again and
again to experience God as the most sacred of all realities, forgiving
those things that prevent us from living the fullness of the life of
God, strengthening our faith as the "pilgrim church on earth," experiencing the justice of God in what is often an unjust world, and
being healed in the myriad ways that only God can offer us. In his
commentary on Vatican II's Constitution on the Sacred Liturgy,
which speaks of the liturgy as the "summit and source" of the church's
life, Josef Jungmann writes that "the highest virtue was not religion
but love; the liturgy was rather a means than an end, the fountain
being Christ and the Holy [Spirit]."[2]

My point is that the liturgy is always about redemption gained for
us once for all in Christ, a redemption experienced here and now in
and for the church through the celebration of the liturgy. Precisely
because it is *liturgical*, the redemption celebrated is always communal,
for and with the whole church. Liturgy is not a private devotion for
personal sanctification only. It is about nothing else than the church's
very identity and vocation—as the redeemed of and in Christ.

The roots of this understanding come from the scriptures, which presume "corporate memory" as a foundation for any act of liturgical prayer (more about "memorial" in Models Three and Four). That liturgical memory is always corporate derives from our identity as inheritors of the Judaeo-Christian tradition, which presumes, asserts, and underscores again and again that we are all part of each other as the chosen people of God. We go to God together. We are members of the one body of Christ. Furthermore every act of liturgy presumes the corporate memory of God's interventions in history that brought freedom, forgiveness, and redemption for God's chosen people in salvation history and to us through the liturgy at which we hear those same foundational stories of salvation "for us and for our salvation" here and now. Once *corporate memory* is assumed as a foundation and axis for all liturgy, then we can begin to develop a theology of the liturgical *actio* (a Latin term that I take to mean "action," "event," "dynamic experience") in general and of the liturgical theology of the Eucharist derived from it in particular.

The Greek word *synaxis* means "assembly," especially an assembly that is gathered for a sacred purpose. *Synaxis* is related to the verb root *synago* meaning "to bring together, [and] to come together." That *synaxis* derives from a verb form with (at least) these two meanings is important to recall in order to underscore the dynamic, event character of all liturgy done at God's gracious invitation and command. From the witness of Justin Martyr (AD 150) through to the teachings of the contemporary magisterium (e.g., the title of section 2 of chapter 5 of the revised GIRM 2002 on the "arrangement of the sanctuary for the sacred *synaxis* [sacred assembly])," appropriate emphasis is always placed on a theology of assembly and the act of gathering as an essential aspect of any theological understanding of what liturgy is and means.

This kind of emphasis is directly related to the "sea change" ushered in with the Constitution on the Sacred Liturgy's assertions that "liturgical services are not private functions, but are celebrations of the Church, which is the 'sacrament of unity,' namely, a holy people united and organized under their bishops... It is to be stressed that whenever rites, according their specific nature, make provision for communal celebration involving the presence and active participation of the faithful, this way of celebrating them is to be preferred, as far as possible, to a celebration that is individual and quasi-private" (nn. 26–27).

The Constitution on the Sacred Liturgy and subsequent magisterial teaching also restored to our liturgical language and experience the manifold presence of Christ in the Eucharist: in the assembly, in the proclaimed word, in the eucharistic species, and in the person of the minister (Constitution on the Sacred Liturgy, *Sacrosanctum Concilium* [SC], n. 7).[3] In addition it put to an end generations of quasi-private experiences of liturgy by asserting that "communal celebrations are to be preferred to a celebration that is individual and, so to speak, private" (SC, n. 27) (more on this under "Active Presence" in Model Nine).

In referring to the "sacred synaxis" (n. 295), the GIRM 2002 adds to the previous 1975 text of the GIRM when it refers to "places where people regularly gather" (n. 293). These assertions underscore the classical definitions of the liturgy as "the church's prayer"—or better the *church at prayer*, which phrasing gives more emphasis to the active participation of the whole church in the liturgy. While some have criticized some of the contemporary emphasis in liturgical literature on "assembly," Pope John Paul II himself uses it in *Dies Domini* when he speaks about the eucharistic *assembly* as the "heart of Sunday."[4] He asserts that "the *dies Domini* ["the day of the Lord" which is the title of the document] is also the *dies Ecclesiae* ["the day of the Church"]." Later he states that "the Sunday assembly is the privileged place of unity: it is the setting for the celebration of the *sacramentum unitatis* ["the sacrament of unity"] which profoundly marks the Church as a people gathered 'by' and 'in' the unity of the Father, of the Son and of the Holy Spirit."[5] This phrase is also repeated in Pope John Paul II's encyclical on the Eucharist (n. 41).

This last assertion deserves emphasis. The liturgical assembly is not of our making. We gather for any and every act of liturgy at God's gracious invitation, having been sacramentally initiated into the body of Christ at baptism. Recall the words of the third eucharistic prayer: "From age to age you gather a people to yourself..." and "hear the prayers of the family you have gathered here before you."[6] We "gather" at the Eucharist because of God's initiating and sustaining grace,[7] to be fed as the body of Christ on the body of Christ. We do not create community. The community that is the liturgical assembly is that which God forges and renews each time we assemble for any act of liturgy.

Furthermore, every act of liturgy presumes not only the church that is gathered in this place and at this time but also the wider church throughout the world. The phrase from the Roman Canon "we offer them for your holy catholic Church" underscores this reality. The naming of the pope and local bishop at every act of Eucharist in the eucharistic prayer serves to remind us of this worldwide community of the church. Our "naming" them is about what the pope and diocesan bishop represent—the whole church throughout the world and the local church at a given location in a diocese. Our naming them also concerns their life and ministry on behalf of the whole church throughout the world and the local, diocesan church. The local assembly gathered for the Eucharist is always part of a larger whole. And the church assembled for liturgy is always part of the church that has gone before us, that is the community of the redeemed in the kingdom of heaven. Thus we can say that ecclesiology and eschatology are intrinsically tied together (more on eschatology under Model Seven). Hence the value of the ending to the preface that states: "and so with all the choirs of angels in heaven we proclaim your glory and join in their unending hymn of praise..."

Thus ecclesiology is the necessary substratum of all liturgy. This presumption of the communal nature of the Eucharist should really lead to an *un*self-consciousness. Through and in the liturgy we are always challenged to be less self-concerned and ever more self-transcendent. We are always challenged to be concerned with "the whole church." This kind of focus—on the other and on the self only in relation to others—offers a challenge to us Americans. Specifically, it has to do with the relationship between freedoms for the individual as highly prized "American" values and the demands of belonging to a church whose very identity is bound up with that which is corporate, communal, and concerned with the common good. At its essence, the Eucharist can be counter-cultural, since it is about prayer in common leading to concern about the good of each other and all others. The celebration of the liturgy is ultimately about communal self-transcendence. Liturgy always presumes prayer with and for each other; it always presumes that we accept the perennial challenges of bearing each other's burdens and of washing each other's feet.

The presumption in most official liturgical books (even before Vatican II) is that we gather at liturgy as the assembly of the local church. The term "local church" is predicated on territory, meaning the diocese in which we live and also, especially in reference to the liturgy, to the local parish to which we belong. Actually, one of the defining characteristics of Catholicism is that it has divided the world into parishes. The theological meaning of such a division is in fact that wherever you may be "you belong" to the Catholic Church, with the parish as a specific manifestation and expression of pastoral concern that one can "belong" and always find in the parish a haven and a home. "Belonging" to the Catholic Church is realized in a particular place. Belonging to a particular diocese and parish reflects our belonging to the church everywhere and at any time. The notion of a diocese and parish based on "territory" is meant to foster relationships with those near whom we live and socialize.

At the same time, it is clear that many Catholics prefer to worship in places other than their ("territorial") parish churches. Hopefully the notion of belonging to a community and a sense of commitment and communal self-transcendence marks these acts of liturgy and such acts of liturgy reflect the lives of the participants as initiated and ever more committed Christians. Even where "picking and choosing" parishes may be possible in some locales (e.g., cities) and sanctioned by some bishops, the main argument of this chapter is not jettisoned —all liturgy is done by and with the whole church. And this same theology is underscored when one celebrates liturgy at other places, e.g., near where one works, recreates, travels for the weekend, as well as when celebrating particular liturgies such as weddings and funerals. But recall what the liturgy always celebrates—*our redemption*. Both terms require humility and presume a challenge. This is to say that the plural *our* is used to remind us that we go to God together and that in addition to praying with and for each other we are also to bear each other's burdens as we live out what we celebrate. And every act of liturgy affirms that we are aware of and continually admit the fact that we stand in need of *salvation*.

The last chapter of the revised GIRM concerning liturgical inculturation indicates that the church universal is not monolithic and that inculturation of the liturgy (accommodation and adaptation to suit various cultures) is presupposed and also, especially at present, an ongoing project. Clearly the Roman rite as we have inherited it was inculturated. Numberless rituals and prayer texts came to "Rome" from other places. One can say that the more expressive aspects of the Roman rite came from areas north of Rome (e.g., the rite for the dedication of churches, Palm Sunday processions, etc.).[8] These "Gallican" customs were both adopted and adapted into the "Roman" rite. Evidence of the inculturation of the liturgy is also writ large in the evolution of the kinds of buildings that have been used for liturgy and the kinds of music used at the liturgy. That inculturation of the liturgy offers opportunities and challenges for the contemporary church is reflected in both the Fourth Instruction on the Proper Implementation of the Liturgy[9] as well as in chapter 9 of the GIRM 2002. But the historical evolution of the Roman liturgy itself attests that we belong to a worldwide and two-thousand-year-old church whose liturgy has been influenced by the adoption of customs from cultures outside of Rome itself.

What is also clear with regard to inculturation is that whatever is said and done in the Roman rite must conform to the adage *lex orandi, lex credendi*. As already noted,[10] in addressing inculturation of the liturgy the GIRM 2002 states that it is important that "the faith be passed on in its integrity since the Church's rule of prayer *(lex orandi)* corresponds to her rule of belief *(lex credendi)*" (n. 397). This phrase is critical for our purposes in this book. It expresses the intrinsic relationship of liturgical prayer and orthodox belief. Initiatives toward liturgical inculturation should always reflect orthodox prayer and belief. Many commentators rightfully observe that at its root the meaning of *orthodoxy* is "correct praise," and that what is intrinsically related to correct praise is "correct belief" expressed in "correct doctrine." Whatever is done by way of continuing the inculturation of the Roman rite must be done in light of developing a common prayer that is orthodox (in every way).

Liturgical inculturation respects that we who are one in Christ come from different locales and cultures. This variety of peoples—in the past up to the present—makes up the mosaic that is Catholicism. This mosaic is never more richly exemplified than in an understanding of the liturgy as essentially corporate, stretching us to embrace all who together form the body of Christ that is sustained by the body of Christ in the Eucharist.

## BROKEN BREAD, SHARED CUP

In the previous model on "Cosmic Mass," when discussing the relationship of the things of this earth that are used in worship, I quoted the words of the *Didache*. There the purpose of quoting the text was to illustrate that human productivity was involved in the making of bread and wine. That same text can function here to illustrate the unity of the church as celebrated and deepened in the Eucharist: "As this broken bread was scattered over the mountains, and when brought together became one, so let your Church be brought together from the ends of the earth into your kingdom . . ."[11] Clearly on a cosmic level the grains of wheat become one in the baked bread to signify the many and various people who make up the church. But church belonging—even as celebrated and ratified in and through the Eucharist—does not always guarantee church unity. Hence the large number of times that the Roman liturgy prays for deeper unity and peace. This is especially true in the invocations of the Holy Spirit for church unity in the Roman eucharistic prayers approved for use after Vatican II (more on this in Model Ten). Invocations such as "may [we be] filled with his Holy Spirit, and become one body, one spirit in Christ" (third eucharistic prayer) make this abundantly clear.

In addition, other words in the eucharistic prayers illustrate the way in which church unity is implied and fostered through our participation in the Eucharist. The words of institution clearly parallel "bread" and "cup," not "bread" and "wine." This is notable theologically.

The text of the Roman Canon reads:

He took bread into his sacred hands . . .
he broke the bread, gave it to his disciples and said
Take this, all of you, and eat it . . .
When supper was ended he took the cup . . . gave the cup to
    his disciples and said
Take this, all of you, and drink from it . . .

The same bread/cup parallel is followed in all the other eucharistic prayers. For example, the fourth states:

> He took bread, said the blessing, broke the bread, and gave it
>  to his disciples, saying:
> Take this, all of you, and eat it...
> In the same way, he took the cup, filled with wine. He gave
>  you thanks, and giving the cup to his disciples, said:
> Take this, all of you, and drink from it:
> this is the cup of my blood...

In the same fourth eucharistic prayer the *epiclesis* for the church states "and by your Holy Spirit, gather all who share this one bread and one cup into the one body of Christ, a living sacrifice of praise." The theological point to be made here is that the breaking of the bread leads to sharing from the one eucharistic bread, a symbolic gesture filled with ecclesiological meaning. We who "take," "bless," and "break" the one bread then share in the body of Christ in the sacrament so that we may live as the ever more unified body of Christ. We also are invited not only to share in the consecrated wine but also to drink it from the (one) cup. This is to say that the liturgical ritual of sharing from one bread that is broken and from one cup that has been poured out for our salvation is a ritual way of underscoring how the Eucharist is essentially a communal experience. The notion of unity expressed in and through sharing one bread and cup reaches back to 1 Corinthians 11 and extends to our present eucharistic prayers and actions. Obviously, this action also brings with it many challenges, among which is the concern as to how we who share from the broken bread and the one cup respond to this gift of unity through the Eucharist as we live the rest of our lives.

It is not a coincidence that the action of breaking bread takes place during the singing of the Lamb of God. This text emphasizes the sacrificial nature of the Eucharist as well as its intrinsic ecclesiology. We who acclaim the "Lamb of God who takes away the sins of the world" also beg "have mercy on us" and "grant us peace," things needed in full measure even for the church on earth as it seeks to become the more perfectly united body of Christ.

In addition to breaking bread for communion, there is another custom observed at this point in the Mass that deserves mention, largely because it deals with underscoring the intrinsic relationship of

togetherness

Eucharist and ecclesiology. It is the dropping of a piece of the consecrated bread into the chalice. This custom originated in a practice
called the *fermentum*.[12] In the early church at Rome (when the Christian population was small), a part of the consecrated bread broken at
the pope's Mass was taken by deacons to other churches in Rome
where it was placed into the chalice during the singing of the Lamb of
God at Masses celebrated at those other churches. The theology of
this ritual gesture concerns church unity—namely that the wider,
whole church is always in union with the Eucharist of the pope. However, as the number of churches grew and it became impossible for the
*fermentum* to be taken to all the other churches in the city, the *fermentum* practice was replaced by the *sancta* practice. What now would
occur was that a part of the consecrated eucharistic bread (broken during the praying of the Lamb of God) was placed on top of the altar,
and the part of the broken bread that was already on the altar from the
preceding Mass was dropped into the chalice. The ecclesiological significance of the *fermentum* now shifted toward an appreciation that
every Eucharist would lead to the next, and the next, and the next, a
continuity signified by dropping a piece of the consecrated bread from
the previous Mass into the chalice at the Mass being celebrated.

To recall the practice of the *fermentum* as we approach receiving
communion can only enhance our appreciation of the way even our
reception of the Eucharist bears on church unity. As we receive communion under the form of consecrated bread, we respond to the
words "Body of Christ" by asserting "Amen." In doing so, we who
now share in the consecrated species are also reminded that we are
also saying "Amen" to the body of Christ that is the church. This is
another example of the multivalence of liturgical language noted as
early as the fifth century in the writings of St. Augustine. "Body of
Christ" here means more than the consecrated species. It also means
that those who are fed by this eucharistic bread are members of each
other in the body of Christ that is the pilgrim church on earth. And
the chalices we use for the distribution of communion under both
species (as opposed to "shot glass"–size individual cups) are themselves important for the symbolic unity they represent. We who drink
from the one cup should live as the more perfectly united church of
God on earth. The fact that permission for communion to be distrib-

uted under both forms of consecrated bread and wine has been increasingly widened in the universal church (in the GIRM 2002, nn. 281–284) and that it has been even more widely expanded by the decisions of the American bishops is important theologically as well as liturgically. The symbolic action of receiving communion by sharing in both species serves as a reminder of ecclesial identity and ecclesial belonging.

## A TRADITIONAL UNDERSTANDING

One of the most important authors writing today on the relationship of ecclesiology and Eucharist is Paul McPartlan. The phrase that best describes his contribution is "eucharistic ecclesiology."[13] He credits the Western theologian Henri de Lubac with coining the famous principle "the Eucharist makes the church." In this context I judge it very significant that Pope John Paul II's encyclical on the Eucharist is entitled *On the Eucharist in Its Relationship to the Church*, and that in it he himself asserts that "the Eucharist builds the Church and the Church makes the Eucharist" (n. 26). This encyclical is truly a meditation on eucharistic ecclesiology. It finds its roots particularly in the patristic tradition and it applies the insights from that tradition to the needs of our day. In some instances it is really an example of liturgical theology in the way it often cites the words and actions of the liturgy as evidence for the strong case the pope presents for the interrelationship of Eucharist and ecclesiology.

As McPartlan points out, this maxim about the Eucharist making the church is of even greater importance for the Eastern theological and liturgical tradition. He specifically notes how central it is to the thought of John Zizioulas.[14] According to McPartlan, de Lubac's research into the patristic and early medieval periods indicates that "a major change in vocabulary...occurred in the twelfth century, severely damaging the patristic link between the Eucharist and the church. Prior to that time the church had been called the *corpus verum*, the *true* body of Christ, and the Eucharist was indicated to be the place where this primary bond was mystically (that is sacramentally, in later terminology) effected by being itself called the *corpus mysticum*, the *mystical* body of Christ."[15] However, once Berengarius of Tours in the mid eleventh century began to provide more or less adequate theological descriptions of the eucharistic elements of bread and wine changed into the body and blood of Christ, the eucharistic *species* themselves then took on the adjective *verum* "and the church had to be content with what was left, namely being called the *corpus mysticum* . . ."[16]

(We who are so accustomed to speaking of the "mystical body of Christ" to refer to the church, not the Eucharist, can find much insight in the fact that "mystical" was a way that the patristic authors referred to the Eucharist.) In addition, while in the patristic era the bishop was presumed to be the one who presided over the eucharistic action with and for the church, by the Middle Ages the emphasis came to be placed on the priest pastor's presidency at the Eucharist and on how to describe the power of God working through him to change bread and wine into the body and blood of Christ. McPartlan states that "if 'the Eucharist makes the church' would be an apt motto for the patristic period, 'the church makes the Eucharist' would better suit the scholastic centuries."[17]

A number of themes emerge from this glimpse into the history of theology. Let us recall that when discussing principles for these models (in Part 1, "A Proposal") I indicated that I wanted to articulate a theology of the Eucharist that reflected a "both . . . and" rhetoric, not one that spoke about "either . . . or." This principle is important to recall here. Obviously, we know that we are the inheritors of the theology of the church and of church structures that have evolved over many centuries. Equally obvious is the fact that some periods—e.g., the patristic and medieval—were more formative than others concerning the theology and practice of the Eucharist. Of particular urgency in Vatican II's considerations of liturgy and ministry (especially of the ordained) was the retrieval of important insights from the patristic era. In fact, many of the liturgical structures and texts in the present Catholic liturgy derive from the patristic era. But we need to be cautious here lest a simplistic "older is better" principle become operative. One of the issues at Vatican II and in the present reformed liturgy was to retrieve insights and practices from the patristic era in order to redirect our attention to some aspects of the Eucharist that may have been eclipsed during the medieval and Tridentine eras.

Recently Frank Senn spoke to the temptation of imitating the past uncritically. In his introduction to a collection of essays in *Liturgy* (the journal of the Liturgical Conference) concerning the use of ancient sources for the revised liturgical rites in both Catholicism and the other Christian churches, he writes:

> The essays in this issue of *Liturgy* do not add up to a program or even a direction for further liturgical revision. They do sound a note of self-criticism within the liturgical establishment that brought us our present liturgical orders and rites. We sometimes acted too precipitously on too little information or on insufficient digging. Churches that use the historic liturgy certainly have to pay attention to history. But it is inadequate to pay attention only for the purpose of replicating ancient orders and retrieving ancient texts in contemporary patterns and books of worship. Those ancient orders and texts were used in a social context just as our orders and texts are—the context of an assembly that was as much enmeshed in the culture of which they were a part as we are enmeshed in our own contemporary cultures. If we use an ancient text or follow an ancient pattern today it should not be just because it is ancient but because it expresses a world view that we share with those who have gone before us in the faith or that we are in the process of recovering.[18]

The key insight here is that the liturgical rites from the patristic era which were used as models for the revision of the liturgical books and rites after Vatican II were regarded as important not simply because they were tried and true but because they offered for our revised rites models that would better exemplify elements of church life and belief from our tradition, elements that had become eclipsed over time. Clearly one example of what had been eclipsed from the late Middle Ages on and needed revival was the intrinsic relationship of ecclesiology to the liturgy, and in particular active liturgical participation of the assembled church in the liturgy.[19]

The involvement and active participation of the community of the church in the Eucharist is repeatedly underscored by the contemporary magisterium. Two examples are particularly notable. The first is from the Constitution on the Sacred Liturgy, which states: "[The faithful] should give thanks to God. Offering the immaculate victim, not only through the hands of the priest but also together with him, they should learn to offer themselves. Through Christ, the Mediator, they should be drawn day by day into ever more perfect union with God and each other, so that finally God may be all in all" (n. 48). The other is from the Constitution on the Church: "the faithful . . . by virtue of their royal priesthood, participate in the offering of the eucharist" (n. 10). These examples reflect what all the eucharistic prayers emphasize by referring to the way that the whole church engages in the act of eucharistic praying. Among others, the contemporary systematic theologian Hans Urs von Balthasar emphasizes the centrality of the active participation of the church in offering the sacrifice of praise that is the Eucharist.[20] The relationship of the ordained and the baptized faithful is subtly noted in the GIRM 2002 when it speaks of the role of the laity in "exercising an office of their baptismal priesthood" (n. 69).

## ECCLESIAL AND LITURGICAL MINISTRY

One of the clearest emphases in the Constitution on the Sacred Liturgy and in all subsequent magisterial documents on liturgical ministry concerns the restoration to the celebration of the liturgy of liturgical roles in addition to that of the bishop or priest who presides over the enactment of the eucharistic liturgy. At the same time, there would seem to be few other aspects of church life today that receive the kind of emphasis in terms of "turf" wars and "who should do what" as does liturgical ministry. At the outset I would like to nuance the subtitle above and argue that in what follows our concern should always be with how liturgical *ministry* reflects church ministering in general as well as how *ministers* serve in liturgical ministry.

In an important study of the patristic evidence detailing the roots of liturgical ministry, Herve Legrand argues persuasively that in the patristic era those who presided at liturgy were those who had a pastoral charge and who exercised leadership in the community.[21] His thesis is that those who led the church theologically, pastorally, and spiritually—almost always the bishops—were those who presided at liturgy, e.g., sacramental initiation (as well as preparation for it and mystagogy after it), the Hours, and the Eucharist. Again what we discover from this kind of historical research is a rich notion of bishops and other liturgical ministers functioning to safeguard the church's identity theologically and spiritually.

One aspect of this leadership and articulation of the faith occurred when bishops presided at the celebration of liturgy. Succinctly put, liturgical ministering derives from and shows itself in (all) other aspects of church leadership and life. This is the theological reason why the GIRM 2002 places such emphasis on the diocesan bishop (n. 22 and throughout) in assertions that are clear advances from the 1975 edition of the GIRM. The theological premise for this emphasis is pastoral leadership of a diocese; when a diocese assembles for liturgy, this kind of ecclesial self-expression offers a model for and a reminder of how liturgy and church life intersect and are always interrelated. Obviously, accommodations to this (patristic) principle can and should apply to parish life and worship today. In particular, they may well offer challenges to some presumptions about our understanding of what liturgical ministry is all about—particularly in relating ministry at the liturgy to the rest of one's ecclesial responsibility and ministry.

For example, the General Instruction on Christian Initiation asserts that "it is the duty of pastors to assist the bishop in the instruction and baptism of adults entrusted to their care..." (n. 13). The rite of infant baptism speaks of the role of the "parish priest (pastor)" in helping to prepare parents for the baptism of their child (n. 8). The rite of marriage states that "as far as possible the pastor himself or the one he delegates to assist at the marriage should celebrate the Mass..." (n. 72). The rite for the anointing of the sick speaks of the duty of "priests, particularly parish priests (pastors)..." (n. 35) when caring for their sick parishioners. The GIRM 2002 states that "pastors...should take into account the many and diverse circumstances of those who are present at a liturgical celebration..." (n. 385). Each of these documents also speaks about other "offices and ministries" in the church, which adds another dimension to the presumed pastoral relationships which the liturgy articulates and celebrates.

Among the things that one can derive from these assertions is that the liturgy is about enacting the saving mysteries of Christ with and among the people as presided over by a pastor, and that this "source and summit" in liturgical ministry has a great deal to do with his pastoral ministry outside the liturgy. Another of the bases for appreciating the liturgy as the "source and summit" of the church's activity is found in day in, day out pastoral encounters which themselves are part and parcel of the life of the parish priest and of those who serve on pastoral staffs. Hopefully they are also appreciated as part and parcel of their spiritual lives. They are certainly part and parcel of what the liturgy as the saving act of Christ is all about.

When liturgy is seen as the "source and summit" of parish life and when liturgical ministries are seen as expressions of serving in other areas of parish life, then the presumed relationship of liturgy and life is evident. There is a world of difference in terms of pastoral liturgical leadership and care between the experience of a priest celebrating Mass in a community he does not know and the experience of a pastor and other liturgical ministers who have an ongoing and direct relationship to the community with which they celebrate the liturgy. This is to suggest that the liturgy is a convergence of preexisting relationships in the church. Liturgical ministers exercise their liturgical ministry precisely as an expression of their ongoing service of the community in myriad ways. To preside at the liturgy is to do so with a pastoral heart. It presumes sets of relationships in terms of church belonging and parish participation. These are then ratified in the celebration of liturgy with church ministers in liturgical roles. The premise is ongoing, sustaining pastoral oversight and care. These are essential correlatives of liturgical leadership and ministry. (More on this in the Conclusion on "A Liturgical Eucharistic Spirituality.")

A related issue concerns what the ministers of the liturgy do to enact the liturgy. *Who* they are and their particular characteristics really should cede to emphasizing *what* they do for the sake of the whole church. In an era of "personalities" and "stardom," we need to recall that liturgical ministry is precisely about that—*ministry*, not minist*ers*. Liturgical ministry is about charisms building up the church, not personal charisma that draws attention to oneself. It is not really about who ministers are in terms of their individual personalities. At the same time, there is an art to being involved in liturgical ministry. A sense of naturalness and expertise in communication (verbal and especially nonverbal) are required characteristics of liturgical ministers. However, whatever each of them does individually is always part of what is done by an ensemble of ministers to foster the participation of the whole church in the act of worship.

With regard to the liturgical ministry of the priest, the GIRM 2002 specifies in a number of places that he acts *in persona Christi capitis* ("in the person of Christ, the head [of the church]"). It would seem clear that a major reason for this insertion in this edition of the GIRM (as opposed to the 1975 edition) is Pope John Paul II's emphasis on this way of describing the role of the ordained priest in the church, articulated specifically in his annual Holy Thursday letters to priests. What is especially notable in this phrase (particularly when compared to the ways in which it has been used in our theological tradition[22]) is the use of *capitis* ("the head"). One of the nuances which this word adds to acting "in the person of Christ" is the reminder that it is always Christ who is head of the church. The addition of *capitis* specifies what this phrase always presumes—that it is Christ as high priest who is the mediator of salvation and that any ministry in the church is always in relation to Christ's high priesthood first and foremost. In fact, Pope John Paul II repeatedly asserts this. One example is contained in the statement in his 2000 letter:

> Those whose task it is to renew *in persona Christi* what Jesus did at the Last Supper when he instituted the Eucharistic Sacrifice, "the source and summit of the entire Christian life" (*Lumen gentium* 11) are thus linked in a special way to the first Apostles. The sacramental character which distinguishes them by virtue of their reception of Holy Orders ensures that their presence and ministry are unique, indispensable and irreplaceable. (n. 5)

That the pope puts the priest's unique liturgical ministry in the context of the rest of the priest's ecclesial ministry is seen further on when he states:

> Our ministry is not of course limited to celebrating the Eucharist: it is a service which includes the proclamation of the Word, the sanctification of the faithful through the Sacraments, and the leadership of God's People in communion and service. But

the Eucharist is the point from which everything else comes
forth and to which it all returns. Our priesthood was born in
the Upper Room together with the Eucharist. (n. 10)

The one who presides and preaches "in the person of Christ,
head of the church" ought to do so humbly, with self-transcendence
and transparency as chief characteristics. The emphasis is not on the
personality (cult?) of the minister but on the person of Christ leading
the assembled church to the Father, through the effective and active
mediatorship of Christ in the power of the Spirit experienced at the
liturgy. At the same time, it is the individual priest's gifts and talents
which are to be placed at the service of the community when he is
presiding and preaching. The goal is not passive or anonymous ministers, nor is it ministry that focuses attention on individual characteristics and personalities. That the contemporary magisterium uses the
adjective *ministerial* priesthood underscores this theology and emphasizes the intrinsic servant role of the ordained.

In light of this usage it is interesting to see how the GIRM 2002
refers to the liturgical assembly as it is engaged in the act of Eucharist. When referring to the general intercessions, it states that "the
people respond in a certain way to the word of God which they have
welcomed in faith and, exercising the office of their baptismal priesthood, offer prayers for the salvation of all" (n. 69). This kind of terminology is certainly congenial with the understanding of Christ's
priesthood experienced in the liturgy by all the baptized, some of
whom are obviously ordained. It is also congenial with that espoused
by contemporary theologians (e.g., John Zizioulas et al.). Finally, it
is a reminder that any and all liturgical roles are meant to image
the church and to serve the assembled church. All liturgical ministers come from the ranks of the baptized and act in service of the
baptized.

One concrete example of how this occurs is the way in which
almost all of the prayers uttered by liturgical ministers are in the
plural—*we, our, us*—and thus are prayed in the name of the whole
church. This is further specified in the description the GIRM 2002
gives to the priest's role in general (n. 31) and to the proclamation of
the eucharistic prayer specifically:

Now the center and summit of the entire celebration begins: namely the Eucharistic Prayer, that is, the prayer of thanksgiving and sanctification. The priest invites the people to lift up their hearts to the Lord in prayer and thanks; he unites them with himself in the prayer he addresses to God the Father in the name of the entire community through Jesus Christ in the Holy Spirit. Furthermore, the meaning of the prayer is that the entire congregation of the faithful joins itself with Christ in acknowledging the great things God has done and in the offering of Sacrifice. (n. 78)

This says a great deal about the importance of the eucharistic prayer in the celebration of the Eucharist itself and of the bishop or priest who articulates it for the whole assembly. Therefore the eucharistic prayer is central to any exposition of a liturgical theology of the Eucharist.

## COMMUNION AND INTERCOMMUNION

Among the things which the prayer after communion at the end of Mass often asserts and reflects is how any particular celebration of the Eucharist should be lived out in our lives (see GIRM 2002, n. 89). One of the petitions often found in these prayers is reflected in the text:

Lord,
may this eucharist
accomplish in your Church
the unity and peace it signifies.
(Prayer after Communion, Eleventh Sunday in Ordinary Time)

What is clear in this text is that while we are still far from experiencing the fullness of the unity and peace in the church which the Lord wills, the Eucharist is our privileged experience of that unity and peace as fully as possible in this imperfect world. Hence our continual need for the Eucharist to strengthen the church. Central to our experience of the Eucharist is the act of receiving the eucharistic species as communion. The lexical root of "communion"—*common union*—and its theological meanings are important correlatives and are worth recalling.

Given the presumption of the close relationship of ecclesiology and Eucharist, we now have the opportunity to reexamine two terms that reflect the theology of the Eucharist: "communion" and "intercommunion." In a sense the latter is a term containing a built-in redundancy, simply because all acts of "communion" relate us to others in the union brought about in Christ. The act of receiving communion is an act of sharing the Eucharist and church life with each other. The commonly used verb form "to take communion" says it more precisely. What we do when receiving communion is to partake in the Eucharist and in so doing to participate in the sacred meal that makes us "one body, one spirit in Christ" (third eucharistic prayer). No act of communion is ever for oneself alone. It always signifies our relatedness to each other through Christ. At the same time, it is always a reminder of what we are not. The "pilgrim church on earth" is not the fully united and perfectly sinless bride of Christ. We are always on the way toward fulfillment and perfection. We feed on the body of Christ in the Eucharist so that the body of Christ on earth can be the ever more complete realization of God's presence with us until we are called to the kingdom of heaven.

Therefore we must always be humble about our virtue and about the journey that still awaits us as we strive to be the ever less imperfect church of God on this earth. There should be no presumption about what we do when "taking communion." In no way do we do this righteously. We do it to allow the bonds of faith and love to grow ever stronger in our hearts and in our lives.

A difficulty often arises, however, when Roman Catholics find themselves in circumstances of worshiping with other non–Roman Catholic Christians and the other Christians find themselves worshiping at a Catholic Eucharist. In these instances the issue of who should/can receive communion arises. It can appear that communion is for "members only" and rhetoric about hospitality and welcoming seem to be given the lie when it comes to not welcoming non-Catholics to eucharistic sharing. However, in fidelity to our theological—and especially our ecclesiological—tradition, this is simply not the case.

It is clear that intercommunion raises numberless issues. One reason for this is that the reception of communion itself reflects a number of theological issues, particularly with regard to ecclesiology —specifically church "belonging." Our purpose in what follows in this section is simply to indicate why the ecclesiology of the Eucharist forbids "open communion" and an "open table." But let us be frank. These are issues that need theological precision and pastoral care. As we have already stated, part of the lived context for this discussion is that the Catholic Church (along with all other churches) has never been nor will it ever be perfect. The key issue in acts of (inter)communion is the degree of belonging to and participation in the church that sharing in the Eucharist presumes and fosters. True to our aim throughout this book, our observations here are theological and are basically about our belief in the Eucharist and about church belonging, that is, ecclesiological. Our concern is not with the legitimate circumstances when exceptions to normal practices may require different action.[23]

Clearly, part of the concern about when we can and should share the Eucharist has to do with what we believe about the Eucharist, e.g., the reality of Christ's presence as reflected in the traditional Catholic term *transubstantiation*. But even where this belief about eucharistic presence may be shared, there are also other understandings about the theology of the Eucharist itself—for example, the sacrificial nature of the Eucharist—that must be presumed. It is clear that an overriding issue here concerns church belonging. Succinctly put, this means shifting the focus from "what I believe" about the eucharistic species to "where I belong" as a member of the church. The issue of communion, especially intercommunion, is always about relating the personal (what "I" believe) with the communal (what church I belong to and why).

Among other things, the Eucharist is always a sign of unity and a source of unity. The latter is based on the bonds which only God can forge among us and which are ratified through the sacramental signs of sharing in communion. Clearly our tradition ritualizes and accomplishes initial belonging to the church and participation in Christ's high priesthood in sacramental initiation (baptism and confirmation leading to Eucharist). This participation is renewed in the Eucharist.

Initial conversion is thus deepened in and through the Eucharist, which leads to greater unity in the body of Christ. Again, the words of the third eucharistic prayer are as consoling and challenging as they are instructive when we pray: "Strengthen in faith and love your pilgrim church on earth." We receive the Eucharist in humility and in the hope that what God draws us into at this holy altar table may be realized in the communion we experience and live in life. The church fed on the Eucharist is always a "work in progress." However, this humble stance is not always obvious to those who celebrate the Eucharist nor is it always obvious when the Catholic Church seems to put up barriers to (inter)communion.

In fact, it is often the case that misunderstandings about "intercommunion" cause major difficulties pastorally. And those difficulties almost always center on hospitality and welcoming people to a specific Eucharist (e.g., funerals, weddings, etc.) rather than on what it means to "belong" and to be a member of the body of Christ, the church. On occasions when we share liturgical services with those who are not initiated and confirmed Catholics or when we ourselves are at liturgical services in other Christian churches, we need to ask: What creed do I affirm and which church community do I belong to? Furthermore, what set of practices and prayer forms am I committed to? The act of taking communion in the Catholic Church is a supreme sign of a number of things: belief in Christ's presence and action as well as profession of belief in the creeds, codes, and practices of the Catholic Church. The act of taking communion is at once most personal and most communal.

One of the chief obstacles to eucharistic sharing across denominational lines is precisely that there are denominational lines within Christianity that divide the Christian church. And a major reason is that all Christian churches do not adhere to the notion of "apostolic succession" that the Catholic Church upholds. Catholic doctrine and practice assert that we can trace the "succession" of our church in general and the ordination of our bishops in particular back to the apostles. Some churches (e.g., Episcopalians, Lutherans, etc.) broke with that succession at the Reformation. At the risk of being too specific, one can assert that it is precisely the issue of apostolic succession —the very doctrine that binds the church as professing the same, orthodox creed believed to have come down to us from the apostles—

that now causes division. The act of taking communion is an act of commitment to the succession of the apostles' teaching and lineage. It also relates to how we understand the nature of the ordained ministry that comes to us from the apostles.

The liturgies of many Christian churches (e.g., Episcopalians, Lutherans, and Catholics) are similar and in celebration we use similar or the same music and have churches that share the same architecture. These facts all point to communality and certainly a high degree of liturgical unity. But the theological issue is not "just" these similarities or how things "look." The theological issue involves understanding the challenge of what it means to take communion. This act reflects church structure and church belonging as well as doctrine about the real presence and one's own personal spiritual life. One challenge that this offers to any of us who share in eucharistic communion is to realize that this act should give the lie to any kind of privatized spirituality or concern for the self only.

That there are degrees of sharing in church life is clear. It is also clear that in certain circumstances receiving sacraments from a minister in a church that is not one's own may be acceptable. Pope John Paul II himself addressed this issue in his encyclical on the Eucharist when he stated:

> While it is never legitimate to concelebrate in the absence of full communion, the same is not true with respect to the administration of the Eucharist *under special circumstances, to individual persons* belonging to Churches or Ecclesial Communions not in full communion with the Catholic Church. In this case, the intention is to meet a grave spiritual need for the eternal salvation of an individual believer, and not to bring about an *intercommunion* which remains impossible until the bonds of ecclesial communion are fully re-established. (nn. 45–46)

Then, in the next paragraph, he repeats what he asserted in his letter of 1995 entitled *Ut Unum Sint* ("that they all may be one"):

> Catholic ministers are able, in certain particular cases, to administer the sacraments of Eucharist, Penance and Anointing of the

Sick to Christians who are not in full communion with the
Catholic Church but who greatly desire to receive these sacra-
ments, freely request them and manifest the faith which the
Catholic Church professes with regard to these sacraments.
Conversely, in specific cases and in particular circumstances,
Catholics too can request these same sacraments from minis-
ters of Churches in which these sacraments are valid.

What is significant is that these texts offer a change from the previous
provisions for special instances of intercommunion. The *Directory for
Ecumenism* issued by the Pontifical Council for Christian Unity in
1993 had an additional provision, namely that "that the person be
unable to have recourse for the sacrament desired to a minister in his
or her own church or ecclesial community" (n. 131).[24] Commentators
have rightly pointed out the fact that John Paul II did not retain this
phrase in his recent writings on the subject.

In their guidelines and study document entitled *One Bread, One
Body*, the Catholic Bishops' Conferences of England and Wales, Ire-
land and Scotland made a distinction between "holy communion and
full communion."[25] This distinction is helpful in that it balances the
fact that we must have a level of agreement in doctrine and practice
to share in the Eucharist of the church with the reality that we are
always deficient and do not always live all that we profess. (This document is also among the most thorough and helpful explanations of
the theology that underscores the Catholic Church's practices regarding intercommunion.)

The *Guidelines for the Reception of Communion* of the American
bishops conference indicate degrees of sharing and the challenge that
eucharistic communion poses for us all. With regard to the situation
of fellow Christians present at Mass, the bishops state:

We welcome our fellow Christians to this celebration of the
Eucharist as our brothers and sisters. We pray that our common baptism and the action of the Holy Spirit in this
Eucharist will draw us closer to one another and begin to dis-
pel the sad divisions which separate us. We pray that these
will lessen and finally disappear, in keeping with Christ's
prayer for us "that they may be one" (Jn 17:21).

Because Catholics believe that the celebration of the Eucharist is a sign of the reality of the oneness of faith, life, and worship, members of those churches with whom we are not yet fully united are ordinarily not admitted to Holy Communion. Eucharistic sharing in exceptional circumstances by other Christians requires permission according to the directives of the diocesan bishop and the provisions of canon law (canon 844, §4). Members of the Orthodox Churches, the Assyrian Church of the East, and the Polish National Catholic Church are urged to respect the discipline of their own Churches. According to the Roman Catholic discipline, the Code of Canon Law does not object to the reception of communion by Christians of these Churches (canon 844, §3).[26]

What is also important to realize here is that there are *degrees* and *levels* of participating in the Eucharist. The very fact that Christians of all denominations regularly find themselves at liturgies in each other's churches means that there is already a presumed level of commitment and cooperation. With regard to liturgical practices, the fact that most Christian churches use (basically) the same set of scripture readings each Sunday is an instance of significant ecumenical cooperation and unity.[27]

While one cannot presume to share in the Eucharist in another church on any regular basis, the fact of sharing in the proclamation of the word, preaching, and intercessory prayer is not nothing. If in fact we can say theologically that these are indeed important aspects of the (inter)celebration of the Eucharist and that Christ is present in the assembly and through the proclamation of the word at the liturgy, then we must assert that engaging in sharing in the word and prayer is itself a sign and source of deepening church unity. The theology of the proclaimed word in the liturgy enhances both our theology of the Eucharist itself (more on this under Model Three, "The Effective Word of God") and our appreciation of what it means that we share its proclamation with fellow Christians. To celebrate the proclamation of the word in common has significance in terms of unity and deepened unity in and through the liturgy. It reflects one level of and (hopefully) an ever deepening unity in Christ. But again, it does not signify complete unity in faith and liturgy because eucharistic sharing

always implies common understandings about the Eucharist, ecclesiology, apostolic succession, etc. At the same time, not to notice the
unity shared in word and prayer is to demean intrinsic parts of the
eucharistic action.

Among the challenges that the intercommunion issue offers us
are to ensure that Eucharist is always seen as an ecclesiological reality and to appreciate the balance between "hospitality" on the one
hand and church tradition and theology on the other, especially
when it comes to intercommunion. This means appreciating that
sharing in the Eucharist reflects sharing doctrine, life, and faith as
well as the sacrament of the Eucharist which itself always reflects
these realities. It also means respecting the different emphases different Christian churches give to eucharistic theology; there are some,
for example, who do not hold to "transubstantiation" and prefer to
speak less philosophically about the presence of Christ in the Lord's
Supper.

## CHALLENGES OF THE CHURCH'S EUCHARIST

To say that common payer is always communal is to assert what is not
always experienced. In fact, it may be most uncommon, especially in
an age and in a place where the individual person is prized over almost
all else. Furthermore, liturgy is not a private devotion, meant (only) to
give me comfort. While comfort and consolation are legitimate things
to experience at and from liturgy, there is also—and, I would argue,
more compellingly—the challenge that all liturgy offers us: nothing
less than communal conversion and communal self-transcendence.
This means that the Eucharist challenges us to change our minds,
hearts, and—yes—our ways and wills to conform to what God has
already revealed and has in store for us. Liturgy is not a refuge from
the world so much as it is an intense moment in time that refocuses
our lives and reminds us that what we celebrate in liturgy should be
borne out in the way we live our lives. Thus, an essential and intrinsic
challenge to every act of gathering for liturgy is dispersing from it to
live in the rest of life what we have celebrated in and through the
liturgy. This means building up the body of Christ which is the
church at the prayer of the liturgy in order that we can become ever

more fully the body of Christ in the world to witness to the reign of God, to the will of God, to the plan of God that all might be saved, renewed, and come to fullness of life in and through what God does for us. To understand the ecclesiology of the eucharistic liturgy may well mean sacrificing what is most personal for what is communal. After all, that which is held in common is meant to support our lives as persons in relationship with each other in faith. To understand the ecclesiology of the eucharistic liturgy may well mean to realize that what concerns me as an individual also affects my faith life in relationship with other believers. This may be a particular challenge to Americans' notions of freedom for the individual in relation to the communal. Some specific examples of tension points in pastoral practice deserve mentioning.

When John Paul II wrote about Sunday Eucharist, he emphasized that it is the *Sunday* Eucharist that is central to the church's life and mission. This centrality has always been affirmed in the church's teaching and practice and is reflected in the 1973 *Directory for Masses with Children*. This document never speaks about adapting the liturgy to children without noting how the Sunday Eucharist of the whole assembly is normative (even when children are dismissed for the Liturgy of the Word). Similarly, according to the revised rites of ordination, ordinations are to take place on Sunday. (In much of our liturgical tradition they customarily took place on Ember Saturdays.) The rationale for celebrating ordinations on Sundays is that it is at the Sunday liturgy that the church assembles. More recently, the phenomenon of having insufficient priests to celebrate Sunday Mass has spawned the phenomenon of "Sunday celebrations in the absence of a priest." One of the key reasons for such worship services is to ensure the unity of the local parish community wherever possible. This is not to denigrate the Eucharist and the opportunity of participating in it in another parish. Among other things, it emphasizes how the unity of the local parish can be jeopardized if the local parish does not regularly gather for Sunday worship.

Some practical applications can flow from the principle of Sunday Eucharist being the "norm." One concerns the practice of celebrating first Eucharist for young people at the Sunday Mass. This is far better both eclesiologically and liturgically than a celebration on any other day and at another time. The reason is quite simple. When children are being prepared to receive the Eucharist, they are being prepared to share in what will be a week in, week out ritual celebration. If in fact Sunday Eucharist is normative, then planning and celebrating a "special" Mass for first Eucharist is both unnecessary and liturgically undesirable. This is because such special liturgies can derogate from the formative nature of the regular Sunday Eucharist as that which will be the ritual weekly fare of those who do celebrate the Eucharist regularly. It is the church's weekly Euchrist that establishes the shape and norm for any other liturgy. The fact that first Eucharist is celebrated at Sunday Mass makes the right statement about where we belong and the value of belonging to the wider parish community.

The very celebration of the Eucharist reveals and reflects a paschal ecclesiology. In our tradition, the views of St. Augustine on relating the Eucharist to communion in the church and his insight that "the whole Christ offers the whole Christ" are pertinent. It is in this framework that the conciliar teaching that the liturgy is the "source and summit" of the church's life makes the most sense. Eucharistic participation is always linked to church life, teaching, and witness. That the Eucharist has been traditionally regarded as the "sacrament of sacraments" reminds us of the ways in which it is indeed the term of initiation, the sacrament to which we are initiated (more on this in Model Five, "Covenant Renewal"). Like every act of liturgy, the Eucharist is always of, by, and for the whole church.

*Discussion/Reflection Questions*

1. How well do I appreciate that almost all of the prayers we use at the Eucharist that refer to our need for God are in the plural? What implications does this have for me when I pray at the Eucharist?

2. It is clear that the church's teaching and discipline about intercommunion can cause hurt feelings and misunderstandings. What can I do to help to explain these positions to non-Catholic friends?

3. There is a fine line between using my gifts and talents at the service of the church at the Eucharist and becoming the center of attention. In what ways can I avoid becoming too focused on my own liturgical role and enhance the roles of others?

*Further Reading*

Herve Legrand, "The Presidency of the Eucharist According to Ancient Tradition," in R. Kevin Seasoltz, ed., *Living Bread, Saving Cup* (Collegeville: The Liturgical Press, 1987, 1982) 196–221.

Hans Urs Von Balthasar, "The Mass: A Sacrifice of the Church?" in *Explorations in Theology III: Creator Spirit* (San Francisco: Ignatius Press, 1993) 185–243.

## MODEL THREE
# The Effective Word of God

*"Then God said 'Let there be light,'*
*and there was light."*
*—Genesis 1:3*

For Roman Catholics in the early 1960s, the clear assertion in the Constitution on the Sacred Liturgy that "the liturgy of the Word and the liturgy of the Eucharist...are so closely connected that they form but a single act of worship" (n. 56) probably came as a surprise. After all, Catholics who grew up in the pre–Vatican II church can remember regularly being instructed that the three principal parts of the Mass were the offertory, consecration, and communion (of the priest). Yet now in this document (and reiterated in other conciliar documents[1]) the bishops at Vatican II were reminding the Catholic faithful of the importance of the proclamation of the word of God at Mass.

In accord with the thesis of this book, our concern in this chapter is with the theological meaning of the proclamation of the word of God at the eucharistic liturgy. Our aim is to present a modest theology of what *happens* when the scriptures are proclaimed at Mass. In particular I will illustrate this dynamic approach to the proclamation of the word by reference to the way the Lectionary structures our

reading. In effect, the Lectionary itself is a statement of liturgical theology. Overall, my thesis is capsulized in the assertion that *when God
speaks, something happens.* Hence the title of this chapter speaks of the
*effective* word of God.

What is notable in contemporary magisterial teaching is that the
proclamation of the word is sometimes referred to as the *table* of the
word of God. This seemingly curious term is found in Vatican II's
Constitution on the Sacred Liturgy. When calling for the proclamation of a greater portion of the scriptures (in effect revising the cycle
of readings we now proclaim at Mass from the Lectionary and the
Book of the Gospels) it states that the reason is so that "richer fare
may be provided for the faithful at the table of God's Word" (n. 51).
The notion that we receive nourishment from this table is repeated
both directly and indirectly in subsequent documents. Take, for
example, the GIRM 2002, which states that "the table both of God's
word and of Christ's Body is prepared, from which the faithful may be
instructed and refreshed" (n. 28) and "in the readings, as explained by
the homily, God speaks to his people, opening up to them the mystery of redemption and salvation, and offering them spiritual nourishment; and Christ himself is present in the midst of the faithful
through his word" (n. 55).[2] What is clear from these references is the
intrinsic relationship of word and sacrament. That we receive spiritual nourishment from each is equally clear.

For a proper appreciation of what happens at the Eucharist we
need to look at *both* what takes place at the ambo or lectern and what
happens at the altar table.[3] This is to say that the vocabulary of traditional Catholic teaching used to describe the eucharistic species—
food—is utilized here to assert the importance of the proclamation of
the word in offering us food and nourishment. Hence the helpful reference to the "table of God's word" in the Introduction to the *Lectionary for Mass* stating that "the Church is nourished at the twofold
table of God's word and of the Eucharist: from the one it grows in
wisdom and from the other in holiness" (n. 10).

What happened in liturgical practice after Vatican II as result of
these assertions was that the proclamation of the scriptures in the vernacular increased in both number and variety. One of the most obvious revisions of the post–Vatican II liturgy has been the expansion of
scripture readings for every liturgical event. In fact, as Msgr. Frederick

McManus has repeatedly noted, the Roman Catholic *Lectionary for Mass* of 1969[4] was such a "success story" that it became the model for the Sunday lectionaries of many other Christian churches and this in itself is a profound ecumenical statement.[5] That the choice of scripture texts to be proclaimed at the Sunday Eucharist is virtually the same among many Christian churches and that these churches collectively believe that when the scriptures are read God acts are certainly very important theological assertions. Words matter. Further, the announcement of God's word in many different churches has implications for the faith of our individual churches and the faith reflected in all the Christian churches.

That Roman Catholics have come to study the scriptures in scripture classes and courses since Vatican II has been a much needed, revitalizing element of Catholic life. That Roman Catholics regularly meet for prayer and discussion about the Sunday scriptures in study groups has been nothing short of a revolution in the way Catholics learn about, pray to, and speak about God. And that Catholics have heightened expectations about the biblical inspiration and theological content of the liturgical homily attests to the achievement of an envisioned aim of the council, the appreciation of God's word as indeed instruction, nourishment, and food.

In the previous chapter I indicated that one of the foundations for the ecclesial nature of the Eucharist is the biblical witness in the Judaeo-Christian tradition that we share a "corporate memory." In that chapter I emphasized the communal, corporate aspect of what it means to "make memory." In this chapter and the next I want to explore what this "act of memory" is all about. My thesis here will be that a constitutive part of all liturgy as an act of memorial is the proclamation of the word of God. More precisely, what I will argue is that the proclamation of the word of God is the *enactment* of the word of God here and now, which action and event become operative for us in a unique way in and through the liturgy.

The words of Jesus at the Last Supper, "Do this in memory of me," are etched in the minds and hearts of all Christians, especially when it comes to participating in the Eucharist. What I should like to suggest here is that the eucharistic act of memory necessarily includes as an intrinsic component the proclamation of the scriptures. While

Roman Catholics never ceased to proclaim the word of God in the Eucharist (as is attested in even the Tridentine Missal), nonetheless the revival of our experiencing that proclamation at the Eucharist is a much welcomed result of the liturgical reforms of Vatican II. I want to argue that, at least in part, to "do this in memory of me" concerns the effective proclamation of and response to the scriptures proclaimed at Mass (and at every liturgical event as prescribed in the current liturgical rites revised since Vatican II). It has always been obvious that to "do this in memory of me" includes what we do in the balance of the eucharistic action in presenting bread and wine, their transformation, and our communion in them.

I suspect that one of the difficulties we have with trying to appreciate the dynamism of what proclaiming the scriptures means is that we are so familiar with printed books and words on a page (or computer screen!) that we presume that the "words" have to do with only conveying ideas and information. In point of fact, the biblical witness and the liturgical experience of the scriptures is based on something very different. It presumes that when the word is announced in the liturgy, precisely through that announcement, *something happens*. Words at liturgy are spoken not simply or primarily for the sake of information. Words are proclaimed at liturgy so that God can do something among us for our sakes and our salvation.

Take for example what happens every year at the Easter Vigil in every Catholic parish in the world. After blessing the new fire and acclaiming the summary of saving history in the *Exsultet* (Easter Proclamation), the Liturgy of the Word begins with the reading from Genesis chapter 1, the account of creation. At verse 3 we hear "Then God said 'Let there be' ..." and what God said came to be, on that day and on the subsequent days of creation. What God said *happened*. The biblical paradigm should be applied to what occurs in the liturgy, namely, that what God says not only happened once and for all but happens still in the here and now when the scriptures are proclaimed. The power of the proclaimed word is that it causes something to occur among us.

In Genesis what happens is the very act of creation. When we hear that text every year at the Easter Vigil we are re-created and given new life. In the book of Isaiah the word renews believers and

accomplishes God's will. In a kind of reprise of the Genesis creation
account, Isaiah asserts boldly:

> For just as from the heavens
>> the rain and the snow come down
> And do not return there
>> till they have watered the earth,
>> making it fertile and fruitful,
> Giving seed to the one who sows
>> and bread to the one who eats,
> So shall my word be
>> that goes forth from my mouth;
> It shall not return to me void,
>> but shall do my will,
>> achieving the end for which I sent it. (Isa 55:10–11)

In the life of Jesus the most significant synagogue service recorded
for us in the scriptures is from Luke's gospel (4:14–20). The evangelist
tells us that Jesus returned to his home town of Nazareth, came to the
synagogue on the sabbath, and "stood up to do the reading" (v. 16).
Jesus read from a scroll containing the text of the book of the prophet
Isaiah. To this day, scrolls containing the Old Testament scriptures are
revered in Jewish liturgy, are lodged in a place of veneration in synagogues, and often are covered with cloths containing gold threads and
precious jewels. These marks of respect show how important these
scrolls are—as God's revelation and self-communication through
words that recount deeds, saving deeds that together constitute a saving history. Luke's gospel states that Jesus then proclaimed this text
drawn from Isaiah 61:

> The Spirit of the Lord is upon me,
>> because he has anointed me
>>> to bring glad tidings to the poor.
> He has sent me to proclaim liberty to captives,
>> and recovery of sight to the blind,
>>> to let the oppressed go free,
> and to proclaim a year acceptable to the Lord.
>> (Luke 4:18–19)

The gospel continues:

> Rolling up the scroll, he handed it back to the attendant and
> sat down, and the eyes of all in the synagogue looked intently
> at him. He said to them, "Today this scripture passage is ful-
> filled in your hearing." (Luke 4:20–21)

What a job description! What an experience of God's action
among us to redeem us! Notice that what Jesus reads as the servant's
role in Isaiah is in fact the role and vocation he accomplishes through
his life and work among us—to save us and redeem us, to set us right
with God the Father, and to reconcile us with each other and the
whole created order. This job description depicts who Jesus is in the
gospel of Luke, especially when after making this proclamation Jesus
says, "Today this scripture passage is fulfilled in your hearing" (v. 21).
It also characterizes the mission and ministry of his followers who, in
the Acts of the Apostles, are to preach and teach what they experienced from Jesus' teaching, preaching, and public ministry. What
Jesus *proclaimed* also *happened*—God's favor was unleashed in this
proclamation through Jesus himself. What Jesus read and did at the
synagogue in Nazareth happened then and there and subsequently
throughout his ministry on earth. He himself *was* what Isaiah had said
God's servant would be. That day the scriptures *became* what they
proclaimed—the making real here and now of God's gracious and
saving acts of salvation—in the person of the Incarnate Word of God.

This is precisely what happens when we experience the Liturgy of
the Word: we revere the books containing the readings, we proclaim
selected texts, and we respond to them in faith, and in so doing we
experience once more and again and again their saving power. What
we hear, *happens*. What we proclaim, *occurs*. What the word says,
*becomes* an act of grace and favor for us here and now, for our salvation
and for our more complete union with God.

Every time we proclaim the scriptures at liturgy "they are fulfilled
in [our] hearing." What we hear as God's good news of salvation
breaks in upon our gathering. Among other things, it challenges us by
melting our stony hearts and leading us to lives of deeper conversion.
Is it any wonder that the refrain to the classic invitatory psalm in the
Liturgy of the Hours (Ps 95) is "If today you hear his voice, harden

not your hearts?" The act of truly hearing and assimilating what is proclaimed depends on the dispositions of our hearts. Hearing and assimilating the word of God often demands nothing less than self-transcendence, which means breaking our icy isolation and turning to others and with them to live what we hear. The proclamation of the word also heals us by giving us renewed, hope-filled hearts to guide our minds and wills so they can be in accord with the will of God.

## Acts of Corporate Memory

We proclaim the scriptures at the Eucharist in order to be reminded of biblical events that occurred for the chosen people. But these are not merely historical reminiscences. These texts are also paradigms. By that I mean that, on the one hand, by their proclamation we are reminded of what occurred once for all time in saving history as God's mighty deeds of salvation. But, on the other hand, we proclaim these scriptures in order that through their very proclamation we can experience here and now that same saving action of God among us just as fully and really as when the biblical events occurred.

But here we need to be clear about what "reminded" means. In biblical-liturgical tradition, a central aspect of "making memory" is that what we proclaim and experience through liturgical actions reiterates and deepens among us what God did (not only "said") once for all in saving history. Hence, the notion of doing this "in memory of me" is only partially concerned with mental recollection. In fact, I would say that mental recall is a small part of what *memorial* means. The biblical background of "making memory" means that when we engage in the liturgy—by both word and sacramental action—God does something. God acts on our behalf. Through liturgical memorial we are drawn into God's eternal act of salvation, re-creation, and redemption.

We do not just "remind ourselves" of what God did. What liturgical memorial involves is God's working through the proclamation of biblical narratives and their complement in sacramental actions to act as savior for us again and again. We do this in liturgy because the liturgy preserves the memory of sacred events in both sacred texts and sacred actions. And in doing this we are preserved from any sort of "self-help" Pelagianism. Liturgical memorial is corporate memory done at God's initiative for us and for our sakes. One clear advantage of the liturgical memorial is that God does not leave us to our own devices to grope for and seek salvation. The gift of liturgy is that it sets before us the key, central, privileged, and unique way in which God works among us here and now to save and redeem us.

Biblical narratives recount the stories of saving history. But saving *history* does not mean what happened a long time ago. Rather, "saving history" means that God did act in the history of humanity definitively and directly for the chosen people of Israel and then most demonstratively in Jesus, and that what occurs in our time is the reiteration of that action in our histories here and now, in the present and for whatever future God has in store for us. In the liturgy we hear what God did in history and in hearing it again and again we are drawn into those same stories. They are paradigms. They occur for us here and now. Through them we are re-created and renewed.

Again, to use the first reading at the Easter Vigil as an example, in Genesis 1 we hear about light being separated from darkness (1:4) and "lights in the dome of the sky, to separate day from night" (1:14). It is in the proclamation of the word at that moment (as well as in countless other moments of the Vigil liturgy) that the light from the Easter candle comes to represent the inner illumination and presence of the light of Christ in our hearts and in our lives. Each reading concludes with the acclamation "Thanks be to God" because what we have heard has occurred one more time in our hearing of it and we assent to that happening among us in the present. God's saving deeds of redemption are perpetuated once again among us. One of the essential ways in which this happens is through the *enactment* of God's word. Sometimes that word of God may be challenging, cleansing, and purgative.[6] Sometimes it may be comforting and encouraging. But always it is a new event and experience of grace and salvation. This is summarized in the revised edition of the General Introduction to the *Lectionary for Mass:* "[T]he liturgical celebration, founded primarily on the word of God and sustained by it, becomes a new event and enriches the word itself with new meaning and power."[7]

When the scriptures are proclaimed in the liturgy, words on a page become words spoken and in being spoken they have an impact and effect on those who listen. One of the reasons why proper training and ongoing formation of readers, deacons, and priests is so important is that the *way* a text is proclaimed can deeply influence the kind of impact that text has on the assembly gathered for liturgy. Theologically, the principle is that *when God speaks, things happen.* When those who proclaim the scriptures do in fact proclaim them clearly and distinctly, they help to give the scriptures new life in this time and place. And when the scriptures come alive they have the power to effect change, to re-create and to renew us.

The proclamation of the scriptures at Mass is like shining light where there was darkness to give new life to what has lost its vigor, to raise up what was bowed down, and to re-create the world according to God's designs, so that what was once chaos is ever again set in right order by God's word. This is the reason why we proclaim the account of creation from Genesis 1 as the first reading at the Easter Vigil. It re-establishes the right order of things in creation—that all of creation is God's gift to us. And how does Genesis describe God's act of creating? By the all-powerful word of God: "And God said..." That same word is so powerful among us in the liturgy that it continues to re-create and reshape us in God's image and likeness. When God speaks, something happens. For that something to happen, however, what is required is an attitude of acceptance. That means we need to be willing listeners of God's word. Some liturgical examples of God's speaking may help to flesh out the kind of theology of proclamation envisioned and presumed as happening in the liturgy.

## THE IMPORTANCE OF A LECTIONARY

One of the reasons why a lectionary is so important is that it structures our hearing and helps us to discover again and again in varied ways and contexts who God is for us. Obviously the God of revealed religion and the God made known through the scriptures is multifaceted and omnipresent. The proclamation of a variety of scripture readings from the Lectionary and the Book of the Gospels helps to disclose various images and likenesses of the God who acts to save us. If this is true for every day at the proclamation of the word at the Eucharist, it is particularly true for those seasons and feasts on which specially chosen readings are proclaimed. When taken together, the very readings we proclaim make a serious theological statement about what the season means.

Consider the season of Lent. Vatican II's Constitution on the Sacred Liturgy decreed that the season of Lent should be revised to emphasize its baptismal and penitential themes (n. 108). Part of the response by those assigned to revise the liturgical books after the council was to study ancient sources containing gospel and other scripture readings and, on the basis of those precedents, to develop a three-year Lectionary cycle for the Sundays of Lent and readings for each of the weekdays of Lent. It is clear that these editors had "baptismal" and "penitential" themes in mind when they revised the Lectionary in light of these ancient sources.

On the first Sunday of Lent in all three Lectionary cycles (ABC) the gospel proclaimed is the account of Jesus' temptation in the desert (Matt 4:1–11, Mark 1:12–15 and Luke 4:1–13). As we hear this account, we ourselves are brought into the (figurative) desert of this holy season to do battle with our own demons and temptations—particularly those to self-promotion and power. What is also notable is that this gospel text is introduced by a verse proper to Matthew's account only, that we "live not on bread alone, but on every word that comes from the mouth of God" (Matt 4:4). This very familiar acclamation marks the proclamation of the word in Lent and is a strong invitation that we need to hear, listen to, and obey the word of the Lord, especially in during this season.

On the second Sunday of Lent in all three cycles the gospel is the account of the transfiguration (Matt 17:1–9, Mark 9:2–10, Luke 9:28–36). What Peter, James, and John experienced in this scene is what we come to experience at every act of liturgy, an announcement of God's word and an experience of Christ's glory that spurs us on in hope until we experience the fullness of Christ's risen glory in heaven. Again, it is important to note that the voice from heaven in all three cycles announces that this is God's Son and that we are to "listen to him." Once more we hear the challenge reiterated—hear, listen, and obey.

On the next three Sundays, the gospel accounts in each of the cycles form a unity.

*handwritten margin note, top: cycles dependent on time of year*

**"A" Cycle.** In accord with the evidence from the ancient evangelaries ("gospel books"), these Sundays now constitute the three important days for the final scrutinies of adult catechumens and candidates. The gospels for the three Sundays reflect a process of deepening conversion based on the account of the Samaritan woman (John 4:5–42) on the third Sunday, the curing of the man born blind (John 9:1–41) on the fourth Sunday, and the raising of Lazarus (John 11:1–45) on the fifth Sunday. This ancient trilogy of texts contains multivalent meanings, one of which concerns preparation for the sacraments of initiation at Easter. After all, where are baptisms done but in water (woman at the well, man cured at the pool of water). What happens at baptism is that we put aside deeds of darkness and walk in the light of Christ (from being blind to being able to see the light). And what results from baptism is that we share in the newness of life in Christ (Lazarus brought to life).

*handwritten margin note, left: conversion*

**"B" Cycle.** Rather than deal with the specific process leading to adult initiation, this cycle of readings is about our identification with the central event of our redemption—the paschal mystery of Christ. Hence we hear the Johannine indication of the import of Jesus' death and resurrection (John 2:13–25) on the third Sunday, the fact that the Son of Man is to be lifted up for our salvation (John 3:14–21) on the fourth Sunday, and the paradox that unless the grain of wheat is planted in the earth and "dies" it cannot bear fruit (John 12:20–33) on the fifth Sunday. If in fact all of Lent is about the paschal process and our living it in our own lives, there can be no better texts than these to highlight this central event of our salvation.

*handwritten margin note, left: redemption*

**"C" Cycle.** Because initiation can be considered a predominant theme in Lent, its renewal in penance and reconciliation is also keenly noted, especially in the Sunday gospels for the third, fourth, and fifth weeks of this cycle. On the third Sunday we hear the parable of the fig tree (Luke 13:1–9) about God's patience in leaving the plant another year to see whether it will bloom again. Where the more earnest gardener might tear it out, the paradoxical advice of the parable is to wait one more year. On the fourth Sunday we hear the familiar and always challenging parable of the prodigal son/father (Luke 15: 1–3, 11–32). Among the clearest lessons to be learned from this parable is that of God the Father's overarching concern to bring us

*handwritten margin note, left: reconciliation*

*handwritten note, bottom: scripture changes but Euch stays the same* back to fullness of life in him. Our inability at times to comprehend this love is seen in the example of the elder son. On the basis of this gospel text we never know whether he was reconciled as was his profligate brother. On the fifth Sunday we hear about Jesus' forgiving the woman taken in adultery (John 8:1–11) (or the woman who took the blame for the man/men who should have been caught in adultery). The poignant scene reveals Jesus' concern with forgiving her and with challenging her accusers at the same time.

In addition to these obviously central texts, the Lectionary is equally careful to structure the first and second readings on the Sundays of Lent. The Old Testament texts all deal with particularly significant events in the history of salvation, especially as these relate to the new covenant in Jesus. (See Lectionary Introduction, n. 97). A glance at the texts of the "A" cycle illustrates this very clearly:

1st Sunday    Creation and Fall (Gen 2:7–9, 3:1–7)

2nd Sunday    Call of Abraham (Gen 12:1–4)

3rd Sunday    Thirst for water in the wilderness (Exod 17:3–7)

4th Sunday    Spirit given to David (1 Sam 16:1, 6–7, 10–13)

5th Sunday    Prophecy of the Spirit to come (Ezek 37:12–14)

Similarly, readings from the letters of the apostles are selected as the second readings to fit the gospel and the Old Testament readings and provide a connection between them. (See Lectionary Introduction, n. 97). Again the cycle of "A" readings is illustrative:

1st Sunday    Justification through faith in Christ (Rom 5:12–19)

2nd Sunday    Salvation calls us to holiness (2 Tim 1:8–10)

3rd Sunday    Our access to God through Christ (Rom 5:1–2, 5–8)

4th Sunday    We are now awake from the death to sin (Eph 5:8–14)

5th Sunday    The Spirit of God dwells in us (Rom 8:8–11)

Given this example, it is clear that we always need to let the scripture readings and the prayers of the liturgy frame and shape how we appreciate what is supposed to be going on in our lives through the liturgy.

## "SPEAK LORD, FOR YOUR SERVANT IS LISTENING"

The proclamation of the word in the liturgy presumes and expects a "dialogical act of listening." Recall the familiar text, "Speak Lord, for your servant is listening," often used as an acclamation to accompany the procession with the gospel book preceding our hearing of the words of the gospel. Its origin in the Old Testament is the call of Samuel (1 Sam 3:1–10, 19–20), a text that is proclaimed every other year right after the Christmas season.[8] The original context for this passage is a time when revelations from God were few and really unexpected. Eli and Samuel were asleep. Three times Samuel heard the voice of God and roused Eli from sleep. Three times Samuel was sent back to bed. Only after the third try did Eli and Samuel realize that it was indeed the Lord who was calling Samuel to spread God's word and thus to renew the dynamic of his speaking to Israel and leading them as his chosen people.[9] The fact that this text of Samuel's "call" is read during the first week of the liturgical year is always poignant and pertinent.

After the appropriate festivities of the Christmas season, we celebrate the beginning of Jesus' earthly ministry by commemorating his baptism in the Jordan by John. Then, the very next week, we hear the call of God to Samuel, a text that can equally apply to us as those who hear and respond to God's call in our own day. God's call to us is to do two things: *to listen* and *to respond* to God's call. Hence the notion of *a dialogical act of listening.* Use of the summary phrase "Speak Lord, for your servant is listening" as an acclamation before our hearing of the good news of salvation reminds us that God's speaking is a direct address and invitation to us to "listen up" and to respond to the power of God's revelation.

It is also worth noting that the full text of the proposed acclamation is "Speak, Lord, for your servant is listening, you have the words of everlasting life." This second part of the acclamation is from John's gospel (John 6:68) and it indicates that what we are about to hear are words that lead us to everlasting life. Not surprisingly, the liturgy juxtaposes two important texts to reiterate a main point: God's speaking makes things happen and our hearing and living of God's word leads us to everlasting life.

What the liturgy offers us is a structured dialogue based on the premise that God speaks and we are to listen *and respond.* The liturgy never offers us the proclamation of God's word alone without eliciting a requisite response on our part. It always offers us the opportunity—the responsibility—to recommit ourselves to what we have heard in and through the liturgy. Thus it is important to look at the structure of the Liturgy of the Word. After the proclamation of a scripture text, the reader ends by saying: "The word of the Lord." Some of us recall that the first rendering of this acclamation was "This is the word of the Lord." This longer phrase was changed for a theological reason.

To explain that reason we need to recall the multivalence of much liturgical language, namely that the words and phrases we use in the liturgy often convey more than one meaning and that sometimes the meanings conveyed reflect a number of important theological ideas. Therefore, when it was decided to eliminate "This is" from the conclusion to the liturgical proclamation "the word of the Lord" it was for a good reason. When the reader says "The word of the Lord" s/he is referring to at least two things—*both* to the actual act of the proclamation of the word *and* to the book from which the reader has proclaimed that text. It was thought that if we continued to use "This is the word of the Lord" we might so emphasize the book from which the scriptures are read that the *event* of the liturgical proclamation of the word would be diminished. At the same time, we need to be clear about proper reverence for both the book containing the readings and the effective proclamation of the readings themselves.

The General Instruction for the Book of the Gospels asserts that "the Book of the Gospels [is] venerated above all the books of readings" (n. 6). The GIRM 2002 presumes that at every celebration of Mass the gospel book is carried in procession, placed on the altar, and then carried in procession to the ambo for proclamation (nn. 172–176). Additional signs of reverence include the carrying of candles to accompany the procession and the incensing of the gospel book. Recall here the reference above to scrolls in synagogues. In the history of Christian art and artifacts there are numberless examples of ornate and beautifully designed gospel books (also called "evangelaries"). To this day at special papal Masses the pope will take the gospel book from the deacon, hold it with both hands, and make the sign of the cross over the gathered assembly after the gospel has been proclaimed. This ritual gesture is now proposed for the church at large in the General Instruction for the Book of the Gospels.

Such a ritual action emphasizes how we should regard and revere the gospel proclaimed from the Book of the Gospels. At the same time, the GIRM presumes that there is another book containing the other scripture readings for the liturgy. This, too, should be revered, but the demonstrative signs of reverence for the gospel book are not to be given to the Lectionary (containing the other scripture texts). This is not to disparage the other texts, especially those from the Old Testament, which fallacy would make us contemporary "Marcionites." (Recall that Marcion and his followers denied the value of proclaiming anything but the gospels. Marcionism was condemned in the second century, principally because the church's revelation is based on both canonical testaments.)

Another meaning of "The word of the Lord" concerns the effective proclamation of the word in the liturgy. What is underscored in our dialogical hearing of the word in the liturgy is the act of proclamation of the scripture readings. Thus, when we assent with "Thanks be to God" to the invitation "The word of the Lord," we are assenting to the active and effective proclamation of the scriptures in the liturgy. We are committing ourselves to allowing them to challenge us, to confront us, and to chasten us. We invite that powerful word to change our minds, hearts, and wills. And at the very same time we invite that same proclaimed word to console us and to comfort us. We invite God's word to turn our experience of defeat to victory and admission of sin to an experience of God's reconciling love. What God says through those texts is as effective and powerful as it was when the events recounted in them happened and when the author(s) crafted them into books for our formation in the faith.

Our response "Thanks be to God" sounds simple enough. And it is something we repeat over and over. But here again we need to look at what we are saying and doing. By saying "Thanks be to God," what we are doing is committing ourselves to the word as proclaimed, with all its paradoxes, challenges, encouragements, and demands. By saying "Praise to you, Lord Jesus Christ" at the end of the gospel, we are committing ourselves to the gospel, especially to its paradoxes, and to doing God's will.

Sometimes at Mass I think it would be interesting to stop and ask whether we really know what we are saying when we assent "Thanks be to God." Are we truly assenting to the proclaimed word of God as the measure of what really matters in life? For example, are we in fact committed to the values reflected in the parable of the laborers in the vineyard when everyone gets the same wage even though all the laborers do not work the same number of hours? In the parable of the prodigal son, are we like the elder brother, the "law and order" son, or do we stand with the father in his overwhelming largesse for the lost child? Are we committing ourselves to God's way of "framing the debate" in terms of mercy outdistancing distributive justice? Are we really committing ourselves to the gospel text at the evening Mass of the Lord's Supper on Holy Thursday when we read in John 13 of Jesus' washing his disciples' feet and inviting us to do what he has done and become willing servants?

These short responses to the scripture readings in the liturgy, "Thanks be to God" and "Praise to you, Lord Jesus Christ," represent a wealth of theology and commitment. At the Eucharist, the proclamation of the word leads us gratefully to the enactment of the memorial sacrifice at the altar table. In fact, that complementary act of moving from ambo to altar table is itself a hopeful and consoling rite. We are the "pilgrim church on earth" and as such know that our lives of faith and faith commitments are not always what they should be. Therefore, among other things, the eucharistic action at the altar offers us the strength we need to live out the commitments we make when we (almost glibly?) acclaim "Thanks be to God" and assent to the gospel's paradoxical truths by acclaiming "Praise to you, Lord Jesus Christ."

### "ONLY SAY THE WORD AND I SHALL BE HEALED"

This text is familiar to all of us, as we say it each time we celebrate the Eucharist and approach eucharistic communion. It is taken from the gospel miracle of the raising of the centurion's son (Matt 8:5–11, a gospel proclaimed every year on Monday of the first week of Advent). In its original setting, the phrase (v. 8) was an act of humility on the part of the one beseeching Jesus' help and it reiterated the man's confidence in Jesus' powerful words. When placed in our Advent Lectionary, this gospel text is a powerful reminder that it is especially in Advent that we are to listen to and ponder the words of the gospel as we await the renewal among us of the incarnation of the word of God at Christmas.

When the text of the centurion, "Only say the word and I shall be healed," is voiced by the assembly at liturgy before coming to communion, it is a subtle but powerful reminder and liturgical expression of the text from the Constitution on the Sacred Liturgy (with which we began this chapter) that "the liturgy of the Word and the liturgy of the Eucharist... are so closely connected that they form but a single act of worship" (n. 56). This is to say that at the very moment when we prepare to receive sacramental communion, this text in the liturgy reminds us that we are healed and strengthened *both* by the proclaimed word *and* by sacramental communion. Or, to put it in a more integral way, we receive sustenance from the word and the altar table, two parts of one act of worship, two complementary ways of receiving God's act of salvation in the Eucharist.

Another way in which the structure of the eucharistic liturgy reinforces the interrelationship of word and sacrament is in the text of the proposed antiphons to be sung at communion.[10] Very often the texts for these antiphons are phrases from the scriptures proclaimed that day in the Liturgy of the Word. Prime examples of what I mean are found in the communion antiphons assigned for the Sundays of Lent. Specifically, the communion antiphon for the First Sunday of Lent comes from the gospel of the temptation account, Matthew 4:4 (originally from Deut 8:3), which is also used as the gospel acclamation in all three Lectionary cycles (as discussed above). The communion antiphon reminds us once more that we live not "on bread alone, but on every word that comes from the mouth of God." This echo from the gospel of Matthew offers at last two theological insights. The first is that, in subtly reiterating the gospel of the day as the assembly processes to communion, the principle of the integrity of word and sacrament is underscored. Second, on this particular Sunday it is significant that this antiphon refers to the word that comes from the mouth of God. What an important reminder that what we proclaim in the scriptures is to be pondered and made one of the bases for our Lenten conversion.

The formative nature of the proclamation of the word of God is demonstrated on the following Sunday, the Second Sunday of Lent, with the antiphon "This is my beloved Son...listen to him" taken from that day's gospel of the transfiguration (Matt 17:5). This again highlights the central place which the Lenten Lectionary in particular and the proclamation of the scriptures at liturgy in general have for the integrity of the theology of liturgy, a theology that is to be reflected in the way we look at and live our lives. What the liturgy proclaims, it enacts. The integrity of word-altar-communion is presumed in the structure of the liturgy of the Eucharist. Clearly, one perennial challenge that the celebration of the Liturgy of the Word offers is to ask the extent to which we really listen to what we hear, whether it takes deep root in our hearts, and whether it is reflected in our lives.

## LISTENING

How well do we really *listen*? Think about it. We live in a society that prizes talk radio, books on tape, personal CD players, and walkmen (or "walkpersons") of every kind and description—all ways that we can (pre)occupy ourselves as well as go about doing other things like exercising, driving, shopping, sewing, or cooking. Given the time crunch we all live under, we often try to do two things at once, so much so that we do not even think about it. But that, in fact, is the question and my point. How well do we really *listen* to what we hear? How seriously do we accept what we hear as true information that is valuable for our formation? What kind of attention do we give to all that we choose to hear?

You and I know what happens when we decide that someone we are talking to has "tuned us out." We don't like it, and if we don't say anything about it at the time we end up feeling frustrated, sometimes angry, bitter, or worse. We feel not taken seriously, ignored, or dismissed. Hence we know the importance of listening, at least when we feel not listened to! With all our high tech means of making sounds for us to hear, the real question is not whether we can *hear*. The more profound and only really important question is whether we choose to really *listen* to what we hear in order to direct the way we think and act.

Is it any wonder that the very first words that St. Benedict uses to begin his *Rule* for monks are "Listen, my son, to your master's precepts and attend to them with the ear of your heart." The Latin term *ascolta* meaning "listen" which begins this phrase is an imperative, a usage that carries with it the sense of command—"Do it!" "Be sure that you listen!" To reinforce that what he is talking about is not a mental exercise, St. Benedict goes on to invite the monks to attend to the master's precepts "with the ear of your heart." What an interesting turn of phrase and juxtaposition, "the *ear* of our hearts."

This reflects the way in many instances liturgical phrases place in relationship things that normally do not "fit" together. Take, for example, the classic psalm verse used often in the Roman liturgy at communion: "Taste and see the goodness of the Lord" (Ps 33:8). What we taste is bread and wine become Christ's body and blood. What we are to "see" through them is something that physical senses or abilities cannot grasp—namely God's graciousness and mercy in feeding us with these transformed eucharistic gifts. Two physical capacities are juxtaposed—tasting and seeing—and the combination of the two means that what we taste and see at the Eucharist is far more than senses can give us. We taste and see sacramental signs of the fullest reality possible—the grace, mercy, and peace of Christ.

Something of the same thing is operative in St. Benedict's "ear" and "heart." Again we have two physical realities. The one is the organ through which we hear; the other is the organ that pumps blood, the principle of life, through our bodies. But what is meant is far more than physical senses or actions. What "ear" signifies is hearing, and St. Benedict's challenge has to do with whether we truly listen to what we hear, whether we choose to be attentive to what comes to us through our ears. This is strengthened by the reference to the heart but not in the sense of a physical organ. For St. Benedict and for so many of us, "heart" means the center of our affections, the source of our self-giving in love, the most sensitive reality that humans experience.

How often do we say "It broke my heart," meaning that we have been terribly hurt. That this usage is metaphorical is obvious. If our heart were in fact "broken," then we could not live or function. There would be no blood pulsing through our bodies. But, as we all know, even taken metaphorically, "a broken heart" can do such damage to us emotionally and psychologically that we would sometimes almost rather die than allow ourselves to be so hurt. No wonder that life-wrenching experiences can be conveyed by referring to our hearts. How often do we hear or say that we have our "heart set on" something or someone?

Take the phrase "half-hearted." We use it to mean things done begrudgingly, with less than our full effort, our full attention, our full commitment. We often use it to refer to another person's lack of dedication to a task or a job. What's even worse is when we use it to refer to the way we relate to another. Then it means withheld love, compassion, or respect.

The metaphorical use of a physical organ to refer to the human reality of depth of commitment—either "half hearted" or "broken"—is significant. We all know well what it means to choose to be half-hearted and to have been so hurt that we say our hearts are broken. Small wonder then, that our continual Lenten prayer (from the psalmist) is for "a humbled, contrite heart" (Ps 51:10). What we mean by a *humbled* heart here is a heart that knows its need for God. Far from groveling before an angry God, Christians pray that we may know our need for God and petition God to reshape and remold us according to the divine image and likeness.

But of course the real challenge when we say this prayer is that we might well get what we ask for—humility and contrition! We say we want these, but when we do receive them we are required to change not only our minds but the very premises of our lives, again symbolized by reference to our *hearts!*

## PREACHING AS CONSTITUTIVE OF THE EUCHARISTIC ACTION

In Model One I quoted some observations that Cardinal Godfried Daneels made at the special consistory in Rome in May 2001 about the loss of a consciousness of *sacramentality* on the part of many today. And I addressed that concern in that section. Here I want to return to the other part of the Cardinal's remarks, namely that "[L]iturgy risks being dominated largely by an excess of words or of being merely a way to recharge one's batteries for *diakonia* and social

action." What is missing, he argues, is "the proper Catholic con-
ception of preaching, which is not primarily marketing rhetoric,
and of *diakonia*, which is not mere philanthropy."[11] My concern
here is with the quality of preaching that accompanies the proclamation of the word at the Eucharist. Specifically, my interest is in
probing what constitutes "good" preaching and what distinguishes it
from "bad" preaching at Mass. As noted in Model One, the phenomenon of the "mega-churches," with their emphasis on music, skits,
"participation" by observation, and the emotional aspects of faith,
contributes to nothing less than a crisis for the survival of Christian
churches that celebrate and value liturgy and sacraments. The sacramental and the symbolic are here jettisoned for the immediate and
the ephemeral. Ongoing conversion to the gospel is replaced by the
quick fix of "self-help problem-solving." Part of what is at stake is
appropriate preaching at the Eucharist.

In his apostolic constitution on the *Missale Romanum*, Pope Paul
VI noted that the proclamation of the word and preaching a homily
at Mass were significant additions to the new order of Mass structure.[12] That such additions are more than a pastoral, ritual nicety and
that there is a clear theological statement being made about the
importance of the proclamation of the word at every liturgy is underscored in the statement in the (revised) Introduction to the *Lectionary
for Mass*, which states:

> The many riches contained in the one word of God are admi-
> rably brought out in the different kinds of liturgical celebra-
> tion and in the different gatherings of the faithful who take
> part in those celebrations. This takes place as the unfolding
> mystery of Christ is recalled during the course of the liturgi-
> cal year, as the Church's sacraments and sacramentals are cel-
> ebrated, or as the faithful respond individually to the Holy
> Spirit working within them. For then the liturgical celebra-
> tion, founded primarily on the word of God and sustained by
> it, becomes a new event and enriches the word itself with new
> meaning and power.[13]

Citing the Vatican II document on priestly life *(Presbyterorum Ordinis)*, this same Introduction states that "the preaching of the Word is

necessary for the ministry of the sacraments, for these are sacraments of faith, which is born and nourished from the word."[14]

In this regard, the words of St. Augustine are pertinent. He argued that sacraments are both "visible words" and "audible symbols." Word and sacrament are uniquely and intrinsically connected. In light of the thesis of this chapter, this means that whenever the scriptures are proclaimed at sacramental liturgy they lead beyond themselves to the enactment of that word in the complementary act that sacramental liturgy implies—no, really requires. This is, when we proclaim the word at sacramental liturgy we necessarily move from ambo to font or altar, or to blessing, anointing, ordaining. The inherent logic of the liturgical theology of the Eucharist requires that we balance the "table" of Christ's body with the table of his word. Here the gospel passage of the disciples on the road to Emmaus in Luke 24 offers a model. The explanation of the scriptures led to recognition of the risen Christ in the breaking of the bread. This complementarity still needs emphasis so that what is enshrined in the biblical revelation is appreciated as what is experienced at the act of the eucharistic liturgy by the proclamation of the word and its complement in what occurs at the altar.

These citations are but representative of the kind of theological emphasis that the revised rites place on the proclamation of the word as constitutive of the act of worship. Thus we limit our theology of any sacrament today when the presumption is sacramental enactment divorced or in any way separated from the proclamation of the word. If in fact the Mass incarnates the presence and action of Christ among us through the proclamation of the word and the enactment of the Eucharist at the altar, then a theological statement is made about what occurs at both ambo and altar table. There is a parallel between the proclamation and preaching of the word and the proclamation and consecration of the eucharistic gifts through the eucharistic prayer.[15] If we are to be true to a theology of the proclaimed word—namely that it is effective—then we need to challenge ourselves theologically into seeing the preaching of the word as constitutive of sacramental efficacy. Given this kind of theology from the Introduction to the Lectionary, one could reasonably argue that there is a certain deficiency when some theologies of preaching do not include explicit and clear reference to the theology of both word and sacramental enactment. Similarly, if the proclamation of the word is regarded as optional or merely introductory to the sacrament —an understanding that is the polar opposite of what the revised liturgical rites say—we underscore a medieval statement of sacramental efficacy. This diminishes the theological power ascribed to the word in the revised liturgical rites. Again, the principle here is that the liturgy establishes a "law of belief," part of which is to give due credit to the word. To see proclamation and preaching as constitutive of sacramental doctrine seems to me simply to draw out what the church's *lex orandi* tells us.

If in fact this kind of theology is to be operative for the proclamation of the word and preaching at Mass, then certain pitfalls need to be avoided. Among them are the following two.

**1. Moralizing.** The "what would Jesus do" theology of preaching puts the emphasis on moralistic problem-solving. The proclamation of the word should lead to changed attitudes (the paradox that suffering brings real life, for example) and a life more deeply converted to the Lord and the gospel. But preachers ought to beware lest they offer a list of things "to do" without helping the assembly realize that they are not on their own in the doing because in fact Christ is uniquely present in the proclamation of the word and the rest of the assembly is engaged in the struggle to live the gospel we have heard.

**2. Didacticism.** Have you even noticed how much time the Liturgy of the Word takes? Often enough I am afraid that its length might seem to diminish the truly Catholic principle and heart of the eucharistic action at the altar and at communion. While not always, it is at least sometimes the case that the heaviness and length of the homily can be a culprit. I am thinking here of homilies that aim primarily to instruct. Clearly we should be educated through homilies. But the kind of education that takes place should be qualitatively different from what happens in a classroom. The Eucharist is the unique ritual event of experiencing the paschal mystery of Christ. Homilies should not resemble class lectures; they should be more than instruction on ideas.

On the other hand, there are things we can keep in mind in preaching that can help to support the kind of theology of the proclaimed word envisioned in the reformed liturgy. Among them are the following three.

**1. *Revelation of God's Kingdom.*** In the end, the homily should help the assembly experience then and there the paradoxes of God's rule and kingdom. If in fact the proclamation of the word is an essential part of God's self-revelation, then it is essential that the assembly sense God's kingdom operative through the homily. The kingdom's paradoxes about the astounding growth of mustard seeds, the return of prodigal sons and daughters, the washing of the feet of the unworthy and the unwashed, the crucifixion of selfish desires, the humiliation of prideful hearts, and the obedience that following a counter-cultural gospel implies—all should be hallmarks of what should be happening when homilists preach at Mass.

**2. *Linking Word and Sacrament.*** Because the theology of the unity of word and sacrament is a hallmark of post–Vatican II liturgical ritual celebration, I would argue that one function of the homily would be to bridge the move from word to altar table. In fact, the ritual action is from word to table, font, marriage vows, ordination rites, absolution, anointing, etc. Therefore, a mention toward the end of the homily as to why we now move forward to the next part of the liturgy would help close any perceived gap between word and sacrament (which would be an unfortunate but lingering legacy from the Tridentine understanding of the parts of the Mass). What may help is a comment such as: "We do not always live the way the gospel directs us. Therefore, we have the consolation and challenge of what occurs at this altar table to strengthen us to live the paradoxes of the gospel in our world, in the all-too-real reality of our lives."

**3. *Obedience.*** As a term, "obedience" often means that which is deliberately irksome and harsh. But, at its root, "obedience" comes from two Latin words, *ob* and *audire* ("to listen"). One of the theological premises of any proclamation of the word is that we live what we have heard. An understanding of the biblically based notion of obedience can help us to see the regular ritual proclamation of the word as a key—not only to obeying God but to leading the Christian life. Here the words of Pope John Paul II in his encyclical *Orientale Lumen* ring true: "When a person is touched by the Word...obedience is born, that is listening which changes life" (n. 10). One model for this, of course, is the Virgin Mary, especially at the scene of the annunciation. Her struggle with the angel Gabriel's invitation (questioning him about "how can this be") and her eventual submission to God's word can serve as a most helpful example of what it means to listen to the word and to put it into practice. Wrestling with the challenge of God's word may well be a constant in our lives. But if we give up that struggle, then the forces of evil will have won because we will have grown indifferent to the word of God.

I began this chapter by referring back to the previous one on "The Church's Eucharist," in which I mentioned the importance of "corporate memory." One of the theses of this chapter has been that the proclamation of the word of God is an act of corporate memory and that an essential part of every act of Eucharist is to listen and to obey the word of God proclaimed at Mass. This event of salvation is renewed daily in the eucharistic memorial. I have argued that the proclamation of the word is constitutive of what it means to "do this in memory of me." The next chapter will presume what we have said here and seek to deepen our appreciation of the biblical and liturgical meaning of what it means to "make memory" of Jesus.

*Discussion/Reflection Questions*

1.  Read, pray over, and discuss the scripture readings for the fif-
    teenth Sunday of the year, Cycle A.

    Isaiah 55:10–11 and Matthew 13:1–23: Draw out the rich-
    ness of Isaiah's vision of what the word of God accom-
    plishes. Discuss what it means to be a hearer of the word.
    Can you identify what kind of "soil" you are for the "seed"
    of the word of God?

2.  Pray over the responsorial psalm for that Sunday, Psalm 65, and
    repeat the refrain, "The seed that falls on good ground will yield
    a fruitful harvest."

*Further Reading*

Introduction, *Lectionary for Mass*, Second Typical Edition, Liturgy Documentary Series (Washington, DC: USCC, 1998) especially chapter 1, which contains a rich theological exploration of the importance of the proclamation of the word at Mass.

Frederick R. McManus, "Pastoral Ecumenism: The Common Lectionary," in Gerard Austin et al., *Eucharist: Toward the Third Millennium* (Chicago: Liturgy Training Publications, 1997) 103–18.

## MODEL FOUR
# Memorial of the Paschal Mystery

*We praise you with greater joy than ever*
*in this Easter season,*
*when Christ became our paschal sacrifice.*
*He is the true Lamb who took away the sins of the world.*
*By dying he destroyed our death;*
*by rising he restored our life.*

*—Easter Preface I*[1]

In this chapter we come to a phrase that might well be considered the "heart of the matter" when it comes to all liturgy—the paschal mystery. In a remarkable book about the Advent liturgy, *The Coming of God*, Maria Boulding asserts forthrightly and simply "all liturgy is paschal."[2] The precise issue in this chapter is how the Eucharist fulfills the Lord's command to "do this in memory of me." Our concern here will be to probe and mine the riches of the simple assertion that the Eucharist is the memorial of the paschal mystery.

It is, I think, beyond doubt that the retrieval of the biblical origins of the concept of memorial and its application have provided the most significant stimulus to developing a dynamic, liturgically based eucharistic theology in our day both within Catholicism and ecumenically. The imperative to "do this in memory of me" is among

the clearest scriptural assertions that undergird the liturgy of the
Eucharist as a communal, ritual action. As in the Passover itself, the
way we make memory in the Eucharist is through the shared word and
a shared meal. In the previous chapter I argued that there is a proper
and necessary *memorial aspect* to the proclamation of the word in the
Eucharist whereby what we hear becomes actualized. What we hear
happens here and now. In this chapter I want to complement those
assertions by saying that in the whole of the eucharistic action the
paschal mystery is actualized and becomes effective for us and for our
salvation. Through the unique medium of the liturgy, especially the
Eucharist, what occurs is that the center and mystery of our faith, the
paschal mystery, is experienced in such a way that the dying and rising
of Christ and *our dying and rising* through, with, and in him are made
real and engage us here and now. This occurs through the action of
the proclaimed word and our participation in what occurs at the altar
where the simple gifts of bread and wine become the body and blood
of Christ, which are then shared in communion. It will be no surprise
that our focus here will again be on how the enacted Eucharist itself is
the means through which we share in the paschal mystery of Christ. It
is the *actio* of the heart of the church's very faith and life.


## MEMORIAL AS MORE THAN "HISTORY"

Commentators legitimately debate the multifaceted meaning of the
notion of biblical "memorial."[3] Among the classic texts that are used
to frame an understanding of this biblical notion are the first two
readings at the Evening Mass of the Lord's Supper (on Holy Thursday night). The first is Exodus 12 (vv. 1–8, 11–14) and the second is
1 Corinthians 11 (vv. 23–26). The key to these texts is how we understand what it means to "make memory" both of the Passover and of
the paschal mystery of Christ. The Exodus text ends with "this day
shall be a *memorial* feast for you" and in First Corinthians the Lord's
command to "do this in remembrance of me" is found after both the
words over the bread and those over the cup (a repetition that attests
to its importance). To understand these texts one needs to appreciate
the biblical dynamism behind issues of telling time and enacting
liturgy.

In everyday speech we often refer to conducting a "memorial service" to honor a deceased relative or friend. By this we mean we want to recall a deceased person's life, especially his or her accomplishments. Not infrequently such services revolve around eulogies—telling stories that reflect well upon the dead person. These celebrations have obvious, beneficial effects for participants and help them to revere their dead. But they are a far cry from the kind of *memorial* that the Bible and the liturgy presume and speak of. Essentially this is because placing emphasis in "memorial services" on a mental recollection of past events is only a fraction of what "making memory" means in our biblical and liturgical tradition (as noted in the previous chapter when considering the "memorial" aspect of proclaiming the word).

What biblical and liturgical commentators try to unpack when they discuss the Hebrew family of terms for making memory *(zakar)* and the Greek terms derived from them *(anamnesis)* is that essentially to engage in a memorial concerns a particular way of understanding history and of telling time. Again, in terms of theology derived from the liturgy, we need to "unpack" the key Greek word for this—*anamnesis* (the opposite of which is amnesia!). And in doing so we need to be clear (and to clarify) some of our presuppositions about what *history* means.

More often than not we presume history to be chronology (from the Greek word *chronos*), meaning the recounting of events that happened in the past. And we also presume that these events are over and done with, at least in terms of determining when and where they happened. Even though some events from the past have definite implications and ramifications for the present—like the signing of the Declaration of Independence for Americans—the events themselves are relegated to the past. They happened once and for all in history. We can recount them in chronological order.

As Thomas Cahill delightfully explains in his recent book *The Gifts of the Jews*,[4] this chronological way of "telling time" in terms of past, present, and future comes from the Jewish understanding of time. It transcends the former cyclical way of "telling time" in other cultures that experienced time as an endless repetition of the planting and harvesting cycles in nature (spring planting, fall harvesting, and time in between). What the Jewish tradition is based on is something quite different, namely that God acted in history and that from then on all time was to be marked as past, present, and future. Thus the importance of salvation history—God has acted definitively in the history of humans to lead, save, redeem, and sanctify. Where, when, and how God acted this way is demonstrable in terms of chronology.

However, where the real genius of the Jewish notion of telling time affects us is in the annual liturgical commemoration of the Passover. This is to say that it is always something we do together; hence the preposition "com" from the Latin *cum*, meaning "with" in *cum* + *memorare*, which gives us "commemorate." For the Jews the Passover is considered as much more than a past event that occurred once and for all. The Passover is also an event that is a present, effective reality. And in being commemorated (literally *remembered together*) in the present, it also necessarily leads to its fulfillment in the future. In biblical phraseology, saving events like the Passover and the death and resurrection of Christ are events that occurred "once for all (time)" (from the Greek term *ephapax* in Hebrews 7:27). The Passover of Israel and the paschal mystery of Christ are both events that occurred once and for all and yet they are also events that by their very nature occur still, here and now, in the unique moment of liturgical commemoration. The Judaeo-Christian understanding of "making memory" in and through the liturgy means that the saving events that occurred once and for all can be and are experienced still, in the here and now, precisely through the privileged medium of liturgy. And these central saving events always point to their future fulfillment. This is captured in the plea of fervent Jews: "May the Messiah come." For Christians it is captured in "Lord Jesus, come in glory."

At the heart of biblical religion and liturgical commemoration are the rabbinic phrases "To remember is to give life—to forget is to let die" and "Remembering is in the doing." Liturgy in Judaism and Christianity is so central precisely because liturgy is the public event whereby participants share in the saving events that occurred in history but that cannot be confined to history (in the sense of chronology). The liturgical notion of making memory is *doing* and participating in *an act of memory* in which the very same events of history that are called "saving" are actualized, that is, realized and experienced once again through the present liturgy. These "saving" events are so extraordinary that they transcend the time and place in which they originally took place. Because they are what they are, we can commemorate them in the act of liturgy. And also, by their nature, they look beyond themselves to their fulfillment in the future. The fact that the liturgy occurs in the present means that saving events of salvation history are experienced here and now in a new act of redemption.

Again, it is the unique mode of *liturgical commemoration* that enables us to experience the same acts of redemption in ever new ways and contexts. Thus liturgical commemoration does not mean that we have to pretend that we were there at the Exodus or at the Calvary of Jesus' death or at the tomb made empty because he rose from it. Nor does it ask that we try to imagine what it was like and how those saving events first happened. That would be anachronistic and a "looking back." What the liturgy does is draw us into those same saving actions in the present so that what we experience is a "here and now" act of salvation based on God's definitive acts of salvation in the Passover and in the Christ event. Liturgical commemoration means that a new event of salvation occurs here and now. It is an act that is intimately joined to what happened in history and to what will happen when liturgy comes to an end and we are called to the kingdom of God forever. All liturgical memorial leads to its fulfillment in the future in God's good time. Christians believe that the fulfillment of the Passover has occurred in Jesus, uniquely in his death and resurrection. For Christians the notion of fulfillment means yearning for the end of time when Christ will come to bring an end to time and to bring time to an end. (More on this under Model Seven, "Food for the Journey.")

Liturgical *memorial* does not involve repeating or redoing anything from the past. Rather, what happened in the past has saving consequences among us in the present. Words such as "enact," "participate in," and "perpetuate" (the preferred term in the Roman Missal) are all helpful ways of describing liturgical memorial. Incorrect words to describe this would be that we "redo" or "reenact" what was accomplished once and for all in a definitive and final way. Notice the precise phrasing used by the GIRM 2002, namely, that "the Second Vatican Council...offered these significant words about the Mass: 'At the Last Supper our Savior instituted the Eucharistic Sacrifice of his Body and

Blood, by which he would *perpetuate* the Sacrifice of the Cross throughout the centuries until he should come again, thus entrusting to the
Church, his beloved Bride, a *memorial* of his death and resurrection'"
(n. 2, italics added).[5] In liturgical memorial we are not going back in
history; rather, history becomes contemporaneous with us, provides us
with a privileged and graced event of salvation here and now, and gives
us a glimpse of what will happen when "all will be in all" and the kingdom of God will have come finally and fully.

At the same time, in liturgical memorial the cyclical notion of
experiencing time (which shaped the way of "telling time" before the
Jews adjusted it) is not neglected. This is to say that the liturgical
commemoration of the events of saving history occur at times that are
determined by the cycles in nature. In the northern hemisphere the
annual commemoration of Passover and Easter are celebrated in the
springtime, a time of the renewal of the earth after the dormancy of
winter. In the southern hemisphere Passover and Easter are celebrated in the fall, a phenomenon that offers its own challenges in
terms of catechesis, not to mention liturgical inculturation and adaptation.[6] But is it not interesting that the phenomenon of celebrating
Passover and Easter toward winter is an example of something that all
liturgy does and is, namely, to point beyond the past and present and
yearn for its future fulfillment. Where Passover and Easter are celebrated in the fall, there is no obvious experience of renewal and
rebirth in nature. When in fact the opposite is happening in nature—
that is, the coming of dormancy and winter—then the celebration of
the liturgy of Passover and Easter can best be understood as a fore-
shadowing of what has yet to happen—namely, the full and final
accomplishment of our salvation. We live the biblical paradox of the
*already* and the *not yet*. The paradox of Christianity is that we can
combine what has occurred and what is yet to be fully realized in
order to assert that yes, we have already died with Christ in baptism, but that no, all has not been fulfilled. Recall the classic text of
Romans 6 (especially vv. 4–5) proclaimed at the Easter Vigil. This text
espouses the Pauline metaphor precisely—we have died with Christ
in baptism... and we shall rise with him (in the future). In the meantime, all liturgy is provisional and promissory of that final coming of
the Lord for which we long when we say "Lord Jesus, come in glory."
So, whether Passover and Easter are celebrated in the spring or fall

does not really matter. And in fact when they are celebrated in the fall the reality of the provisional nature of all liturgy is underscored. They are in effect liturgical commemorations of saving events from the past that are made "current events" in and through the liturgy and they are oriented to their future fulfillment. (Again, more on this in Model Seven, "Food for the Journey.") The point to be made here is that a liturgical telling of time presumes an understanding that is both chronological (what happened once and for all in history) and cyclical (the way we commemorate such an event is based on the rhythm of the seasons, which recur annually).

In a sense, the image of a spiral can help to illustrate this point. One could envision the liturgy as a spiral that is both circular and elongated. The elongated part represents the evolution of human history —chronology. The circular part delineates what recurs annually— cyclical time. The spiral combines both chronological and cyclical time-telling. Extension of the spiral depicts the combining of repeated, annual commemorations of events of our salvation (Christ's death and resurrection) with the evolution of human history from creation, through the Exodus, to the Christ event, and until the end of time. The spiral is thus an apt image for the way liturgy always combines what happened in human chronology with the way it is commemorated annually, according to the rhythm of the seasons.

The texts of the eucharistic prayers almost always insist on the fact that in the liturgy we recall the past, summon the future, and experience here and now a new event of salvation. There is a delicate balance that should be achieved in keeping these three things in proper relationship. By this I mean that in recalling the past deeds of saving history in the Eucharist we are not to pretend that we were there when those events first happened, or that what the liturgy does is to transplant us back to that time and place. Liturgical memorial is a true experience of Christ's unique paschal mystery in that it recalls the past in such a way that all God accomplished then and there is experienced here and now in a new act of salvation. In the Eucharist we experience and take part in Christ's dying and rising in such a way that this unique, once for all *(ephapax)* act of salvation occurs still.

The biblical and liturgical understanding of memorial requires that we move beyond notions of memorial as reminiscence, as an imitation of past events, as only a mental thought process involving reflection on history as chronology. In addition, one of the central issues here is the irreversibility of time—past, present, and future—and how the cycles of nature help to frame the liturgical commemoration of irrepeatable yet perennially experienced events of salvation. What we experience in and through the memorial of the paschal mystery in the Eucharist is always the same, yet ever new.

## WHO REMEMBERS

Liturgy is something that persons of faith do in common. The essentially ecclesial nature of all liturgy is self-evident in the enactment of the Eucharist as the action of the church. What we do in the act of "making memory" in the Eucharist is to be drawn into the very paschal dying and rising in Christ. Thus it seems fairly obvious that the answer to the question of "who remembers" is the faith community of the church. However, in a stimulating study on eucharistic memorial, the scripture scholar Joachim Jeremias takes a somewhat different position. In his book *The Eucharistic Words of Jesus*[7] he argues that the translation of the Greek for "do this in memory of me" really should be changed so that the emphasis is placed not on what the church does but rather primarily on what God has done and does. Jeremias prefers an adjustment to read "that God may remember me." And, in doing so, Jeremias places the emphasis on what God does for us in Christ and what God continues to do among us through the liturgy.

Clearly this "translation" is unique and many scripture scholars fault Jeremias for it. However, from the perspective of *liturgical* memorial, what Jeremias has to say is crucially important for an adequate understanding of making memory in the liturgy. This is to say that all liturgy is done at God's gracious initiative. What the community of the church does is respond to God's initiating and sustaining grace. This understanding of liturgical memorial places emphasis both on God's initiative and on the church's active and conscious response in and through the liturgy. This is important to underscore so that the act of liturgy is always respected as that which Christians do in memory of the Lord in response to God's inviting, sustaining invitation and action.

A main concern enunciated time and again in Vatican II's Constitution on the Sacred Liturgy was that the reason for revision of the sacred liturgy was that the assembly could take part fully, consciously, and actively.[8] Admittedly, some have criticized certain examples of the celebration of the reformed liturgy for being too focused on what the assembly does and for being insufficiently focused on the Godward dimension of liturgy.[9] And some of those criticisms need to be addressed, lest the "new" liturgy appear to be primarily something that humans do, something primarily focused on us. However, one difficulty is that sometimes these criticisms have been based on a critique of the conciliar mandate itself that the liturgy be fully, actively, and consciously participated in. The conciliar mandate remains, even if some of the ways in which the liturgy is celebrated may be faulted. "Active participation" is the assembly's right and vocation, simply because if the liturgy is the privileged school of faith and a central means of salvation, then it must be participated in so that what it says and does may be experienced as fully as possible and appropriated as faithfully as possible.

At the same time, one also needs to realize that "active participation" should not be perceived to mean only human activity. At its root, participation means that we "take part in" the very life of God. The adjective "active" means that what liturgy always is and does—make us sharers in the life of God—should be apparent in our experience of liturgy, specifically in the way we engage ourselves in what we say and do liturgically in common prayer, song, gesture, and silence. Again, true to our thesis, a proper appreciation of active participation places emphasis first on what God does in the liturgy and then on what we do in response through the liturgy. Similarly, liturgical memorial is fundamentally about what God does for us as well as about what we do to experience that saving act of grace here and now.

Returning to the Jeremias thesis, the obvious question is: What does it mean to say that God *remembers*? The answer, in effect, comes from the theology of memorial articulated from biblical and liturgical sources. What biblical and liturgical memorial implies is that God's remembering is God's own acting benevolently among us. God's remembering is what gives us life. God's act of remembering makes life worth living. In biblical rhetoric, when we ask God to "remember" us we are asking that the divine life in us be sustained and deepened.

And when we ask that God "forget" things, such as our sins, we are asking that they be forgiven, blotted out, and taken away. Recall the rabbinic phrase that says, "To remember is to give life, to forget is to let die." Again, the issue is that liturgical memorial transcends mental recollection. It has everything to do with what God does for us in benevolence and in grace. Liturgical commemoration, therefore, offers us a wide spectrum in terms of combining our act of remembering God with God's act of remembering us—provided that both are placed in a tandem relationship with God's initiative as its foundation.

Returning to the human side of the matter, it is crucial that liturgical memorial be appreciated as what is done and said by the whole church. In fact, all liturgy is ecclesial and all liturgy is paschal. Or, to put it somewhat differently, all paschal liturgy is the church's liturgy. In effect, liturgical memorial is always liturgical *commemoration*. Every eucharistic prayer presently in use in the Roman rite contains the command "Do this in memory of me." What is helpful is to recall that the Latin for this phrase is *Hoc facite in meam commemorationem*. The last word means that to do this is to commemorate—to make memory together. The essential point here is that Eucharist is about what the church does together in making memorial of the paschal mystery of Christ.

## WHO/WHAT IS REMEMBERED?

In determining who/what is remembered we return to one of the premises of this book, namely *lex orandi, lex credendi*, what we pray (at the liturgy) is what we believe. Hence the value of combing and pondering what the texts of the eucharistic prayers presently in use in the Roman rite say about memorial. The GIRM 2002 asserts that the eucharistic prayer is "the center and summit of the entire celebration" (n. 78).[10] Therefore, this prayer in particular has special meaning for our purposes here. One of the advantages in the present reform of the liturgy of having the eucharistic prayer proclaimed aloud and in the vernacular (practices that had not been in use for centuries) is to enable eucharistic communities to hear and appropriate what the prayer says and what the prayer does. In effect that is what this prayer (of prayers) is about—saying and doing.

The GIRM 2002 asserts that in the eucharistic prayer the priest "performs the commemoration" and renders thanks "in the name of the whole people" (n. 2). Note that the role of the priest is to pray "in the name of all the people" and that the *anamnesis* is understood to be central to the whole action of making Eucharist (see GIRM 2002, n. 79). Now it is essential that we be clear here. While asserting that the *anamnesis* is central to the eucharistic prayer and (even) that the eucharistic prayer is the center and summit of the whole Eucharist, it would be a mistake to isolate either the *anamnesis* part of the prayer or the eucharistic prayer itself from the rest of the whole eucharistic liturgy. In fact, these specific instances of *anamnesis* are constitutive parts of a cohesive celebration of word and Eucharist, closely joined together as one act of worship.[11] That all of the memorial aspects of the eucharistic rite merit special attention is important, especially for remedial reasons. By this I mean that since the Roman Canon was said silently by the priest for centuries and is at present proclaimed aloud for all to hear, it is now time to claim the centrality of this prayer in both eucharistic celebration and theology. In so doing we can draw on its theology to better appreciate what it is that the Eucharist is and does.

Recall one of the premises of the last chapter: When God speaks, something happens. In a parallel way, we can say that when the priest prays the eucharistic prayer, God works to transform bread and wine into the body and blood of Christ. However, again to avoid a minimalist understanding of this prayer, it would be inappropriate to look to that transformation as the sole "use" for the prayer. In fact, the eucharistic prayer is a lyrical, poetic prayer expressing praise, thanks, blessing, and honor to the Triune God for our relationships with God, creation, and each other, especially by recounting the great deeds of salvation that God has accomplished and accomplishes still through the act of making Eucharist.

These "great deeds" of salvation are termed the *magnalia Dei*. In proclaiming them in every eucharistic prayer we engage in an act of memorial whereby what we proclaim occurs still, in particular (but not exclusively) in the transformation of the eucharistic gifts, a transformation that is itself for the purpose of eucharistic communion. Hence the theological value of the dynamism of the verbs that frame the institution narrative: "take"/"eat," "take"/"drink." At the same

GIVE = MODEL SEVEN

time, another set of verbs gives shape to the whole eucharistic action: "take, bless, break, give." (Recall here what was said in Model Two, "The Church's Eucharist," about "taking" and "eating/drinking.") These verbs are ritualized in the structure of the Eucharist itself. "Take" involves the act of presenting gifts (and preparing the altar), "bless" involves the act of transforming eucharistic gifts (in and through the eucharistic prayer), "break" involves the breaking of the eucharistic bread, and "give" involves the act of eucharistic communion itself. A good way to appreciate the value of these words and actions is to see them as concentric circles. The words "take/eat/drink" are located in the structure of the eucharistic action "take, bless, break, give," which is framed within a whole Eucharist from the introductory rites, to the proclamation of the word of God, through the action at the altar and communion, to concluding rites.

One application for the present examination of what the eucharistic prayers "say" about memorial specifically is to be sure that we keep them in perspective with the rest of the whole eucharistic action, which itself can legitimately be termed an "act of memory." The concepts articulated here shape what the Eucharist is and does through the eucharistic prayer, whose genre is that of a lyrical hymn of praise and thanks based on memorial of the great deeds God has done for us and for our salvation (*magnalia Dei*), which include transformation, memorial, offering, and supplication. Thus the eucharistic prayer is best not regarded as a "formula" that works "automatically." It is a prayer that acclaims God and draws us into the eucharistic action and dynamism.

Notice the title of this section. It concerns *who* and *what* are remembered. What we see in the eucharistic prayers is that liturgical prayer never separates Christ's paschal mystery from our being incorporated into it. This underscores the theology of memorial we have articulated thus far in this chapter, that what happened once for all in saving history is always at least two things. The eucharistic action is always both the selfsame paschal sacrifice of Christ and at the same time a new action, a new event of salvation and sanctification in the here and now. Every act of liturgical memorial places proper emphasis on what has been accomplished, what is being accomplished, and what will yet be accomplished when God will be all in all and we are drawn to the kingdom of heaven for eternity. In essence, what the *reasoning*

eucharistic prayers say we "make memory of" (especially when all the prayers are considered together) is the obedient life, betrayal, humiliation, suffering, passion, death, resurrection, ascension, and second coming of Christ—and of our participating (taking part) in those paschal events through the Eucharist.

Let us look at the eucharistic prayers and see which aspects of the paschal mystery are emphasized in which prayers. Recall that when the "great deeds of salvation" are articulated in prayer they are realized here and now for our sanctification and salvation. The "doing" of memorial means that the things made memory of are present in all their dynamism and fullness.

Pride of place in terms of the Western liturgical tradition goes to the Roman Canon. Even when it was said silently by the priest, it contained, and still contains, the assertion:

> [W]e, your people and your ministers
> recall his passion
> his resurrection from the dead,
> and his ascension into glory...[12]

This clear articulation of the passion, death, resurrection, and ascension remains a very helpful summary of what Christ accomplished for us and the way he accomplished it. The church's *lex orandi* therefore can be seen as supplying an important understanding about the entirety of the paschal mystery. This is especially important, given the emphasis from Trent on the Mass as the unbloody sacrifice of Calvary. The Roman Canon always said more than that, and its notable feature is the assertion that Christ's ascension was an intrinsic part of the paschal mystery. Rather than viewing the ascension event as Christ's leaving the disciples, the church's liturgical tradition has always placed emphasis on the ascension as the unique moment of Christ's returning to God the Father's right hand in glory to make intercession for us. In fact, citing the ascension in this way underscores Christ's high priesthood and eternal intercession. Implications for a theology of eucharistic intercession and for the theology of the ordained priesthood are obvious here.

The second eucharistic prayer in use in the present Roman rite also deserves special attention because it dates from the earliest period of the Western liturgical tradition and is often ascribed to the third-century author Hippolytus of Rome.[13] Its simplicity is striking when it states:

> In memory of his death and resurrection...

In commenting on the laconic style of this prayer, scholars have noted that it was really meant to be an outline, a brief summary of what a eucharistic prayer should be. It was common at this stage of the evolution of liturgical practice that celebrants would elaborate on this text and embellish it where deemed appropriate.[14] Like the Latin text of the Roman Canon, it begins with the word *memores*, a Latin term meaning "we make memory."

The inspiration for the third eucharistic prayer is a composite of non-Roman sources.[15] This prayer gives us a fuller appreciation of the sweep of the paschal mystery when it states:

> Father, calling to mind the death your Son endured for our
>     salvation
> his glorious resurrection and ascension into heaven,
>     and ready to greet him when he comes again...

Even while appreciating the richness of this prayer, it is necessary to indicate the weakness in the present translation of its first words. The Latin text is actually: *"Memores, igitur, Domine."* This is to say that it repeats the same Latin term for "making memory" from the Roman Canon and the second eucharistic prayer, and in light of its Greek (and Hebrew) roots would require a much more enriched verb than "to recall," especially since "recall" more than hints at a mental recollection. In its place I would suggest that greater fidelity to the Latin would be achieved by having this phrase read "We commemorate..." This language respects the breadth of the notion of memorial as a communal event and experience of salvation.

The assertion that this death was "for our salvation" indicates again how liturgical prayers never simply describe Christ's paschal mystery. Rather, they always draw us into experiencing it in all its fullness through the action of the Eucharist. The particular addition in this prayer of "and ready to greet him when he comes again" is

very significant theologically, since it incorporates into the eucharistic
prayer an essential part of the paschal mystery—its fulfillment at the
second coming. The fact that it is articulated here has significance for
a theology of the Eucharist as anticipatory of the kingdom yet to
come. We will discuss this more fully under Model Seven, "Food for
the Journey." For now it is important to emphasize that the memorial
section of the fourth eucharistic prayer states:

> Father, we now celebrate this memorial of our redemption.
> We recall Christ's death, his descent among the dead,
> his resurrection, and his ascension to your right hand;
> and looking forward to his coming in glory...

What may be regarded as the building blocks from the first three
eucharistic prayers are summarized and synthesized here. While "we
recall" (for the Latin *recolimus*) is as weak as "calling to mind" in the
third prayer, at least it is introduced in this prayer by the strong assertion that we "now celebrate this memorial of our redemption..."[16] As
is traditionally the case in liturgical texts, the verb "to celebrate" is
less energetic and preoccupied with what we do than is the common
contemporary understanding of the term. Rather, liturgical tradition
would underscore how "celebration" is a public act done in common
to ensure solidarity and communion with God and with each other
through the unique paschal mystery of Christ.

This same sense of what we "celebrate" is articulated in the second eucharistic prayer for Masses of Reconciliation. It states:

> We celebrate the memory of his death and resurrection
> and bring you the gift you have given us, the sacrifice of
>     reconciliation.

What is interesting in this assertion is that it combines Christ's paschal victory with our experiencing it in and through the Eucharist as a
source of reconciliation—with God and each other.

The way the memorial part of the first eucharistic prayer for
Masses of Reconciliation articulates what we are doing in the Eucharist is notable, since it places emphasis on memorial as an action. It
reads:

We do this in memory of Jesus Christ,
our Passover and our lasting peace.
We celebrate his death and resurrection
and look for the coming of that day
when he will return to bring us the fullness of joy.

We have here a highly balanced and inclusive notion of eucharistic memorial in terms of what Christ accomplished and accomplishes among us through the Eucharist. This prayer too underscores that eucharistic memorial is also something we do (but again, always at God's gracious invitation).

In addition to revisions involving the traditional parts of the eucharistic prayer, one of the new features to the eucharistic prayers after Vatican II was the insertion of the acclamation after the words of institution. This part of the eucharistic liturgy is often termed the "memorial acclamation," precisely because it articulates in a summary way what the eucharistic action is all about in terms of drawing the praying church into the event taking place, that is, our being made sharers in Christ's paschal mystery. When those responsible for revising the Roman Canon studied its strengths and defects,[17] it was determined that there should be a place within the prayer itself when the assembled community could actively participate in what was being articulated in the eucharistic prayer by means of an additional acclamation (understanding that the Great Amen was the first and only acclamation from the second century onwards and that the Sanctus acclamation had been in use from at least the seventh century[18]).

Pastorally it is clear that the articulation of the community's participation in the paschal mystery through the memorial acclamation is an important element in the present reform of the eucharistic liturgy. However, it needs to be said that not all of the present texts of the acclamations capture the dynamism and urgency of the Latin originals. While "Christ has died, Christ is risen, Christ will come again" is offered as the first option in the (present) English language Sacramentary, it is more an assertion than an acclamation. In fact, the Latin text reads: "*Mortem tuam annuntiamus, Domine, et tuam resurrectionem confitemur, donec venias*," which in a literal translation would read: "We acclaim your death, O Lord, and we confess your resurrection, until you come again." The sense of the Latin is that what we do in acclaiming and acknowledging the power and dynamism of Christ's death and resurrection is the core of our faith and hope until his second coming, which return we await and look to in expectation. An acclamation does not describe the paschal mystery. It describes how we participate in it and how we also long for its fulfillment. The phrasing of the present third acclamation,

*we are involved*

> When we eat this bread and drink this cup
> we proclaim your death, Lord Jesus,
>    until you come in glory

is a useful translation and certainly combines the action of Eucharist with the paschal mystery, including Christ's second coming.[19]

The fourth option:

> Lord, by your cross and resurrection
> you have set us free.
> You are the savior of the world

is again more of a statement than an acclamation. The Latin text[20] contains the urgent plea *"salva nos,"* that is, that the Lord would save us (now). The lack of such an imperative in the present translation diminishes the dynamic character of the eucharistic acclamation.

The second option for the memorial acclamation is most useful theologically but is a debated inclusion into the present *Sacramentary for Mass*. It reads:

> Dying you destroyed our death,
> rising you restored our life.
> Lord Jesus, come in glory.

The fact that this text is not a translation from any Latin original has prompted some to criticize its inclusion in the eucharistic rite. My own sense, however, is that it has been a very useful acclamation, precisely because it combines a number of elements constitutive of eucharistic memorial in a succinct way. The fact that it derives from the first of the Easter prefaces suggests its theological value and liturgical appropriateness. That text (repeated from the head of this chapter) states:

> We praise you with greater joy than ever
> in this Easter season,
> when Christ became our paschal sacrifice.
> He is the true Lamb who took away the sins of the world.
> By dying he destroyed our death;
> by rising he restored our life.

The addition in the acclamation of "Lord Jesus, come in glory" is most helpful, especially in the Roman rite whose prayers had been less focused on the second coming than those of other (especially Eastern) rites.

In summary, we can assert that what the liturgy says is what we believe and that what these parts of the eucharistic prayer say and do are crucial for our understanding and appropriation of what it means that the Eucharist is the memorial of the paschal mystery—of Christ's paschal mystery and the mystery of dying and rising that occur in the lives of all believers.

## IMPLICATIONS

Clearly there are a number of implications to be derived theologically and spiritually from the notion that the Eucharist is the memorial of the paschal mystery. Among others, I offer the following four.

### 1. Ecumenical Eucharistic Theology and Agreement

When the theologian Max Thurian was a member of the ecumenical community at Taize and a participant in ecumenical research and dialogue on the Eucharist,[21] he stated that the notion of eucharistic memorial was the single most important aspect of eucharistic theology and liturgy to influence ecumenical relations since the Second Vatican Council. This central concept of eucharistic memorial was particularly helpful when Catholics were asked thorny questions by members of the churches of the Reformation, questions such as: Is the term "transubstantiation" the only and necessary way to describe eucharistic presence? and What does it mean to call the Eucharist a "sacrifice"? In examining the tradition of eucharistic prayers, participant churches came to realize that long before and long after "transubstantiation" was coined as a term for eucharistic presence, the texts of the liturgy spoke of "take...eat...drink...[and] do this in memory of me." Thus it was possible to engage in a biblical and liturgical refocusing of the question of eucharistic presence based on the evidence of the scriptures and the church's *lex orandi*. With regard to the Eucharist as "sacrifice," what is required is a recontextualizing of the question within the dynamism of liturgical memorial, where the articulation of what we make memory of uniquely through the liturgy leads immediately to references to what we now offer. (More about this in Model Eight, "Sacramental Sacrifice.")

The key point made by Thurian continues to need to be made, namely that eucharistic memorial can help to define not only a tradition's own understanding of the Eucharist but also what the Eucharist is and means across denominational lines. The notion of eucharistic memorial has offered a way forward for ecumenical understanding and relations based on commonly held assumptions that stand behind conventionally held positions and terms. It is not uncommon to see in ecumenical statements notions of "remembrance" and "memorial" as pillars of agreement on the Eucharist.[22]

## 2. "Communion Services"

When posing some of the contemporary questions about the Eucharist in Part 1 ("Questions: Polls, Practices, Polarizations"), I noted that the decline in the numbers of ordained priests means a decline in the availability of the regular celebration of the Eucharist on Sundays (at least in some places) and that attempts to deal with this problem have given rise to the (USA) ritual *Sunday Celebrations in the Absence of a Priest*. Whatever can be said in favor of such services in terms of addressing a pressing pastoral, liturgical need, it is necessary to point out that these services are simply not the same thing as the celebration of the liturgy of the Eucharist. Again, the phrase from Pope John Paul II's encyclical on the Eucharist is clear when it speaks about "the sacramental incompleteness of these celebrations" (n. 32). The very core of the eucharistic *actio*, framed by the verbs "take, bless, break, and give" is jettisoned, because there is no action of taking and blessing the bread and wine. Distribution of communion from the reserved sacrament is not the same thing as participation in the fullness and breadth of the eucharistic action.

To be even more precise, some commentators have pointed out that what is clearly lacking in such services is the eucharistic prayer, specifically the *anamnesis*, which is the "center and high point" of the celebration of the Eucharist. Such "communion services" are not the *actio Christi* and the *actio ecclesiae* which is part and parcel of the church's traditional understanding of what the Eucharist is and does.

## 3. Eucharistic Devotions

In the same section of Part 1 ("Questions: Polls, Practices, Polarizations"), I indicated the phenomenon of the proliferation of eucharistic devotions, specifically exposition of the sacrament, adoration, and benediction. I also indicated that the presumption of the rite for the worship of the Eucharist outside of Mass was that such practices are derived from and should lead to participation in the act of the Eucharist itself. The irenicism and theological cogency that characterize such official documents do not always mark the rhetoric about these practices at present.

It would seem that the directives from the liturgical reforms after Vatican II to the present—ensuring that eucharistic devotions be seen as extensions of the Eucharist and lead to fuller participation in it— can be sustained simply by recalling what the Eucharist says and does. Simply put, this means that the eucharistic prayer is the high point of what the Eucharist says it does. In other words, when we proclaim a eucharistic prayer containing a section named "memorial," we realize that in and through that very proclamation we are drawn into that memorial. It is not something that we are invited to ponder, for example, during adoration. It is, rather, something that happens in the proclaiming of the prayer. Furthermore, because the basic structure of the Eucharist contains the verbs "break" and "give," then any eucharistic devotion will necessarily be less than the fullness of the eucharistic action.

Again, true to a premise of this book, the issue is "both...and," with the theological weight always given to the enactment of the Eucharist. To choose "either...or" would be to diminish the church's liturgical and devotional life. And where eucharistic devotions do take place, the structure and liturgical normativity of the rite for the worship of the Eucharist outside of Mass should be presumed. Not coincidentally, part of the prayer said by the priest or deacon before benediction reflects the theology of eucharistic memorial articulated here when it speaks of "this memorial of your passion and cross."

## 4. A Paschal Lens on Life

As noted above, the eucharistic memorial acclamation derived from the first Easter preface places appropriate emphasis on our participating in Christ's paschal mystery. The key is in the pronouns.

> Dying you destroyed *our* death,
> rising you restored *our* life . . .

The verb forms of "dying" and "rising" point to the specific nature of liturgical memorial, namely that through the act of liturgy we are made sharers in the paschal dying and rising of Christ. Put more personally, we can say that in the Eucharist we are so conjoined to Christ that the sufferings of our lives, the dying to self and selfishness and to the ephemeral things of this world and, yes, our need to stare death in the face and stare it down, all occur. What "we remember" is what God did in Christ; what we do in the Eucharist is allow our lives to be reshaped and reformed in that image and likeness.

We place lenses on our eyes to see as fully and accurately as we can what there is to see. One of the purposes of celebrating the Eucharist is to place *paschal* lenses on our eyes. Why paschal? Because when the dying and rising of Christ is the prism through which we look at life, through which we evaluate ourselves, our lives, and everything in them, then we can say that the paschal mystery becomes the true measure of who we are and what we are about. These paschal lenses help us to see what is really real. The perspective is faith, not just eyesight. "We walk by faith, and not by sight . . ."

The challenge here is to allow Christ's obedient life, suffering, passion, death, resurrection, and ascension to be the prism we use to evaluate what really matters in our lives. The celebration of the Eucharist is crucial if we are to allow this way of looking at life to be "second nature." But because it is often not second nature, we need the repeated ritual enactment of Christ's paschal mystery to take deep root in our lives. It can then become the way we measure success and failure, happiness and suffering, hopefulness and despair, triumph and humiliation. And, more often than not, what happens is that apparent failure in the world's eyes is the very thing that leads us to deeper conversion to Christ; that what is apparent despair is a dark night of the soul leading to a new appreciation of the brilliance of Christ's light; that what we experience as humiliation is really a purgation leading us to a fuller life in God's sight, even if that is not the way others see it or us.

The last part of the memorial acclamation, "Lord Jesus, come in glory," leads to a plea for final and complete fulfillment in what is yet to be. It is also a most hopeful assertion in terms of what eucharistic memorial is about, namely a privileged and, yes, always provisional experience of dying and rising through, with, and in Christ. Thus, a paschal lens on life helps us to see what is really real and to conform our lives to that amazing and sustaining vision. We need regular and repeated eucharistic celebrations of the memorial of Christ for this to happen.

The argument set forth in this chapter is that the memorial of the paschal mystery is the axis, the center for all that the Eucharist is and does. The Eucharist is the measure of life in which we put time, place, history, and fulfillment in proper perspective. But we do this adequately (not to say fully) only when we do it by allowing our real lives to be merged into the memorial of Christ's dying and rising. For this we always need the food of the Eucharist. If, in the words of Maria Boulding (quoted at the beginning of this chapter), "all liturgy is paschal," it is certainly all the more true that every Eucharist is at its heart the memorial of Christ's paschal mystery and of the paschal mystery lived out in our lives.

*Discussion/Reflection Questions*

1. Read and pray over Exodus 12 and 1 Corinthians 11. The first two readings for the Evening Mass of the Lord's Supper on Holy Thursday are taken from these passages. They are of central

importance for appreciating the notions of memorial and time as these are proclaimed at this important liturgy.

2. Think about what you normally mean when you use the word "memory" and discuss how a biblical and liturgical understanding of this word would offer challenges to its customary usage.

*Further Reading*

Jerome Kodell, *The Eucharist in the New Testament* (Wilmington: Glazier, 1988; now published by The Liturgical Press).

MODEL FIVE
# Covenant Renewal

> *Take this, all of you, and drink from it:*
> *this is the cup of my blood,*
> *the blood of the new and everlasting covenant.*
> —*Institution Narrative,*
> *Eucharistic Prayers of the Roman Rite*

Covenants is the title of the first half of a cycle of medieval English miracle plays. The theology of this "play" is clear—God's overarching love extended to Israel and now to us through a series of covenants that he initiated and into which believers are drawn. The covenants portrayed include Adam and Eve, Cain and Abel, Noah with his wife and "family," and finally the most poignant of all, Abraham's sacrifice of Isaac. When this medieval play is produced and performed in a church, the dialogue between Abraham and his youthful son take place as the son approaches the altar. Isaac winces with pain as his father Abraham sweeps a bright, stainless, new butcher's knife before his unseeing eyes. Isaac says to his father:

> Is it God's will you kill me with your knife? . . .
> Then you must do what God has bid.
> But tell not my mother what you did.

Their dialogue ensues. Finally God announces:

> Abraham, thou art spared to sacrifice thy son today,
> But know that, free of sin, one day,
> For to win all mankind's grace
> My own lad will be taken to a place
> Of sacrifice, and for all men good and ill,
> Will be done to death upon a hill.[1]

While poignant at any time and in any place, these words spoken at or near an altar in church take on a particular poignancy because it is at the altar that we speak the words of the eucharistic prayer referring to what we are doing as the renewal of the "new and everlasting covenant" in the blood of Christ. The Abraham/Isaac, God the Father/ Jesus the Son typology is recalled and enacted each time we celebrate the covenant renewal of the Eucharist.[2] Hearing such a text from a mystery play at the altar can help to shape our hearing of the words from the Roman Canon:

> Look with favor on these offerings
> and accept them as once you accepted
> the gifts of your servant Abel,
> the sacrifice of Abraham, our father in faith,
> and the bread and wine offered by your priest Melchisedech.[3]

Covenants indeed—in and through Abraham and our other forebears in the faith to Christ's "new and everlasting covenant" in and through the Eucharist.

We come in this chapter to a consideration of the Eucharist under the term *covenant renewal*—an obviously multifaceted concept given our biblical and liturgical tradition. Our premise here is that every Eucharist commemorates (in the fullness of the meaning of that term as described in the last chapter) and celebrates God's covenant relationship with fallen yet graced humanity. God's overarching initiative in love always transcends our response. In faith we use the term "covenant" to signify bondedness, irrevocable relationship, and unbroken union as well as God's invitation to us and our response enacted through the Eucharist.

Of all the models discussed in this book, this is this one that particularly concerns the relationship of baptism to Eucharist. That is to say that we are concerned here with how the Eucharist renews and deepens the conversion first forged, signed, and sealed among and for believers through the waters of baptism. Sacraments of initiation are classically celebrated at the Easter Vigil. This is the reason why the Constitution on the Sacred Liturgy of Vatican II required that the liturgical readings, rites, and prayers of the Lenten season be revised so that the faithful might more diligently "listen to the Word of God and devote themselves to prayer [in order] to celebrate the paschal mystery. The baptismal and penitential aspects of Lent are to be given greater prominence, in both the liturgy and liturgical catechesis" (n. 109). In asserting that "more use is to be made of the baptismal features proper to the Lenten liturgy; some texts and rites from an earlier era are to be restored..." the council fathers asked that the classic prayers and rites of the adult catechumenate from the patristic era be restored.

Hence the theological and spiritual importance of the "success story" in the church today of the revised Order for the Christian Initiation of Adults with its rite of election, scrutinies, and the proclamation of gospel passages that "structure" the candidates' last Lent before initiation: temptation, transfiguration, the Samaritan woman (John 4), the cure of the man born blind (John 9) and the raising of Lazarus (John 11).[4]

The following treatment of "biblical covenants" is taken from another aspect of the present Lenten Lectionary structure. Our treatment of biblical covenants is shaped by what the Lenten Lectionary offers as premier examples and paradigms leading to the renewal of the new covenant in the sacrifice of Christ commemorated during the paschal triduum. As the *Lectionary for Mass* states with regard to the structure of the first reading on Sunday: "The Old Testament readings are about the history of salvation, which is one of the themes proper to the catechesis of Lent. The series of texts for each year presents the main elements of salvation history from its beginning until the promise of the New Covenant" (n. 97).

We will be concerned here primarily with the first readings in the "B" cycle of the Lectionary, all of which clearly proclaim and reaffirm biblical covenants. However, the primary Old Testament narrative that helps frame the reason for Christ's incarnation and paschal mystery is the first reading proclaimed on the First Sunday of Lent in the "A" cycle, "the creation of our first parents, and sin" (as described in the subtitle to the reading in the Lectionary). That the second reading for this same Sunday is the Pauline theology of the second Adam in Romans 5 (vv. 12–19) is significant not only for appreciating the theology and practices of the season of Lent but also for understanding how the Bible itself interprets the fall and its being overturned in and through Christ. In what follows our concern will be with the light shed by the liturgical context on how to interpret such multilayered and multifaceted texts[5] and what such texts have to "say" about the notion of covenant religion, especially as it affects cultic observances as responses to such covenants.

## BIBLICAL COVENANTS IN THE LITURGY

Obviously the idea of "covenant" and the phenomenon of "covenant-making" is central to the biblical tradition. By way of comparison and contrast, it would be important here to indicate that this word (and reality) is far different from what we refer to as a "contract." In our common understanding (and observance!) of them, "contracts" are documents that bind equal parties to perform and accomplish what they commit themselves to. Hence we sign contracts as documents of agreement and commitment. The biblical reality of *covenant* is not the same.

While our concern here will be with *covenants* established between God and believers, it is important to note that covenants between parties (individuals and tribes) mark much of the history and rhetoric of the Old Testament. The covenanting parties bound themselves by ritual agreement which included (often terrible) consequences for the party violating the covenant. However, parties to such covenants among humans and tribes (as described in the Old Testament, e.g., Abraham with the Canaanites Eshcol and Aner in Gen 14 or with Abimelech in Gen 21) were not necessarily equals. This is certainly true of the covenant(s) established between God and Israel and the new covenant in the blood of Christ. Yet obligations were imposed on all who committed themselves to such covenants. For Israel in particular, the most important obligation was to worship no other god but Yahweh and to observe the standards of cult and conduct which Yahweh required.

Given our contemporary increased appreciation of the role of Abraham in Islam, these biblical texts from Genesis deserve special attention because of their focus on this paragon of faith, whose faith profession and commitment are important exemplars for the revealed religions of Judaism, Islam, and Christianity. (At the same time, however, our concern here will be with the way the Catholic liturgy uses the Abraham paradigm as the model for our faith response to word and sacrament.)

What follows in this chapter is itself an example of the *lex orandi, lex credendi* principle at work, namely that what we hear proclaimed in the liturgy shapes how we understand the biblical and liturgical notion of covenant renewal through the Eucharist. The *Lectionary for Mass* makes theological statements about feasts and seasons. Here we turn to part of the "statement" made during Lent about covenants.

### Genesis 2:7–9, 3:1–7 and Romans 5:12–19
*(Readings for the First Sunday of Lent, Year "A")*

If in fact much of the biblical witness about covenants concerns obeying terms of commitments and worshiping the one true God, it is obvious that the Genesis account of the fall is the classic "set up" for all covenant stories that follow. Understandably, the dialogue between "the serpent" and Eve has been recounted in literature and the arts in numberless ways. The cunning serpent's inquiry, "Did God really tell you not to eat from any trees in the garden?" and the assurance that even if you do eat from that one "you ... will not die" sets the pattern for other stories of additional temptations and falls in the scriptures. Indeed, Eve sees the tree in a new light—"The tree was good for food, pleasing to the eyes, and desirable for gaining wisdom." What was forbidden becomes desirable. "So she took some of its fruit and ate it." She disobeyed God and deleterious consequences followed for her, for her husband, and for us all. Banishment "east of Eden" (recall the Steinbeck novel with this title) and that we are "poor banished children of Eve" (from the prayer *Hail Holy Queen*) are typical ways of describing how this sin became "original" for all who followed Adam and Eve.

Quite understandably, the account of the fall proclaimed on this First Sunday of Lent is followed by the classic Lenten psalm, Psalm 51, with the refrain "Be merciful, O Lord, for we have sinned." What is obviously disaster in the Genesis text is reshaped into a hopeful cry in the psalm through such phrases as "in the greatness of your compassion wipe out my offense" and "a clean heart create for me O God." The dynamic in the juxtaposition of these texts—humanity's fall yet hope in God—reflects biblical, covenant religion. We are never equals with God in the covenant, yet in covenant faith we are able to presume to cry out for mercy and a renewed heart. When we hear the gospel of the temptation of Jesus at this same liturgy (Matt 4: 1–11) we experience once again the power of triumphing over temptation.

One of the hopeful motifs clearly apparent in the Easter Proclamation (the *Exsultet*) is that what we celebrate at Easter is the fall overcome. The fall of Adam is called a "necessary sin" in this hymn, necessary so that we could receive so great a redeemer—God's only Son. The reference in this proclamation that Christ's *blood* has "paid for us the price of Adam's sin" is significant given that Old Testament covenants were often ratified by the blood of animals. Such is the biblical context for the blood of the Passover lamb being sprinkled on the doorposts so the avenging angel would pass by. And how fitting it is that the complete description of this event in Exodus 12 is proclaimed as the first reading at the Evening Mass of the Lord's Supper on Holy Thursday. Thus what could be construed as death-dealing in the slaughter of lambs at Passover becomes life-giving through the use of blood to save. The *Exsultet* continues:

> This is our passover feast,
> when Christ, the true lamb is slain,
> whose blood consecrates the homes of all believers.[6]

In this same proclamation we assert that the power of Christ's resurrection solemnly commemorated on this holy night "restores lost innocence." The innocence lost by Adam and Eve is restored through *vs. all-knowing*

Christ, the innocent one who went to his death for our salvation. The relationship between the sin of our first parents and the redemption Christ won for us is summarized in the second reading from Romans 5 to follow on this First Sunday of Lent.

One central key to interpreting both Genesis and Romans is the relationship of obedience and disobedience to the word and command of God. It is summarized in the last verse of the Lectionary's text from Romans, which reads:

> For just as through the disobedience of the one man
> the many were made sinners,
> so, through the obedience of the one,
> the many will be made righteous. (v. 19)

The notion of *obedience* is at the heart of the matter about covenants in biblical religion. God's will is made clear and believers commit themselves to it. But not always, and sometimes not forever. As numberless biblical stories—especially the one about the worship of the golden calf in Exodus 32—recount, there can be a fickleness to the covenant responses that human beings try to make in response to God. Thus in chapter 32 of Exodus the real issue is not the worship of a man-made idol. The real issue is about asking ourselves what gods we want to follow and what gods we really want to worship. The golden calf stands for an idol that makes no demands on believers. The golden calf stands for the gods of our own making—self-absorption, catering to our wills and ways, nurturing only the self.   *discipline*

Hence the centrality of the value of obedience in biblical religion. Recalling what we argued in Model Three about the liturgical proclamation of the word of God, it is in hearing and obeying that word that we become more faithful believers. "Thy will be done" becomes a necessary part of every Eucharist, not only in the Lord's Prayer, but in every acclamation we utter in response to the scriptural texts that are proclaimed at the liturgy. Those acclamations are the way we daily say "thy will be done" in terms of assenting to and living according to the word proclaimed at liturgy.

Is it any wonder that the Abraham/Sarah cycle from Genesis (and as capitalized on and used in the epistles such as in Romans 4 and Galatians 3) becomes a key to unlocking the notion of covenant and covenant renewal as proclaimed and celebrated in the eucharistic liturgy?

As noted above, this is particularly the case in the readings proclaimed on the Sundays of Lent. In fact, the first part of the Abraham cycle from Genesis 12 is the first reading on the Second Sunday of Lent in the "A" cycle, (vv. 1–4a). It recounts the call of Abram, whose name was later changed to signify the change that God made in his life and vocation. Cannot the same be said of those preparing for baptism at Easter who will be called by name to signify a radical change in their life and vocation as derived from sacramental initiation? In addition, it is also notable that the Abraham/Sarah cycle from Genesis is the source for the first reading on the Second Sunday of Lent in the "C" cycle (Gen 15), with the explicit use of the word "covenant" and reference to divine initiative in its Lectionary subtitle, "God made a covenant with Abraham, his faithful servant."

However, as noted above, it is primarily in the "B" cycle of the Sunday Lenten Lectionary that the first readings deal with covenants. Hence we offer an overview of these texts to glean further insight into biblical covenants as proclaimed in and through the liturgy.

### Genesis 9:8–15
*(First Sunday of Lent, Year "B")*

The subtitle for this text in the Lectionary is "God's covenant with Noah when he was delivered from the flood." This is significant because from all that is contained in this section of Genesis (chapters 5 through 9) that speak about the depravity of humans after the fall and "how great was man's wickedness" (6:5), the Lenten Lectionary offers us verses for our Lenten proclamation about hopefulness and redemption. The assurances that "never again shall all bodily creatures be destroyed by the waters of a flood" (9:11) and "the waters shall never again become a flood to destroy all mortal beings" (9:15) are of central importance in this text. These same assurances and positive features frame how the Lenten Lectionary underscores divine initiative and God's overarching concern to save us from all that would do us harm. The covenant as forged with Noah and his family is now renewed among us through this proclamation on the First Sunday of Lent, the day of the annual rite of election of catechumens and candidates.

That the liturgy always underscores the saving aspects of biblical covenants is exemplified in the prayer for blessing water at Christian initiation, when it says:

> The waters of the great flood
>> you made a sign of the waters of baptism
>>> that make an end of sin and a new beginning of goodness.

The point is clear. Where sin abounds, even after sharing in the covenant of baptism, God's grace always abounds even more. This is captured in the responsorial psalm that follows this text when proclaimed on this First Sunday of Lent, Psalm 25:10: "Your ways, O LORD, are love and truth for those who keep your covenant." Other verses from this psalm refer to knowing God's ways and being formed in divine truth (v. 4) as well as asking that God's compassion "from of old" be given to us "because of your goodness, O LORD" (vv. 6–7). Thus we can say that the liturgical proclamation about covenants reflects divine compassion and an invitation to greater fidelity in living according to God's word. We hear this text in the context of the Eucharist where all covenants are viewed in light of Jesus' "new and everlasting covenant," which is renewed each time the Eucharist is celebrated.

## Genesis 22:1–2, 9a, 10–13, 15–18
### (Second Sunday of Lent, Year "B")

Once again the subtitle for the reading in the Lectionary summarizes a key theme. Today it is chosen from the familiar text of the Roman Canon: "the sacrifice of Abraham, our father in faith." By using the words of the Canon in this subtitle, the Lectionary indicates how central this passage is in biblical religion and in our liturgical tradition. The fact that the phrase "the sacrifice of Abraham, our father in faith" was spoken for some fifteen hundred years in the Catholic liturgy when the Roman Canon was the only eucharistic prayer used indicates the supreme importance of this text for understanding what the liturgy celebrates. Clearly the Abraham/Isaac relationship and this act of obedience to God's will and word has classically offered an Old Testament background to the God the Father/Jesus his Son act of sacrifice. Jesus the Son, doing his Father's will and accepting the cup of suffering, mirrors biblical covenant commitments even to the point of death. The very use of "beloved son" (v. 12, recalling "your son Isaac, your only one" in Gen 22:2) indicates a special, unique description of Isaac, the same description traditionally ascribed to Jesus in the Bible and liturgical tradition.

That God put Abraham to the test and that, in the words of the Lectionary reading, he replied "Here I am" (v. 1) to do what he was commanded offers a paradigm for biblical writers about commitments to and the fulfillment of God's commands. This same kind of phraseology is used in the call of Isaiah "Here I am . . . send me" (Isa 6:8), reiterating the importance of hearing and responding to God's word and will, especially in a season like Lent. This notion is reinforced in the last line of the reading, which follows upon the promise of "descendants as countless as the stars of the sky and the sands of the seashore" in the assertion "all this because you obeyed my command" (v. 18).

That following the Lord's will often requires great personal sacrifice and hardship is reflected in the responsorial psalm (Ps 116) containing the phrase "precious in the eyes of the LORD / is the death of his faithful ones" (v. 15). The death required in Abraham's case was not the physical death of Isaac, it was the more demanding and radical death to self-will and self-absorption. The second eucharistic prayer uses the phrase "before he was given up to death, a death he freely accepted" in a modestly phrased but significant assertion of this perennial challenge and biblical paradigm. Its placement before the institution narrative at the Eucharist makes it a subtle yet important reiteration of the way the Eucharist functions as a renewal of the conversion fostered by the word of God, complemented in sacramental initiation, and then continually celebrated at the Eucharist.

### Exodus 20:1–17
*(Third Sunday of Lent, Year "B")*

The next "biblical covenant" text contains the promise of the Lord's active and dynamic presence to Israel and the required response of believers in "the law... given through Moses" (as is stated in the reading's subtitle). The familiar "ten commandments" follow upon the assertion and commitment from God's side "I, the LORD, am your God, who brought you out of the land of Egypt, that place of slavery..." (v. 2), a text that recalls how biblical religion is predicated on a God who acts in history. Again, what is operative here is the paradigm of God's initiative. The reference to "slavery" was used by the Jewish commentary, the *Mishnah*, as well as by other texts in discussing how through the liturgical commemoration of Passover (recall the last chapter) believers in the present should act as though they had personally gone forth from Egypt, from slavery to freedom, from estrangement to union with God.

What this introduction also does is frame the commandments as responses to God's overarching invitational love and his constant, abiding, and amazing grace. The first command to follow also reiterates the familiar biblical challenge in covenant religion—"You shall not have other gods besides me. You shall not carve idols for yourselves..." (vv. 3–4). This reference presages the poignant betrayal of the covenant in Exodus 32, with the molten calf, crafted because of the pride of those who worked to worship their own will. Quite the opposite is the constant assertion of the biblical witness proclaimed in our liturgical tradition.

The major burden of this text is Israel's—and our—response to God's invitation in covenant living and religion. The Lectionary reading begins with the words: "In those days, God delivered all these commandments..." (v. 1). While we normally refer to the number "ten" when describing the commandments, in point of fact they are disproportionate in length in that the first one takes up verses 2–6 and concerns the worship of the one, true God. The third, about sabbath rest, is also somewhat disproportionate, because it describes why and how the sabbath should be observed (vv. 8, 10). "Keep holy the sabbath day" by "no work" (vv. 8, 10) is the clear command. One recalls here the challenges of Pope John Paul II in *Dies Domini* about the importance of leisure and recreation for Christians on Sunday, and especially for the celebration of the Eucharist.[7]

The verses for the responsorial psalm, taken from Psalm 19, state that "the law of the LORD is perfect, / refreshing the soul" (v. 7), that "the decree of the LORD is trustworthy" (v. 8), that "the precepts of the LORD are right" (v. 9), and that "the ordinances of the LORD are true" (v. 10). These are helpful reflections on the fact that the revelation of God's precepts is just that—revelation. God's precepts, commands, and laws should be understood as expressions of divine revelation in the context of the covenant. The commandments concretize aspects of human behavior; their wisdom comes from the fact that they are part and parcel of God's self-revelation.

Such is the theology of the refrain to the psalm, "Lord, you have the words of everlasting life," words spoken by Peter in the gospel of John (6:68c). It is to be noted that this reference to God's word comes at the end of John 6, the chapter containing the miracle of the multiplication of the loaves and the "bread of life" discourse (which itself says a great deal about the value of the proclamation and exposition of God's word in the liturgy).

### 2 Chronicles 36:14–16, 19–23
*(Fourth Sunday of Lent, Year "B")*

Probably the least familiar of the "covenant stories" in these first readings for the Sundays of Lent in the "B" cycle is that which ends the two books of 1 and 2 Chronicles (which books lead into Ezra and Nehemiah). In the two Chronicle books the author idealizes David's rule and role; hence he exalts the Davidic covenant. One of the main theological themes of the Chronicle books is that we in the present must always learn from the past, which in this instance means covenant fidelity and listening attentively to the word of the Lord as proclaimed by the prophets. Thus prophecy is less forecasting the future than it is interpreting the present on the basis of traditional, covenant religion, since such interpretation leads to deeper commitment to God and more faithful and fruitful lives.

As indicated in the Lectionary subtitle, the reading concerns "the wrath and the mercy of the Lord . . . revealed in the exile and liberation of his people." Familiar covenant themes thus recur here. The indictment of adding "infidelity to infidelity" and "polluting the LORD's temple" is poignant. Such actions obviously strike at the heart of biblical, covenant religion. The "seventy years" prophesied by Jeremiah are fulfilled. And it is also in fulfillment of Jeremiah's prophecy that Cyrus is pictured as the one who commissions the Jews to go to Jerusalem and there build a temple for the Lord (v. 23). The assertion that the Lord "had compassion on his people and his dwelling place..." is important, again to reiterate that what we do in covenant religion in keeping our commitments is always done at God's invitation and with God's sustaining support. What the Chronicler describes in this text is a new beginning, a new start in living according to God's covenant designs.

When proclaimed during the season of Lent, this text offers believers an invitation to greater commitment to listening to and observing the word of the Lord, which is so central to covenant religion. The proclamation of the word effects something. In the books of Chronicles that word effects a rebuilding of God's temple, not in bricks and mortar but rather in the new temple of committed human hearts.

The Babylonian exile is rehearsed in the verses of the responsorial psalm, Psalm 137. Recounting their history, principally their election by God and the ways in which God has supported them, this text was a means for Israel in every generation to realize that saving history is not over and done with. In fact, it is still experienced in the here and now of covenant renewal established through the liturgy. That same thing can be said to happen when we celebrate the liturgy. When we pray a psalm such as this one, the events it recounts are made effective again (or still). In the Lenten journey we use this very psalm to invite greater fidelity to God after any (figurative) exile of our own lack of faithful response to the God of the covenant.

### Jeremiah 31:31–34
*(Fifth Sunday of Lent, Cycle "B")*

The last of our series of biblical texts of the covenant and its renewal through the church's liturgy is the familiar prophecy of Jeremiah, subtitled in the Lectionary "I will make a new covenant and remember their sin no more." The divine initiative upon which all covenant relationships is based is reflected in the phrase "I will make ...says the LORD" (v. 31). That it is termed "new" invites one to see beyond any kind of legalistic notions of one's responsibility in observing the obligations that the covenant relationship requires. That the institution narrative we use at the Eucharist contains explicit reference to "the new covenant in my blood…" specifies that for Christians this covenant is expressed through the paschal sacrifice of Jesus.

Any seemingly sharp contrast between the "old" and "new" covenants in the phrase referring to "the covenant I made with their fathers" (v. 32) and this "new" one is somewhat mitigated when we realize that the "new" covenant is also "with the house of Israel…" (v. 32). The point here is more about continuity in purity of heart and purified intentions rather than any distancing of God from choosing—again and again—the house of Israel as the specially chosen and blessed of all peoples. Christians who hear this text about a "new" covenant written "on their hearts" should not be quick to presume that this means us and not the Jews. In fact, the opposite is the case. We inherit the new covenant from our Jewish forebears in the faith.

This is to say, in the often quoted phrase of Pope John XXIII, that we are all "spiritually Semites." Thus the more we reach to and realize our common Jewish roots in covenant religion's continuity as opposed to any presumption that Christians are the "new" chosen race, the more accurate is our assessment of our real faith lives and vocations in covenant religion. Here one recalls the phrasing of the invitation to prayer at the Good Friday liturgy "for the Jews":

> Let us pray
> for the Jewish people,
> the first to hear the word of God,
> that they may continue to grow in the love of his name
> and in faithfulness to his covenant.

The promise with which the Jeremiah text concludes, "I will forgive their evildoing and remember their sin no more" (v. 34), reflects, once again, the import of divine forgiveness to help us live in fidelity to the covenant. We also see the biblical notion of "remembering" as a divine action that takes effect and does something within us that only God can do—forgive our sins. One recalls here, once more, the poignancy of the words of the institution narrative at the Eucharist, about Christ's

> blood of the new and everlasting covenant.
> It will be shed for you and for all
> so that sins may be forgiven.

In terms of liturgy and sacraments we can say that the sin-forgiveness that was first accomplished in water baptism is now recalled and reiterated through the Eucharist, the sacramental celebration of the sin-forgiving sacrifice of Christ himself. Part of the dynamism of the Eucharist as a sacrament of covenant renewal is that it is a sacrament of the forgiveness of sins. This is especially the case when texts such as this are read during Lent—the period of preparation for and the renewal of baptism.

That God's compassion is both presumed and invoked in the verses of the responsorial psalm, Psalm 51, is thus entirely appropriate as a reflection on the last verse of the reading and an expression of one of the ways in which this text can and should be personally appropriated by all who hear it. The refrain "Create a clean heart in me O God" (from Ps 51:12a) reiterates one of the main points in the Jeremiah text—namely that the "new" covenant will involve the law being written upon "their hearts." For us who pray this psalm, what is required is a deep personalization and appropriation of God's law so that it is seen not as something irksome or an imposition but as something we welcome as God's personal revelation and invitation to respond fully to him in faith—a faith that does nothing less than shape our whole lives. Such is the most adequate way of living according to God's covenant—whether founded on the covenants of Adam and Eve, Cain and Abel, Noah with his wife and "family," and Abraham and Isaac, or now, most poignantly of all, on the covenant in God's only and beloved Son, Jesus Christ.

That this latter covenant involves the shedding of blood requires some explanation, again with an eye toward giving appropriate background to how we understand what it means to say "the blood of the new and everlasting covenant..." in the eucharistic prayer.

## Life Blood—Blood and Water

For several years the American Red Cross used the phrase "Save lives, give blood" in its advertising campaigns for blood donors. The truism contained in this phrase for biblical religion is that blood signifies *life* and that when a biblical covenant was sealed in blood it was to signify the life and vitality that would derive from that covenant. Recall that in the Exodus 12 text (discussed in the previous chapter) it was the blood sprinkled on the doorposts that signified who the inhabitants were—members of God's covenanted people—and served as the sign that they were to be spared by the blood of the lamb. The slaying of the Passover lambs gave families the ability to roast the meat and share in the life-giving meal of the Passover. It is not coincidental that in the gospel of John Jesus dies on the cross at the moment when the lambs are being butchered for Passover (John 19:28–37). Now the ratification of the new covenant was to be through the blood of the Lamb of God who takes away the sins of the world (also from the gospel of John, 1:29). This positive evaluation of what is obviously an ignominious death—on a cross, after betrayal by one's friends—images the paradox of Christianity. That is, from what appears to be an avenging death comes restorative life with God and each other through the now-risen Christ. It is clear that in biblical religion the shedding of blood is not primarily about the destruction of the victim. It is about the new life of grace that comes from the blood of the lamb.

Hence the positive theology of the texts of the eucharistic prayers and the rites at communion. Again, it is the "blood of the new and everlasting covenant" that is actualized and made real through the eucharistic prayer and action. In this connection, what the GIRM 2002 says about communion under both species is significant:

> Holy communion has a fuller form as a sign when it is distributed under both kinds. For in this form the sign of the eucharistic banquet is more clearly evident and clear expression to the divine will by which the new and eternal Covenant is ratified in the Blood of the Lord, as also the relationship between the Eucharistic banquet and the eschatological banquet in the Father's kingdom. (n. 281)

The repeated acclamation addressed to Christ before communion is "Lamb of God, you take away the sin of the world, have mercy on us." And when the priest raises the eucharistic species, he uses a text combined from John 1:29 and from the Book of Revelation 19:4 acclaiming the supper of the Lamb. The proposed revised translation of this text brings out the eschatological aspect of the Eucharist when it says:

> Behold the Lamb of God
> who takes away the sin of the world.
> Blessed are those called to the supper of the Lamb.

It is notable that the previous GIRM stated that the priest was to hold the consecrated bread over the paten (n. 115). The revised GIRM 2002 (n. 157) has adjusted this in specifying that the priest is to hold the consecrated bread above the paten or the chalice and invite the assembly to communion. This latter option of holding both the consecrated bread and chalice is a helpful ritual adjustment because it combines both bread and cup in what the people look at when they are invited to communion. While our liturgical tradition has always upheld communion under both species by the priest, the custom in the West from the ninth century onward was to limit communion from the chalice by the non-ordained. The restoration in the GIRM 2002 of the numerous opportunities for communion from the chalice by the non-ordained[8] indicates the possibility that the whole assembly can regularly participate in sharing both the eucharistic bread and cup, a participation that is a more complete sign of what the eucharistic communion always is—namely a sharing in communion under both species as a participation in the dead and risen Christ. From the point of view of the theology of covenant renewal at issue in this chapter, taking eucharistic communion under both forms is an excellent practice to reflect the Lord's command to "take and eat...take and drink..." of the body and blood poured out for the forgiveness of sins.

That Christ's blood is life-giving is presumed as well as articulated in the passages from the Johannine corpus that speak of blood and water. John 19:34 states that a soldier pierced the side of Christ and that "immediately blood and water flowed out." Commentators often assert that this verse was explicitly included in John's gospel to underscore the reality of the physical death of the human Jesus. This was to counteract any tendency to view Christ only as divine and hence as not capable of suffering or dying or enduring pain. At the same time, this text has traditionally been used to describe the liturgical celebration of the Eucharist as a sharing in the reality of the death and resurrection of Jesus.

The central, primal element here is water. This is the only element that humans need to survive. The reference to baptism reminds us of Jesus' baptism in water, which establishes why we use water in our rites of Christian initiation. It is not a coincidence, therefore, that Exodus 17:3–7 about water from the rock would be read during the Lenten season, specifically on the Third Sunday of Lent in the "A" cycle, in a reading that sets up the (classic) gospel for this day, the account of the Samaritan woman (John 4). While the symbolism of the account centers on water with its life-giving properties (the Israelites needed it in order to survive), the way the text is written involves obedience to the Lord. The dialogue involves grumbling and questioning why the people should follow Moses. Moses seeks divine help, and he receives it. In obedience to the Lord's command, he strikes the rock and water flows from it to slake the people's thirst. The seemingly insignificant reference to location leads to the more complete description of what occurred there. The Lectionary reading concludes with these words:

> The place was called Massah and Meribah
>     because the Israelites quarreled there
>     and tested the LORD, saying,
> "Is the LORD in our midst or not?" (Exod 17:7)

These same places are named each time the church uses Psalm 95 as the invitatory to the Liturgy of the Hours: "Harden not your hearts as at Meribah, / as in the day of Massah in the desert..." (v. 8). This same psalm is the responsorial psalm on this Third Sunday of Lent. The key, once again, concerns living according to God's covenant. At water baptism and its renewal at the Eucharist we are asked to take our stand in faith with the Lord, with the Lord's word and will. The sacramental bond of this commitment begins at baptism; it continues and (hopefully) is deepened in the celebration of the Eucharist.

The symbol of water also figures prominently in 1 John 5:8 which speaks of the Spirit, water, and blood, which many early liturgical commentators and rites (e.g., the East Syrian baptismal tradition) use as a reference to the sacraments of baptism and Eucharist. Clearly water refers to baptism, and blood refers to the Eucharist, both of which are made possible by the outpouring and invocation of the Holy Spirit. Well-designed church buildings establish a fitting place for baptism and for the Eucharist, thus indicating the connection between these two sacraments. Specifically, the placing of the baptismal font near the door of the church obviously signifies our initiation into the church by water baptism. When we dip our fingers into that font and make the sign of the cross upon entering the church we recall the covenant of baptism and look for the sacramental renewal of that covenant in the Eucharist. While customarily we think of the body of Christ as the eucharistic bread, these scriptural allusions and liturgical customs remind us that eucharistic participation has always joined bread and cup, body and blood. They also remind us of the fundamental theological reality—that the celebration of the Eucharist is always a renewal of the covenant of baptism.

It is therefore most helpful when those responsible for building or renovating churches make the location and usefulness of the baptismal font a high priority in that construction. The very design of church buildings expresses and reflects our sacramental and liturgical theology. If this is true for the placement of the ambo for the proclamation of the word, it is equally true for the placement of the baptismal font. Obviously closely related to the location of the font is its use with generous amounts of water. The revised rites for both adult and infant baptism always indicate that immersion *or* infusion with water may be used. The fact that immersion is always mentioned first in these revised rituals says a great deal about it being a preferred option to symbolize baptismal washing and the sacramental ratification of one's first participation in the covenant of baptism. The use of the rite for blessing and sprinkling with holy water at Sunday Eucharist does this for the Eucharist as a sacrament of covenant renewal.[9]

## A SACRAMENT OF INITIATION

The Eucharist is *a* sacrament of initiation. While we customarily think of baptism and confirmation as sacraments of initiation, it is the Eucharist which is the sacramental term of that process, the final end of the catechumenate. Initiation through the celebration of water baptism and chrismation leads to the altar table. This is underscored at every Eucharist by the words "new and everlasting covenant," which are given particular emphasis in the Rite of Blessing and Sprinkling with Holy Water on Sundays. Recall some of the phrases used in this rite. To introduce it, the priest says explicitly:

> This water will be used
> to remind us of our baptism.
> Let us ask God to bless it
> and to keep us faithful
> to the Spirit he has given us.

In the first prayer to bless the water, two specific phrases are worth noting. The first is that this blessing is most fitting on a Sunday, with the phrase: "on this day which you have made your own." The second is an eschatological reference to coming "into your presence to receive your gift of salvation." Combining these insights, we can say that the issue is an appreciation of Sunday as the day for initiation sacraments. That is, as the revised rituals all explicitly state, baptisms should take place on Sundays. And, as Pope John Paul II has recently reminded us in chapter 2 of *Dies Domini*, the Sunday Eucharist should be qualitatively different from weekday celebrations. Its ritual structure and musical components should all speak to Sunday as the day of the Lord.

The third of the blessing prayers, designed for the Easter season, heightens our awareness of how the Eucharist deepens what was begun at baptism:

> Hear our prayers and bless this water
> which gives fruitfulness to the fields
> and refreshment and cleansing to man.

You chose water to show your goodness
when you led your people to freedom
through the Red Sea
and satisfied their thirst in the desert
with water from the rock.
Water was the symbol used by the prophets
to foretell your new covenant with man.
You made the water of baptism holy
by Christ's baptism in the Jordan:
by it you give us a new birth
and renew us in holiness.
May this water remind us of our baptism,
and let us share the joy
of all who have been baptized at Easter.

That there is always an eschatological aspect to all sacraments, and
here especially to the Eucharist, is noted in the conclusion to the rite
when, having sprinkled the assembly with blessed water, the priest
prays:

May almighty God cleanse us of our sins,
and through the eucharist we celebrate
make us worthy to sit at his table
in his heavenly kingdom.

We began this chapter by referring to the multifaceted biblical
reality of covenants forged, ratified, and renewed. The seemingly simple assertion in the eucharistic prayer about "the new and
everlasting covenant" certainly speaks volumes when placed against
its biblical background and when seen in light of the liturgical celebration of the sacraments of initiation. Our bondedness to and with
God through the covenant is sacramentally begun at the bath of baptism and sacramentally renewed through the bread and cup of the
Eucharist. That this radical, initial conversion is signified in the water
of baptism, the single element needed to sustain life, is obviously significant symbolically and in sacramental reality. That this conversion
is deepened by the "daily bread" of the Eucharist is also significant

anthropologically and sacramentally. That is to say, we dine with others in order to preserve human and social life. We dine at the Eucharist to be sustained in the divine life of God begun at baptism and culminating at the "supper of the Lamb" (Rev 19:4).

But the basic premise of all of this is that we have responded and continue to respond to God's invitational word and grace in our own personal and communal conversion. In a real sense, the Christian life (even for those baptized as infants) is always about "convert-making" and "convert-keeping." In the very celebration of the Eucharist the church offers us the opportunity to recommit ourselves to God's covenant—in hearing and obeying the word of the Lord and in celebrating the eucharistic action. The Eucharist is thus a sign of our conversion to the covenant and a means for that covenant to be renewed in our lives. In the words of the first eucharistic prayer for reconciliation:

> Yet, before he stretched out his arms between heaven and earth
> In the everlasting sign of your covenant,
> he desired to celebrate the Paschal feast
> in the company of his disciples.

We come as disciples to the Eucharist to renew our commitment to the covenant that will last until no more covenants are needed and we will have met the Lord in the kingdom.

*Discussion/Reflection Questions*

1. It is clear that Christ's blood was shed for our redemption and that sacraments, especially baptism and the Eucharist, renew that life within us. How well then do I respond to God's covenant love in terms of living a life of concern for others?

2. The shedding of blood in the biblical tradition most often refers to its positive results—union with God. How does this understanding help me to appreciate the myriad and frequent references to *blood* in the liturgy of the Eucharist?

3. How could a biblical catechesis on the covenant texts from the Lenten Lectionary (as described here) be used in RCIA programs to help those to be initiated at Easter better understand what it is they are going to do at the Easter Vigil?

*Further Reading*

Read and pray over the biblical texts from the Lectionary presented in this chapter. Use a biblical commentary to learn more about what they mean. Then pray over their accompanying responsorial psalms to better appreciate the implications of these readings for our spiritual lives.

## MODEL SIX
# The Lord's Supper

*Behold the Lamb of God*
*who takes away the sins of the world.*
*Blessed are those called*
*to the banquet of the Lamb.*
—*Invitation to Communion*[1]

We come now in this model to a consideration of the ritual dining that ratifies our commitment to God and to each other in and through the Eucharist. This model considers the rhetoric of using plural words (especially pronouns) in Christian liturgy through which we dare to call God "our" Father and "our" Lord. It also reassesses the ritual action through which we participate in the sacramental representation of the paschal mystery in the eucharistic supper. These usages—in word and action—are relational. They concern relationships with God and with each other. The liturgy "speaks" to us in at least two ways—words and actions. In accord with our thesis, our purpose here will be to underscore aspects of what the eucharistic liturgy *says* and *does*. In saying words, the liturgy does something; in doing something, the liturgy also says something.

## "OUR" LORD

**Our.** The texts of the eucharistic liturgy in the Roman rite are clear in their repeated use of the pronoun of relationship "our" when referring in prayer to God, "through Christ our Lord." Take, for example, the texts in the eucharistic prayers that precede the words of institution. When referring to the eucharistic offering, the Roman Canon states:

> Let it become for us
> the body and blood of Jesus Christ,
> your Son, our Lord.

Eucharistic Prayer II contains the *epiclesis* that states:

> Let your Spirit come upon these gifts to make them holy,
> so that they may become for us
> the body and blood of our Lord, Jesus Christ.

Eucharistic Prayer III (also in an *epiclesis*) states:

> And so Father, we bring you these gifts.
> We ask you to make them holy by the power of your Spirit,
> that they may become the body and blood
> of your Son, our Lord Jesus Christ
> at whose command we celebrate this eucharist.

And Eucharistic Prayer IV (also at the *epiclesis*) states:

> Father, may this Holy Spirit sanctify these offerings.
> Let them become the body and blood of Jesus Christ our Lord,
> as we celebrate the great mystery
> which he left us as an everlasting covenant.

In addition to the eucharistic prayer, all of the other presidential prayers in the Roman rite end with references to "our Lord." The opening prayers (termed *oratio* in the *Missale Romanum*) most usually conclude with

We ask this through our Lord
    Jesus Christ, your Son,
who lives and reigns with you and
the Holy Spirit, one God, for ever and ever.[2]

Fortunately, the proposed revision of the Sacramentary restores "in the unity of the Holy Spirit" in order to translate the Latin *in unitate*. This is a better rendering than the present translation "*and* the Holy Spirit..." (emphasis added). This proposed change helps to underscore the point of how the words in liturgy reflect sets of relationships —namely our relationships to God and to each other—and assert belonging. By stating "in the unity of the Holy Spirit..." the liturgy articulates that we share in the very life of the Triune God in and through the liturgy and that it is "we" who share in it, the whole church. Thus "in the unity" refers to our relatedness to the Trinity and to each other as members of the liturgical assembly and of the church at large.[3]

Both presently and in the proposed revised *Sacramentary for Mass*, the prayers over the gifts (termed the *oratio super oblata*) end with "grant this through Christ our Lord."[4] Similarly, the prayers after communion (termed *post communionem* in the *Missale Romanum*) end with the phrase "Grant this through Christ our Lord."[5]

The point here is based once more on the *lex orandi, lex credendi* principle. What we pray is that "we" ask the Father to grant us what we need "through Christ *our* Lord" (emphasis added). What we seek from God is something we cannot accomplish ourselves. What we need is the action of God—Father, Son, and Spirit—to accomplish this among us here and now. But in making these prayers with these phrases we also are asserting—simply by the pronouns we use—that we are committed to Christ as *our* Lord and that we recommit ourselves to him as we beseech his help. Thus it is an assertion of faith that *the* Lord is *our* Lord in the sense that we invite God to possess us once more through the commitments we bring to and express through the liturgy, specifically through the prayers we say in the liturgy. The repeated use of *our* here is most important; it is a pronoun of relationship—of our relationship to each other as well as to the Triune God through Christ. The simple repetition of the pronoun "our" reiterates the uncommon assumption that we dare to call and claim God as "ours" and that in so doing we are committing ourselves once more to covenant relationships and commitments.

We call the study of God "theology," a term from the Greek meaning literally words about God—*theos* for "God" and *logos* for "word(s)." Compared with names for God the Father and the Holy Spirit, it is clear that because of the incarnation and the fact that Jesus walked this earth we have an enormous number of names for the second person of the Trinity. Among these are "Jesus," "Christ," "Messiah," "Savior," "Redeemer," "Son of God," "Son of Man," etc. The liturgy uses all of these in the scriptures proclaimed and the prayers prayed. But from all of them the church's wisdom determines that the mediatorship of Christ in liturgical prayer is expressed in the formula "through Christ our Lord." A number of things are "said" simply by the use of "Lord" in these prayers.

*Lord.* Because of its importance as the "overture" to the Easter triduum and because of the richness of its scripture readings and liturgical prayer texts, I have repeatedly made reference to the Evening Mass of the Lord's Supper on Holy Thursday night. What is notable is the way it uses "evening" as the designated time and "Lord" as the author and object of this commemoration.

The setting for the Mass—*evening*—refers to the way Jews tell time. Days begin with sunset, not sunrise, hence the refrain to the account of creation in Genesis 1 "and it was evening and morning the . . . day." Sabbath meals begin after sunset, as does the annual Passover. To this day the Christian liturgy retains the value of celebrating evening prayer on the evening before Sundays and special feasts. This is to say that something new begins with an evening liturgy that looks to the eucharistic liturgy of the day to follow. Thus the Easter triduum is begun with this evening Mass. But what is more intriguing theologically and liturgically is the rest of the title—"the Lord's Supper."

"Lord" has a number of meanings in the Bible. In brief we can say that essentially in the Old Testament it is a title of honor for a god, a king, a person of superior rank, such as, for example, the owner of a slave.[6] Some of the Old Testament uses derive from the title "Adonai" (a title used as one of the "O" antiphons at the end of Advent).[7] In the New Testament, "Lord" signifies authority and power. This title for

Christ is more frequently used in the Pauline letters than anywhere else in the New Testament, which is not surprising given that the gospels concern the words and deeds of the earthly Jesus. "Lord" is a title that most usually signifies exaltation. So, for example, the hymn in Philippians 2:5–11 indicates that God "exalted" Jesus and we can call him "Lord" because of his obedience and because of what he suffered as a result of obeying the will of God.

When St. Paul recounts the institution of the Eucharist (1 Cor 11:23–26), he does so by using a preexisting narrative beginning with the words "the Lord Jesus..." Theologically the combination of these names means that the author is recounting what Jesus did while on earth, but also that we now can acknowledge him as the exalted Lord, a status given him after his having endured his passion and death—which led to his resurrection, ascension, and exaltation to the Father's right hand in glory. Therefore it is significant that the title for the Holy Thursday liturgy is "Evening Mass of the *Lord's* Supper," not the "Last Supper." (The same theology is behind the title for the Good Friday Liturgy: "Commemoration of the Lord's Passion."[8])

The title could not be "Last Supper" simply because all liturgy is about the total paschal mystery of Jesus, not just one or another event, all of which together comprise the whole paschal mystery. Where "Last Supper" would have us focus on the night before Jesus' passion on Calvary, "Lord's Supper" appropriately has us focus on the whole paschal mystery which is commemorated in a particular way each year at the triduum. That this liturgy is the "overture" to the triduum is seen in the proposed entrance antiphon for this night. Adapted from Galatians 6:14, the antiphon summarizes the whole paschal mystery yet focuses on the cross and incorporates important titles of Jesus: "We should glory in the cross of our Lord Jesus Christ, for he is our salvation, our life and our resurrection; through him we are saved and made free." The liturgy on this night is not only about the commemoration of the last supper—as rich and profound as this would be. Placed within the perspective of the commemoration of the totality of the paschal mystery, particular aspects of this evening liturgy can be put into proper focus. Clearly this liturgy emphasizes the memorial (with the first reading from Exodus 12) and service (with the gospel from John 13) aspects of the Eucharist. That this mystery is enacted in the church, presided over by ordained priests, is also a key theme that has evolved over time in association with this liturgy.

It is worth noting that the cause of a great deal of controversy and consternation since the liturgical revisions of Vatican II at this liturgy, namely whose feet can be washed, is at least ironic because what is really at the heart of this liturgy is the building up of the church through the celebration of the Eucharist. Unfortunately, all too often in the recent past the decision about whose feet can be washed has had the opposite effect. Furthermore, the theology of this liturgy, like that of every act of liturgy, is multivalent—it sustains a number of theological ideas and it celebrates those realities. To place too much emphasis on any single dramatic aspect of the liturgy which "imitates" what Jesus did while on earth, like washing feet or carrying palms in procession, is to risk losing the symbolic center of all liturgical participation and to place emphasis on historical reminiscences. Liturgy is not about re-enacting anything or reminiscing about any events. It is about a multivalent commemoration of Christ's paschal mystery and our appropriation of it through sacred signs and symbols.[9]

It was only with the reform of Holy Week in 1955 that the option was given for parishes to conduct the washing of the feet—the *mandatum*. At that time the Sacred Congregation of Rites noted that the traditional significance of the rite of foot washing was "to show the Lord's commandment about fraternal charity..." The Congregation at that time asked that the faithful should be instructed on the profound meaning of this sacred rite and should be taught "that it is only proper that they should abound in works of Christian charity on this day."[10] What was notable in this revised liturgy was that the foot washing was optional and that the catechetical emphasis was on fraternal charity. What was not optional was the celebration of the Eucharist, including the transfer of the Eucharist to the repository for veneration and for communion on Good Friday. In addition, the ritual in 1955 made no mention of the rite signifying Jesus' washing the feet of twelve disciples.

The Roman rite has always been resistant to adding features that reenact one or another aspects of Christ's paschal mystery. For example, it was only in the eleventh century that Rome adopted the practice of carrying blessed palms in procession on the Sunday before *process of lent leading to Lord's supper*

Easter (a practice that came to Rome from Gaul, which itself received the custom from Jerusalem). And even here it is noteworthy that after the procession, when the assembly has gathered in church, from the opening prayer of the Passion (Palm) Sunday Mass there is no mention of Christ's entry into Jerusalem or any hint of triumph. The balance of the liturgy focuses on Christ's obedience, humiliation, and death (but always from the perspective of his resurrection and exaltation). The point to be made here is that the Roman rite was hesitant to include a dramatic element that might overshadow the balance of the ensemble of signs and symbols—in their breadth and multivalence—that constitute the liturgy.

Similarly, while the washing of the feet has multiple meanings and settings, it was only in the 1955 ritual that it was offered as an option for usage in parishes. From prior history we know that the pope washed the feet of some poor people at a special meal on Holy Thursday and gave them money for sustenance. Thus a theology of fraternal charity was exemplified, but the foot washing did not occur at the Eucharist.[11] In monastic communities it was common that the abbot or abbess would wash the feet of the entire community in the chapter room at some point on this day. Here the theology would be in imitation of Jesus who as "Teacher" and "Lord" washed his disciples' feet. One aspect of the theology reflected in this ritual is role reversal. The master becomes the disciple. The disciple is given an honor customarily given to the master. All "masters" must realize that they are servant disciples.

An additional layer of meaning came to prominence in the Holy Thursday liturgy in the Middle Ages, with its theology of ordination emphasizing the power of priests to consecrate the Eucharist. Thus it was not surprising that rites on Holy Thursday should be linked to a theology of sacramental ordination. From these historical insights we see "multivalence at work." Clearly foot washing came to carry with it a number of theological meanings. The Roman rite was traditionally hesitant about adopting such a dramatic gesture as the washing of the feet because of its uniqueness in celebration (done once a year, therefore inviting particular attention and interest) and because all liturgy is the enactment of the whole paschal mystery—not one or another aspect of it "out of context." Thus it was judged that to have such a dramatic gesture as an essential part of the liturgy might well derogate from the poignancy of celebrating all of the paschal mystery, whole and entire, at this (and every) Eucharist.

In the post–Vatican II liturgical revisions, the option of washing feet remains. But note that it is an option; the rubrics state "depending on pastoral circumstances, the washing of the feet follows the homily." Then they refer to "the men *(viri selecti)* who have been chosen…" and what they should do. Often enough in recent years the controversy has centered on what the Latin term *vir* ("man") means and increasingly the interpretation has been that this does in fact mean the male gender, not generic humankind (for which the term would be *homo*). However, the U.S. Bishops' Committee on the Liturgy issued a statement in 1987 indicating that the feet of both men and women could be washed. Specifically, the committee stated that this custom, which had grown prevalent in the previous decade or so, signified an appropriate emphasis on fraternal charity and humble service. Therefore the inclusion of women as well as men, even though not specified in the rubrics, was considered a legitimate action in the United States.[12]

It would seem clear that the custom in some dioceses at present to limit the washing of the feet to twelve men would be because of a strict interpretation of the precise wording of the rubric, "men" *(viri)*. It would appear that at least one other theological understanding is also at work here, namely that Jesus' disciples at the Last Supper were all male and that the command to "do this in memory of me" (from the second reading from 1 Cor 11:24 and repeated in 25) refers to ordination, which is reserved to males. Whether or not this is made explicit, I would also think that Pope John Paul II's emphasis on the way the priest acts at the Eucharist "in the person of Christ" *(in persona Christi)*, where Christ's maleness is emphasized, would make the washing of the feet a ritual to support vocations to and in the priesthood.

This overview indicates the power of liturgical commemoration (as opposed to historical reminiscence) and of multivalence (rather than a single meaning given to a symbolic gesture in the liturgy). But what occurs when the foot washing is reserved to males is a perceived exclusion of women and at least an eclipsing of the notions of fraternal charity and humble service that should mark every celebration of the Eucharist, but especially that on Holy Thursday night. In addition, the restriction of this rite to *twelve* men, though customary, is not found in the Missal. It simply states "some men" (*viri selecti*).

In fact, what is arguably a more traditional underlying theological understanding for Holy Thursday is reflected in the other rubric that follows: "At the beginning of the liturgy of the eucharist, there may be a procession of the faithful with gifts for the poor." As already noted, there is historical precedent on Holy Thursday for the pope to feed and to give gifts to the poor, a practice that challenges us to take this rubric seriously and in observing it to emphasize this traditional aspect of the theology of this day. Taking up such a collection would emphasize a liturgical theology of Holy Thursday night which would link eucharistic sharing with ministering to and caring for others (which understanding is essential to any appreciation of the celebration of Eucharist).

## SUPPER

As we come to this consideration of "supper," it is important to recall that we are dealing with a term that includes a number of meanings and that the supper-meal context is crucial for any interpretation of the Eucharist. A major difficulty arises today when rhetoric about the Eucharist separates what is inseparable (*table* from *altar*). Depending on one's interests, this separation can caricature another appropriate way of describing this multifaceted reality. Is there no more clear instance of polarizing rhetoric that the separation of *sacrifice* from *meal*? A major premise for eucharistic theology derived from the liturgy (as I have already argued) is that at its heart the liturgy of the Eucharist is about the dynamic action enshrined through the use of the verbs "take, bless, break, (and) give." Here we will be concerned with the actions at the altar of "breaking" and the "giving" of eucharistic communion.

The Eucharist is about dining, not just the taking of food (as was argued in Model One, "Cosmic Mass"). This human action of taking a meal together provides the theological and liturgical context necessary to interpret what is taking place in the act of eucharistic communion. All of these verbs "take, bless, break, give"—but *taking* and *giving* in particular—draw from the understanding that the Eucharist derives from the Jewish sabbath meal and the Passover seder. We are reminded of this in the words of the eucharistic prayer which explicitate that what Jesus was doing was done "at supper."

Before the words over the cup, the Roman Canon states: "When supper was ended..." This same usage is found in a number of other eucharistic prayers in use in the Roman rite (specifically the second and third).[13] Eucharistic Prayer IV introduces the words over both bread and cup with "While they were at supper..."[14] This phrase is something of a transition between the recounting of the events of saving history and Christ's love for his disciples to this moment of recounting the events of the Last Supper and the institution of this meal in the new covenant. The usage from the Canon and the other prayers indicates the structure of the Passover meal[15] where what is declared over the bread is separated from what is declared over the cup of wine, because between these solemn declarations at the Passover is the sharing of the (seder) meal itself. The declaration "[T]his is the cup of my blood..." likely occurred as the third cup of wine was taken at Passover. This phrase was a solemn declaration of the new covenant in Jesus, poignantly stated precisely at the moment when God's covenant relationship would be "recalled" during the Passover meal. The fact that all the institution narratives (Matthew, Mark, Luke, and Paul) refer to Jesus' taking a *cup* is theologically important. (Recall our argument about this from Model Two, "The Church's Eucharist.") The issue here is not only that it is Christ's blood that was shed but also that through the Eucharist the church is now able to participate in his unique self-offering and sacrifice by sharing the common cup. "Cup" here signifies unity—we share in the one bread and the one cup and through this act of dining we participate (literally "take part in") the eternal sacrifice of Christ.

For the Jews, to be invited to dine with another was a sign of deep and intimate relationship. To be invited to share in the sabbath meal and especially to share in the Passover meal was a sign of deep bondedness—in effect to be considered "one of the family." Table sharing signifies a relationship; it is not just about consuming food. Thus, to hear these words from the Last Supper narrative in the eucharistic prayer is a significant reminder of the powerful bonds forged and sustained with Jesus at table during his earthly ministry and after his resurrection, experiences that form the basis for what the church does in enacting the Eucharist. This kind of bondedness and presumed intimate relationship makes Judas's betrayal even more harsh and ironic. One who was a chosen follower and table companion turns out to be the betrayer. That the act of betrayal takes place after having shared a last meal with Jesus and the other disciples is poignantly described in the words of Psalm 41: "Even my friend who had my trust / and partook of my bread, has raised his heel against me" (v. 10).

The fact that all the eucharistic prayers in the Roman rite assert what is found only in Matthew's account, namely that Christ's blood is "shed for you and for all so that sins may be forgiven" (cf. Matt 26:28) is most significant. It underscores how the paschal mystery of Christ is the source of reconciliation and forgiveness. Because of Judas's action, the table of the last supper became the scene of "the unkindest cut of all" in ignominious betrayal. In contrast, the altar where the Lord's Supper is enacted is now the place of betrayal overturned and reconciliation established once more.[16]

What is central here is that what is accomplished occurs through sharing in a meal. One of the most interesting studies of Jesus' use of meals in the New Testament (specifically the gospel of Luke) is by Robert Karris.[17] In Karris's study the gospel of Luke is structured around instances of dining and meal taking, both during the life and ministry of Jesus of Nazareth and after his resurrection. From the finding of the child Jesus in the manger (literally "feed box") in Luke 2:12 to the meal with the disciples at Emmaus (Luke 24:13–35), significant revelations about who Jesus is and his rule and kingdom occur at meals. Take, for example, the kingdom parables of the lost coin, the lost sheep, and the prodigal son. They are joined together and occur in the context of Jesus taking a meal with "tax collectors and sinners" (Luke 15:1–3). For Karris, it is most often at table that Jesus shows particular compassion to those in need.

Clearly one of the most memorable and moving post-resurrection accounts in the gospels is that of the disciples on the road to Emmaus. From as early as the patristic era, commentators on this text have noted how word and table fellowship are linked. The risen Jesus' recounting and interpreting the scriptures for the disciples on the road and then their recognition of him "in the breaking of the bread" mark the two major parts of the eucharistic liturgy. That this gospel may be proclaimed at the Eucharist on Easter evening and is read over two days of the Easter octave (Wednesday and Thursday) indicates the priority this text has for enabling us to appreciate how the Eucharist is the way Christians in every generation share in Christ's paschal dying and rising. Table fellowship preceded by sharing the word is the classic way Christians participate in the mystery of Christ's death and resurrection.

Hence the value of the way the eucharistic prayers refer to sharing the Lord's "supper" in the Eucharist. But, as always, it is imperative to realize that each and every sharing of the Lord's Supper at the Eucharist leads to sharing in God's presence in the kingdom of heaven. There, "sacraments shall cease." When we enter God's kingdom finally and fully, we will no longer need signs and symbols, for we will have met the Lord face to face. Until that time, the eucharistic banquet is our life in God through Christ, and we need the Eucharist as the most privileged share we can have on earth of the "supper of the Lamb" we yearn for in eternity. The fact that the Book of Revelation uses "supper" to refer to this accomplishment indicates how important the eucharistic supper is for "the pilgrim church on earth." (More on this in the next chapter, Model Seven, "Food for the Journey.")

Human beings need food and drink to sustain human life. Christians profess belief in Christ, specifically his paschal dying and rising, which "mystery of faith" gives us life and hope here on earth until we are called to eternity. Hence the significance of the fact that at the Eucharist we share a meal rich in symbolism: bread and wine taken, blessed, and shared in this sacred meal is the dynamic invitation and fullness of Christ's paschal mystery available to us here on earth. This is true each time we celebrate the Eucharist, and it is especially true when we celebrate the Evening Mass of the Lord's Supper each year.

## THEOLOGICAL ISSUES

On one level the actions of breaking the eucharistic bread and giving the vessels with consecrated bread and wine to ministers for the

distribution of communion are precisely that—preparation of the
sacred species for communion. On a much deeper level, however, we
need to focus first on a number of theologically important issues that
underlie these actions. Specifically, these issues include the theology of
church unity, sacramental and liturgical integrity, and the relationship
of liturgical ministry to church ministry. After that we shall address the
protocols for the distribution of communion as enunciated in the
revised GIRM and in the American *Norms for the Distribution and Reception of Holy Communion*.[18]

***Church Unity.*** St. Paul's assertions in 1 Corinthians 10:16–17 (proclaimed as the second reading on the Solemnity of the Body and
Blood of Christ in the "A" cycle) offer the classic text that indicates
the relationship of breaking bread and church unity.

> The cup of blessing that we bless,
>     is it not a participation in the blood of Christ?
> The bread that we break,
>     is it not a participation in the body of Christ?
> Because the loaf of bread is one,
>     we, though many, are one body,
>     for we all partake of the one loaf.

That the eucharistic cup is referred to first is probably due to the fact
that at Passover meals declarations of prayer made over cups of wine
occur four times and a declaration over the bread occurs once. What is
noticeable about the reference to the "cup" is that it is a reference to
the sharing from it, a "communion" signifying unity in and through
Christ. That this text also uses the term "participation" is very important, given the theology of what "participation" means in terms of
truly taking part in the paschal triumph of Christ through the Eucharist. The parallel text about the bread being a participation in the body
of Christ has ecclesial overtones as well, given its obvious reference to
the bread being eaten at this meal. For Paul, "body of Christ" is a signature metaphor for the church, with each part contributing to the
whole. The final verse of this text utilizes the obvious symbolism
intrinsic to the reality of bread itself, namely that baking and sharing

from one loaf signifies unity in and through Christ. When we share in the one loaf at the Eucharist we partake not only of the one loaf but also in the one Christ. Theologically the same thing can be said about many grapes being crushed and fermented to make wine.[19]

The requirement that we break bread at every Eucharist for distribution in communion recalls the relationship of the Eucharist both to cosmos and to the church (recall here the discussion above of Models One and Two). We who through the Eucharist partake of what was baked as one bread seek to be made more fully one in Christ and with each other as members of Christ's body, the church. In a sense, to state that our concern is to "build up" the church through the Eucharist is at least redundant, if not in fact unnecessary. It is the presumption of the liturgical theology of breaking and sharing from the one bread of Christ in the Eucharist. Without the notion of building up the church, the Eucharist cannot be understood to be the Eucharist. We repeatedly celebrate the Eucharist for the pilgrim church to be less imperfect and more fully the body of Christ on earth. Until the kingdom comes we are privileged to share in the Eucharist to make us the less imperfect church which one day will join the saints in God's eternal kingdom.

***Sacramental and Liturgical Integrity.*** Those who remember the Tridentine Mass will recall that the breaking of bread concerned the priest's host only and that, since no one except the priest received under both forms, there was no bread breaking and cup pouring for the laity. In addition, at the Tridentine Mass it was not uncommon for priests (only) to go to the tabernacle, not to the altar, to get the hosts needed for communion at Mass. The custom was to distribute both from hosts consecrated at the altar at a particular Mass and from those reserved in the tabernacle, with no differentiation between the two. On one level this can be understood to reflect church teaching that what was consecrated was the body of Christ and was to be revered as such.

On another level, however, as early as the pontificate of Pope Benedict XIV, taking hosts from the tabernacle was regarded as an abnormality for theological reasons. Benedict was pope in the late eighteenth century, two centuries after the council of Trent had delineated key formulations about the Eucharist. Among other things, because of the state of the celebration of the Eucharist and the controversies during the Reformation about what the Eucharist is, the fathers at Trent made several key assertions about the Eucharist that were to become central to the theological explanation and liturgical celebration of the Eucharist. Among these were the assertions that the eucharistic presence of Christ should be described as *transubstantiation* and that in the Eucharist a sacrifice is offered.[20] These tenets were to be seen as correlatives and were not to be seen among the faithful as "separating the inseparable"—that is, the notion of real presence from that of sacrifice. (More will be said about this in Models Eight and Nine.)

What Benedict XIV witnessed in the celebration of Mass was the common practice of distributing communion from hosts in the tabernacle, that is, hosts that had not been consecrated at a particular Mass for distribution at that Mass. The difficulty that Benedict XIV perceived was that the faithful would come to understand that the sacrament of the Eucharist was available in the tabernacle and that the eucharistic sacrifice was experienced (only) at Mass. For him, the liturgical practice of distributing communion from the tabernacle could easily cause confusion because it separated sacrifice from presence. In order to avoid any such misunderstanding, the pope decreed that (to the extent possible) the communion of the faithful at every Mass should be from hosts consecrated at that Mass. He judged that this practice would help to underscore the integrity of eucharistic theology. This same admonition has been in the papal magisterium since. In the twentieth century it was reiterated, especially by Pope Pius XII. The practice is presumed to be normative in the post–Vatican II revised eucharistic liturgy. (It is especially emphasized in the revised edition of the GIRM 2002.)

With regard to the gestures at Mass, Trent stipulated that priests were to observe the rubrics extremely carefully, not to say punctiliously. This was in reaction to some very varied practices, including that of priests overly prolonging the elevation of the consecrated host and chalice. Because the faithful did not normally partake in eucharistic communion, many of them wanted to see the consecrated host for as long as possible. This is what some commentators have called "ocular communion." However, prolonging the elevation caused a diminishment in the *actio*, which was the proclamation of the Canon, the consecration of the species, and the elevation at the Great Amen. Thus the theological wisdom found in the clarity of the Missal's rubrics after Trent that this gesture should be done reverently, but efficiently, and should not be overly prolonged.

In the Missal of Pope Paul VI what is clear is that the gesture that follows the words of institution is not called an "elevation"; rather, it is called the "showing" *(ostensio)* of the species to the faithful. Thus it is helpful to look at the way the GIRM 2002 structures the gestures to be used at the Eucharist. First it indicates that when presenting bread and wine (note the term "presenting," not "offering"), the priest is to hold them "slightly raised" (n. 141) over the altar. After the words of institution he "shows the host and then the chalice" (n. 150). At the end of the eucharistic prayer, "the priest takes the paten with the host and the chalice and elevates them both while alone singing or saying the doxology" (n. 151).

There is an important point made here through the symbolic gestures of the liturgy, and it is that holding up the elements at the end of the eucharistic prayer is the most traditional of the gestures having to do with the eucharistic species and the most important theologically. The raising of the paten and chalice at this point accompany the doxology of explicit praise: "Through him, with him, in him all glory and honor are yours." At the same time, the act of elevation itself at this point has also traditionally been understood to carry a sacrificial connotation. This is to say that at the end of the prayer, with the species of the Eucharist consecrated, we now offer back to the Father what he has offered to us "through, with, and in" *Christ our Lord.* Then before communion the GIRM 2002 instructs the priest to take the host "consecrated in the same Mass and [hold] it slightly raised above the paten or above the chalice..." (n. 157). This gesture parallels that at the presentation of the gifts. What were first taken as gifts from this good earth are now raised together and offered back to the Father. The bread and wine, the result of the paschal processes of baking and fermenting, are now the sacramental representation of the paschal mystery of Christ, whose sacrifice replaces all others and reconciles us with the Father. This final doxology and elevation signal the invitation to the assembly to ratify and commit themselves once more to what has occurred throughout this prayer—a lyrical, poetic prayer of praise and thanks through which the gifts from this good earth have become the gifts that will lead us to eternal salvation.

For our purposes, at least two important corollaries follow. One is that liturgical practice has traditionally been perceived to have theological implications and consequences. The words *and ritual gestures* of the liturgy "say" a number of things theologically. Hence it is important that what is done liturgically reflect as adequately as possible the theology inherent in the liturgy, including its ritual prescriptions. These rubrical distinctions—"slightly raised," "showing" and "elevation"—are ways in which the GIRM makes statements about the theology of what occurs when we "take, bless, break, and give" in the Eucharist. The most important gesture is at the end of the eucharistic prayer. The second point to be made is that there is an integrity to eucharistic doctrine, a unity requiring that essential parts be factored into our understanding of this sacrament. Specifically, from Benedict XIV on it was for the important *theological* reason that we cannot separate the inseparable—sacrament from sacrifice—that the species to be distributed at Mass should be consecrated at that Mass. What can be caricatured as an unrealistic liturgical nicety—consecrating enough eucharistic bread and wine at Mass for communion at that Mass—is in fact about the integrity of the enactment of the Eucharist. The *Norms for the Distribution and Reception of Holy Communion Under Both Kinds in the Dioceses of the United States of America* state:

> When Holy Communion is to be distributed under both species, careful planning should be undertaken so that enough bread and wine are made ready for the communication of the faithful at each Mass. As a general rule, Holy Communion is given from hosts consecrated at the same Mass and not from those reserved in the tabernacle. Precious Blood may not be reserved at one Mass for use at another..." (n. 30)[21]

Again, the issue here concerns the integrity of the liturgical action for a theological reason—not separating real presence from sacrifice.

***Liturgical-Church Ministry.*** I noted in Model Two, "The Church's Eucharist," that a rule of thumb for liturgical ministry is that what occurs in the ministries that enact the eucharistic liturgy should reflect ministry in the church outside the liturgy. The principle here is that the ministry of presiding over the liturgy, whether of bishop or priest, reflects the office of leadership, specifically oversight and responsibility for the church in the life of the church in general. It is that role which supports the role of liturgical presidency.[22] Those who exercise the charism of teaching and leading are obviously those who preside over and preach at the liturgy. The presumption in almost all of the revised liturgies from Vatican II is that the one who presides is the parish priest/pastor, a presumption that reiterates this key liturgical, theological insight. (On occasion the general instructions to the revised liturgies will speak of the "priest" without specifying "parish priest/pastor.")

Studies of the history of the diaconate reveal that those who exercised leadership and responsibility for the church's charitable and social concerns were those who assisted the bishop in the role of deacon. He who proclaimed the gospel and led the intercessions was the one who exemplified the social justice aspects of the gospel and knew who needed to be prayed for because of his ministry to the poor and the marginalized, the sick, and those who had died. The history of the ministry of reader indicates that those who proclaimed the scriptures at liturgy were also those who taught the word of God as catechists outside the liturgy.

In our own day, the expansion of the role of those who distribute the Eucharist has as much (or even more) to do with ministering to those in need outside of liturgical assemblies as it does with communion distribution at regular eucharistic celebrations in church. This is to say that the proliferation of commissioned eucharistic ministers enables the homebound to receive the Eucharist regularly because of this ministry. The visits, consisting of prayer, scripture reading, reflection on the scriptures, and the rite of distribution of communion, are an extension of Sunday liturgy. What these ministers have done and do at Sunday Eucharist in distributing communion is thus extended to church service outside the liturgy as well. Obviously, eucharistic ministers offer demonstrable service in offering the consecrated species to the assembly. But there is also the possibility that those who minister at the Eucharist can help to prepare for the liturgy by baking the bread for the liturgy. While the custom of the Catholic Church that the eucharistic bread be unleavened is always to be upheld, there is nothing (even in recent legislation)[23] to suggest that members of the assembly should not or ought not bake the eucharistic bread. Such a practice would signal a level of eucharistic participation that exists prior to the celebration of Mass itself.

Closely related to this is the concern in the GIRM 2002 (and the American *Norms*, n. 33) that

> [t]he meaning of the sign demands that the material for the Eucharistic celebration truly have the appearance of food. It is therefore expedient that the Eucharistic bread, even though unleavened and baked in the traditional shape, be made in such a way that the priest... is able in practice to break it into parts for distribution to some of the faithful. Small hosts are, however, in no way ruled out when the number of those receiving Holy Communion or other pastoral needs require it. The action of the fraction or breaking of the bread, which gave its name to the Eucharist in apostolic times, will bring out more clearly the force and importance of the sign of unity of all in the one bread, and the sign of charity by the fact that the one bread is distributed among the brothers and sisters. (GIRM 2002, n. 321)

With regard to the specific issue of who the appropriate eucharistic ministers are, the present Missal retains the language from the former GIRM and other subsequent documents. It states that the "ordinary ministers" of the Eucharist are the bishop, priest, or deacon and that "extraordinary/special ministers" are those used regularly or those called forward when a sufficient number of priests and deacons is not present (n. 162). This latter category includes acolytes, commissioned ministers, and those commissioned for the occasion.

Not unlike (most) other post–Vatican II treatments of ordination and ministry, these assertions can be read in two ways. The first assures that ordination and those ordained be safeguarded and sustained, hence their being named "ordinary ministers." The other is to make sure that the liturgical assembly is adequately served and that rites of communion not be delayed. Hence the reference to "extraordinary" ministers, a category that includes those who have been specifically trained and prepared and who exercise this ministry regularly. Yet there is also reference to those asked at a particular liturgy to assist with communion distribution. The Missal clearly envisions that, when there are large numbers of communicants and an insufficient number of ordinary and commissioned ministers, the priest may, on an ad hoc basis, ask additional laypersons to assist in ministering at communion. The American *Norms* state:

> When the size of the congregation or the incapacity of the bishop, priest, or deacon requires it, the celebrant may be assisted by other bishops, priests, or deacons. "If such ordinary ministers of Holy Communion are not present, the priest may call upon extraordinary ministers to assist him, i.e., formally instituted acolytes or even some of the faithful who have been commissioned according to the prescribed rite. In case of necessity, the priest may also commission suitable members of the faithful for the occasion" (cf. GIRM, no. 108). Extraordinary ministers of Holy Communion should receive sufficient spiritual, theological, and practical preparation to fulfill their role with knowledge and reverence. (n. 28)[24]

The key issue here is that communion distribution should be done with reverence and care, but that it should not be overly prolonged. Having sufficient numbers of eucharistic ministers who are well prepared can enhance the level of reverence and decorum that should accompany this action, particularly so that the rite need not be done in a rushed manner.

### SIGN VALUE OF TWO SPECIES

From the writings of St. Augustine through the masterful synthesis of St. Thomas Aquinas through to the teachings of the contemporary magisterium, traditional Catholic language about sacraments refers to them as *signs*. In fact, St. Thomas Aquinas begins his reflection on "sacraments in general" by stating that sacraments belong to the category of signs.[25] The use of such language serves as an important reminder that "signs" have critical theological meanings and that signs and symbols used in the liturgy make theological statements about what is being celebrated. Thus the importance that the post–Vatican II revised liturgy places on the use of signs and symbols (e.g., immersion at baptism for cleansing, regeneration, new birth, etc.) is for the sake of theology—itself a mainstay of Catholic life.

One of the clearest examples of emphasis on the role of signs as used in the Eucharist has been the expansion of the opportunities for Catholics to receive communion under both species. In the previous model on "Covenant Renewal" I quoted a section of the GIRM 2002 on the significance of communion under both species. I quote it here again, this time for what it says about the sign value of eucharistic participation:

> Holy communion has a fuller form as a sign when it is distributed under both kinds. For in this form the sign of the eucharistic banquet is more clearly evident and clear expression to the divine will by which the new and eternal Covenant is ratified in the Blood of the Lord, as also the relationship between the Eucharistic banquet and the eschatological banquet in the Father's kingdom. (n. 281)

Note especially the phrase "fuller form as a sign." This speaks to the heart of Catholic theology and practice. What was required of the priest at Mass—to communicate under both forms—is now possible for the whole assembly with great frequency, at the times and places determined both by the Holy See and by the diocesan bishop.[26] The GIRM 2002 further states that "the faithful should be encouraged to seek to participate more eagerly in this sacred rite, by which the sign of the Eucharistic banquet is made more fully evident" (n. 282).

In addition, the fact that the faithful have the option of receiving the eucharistic bread in the hand underscores the sign value of taking the Eucharist as food and drink. This practice serves to underscore the meal-sharing aspect which is obviously at the heart of what the Eucharist is. This is noted in the American *Norms*, which state:

Holy Communion under the form of bread is offered to the communicant with the words "The Body of Christ." The communicant may choose whether to receive the Body of Christ in the hand or on the tongue. When receiving in the hand, the communicant should be guided by the words of St. Cyril of Jerusalem: "When you approach, take care not to do so with your hand stretched out and your fingers open or apart, but rather place your left hand as a throne beneath your right, as befits one who is about to receive the King. Then receive him..." (n. 41)

The Lord's command "take and eat...take and drink..." is now able to be fulfilled across the board for all in the liturgical assembly. This speaks volumes about the nature of the eucharistic liturgy—especially when viewed through the classic Catholic optic of the *sign value* of sacraments. Again, this is underscored in the American *Norms*, which state:

At the same time an appreciation for reception of "the whole Christ" through one species should not diminish in any way the fuller sign value of reception of Holy Communion under both kinds. For just as Christ offered his whole self, body and blood, as a sacrifice for our sins, so too is our reception of his Body and Blood under both kinds an especially fitting participation in his memorial of eternal life. (n. 16)

It is clear that the assertions in the Missal and the American *Norms* do not require the faithful to receive under both forms. To say that would go against the Catholic doctrine of *concomitance*—which asserts that when one receives one species in the Eucharist, one receives the whole Christ present in and through the Eucharist.[27] The GIRM 2002 (n. 282) does go on to say:

[Pastors] are to teach, furthermore, that the Church, in her stewardship of the Sacraments, has the power to set forth or alter whatever provisions, apart from the substance of the Sacraments, that she judges to be most conducive to the veneration of the Sacraments and the well-being of the recipients, in view of changing conditions, times, and places. At the same time, the faithful should be encouraged to seek to participate more eagerly in this sacred rite, by which the sign of the Eucharistic banquet is made more fully evident.

What one sees here is a development in the direction of restoring a eucharistic practice whereby the entire assembly, ministers and faithful, can and should receive communion consecrated at the Mass being celebrated and in which the faithful are encouraged to participate in the eucharistic sacrament under both forms of consecrated bread and wine. The American *Norms* clearly give preference to the distribution of the consecrated wine from the chalice:

> Among the ways of ministering the Precious Blood as prescribed by the GIRM, Communion from the chalice is generally the preferred form in the Latin Church, provided that it can be carried out properly according to the norms and without any risk of even apparent irreverence toward the Blood of Christ. (n. 42)[28]

## PASTORAL IMPLICATIONS

In accord with the present Missal and the American *Norms* for holy communion, some specific practices surrounding the frequency and administration of communion under both forms deserve mention specifically because they imply theological issues.

*"Body of Christ."* One of the more noticeable changes from the Tridentine Mass to the post–Vatican II Mass structure was the change in what the priest said as he gave holy communion to the faithful. The restoration of the traditional "Body of Christ" with the communicant's reply "Amen" ended hundreds of years during which the priest said (in Latin) "May the body of our Lord Jesus Christ preserve your soul unto life eternal." Note that the present (restored) usage says "Body of *Christ*," not "of *Jesus*." This harkens back to our assertions at the beginning of this chapter—that what we are com-

memorating is the whole paschal mystery, not "just" the historical life of Jesus. Using the title "Christ" is meant to underscore all that we profess and believe about the preexistent Word of the Father, the historical Jesus, and the exalted, resurrected Lord. The assertion "Body of Christ" also contains important ecclesiological meanings. St. Augustine invites those who respond "Amen" to commit themselves to affirming the reality of Christ present in the Eucharist as well as to affirming that the Eucharist is for building up the body of Christ, the church. This is another instance of deliberate mutivalence in liturgical language.

In addition, "Body of Christ" refers to the feast celebrated on the Sunday after the Solemnity of the Trinity (in many national liturgical calendars including that of the United States). However, the title of the feast has been changed to "Solemnity of the Body and Blood of Christ." This is significant both historically and theologically. Stories abound about when and how the feast of "Corpus Christi" began and the reasons why it was instituted.[29] Whatever may be made of the origins of this festival, what is important to note theologically is that the title reminds us of how the Eucharist is about honoring Christ as present and active among us and that we should always presume that the Eucharist is about the body *and blood* of Christ. That two species are presumed in the enactment of every Eucharist is enshrined in the title for this feast and has thankfully been restored in much pastoral practice for all in the assembly to share in.

*Gestures.* The American bishops have determined the following regarding the distribution of communion:

> The faithful are not permitted to take up the consecrated bread or the sacred chalice themselves and, still less, hand them on to one another. The norm for reception of Holy Communion in the dioceses of the United States is standing. Communicants should not be denied Holy Communion because they kneel. Rather, such instances should be addressed pastorally, by providing the faithful with proper catechesis on the reasons for this norm.
>
> When receiving Holy Communion in the hand, the communicant bows his or her head before the Sacrament as a

gesture of reverence and receives the Body of the Lord from
the minister. The consecrated host may be received either on
the tongue or in the hand at the discretion of each communicant. When Holy Communion is received under both kinds,
the sign of reverence is also made before receiving the Precious Blood. (GIRM 2002, n. 160)

These directives follow what is fairly standard practice in the
church universal. The rationale for standing is to show reverence
(one stands when someone enters a room) rather than kneeling to
show penitence. The fact that the kneeling posture for communion in
the Tridentine Mass has been changed to the former practice of
standing makes the theological statement that receiving communion
is less an act of penitence than it is a multivalent act in which processing and the posture of standing have important significance. The act
of procession to and from reception is a sign of the pilgrim church as
it journeys to the kingdom of heaven. In the meantime, the act of
processing at all liturgies is an expression that we are truly pilgrims
on this earth and stand in readiness for the coming of God's kingdom
in its fullness.[30]

Where the former GIRM called for a "sign of reverence" to be
made before sacramental communion, it left it ambiguous as to what
people were to do. In fact, they often chose a number of different gestures (including kneeling for communion). The American bishops
have now determined that one should bow one's head before receiving. This again underscores appropriate reverence for the eucharistic
species and yet does not emphasize the penitential gesture of kneeling
(a practice that can result in people walking into one another). The
specification of showing a sign of reverence for both species follows
the custom where in the rite of concelebration all priests are to show
due reverence to both species as they receive each of them.

*Act of Giving/Receiving.* What is clear in all the norms for communion in the Missal and in the American *Norms* is that communicants
always receive from a minister. No one takes the Eucharist to oneself
(except for the priest who receives reverently at the altar). The customary act of human hospitality in offering food and taking it is here
enhanced to reflect the act of dining at God's gracious invitation. In

order to provide for a sense of decorum, the *Norms* speak about having sufficient numbers of eucharistic ministers. All should have received "sufficient spiritual, theological, and practical preparation to fulfill their role with knowledge and reverence" (*Norms*, n. 28). As in every liturgical ministry, what should be uppermost is that one is a *minister* and that one's role is that of service and self-transcendence. One should be gracious and invitational, yet one should also guard against allowing one's personality to become too important or using this occasion as a time to greet people. A sense of decorum and reverence should always characterize liturgical ministry, especially as the pilgrim church comes to receive its saving Lord in communion.

When attempting to "unpack" the theological implications of the rites of communion, we must keep in mind that the overriding liturgical and theological principles concern the value of giving and receiving the eucharistic species, of sharing in Christ's paschal victory through eucharistic communion. The consummation of the eucharistic sacrifice is our participation in the ritual of communion—literally our taking part in the Mass through taking communion in common. The act of taking the Eucharist is always an act of giving and receiving. This reflects the theology of the Eucharist itself—that we who communicate and partake in the Eucharist do so at God's gracious and continual invitation. We come to receive from the Lord what makes us draw ever closer to him. In the end, the act of communion underscores what every act of Eucharist is—a sharing in the Lord's Supper.

*Discussion/Reflection Questions*

1.  Read and reflect on the treatment of the Eucharist in the *Catechism of the Catholic Church* (nn. 1322–1419). Look for words and phrases that emphasize that the Eucharist is about our communion in the Lord's Supper.

2.  Read and reflect on what St. Paul recounts in 1 Corinthians 10 and 11 about church life and sharing in the Lord's Supper. Note that dissensions caused Paul to chastise the community at Corinth.

What dissensions are (unfortunately) evident in the church today (parish, American church, etc.)? How can we be strengthened to deal with these dissensions through the very Eucharist we celebrate?

## Further Reading

Francis J. Moloney, *A Body Broken for a Broken People: Eucharist in the New Testament*, rev. ed. (Peabody, MA: Hendrickson Publishers, 1997; orig. pub. Victoria: Collins Dove, 1990, 1997).

## MODEL SEVEN
# Food for the Journey

*O sacred banquet, in which Christ becomes our food,*
*the memory of his passion is celebrated,*
*the soul is filled with grace*
*and the pledge of future glory is given to us.*
    —O sacrum convivium *(St. Thomas Aquinas)*

Twenty-first century Americans, equipped with so many high tech resources for instant communication and immediate results, can be very impatient. "Are we there yet?" is not only a question of children to parents or grandparents on a car trip, it is a refrain of a people who like to "get it done" *now*. Whatever can be said about the communications revolution and the incredible accomplishments we see today in commerce, education, and society at large because of the speed of communications, it is still a tenet of the Judaeo-Christian tradition that, indeed, we are not "there" yet. Yes, God has acted definitively in human history to change its course. God acted definitively to call the people of Israel as a special possession and lead them through exodus and exile to freedom. God acted definitively to call the "new Israel" to salvation and redemption through the "new exodus" in Christ's paschal mystery and triumph. The Passover has happened and the "new" Passover in Jesus has been accomplished. But

there is always a "not yet" in biblical religion. Whether it is the acclamation "next year in Jerusalem" or "Come, Lord Jesus," people of
covenant faith pray and yearn for all to be accomplished—as we pray
daily in the Lord's Prayer, "Thy kingdom come."

The purpose of this chapter is to focus on the way in which the
Eucharist ritualizes and realizes all that has been accomplished in and
through Christ even as the church yearns for the fulfillment of (even)
the Eucharist—as we long for Christ who has died and who is risen to
"come again." We Catholics are firmly committed to the phrase "the
real presence" of Christ in the Eucharist (more on this in Model Nine,
"Active Presence"). But this chapter deals with another tenet of our
faith, that the real presence in the Eucharist leads to its completion in
the kingdom of God for all eternity.

Our human experience is that we lack the full realization of
Christ's promises in our lives. We live in the perennial challenge of
the "already" and the "not yet." We are (already) members of Christ's
family, but we have yet to achieve (actually, to be more theologically
precise, we should say "receive") the fullness of that reality in our
lives. In the meantime, the Eucharist—this most central, sacred, sacrificial sacrament—is the place where the church realizes as fully as it
can this side of eternity the fullness of God's kingdom among us. The
classical ending to many early and patristic liturgies was *maranatha*,
"Come, Lord Jesus."[1] Until that time when the Lord comes again we
need the Eucharist so that, at God's invitation, we can realize among
us as fully as possible the paschal victory of Christ—past, present, and
future—with its final, future completion something we yearn for at
every liturgy.

Our concern in this chapter will be with the incompleteness of
the Christian life as experienced in the liturgy. We will look at the
*eschatological* elements of the Eucharist specifically and of other
revised rituals—namely the *Rite for the Pastoral Care of the Sick: Rites of
Anointing and Viaticum* and the *Rite for the Dedication of a Church*. We
will be concerned with the hopefulness that springs from every liturgical celebration of the Eucharist until the second coming.

## ESCHATOLOGY

In theological parlance, *eschatology* refers to that aspect of our faith that deals with what happens to us after death and what belief in the afterlife has to do with our lives here on earth. Taken from the Greek term *eschatos* (meaning "furthest," or "last"), this aspect of theology reflects on Christ's second coming—"Christ will come again"—and what implications that tenet of our faith has for us here and now. Given the meaning of "eschatology," is it any wonder that Christ himself is called the *eschatos*, the promised one who came once in human history and who will come again at the end of time? When Christ comes in glory at the end of time, all of us will be judged and led to eternity. Hence, eschatology has classically been understood as dealing with God's judgment of us and our being led to heaven, hell, or purgatory. Traditional Catholic theology asserts that before Christ comes again and at the moment of our individual death, God will judge us in a "particular" way and then, at the second coming, we will be judged finally and for all eternity. (Classical theological manuals dealt with these issues under the title "the last things" which translates the Latin *de novissimis*). It is therefore essential that when we celebrate the memorial of Christ's paschal sacrifice at the Eucharist we realize the importance of references in the prayers to Christ's second coming.

As noted in Model Four, "Memorial of the Paschal Mystery," the eucharistic prayers in the present Missal include eschatological references in the memorial acclamations and in the *anamnesis* parts of some of the eucharistic prayers added to the church's *orandi* since Vatican II. For example, the third eucharistic prayer refers to

> his glorious resurrection and ascension into heaven,
> and ready to greet him when he comes again...

and the fourth states:

> We recall Christ's death, his descent among the dead,
> his resurrection, and his ascension to your right hand;
> and, looking forward to his coming in glory...

Such inclusions are nothing short of revolutionary, given the durability of the Roman Canon, which did not contain such explicit eschatology and was proclaimed for fifteen centuries. The text of the "memorial" section of the Roman Canon ends with the phrase "We ...recall his passion, his resurrection from the dead, and his ascension into glory..." The added phrases in the other (newer) eucharistic prayers are most welcomed. Also most welcome is the invitation to communion, "Happy are they who are called to his supper" (from Rev 19:9).

One other place where the Roman liturgy often enough reflects eschatology is in the prayers after communion. See, for example, texts such as the prayer after communion on the Feast of St. Barnabas:

> Lord
> hear the prayers of those
> who receive the pledge of eternal life
> on the feast of St. Barnabas.
> May we come to share the salvation
> we celebrate in this sacrament

or that for the Solemnity of the Body and Blood of Christ:

> Lord Jesus Christ,
> you give us your body and blood in the eucharist
> as a sign that even now we share your life.
> May we come to possess it completely in the kingdom
> where you live for ever and ever.

In addition, repeated phrases in prayers after communion such as "and so enter your kingdom" and "bring us to the eternal life we celebrate in this eucharist" evidence the way in which the celebration of the Eucharist is to lead to its fulfillment in the kingdom.

At the same time, it must be acknowledged that the present Order of Mass in particular and the prayers of the Roman Missal in general contain comparatively few specific references to this aspect that is intrinsic to eucharistic liturgy and theology. This, I think, is unfortunate and is especially apparent when we compare our liturgies with those from the Eastern liturgical traditions. But, given the context for all liturgy—that we pray in expectation of Christ's second coming—the eschatological can be said to be intrinsic to every act of liturgy. And, as will be seen in what follows, at certain times the liturgy places greater emphasis on this aspect of the faith than at other times.

## FULFILLED BUT NOT YET COMPLETE

In biblical theological circles it is not uncommon to interpret salvation history as consisting of a dynamic of *promise* leading to *fulfillment*. In this framework, the Old Testament prepares for what is to come. What the prophets prophesied came to be in and through the incarnation and paschal victory of Jesus. What was promised to our forebears in the faith, from Abraham and Sarah through all the prophets, came to be fulfilled in and through Christ.[2] Of all the liturgical seasons, it is Advent–Christmas–Epiphany that offers us an annual reminder of what we know to have happened and what has yet to happen in saving history. Christ was foretold by the prophets as our redeemer, he came in the flesh (emphasized in John 1:1–18, the gospel for Christmas Day, especially at v. 14), was revealed as Savior of all nations (Epiphany) and undertook a mission and ministry (begun at his Baptism) that we call the paschal mystery. All this has been accomplished. But our salvation, our redemption, our sanctification is not yet finally or fully completed. The Advent season begins on a specifically eschatological note—when Christ will come again to judge the living and the dead, as is seen in the gospels for the three Lectionary cycles on the First Sunday of Advent, specifically Matthew 24:37–44 (Year "A"), Mark 13:33–37 (Year "B"), and Luke 21:25–28, 34–36 (Year "C"). This is also clearly underscored in the preceding week, on the Solemnity of Christ the King, where in Year "A" the gospel from Matthew 25:31–46 is about the last judgment, the separation of the sheep from the goats.

However, let us also be clear that this overarching understanding of salvation history does not mean that the value of the Old Testament is found only in its relation to the New or exclusively in the way it helps us to interpret who Jesus is. Clearly all scripture, not just the New Testament, has been written for our instruction. Those of Jewish faith were the first to share in God's covenant, a covenant that has not been taken away. Hence the point to be made here is that one legitimate way of understanding the historical nature of Christianity is to see it as the fulfillment of what was prophesied in the Old Testament. The very fact that we still proclaim the Old Testament in the liturgy (especially in Advent and in Lent) means that we hear those challenging and formative words in a number of ways, among which is promise-fulfillment-and (still) incompletion. But at the same time we need to respect that, when proclaimed at the Christian liturgy, these texts should be respected for the challenge they bring to bear among us on their own terms. Thus they should not be seen only as the fulfillment of a promise but as perennial challenges to the church here and now and in any age. The prophecies of Isaiah and Jeremiah can and do stand on their own as challenges to us who believe in Christ. The prophetic voices need to be heard still because the injustices they name and indict still need to be named and indicted. And our conversion is meant to be deepened in our hearing of them. Thus, at the Eucharist on Friday and Saturday after Ash Wednesday, when we read Isaiah 58 about the kind of fasting God wants, we need to respond to Isaiah's challenge even though (or especially because?) Christ has indeed come to set us right with God his Father.[3]

This discussion leads us to examine the ways in which we often use *fulfillment* to mean the end of the process when in fact *fulfillment* really means that God's definitive Word has been spoken and become incarnate among us in Jesus, whose rule and kingdom are both gifts and realities that make demands upon us. What we experience in life—yes, even the Christian life—is that all has not been fulfilled in the sense that all is not totally congruent with the will of God and that God's rule and kingdom make demands on and among us. In classical theological language this is because of the "effects of original sin." Ever since our first parents were banished from the Garden of Eden we have felt incomplete. We have to suffer. Life is imperfect. But recognition of this reality does not mean that Christ's paschal victory is in any way mitigated. What it does mean is that we have to face up to the fact that life is incomplete and that only when Christ comes again will all things come to fruition. Then God's fulfilled promises will be brought to completion. It is then that all human limitations will come to an end and "all will be all" in Christ.

If we were perfect and life was complete there would be no need for grace, mercy, liturgy, or sacraments. The phrase "O Lord at length when sacraments shall cease..." from the familiar hymn *At That First Eucharist* is the refrain of all liturgy. Sacraments will cease when we, the redeemed, meet the Lord in the kingdom of heaven. We need to realize that we live in God's grace in the meantime, the time between Christ's first and second coming. We look for the fulfillment of Christ's mission among us. We still await the completion of all he came to accomplish. Why else would there be need for liturgy or the Eucharist? And why else would this prayer be structured in such a way as to remind us always of what is yet to be?

Because we are not perfect, and all has not been completed, the church's liturgy serves as our participation in all that Christ has accomplished and what will be "as we wait in joyful hope for the coming of our Savior, Jesus Christ" (embolism to the Lord's Prayer at Mass). The very act of liturgy itself and, more specifically for our purposes, what liturgical texts say are important for how they remind us of all that has yet to come to pass. Marianne Micks wrote of this dimension in her wonderful and aptly titled book on the theology of liturgy, *The Future Present.*[4] What the liturgy offers us here and now is the fullness of what will yet be accomplished. But until time comes to an end when Christ comes again, the liturgy is the supreme experience of what has yet to be revealed. Our "future" in God is already "present" in the liturgy. We cry "thy kingdom come" for that kingdom to be completed and for us to be drawn into it forever.

What the liturgy is, therefore, is the *unique and privileged* experience for the church of God's kingdom among us. As such it is irreplaceable. Without it we cannot live the life of God. It is the supreme moment for the church's self-realization on earth of what it hopes to be drawn into at the end—the community of the finally and fully redeemed in the kingdom of heaven forever. But, at the same time, the liturgy is also *promissory* and *provisional*. It is promissory in the sense that it is God's "down payment" on what we will experience in its fullness in the kingdom. It leads to that final consummation and final reality. It is provisional, and Christ's real presence, as "really real" as it can be, is also provisional, because this real presence—especially through the enactment of the Eucharist—leads to its completion at the "supper of the Lamb."

Hence the value of the prayer after the blessing and sprinkling
with holy water at Sunday Mass:

May almighty God cleanse us of our sins,
and through the eucharist we celebrate
make us worthy to sit at his table
in his heavenly kingdom.

Note the reference to table fellowship: we yearn for what lies beyond
even what the Eucharist—this sacrament of sacraments—can offer us.
We yearn for the day the church is assembled not at the altar/table in
church at the Eucharist but rather at the final banquet in God's kingdom forever. No wonder that from the patristic era onward the
phrase of the Lord's Prayer at Mass "give us this day our daily bread"
has been interpreted to mean that at the Eucharist we glimpse what
we shall experience fully in the kingdom. But before "thy kingdom
come" in fact is realized, what we experience in the Eucharist is the
closest we can get to that final fulfillment. The Eucharist is indeed
both "the future present" and also the present lived in the sure hope
that the kingdom will come and we will be called to meet the Lord in
the kingdom of heaven.

One of the more helpful discoveries in studying patristic com-
mentaries on the Eucharist has been the way many of the fathers were
able to assert what might be termed "levels" of real presence in the
Eucharist.[5] In such expositions the Eucharist is respected as a chief
means for experiencing the fullness of the risen Christ until that day
when we experience the completion of the Christian life and share in
the eschatological banquet in the kingdom of God. Holding in tension the "already" of Christ's presence and the "not yet" of that same
presence is no mean feat. But it is presumed in our theology and
needs to be sustained. The action of Christ through the real eucharistic presence is a continual reminder that the kingdom has not yet
come in its fullness. Hence we can say that every Eucharist contains
the real presence of Christ; and yet, at the same time, every Eucharist
looks to the completion of that sacramental presence when we will be
guests at the supper of the Lamb in the kingdom forever.

In terms of an eschatological understanding of the Eucharist we
can say that eschatology concerns more than being aware of what will

happen at the end of time. It also concerns what our life on earth
means here and now in light of the hopefulness that comes from
belief in Christ and his second coming. Eschatology is about the *now*
as much as it is about *what will be*, that is, what will be revealed at the
end of time. What (always) matters in the Christian life is how what
has happened in the incarnation and paschal mystery of Christ and
what will yet happen in his second coming come to bear on the present. What does our belief in Christ's coming among us—his dying,
rising, and ascension and then his second coming—mean as we live
each day we are given on this good earth? The pressing issue of
eschatology is not only what *will* happen but also what happens *now* in
light of what we believe.

Fundamentally, like all Christian theology, eschatology concerns
the community of the church and how the church should live here and
now. This is to say that there is always an eschatological edge, an
eschatological challenge that makes demands upon us to live our faith
in Christ who has come and who will come again at the end of time.
The issue is the "in between" of human life in light of who Christ is.
In fact, one of the contributions of liturgy itself is that by its nature it
is a continual reminder of the corporateness of our faith stance and the
corporateness of our belief in Christ dead, risen, and to come again.

## LITURGICAL PRACTICES

### Viaticum

In my opinion, one of the "success stories" of the post–Vatican II
reform of the liturgy in the church in the United States is the revised
*Rite for the Pastoral Care of the Sick: Rites of Anointing and Viaticum.*[6] The
first three chapters of this ritual concern visiting the sick to bring
them the Eucharist. The opening up of this ministry to the non-
ordained has led to a wide range of people taking responsibility for the
pastoral care of the sick and to increased frequency of the reception of
communion by the homebound, especially on Sundays. In addition,
the shift away from deathbed "extreme unction" to the anointing of
the sick at any time in our lives when we are seriously ill has led to the
proliferation of communal celebrations of anointing with the Eucharist

(which is presupposed and the preferred way of caring for the sick[7]) as well as a revised rite for those individuals who are near death.

With regard to those who are dying, this revised ritual makes clear the lesser known but firm Catholic view that anointing, penance, *and* viaticum are all part of the "last sacraments" given to a dying person. The *Catechism* asserts that "as the sacrament of Christ's Passover, the Eucharist should always be the last sacrament of the earthly journey, the 'viaticum' for the 'passing over' to eternal life" (n. 1517). In traditional Catholic theology, viaticum has been an intrinsic part of the "last rites." However, it was not uncommon that "extreme unction" was really regarded as the "last rites" (despite the fact that the plural form— *rites*—indicates that this means more than a single sacramental ritual).

Just as ministry to the sick at home is "people to people" and "family member to family member," so the rites for viaticum and prayers for the dying are not confined to the ministry only of the ordained. The prayers for the dying can be said by family and friends at a person's deathbed. Prayers that accompany viaticum are particularly poignant in terms of the notion of journey and hopefulness that they reflect. For example:

> God of peace,
> you offer eternal healing to those who believe in you;
> you have refreshed your servant N.
> with food and drink from heaven:
> lead him/her safely into the kingdom of light.

> All-powerful and ever-living God,
> may the body and blood of Christ your Son
> be for our brother/sister N.
> a lasting remedy for body and soul.

> Father,
> your Son, Jesus Christ, is our way, our truth, and our life.
> Look with compassion on your servant N.
> who has trusted in your promises.
> You have refreshed him/her with the body and blood of Your Son:
> may he/she enter your kingdom in peace.

What is notable in these prayers is the sense of healing, despite the fact that, by its very name, viaticum implies that death is near. What this means sacramentally is that rites of anointing and viaticum are rites of healing, but not necessarily of curing. To make this distinction can be most helpful in pastoral care and in a pastoral theology of rites for the sick. From a liturgical-theological perspective on the Eucharist, it is particularly notable that the first two prayers refer to both the species of "food and drink" and "the body and blood of your Son." The prayers for the commendation of the dying are very moving and uplifting. The prayer "when the moment of death seems near" is particularly fitting:

> Go forth, Christian soul, from this world
> in the name of God the almighty Father,
> who created you,
> in the name of Jesus Christ, Son of the living God,
> who suffered for you,
> in the name of the Holy Spirit,
> who was poured out upon you,
> go forth faithful Christian.
> May you live in peace this day,
> may your home be with God in Zion,
> with Mary, the virgin Mother of God,
> with Joseph, and all the angels and saints.

Among the theological points that are made in these prayers and in what is termed the "Continuous Rite for Penance, Anointing and Viaticum,"[8] the communal rite of anointing at a Eucharist is a counter-cultural challenge that reminds us all of our human fragility. In a culture that more often would want to cover over death, these prayers and these rites urge us to realize that the sick to whom we minister are in fact ministering to us at the same time. In their fragility they are telling us—who think we are "well"—that for us too, suffering and death are still to be faced, not denied or (what is even worse) ignored. The use of this ritual for viaticum reminds us that in a real sense every act of communion is viaticum, that is, food for the journey to everlasting life. One day, in fact, it will be our last communion—

viaticum in the strict sense—and we will meet the Lord face to face. The Eucharist is the church's eschatological, promissory reality— food for the journey to everlasting life. Is it any wonder that so many classical liturgies ended with the plea *maranatha*—"Come, Lord Jesus"? How very fitting, therefore, that the Lord's Prayer precedes every act of receiving communion, whether at Mass or at home visits, with the apt petition "Give us this day our daily bread..." In the meantime, the assertion in one of the invitations to communion at viaticum outside of Mass is worth recalling:

> Jesus Christ is the food for our journey;
> he calls us to the heavenly table.

Once more, at the very act of eucharistic communion we are drawn to realize the fulfillment of this action in the kingdom of heaven. In a real sense what we name as "viaticum"—our last reception of the Eucharist—can in effect be used for the Eucharist every time we receive it. Every act of eucharistic communion is viaticum until our last communion, the last time we receive Christ as our hope for the journey to life eternal.

## Location of the Altar

There is debate today about the location of the altar in our churches, with some engaging in fervent appeals for the altar to be placed against the wall of the sanctuary and having the priest not face the congregation during the eucharistic prayer and rites before communion. The historical precedent of the priest facing "toward the east" (from the Latin phrase *ad Orientem*) is invoked to support this proposal. Whatever is said by way of fact or evidence in such discussions, I think it important to recall that the phrase *ad Orientem* originally meant that church buildings and those who shared in the Eucharist faced east because that was understood to be the direction from which Christ would return at the second coming. The logic was that, since the sun rises in the east, that is where Christ will come from at the end of time as the (definitive) light of the world. Alternatively, the west was imaged as the place of darkness (the sun sets in the west) and therefore the realm of Satan.

However, with the passage of time and the need for increased numbers of church buildings, it was no longer possible for all churches to be positioned on an explicit east/west axis. Thus, what diminished was the presumed sense that those at the Eucharist faced east. In a way this is regrettable, since the architecture and location of the altar could be presumed to reflect a theological truth, namely the eschatological emphasis of the Eucharist, of all liturgy, and of the whole Christian life. When the *ad Orientem* argument is used today as the basis for appeals to not have the priest face the congregation, what is often left out is the rest of what occurred when the priest did face the east. When Mass was celebrated *ad Orientem* in the patristic era, the posture of the congregation was standing, everyone listened to the words of the priest, especially during the eucharistic prayer, and there were no elevations at the words of institution. If one determines that the *ad Orientem* precedent should be imitated, does that mean that these other practices should be revived as well?

In addition, it is notable that the revised GIRM 2002 adjusts what was said in the 1975 GIRM about the location of the altar. The new GIRM says:

> The altar should be built apart from the wall, in such a way that it is possible to walk around it easily and Mass can be celebrated at it facing the people, which is desirable wherever possible. (n. 299)[9]

What is underscored when the Eucharist is celebrated facing the people is that aspect of eucharistic theology that emphasizes it as a sacred *meal*. This should never be jettisoned or mitigated. That by its very nature the altar also emphasizes the sacrificial nature of the Eucharist is also equally clear. My sense is that the "both...and" of the Catholic tradition on the Eucharist can be enhanced by an appreciation that when Mass is celebrated at the altar with the priest facing the people both facets of eucharistic theology can be evident—meal and sacrifice.[10]

### *Sancta* Custom

It was noted when discussing Model Two that the practice of the priest dropping a particle of the broken consecrated bread into the chalice originated with a custom known as the *fermentum*, meaning that a part of the consecrated bread broken at the pope's Mass (as evidenced as early as the fifth century) was taken by deacons to other churches in Rome where it was placed into the chalice at the Eucharist being celebrated at those other churches.[11] The theology here is church unity—namely that the whole church is always in union with the Eucharist of the pope. When the number of churches grew, making it impossible for the *fermentum* to be taken to all the other churches in the city, the *fermentum* practice was replaced by the *sancta* practice. What now would occur was that a part of the consecrated eucharistic bread (broken during the Lamb of God) was placed on top of the altar, and the part of the broken bread that was already on the altar from the preceding Mass was dropped into the chalice.

The ecclesiologcal significance of the *fermentum* now shifted toward an appreciation that every Eucharist would lead to the next, and the next, a continuity signified by dropping a piece of the consecrated bread from the previous Mass into the chalice at the Mass being celebrated. In this sense we can say that the eschatological dimension of every act of Eucharist was now underscored by this (new) practice. The theology at work in these symbolic actions was both ecclesiology and eschatology. It is not coincidental that today, when the priest drops a piece of consecrated bread into the chalice, this action precedes the invitation to communion, "the supper of the Lamb," and the prayer after communion which so often deals with being led beyond this Eucharist to life everlasting.

For our appreciation of the multifaceted reality of the Eucharist, holding in mind both historical precedents—*fermentum* and *sancta*—can help us to appropriate some of the ecclesiological *and eschatological* meaning inherent in the act of receiving the Eucharist.

## Liturgical Prayers

Every liturgical prayer announces what we need, but it does so in confidence and hope because we pray to the God who can grant what we ask. Every liturgical prayer begins by naming and acclaiming God's attributes. Then it moves to naming what we lack or what we yearn for, which can be granted us only by God. We then ask for that gift (or those gifts) to be granted. We end all liturgical prayers by explicitly saying we ask this "through Christ our Lord" or in the name of the Triune God: "through our Lord Jesus Christ, who lives and reigns with you in the unity of the Holy Spirit, one God, forever and ever" (recalling again that "in the unity of" is an ecclesiological reference). When it comes to the "not yet-ness" of the Christian life and our imperfections, we are reminded in such prayers that the liturgy offers us the consolation of being a part of a community far greater than we know—the whole community of the redeemed. The food that we take as "food for the journey" is essentially a food that we share in as brothers and sisters of each other in faith. All liturgical prayers remind us that we are not alone. Hence, any eschatological emphasis in the Eucharist is a communal eschatology. It is not about "my judgment" or about "my salvation" only. It is about our being a part of the community that stands in need of complete redemption in and through Christ. This is what the liturgy celebrates and is.

Take, for example, the opening prayer on Christmas day:

> O God,
> you wonderfully created human nature
> and even more wonderfully restored its dignity.
> Give us the grace to share in the divinity of Christ,
> who humbled himself to share in our humanity.[12]

Note the identification of Christ with human nature and the prayer that we humans share the fullness of divinity through Christ. This is the paradox and heart of the Christ event—not only that he has come and accomplished our salvation but that we can share the very life of God even here on earth, even as we long for the completion of our earthly sojourn. This opening prayer is complemented by the prayer after communion on Christmas day:

> Merciful God,
> grant that the Savior of the world,
> who was born this day
> to bring us new and divine life,
> may bestow upon us the gift of life everlasting.

What is explicit here is what many prayers after communion ask for—that we might share the completion of our earthly life by being called to eternal life in God. In the meantime, through such prayers we acknowledge that what we have celebrated in the liturgy of the Eucharist and receive in communion is food for this journey.

Obviously, longer prayers can speak more fully of God's attributes, saving history, and what we need from God. The structure of these prayers is the same in almost all post–Vatican II revised liturgies: acclaiming divine attributes, *anamnesis* of saving history, *epiclesis* for God's particular blessings among us here and now, and final doxology.

A good example is the preface for the Dedication of a Church from the *Sacramentary for Mass*, used on days commemorating the dedication of a particular parish church or the Church of St. John Lateran on November 9th. What is most intriguing is that this prayer draws minds and hearts beyond the edifice to what liturgy, sacraments, and the church are meant to serve, the final fulfillment of God's kingdom among us. The preface says:

> We thank you now for this house of prayer
> in which you bless your family
> as we come to you on pilgrimage.
> Here you reveal your presence
> by sacramental signs,
> and make us one with you
> through the unseen bond of grace.
> Here you build your temple of living stones,
> and bring the Church to its full stature
> as the body of Christ throughout the world,
> to reach its perfection at last
> in the heavenly city of Jerusalem,
> which is the vision of your peace.

Much of the same theology is reflected in the prayers contained in one of the most eschatologically oriented rites of the Roman rite, the *Rite for the Dedication of a Church and an Altar.* Note in particular the prayer for the dedication of the altar in the new (or newly renovated) church:

Father in heaven,
source of holiness and true purpose,
it is right that we praise and glorify your name.
For today we come before you,
to dedicate to your lasting service
this house of prayer, this temple of worship,
this home in which we are nourished by your word and your
    sacraments.
Here is reflected the mystery of the Church.
The Church is fruitful,
made holy by the blood of Christ:
a bride made radiant with his glory,
a virgin splendid in the wholeness of her faith,
a mother blessed through the power of the Spirit.
The Church is holy,
your chosen vineyard;
its branches envelop the world,
its tendrils, carried on the tree of the cross,
reach up to the kingdom of heaven.
The Church is favored,
the dwelling place of God on earth:
a temple built of living stones,
founded on the apostles
with Jesus Christ its corner stone.
The Church is exalted,
a city set on a mountain:
a beacon to the whole world,
bright with the glory of the Lamb,
and echoing the prayers of her saints.

Lord,
send your Spirit from heaven
to make this church an ever-holy place,
and this altar a ready table for the sacrifice of Christ.
Here may the waters of baptism
overwhelm the shame of sin;
here may your people die to sin
and live again through grace as your children.

Here may your children,
gathered around your altar,
celebrate the memorial of the Paschal Lamb,
and be fed at the table
of Christ's word and Christ's body.
Here may prayer, the Church's banquet,
resound through heaven and earth
as a plea for the world's salvation.
Here may the poor find justice,
the victims of oppression, true freedom.
From here may the whole world
clothed in the dignity of the children of God,
enter with gladness your city of peace.[13]

What is striking in this prayer is the elaboration on a theology of what the church is here and now and what it yearns to become in the kingdom in eternity. Again, the tension between the "already" and the "not yet" is not only sustained here but is one of the prayer's clearest emphases.

## HOPE FOR THE JOURNEY

In the early 1980s the distinguished church historian and professor Martin Marty published a book that was unlike his others. Entitled *A Cry of Absence: Reflections for the Winter of the Heart*,[14] it was a series of reflections on God's absence as reflected in the book of the Psalms. Again and again, in poignant and yet encouraging style, Marty reflects that it is simply overly facile to presume that believers always experience God's presence. In reality, more often than not, what they experience is God's absence. He wisely cautions against an overly optimistic theology or an incarnational theology that so emphasizes God's presence to us that it can leave us ashamed for not feeling that close to even the incarnate and revealed God.

Something of the same can be said, it seems to me, about the reality of struggling to believe in the real presence of Christ in the Eucharist when a feeling of absence is more real. Yet it is Marty's genius to reflect on such a "winter of the heart" in light of the psalms ("My God, why have you forsaken me?") and to argue that, rather than a fall from grace, an experience of God's absence can in fact be God's grace at work. The challenge is to name that absence and to pray in hope for a deeper experience of God in the midst of the struggle.

The same can (and should) be said of faith in the Eucharist. While never mitigating any of our faith in the eucharistic presence of Christ, it might be more helpful pastorally to help people name the absence of God, an emptiness that can be filled only by coming to believe even ever so weakly that God is indeed with us as Emmanuel. The gift of eucharistic presence is that God is indeed present to us in ways beyond our imagining, even (especially?) when we do not experience it. Often enough the hopefulness that comes from a glimmer of light at the end of the tunnel is more important than a fluorescent lit path or bright sunshine. It is then that the Eucharist is not a superfluous extra; it is literally our life blood, the thread that tethers us to the lifeline of grace and life in Christ.

Hence the value of such petitions as "strengthen in faith and love your pilgrim church on earth," a prayer that names our status as pilgrims yearning for the fulfillment of all our hopes and dreams in Christ. As pilgrims we will never experience God totally and fully in this life, even at the Eucharist. But it is the Eucharist (above all) that offers us the promissory reality of what is to come. In God's kingdom all our longings will be fulfilled and the winters of our discontent will be turned into the eternal spring of life in God.

As an eschatological reality, the Eucharist is the sacrament that both offers us grace for strength to lead the Christian life and leads us to its fulfillment in the kingdom of heaven. It is therefore the future present for the sake of our present lives and our future lives in God's kingdom forever. In this connection, when I see notices for "healing Masses" I sometimes wonder whether they might suggest that every Eucharist is not about healing. Furthermore, it would seem important not to overstress "healing" so much as to diminish other aspects of eucharistic theology and practice, such as, for example, hope for the journey to the kingdom.

What is imperative in the meantime is to appreciate what the Eucharist offers us and what it challenges us to under this eschatological dimension.

## LIFE RELATION OF THE EUCHARIST

In effect, I would argue that the most useful imperative for appreciating the life relation and social justice implications of the liturgy derives from its nature as eschatological. The fact that it names and celebrates that "we are not there yet" is its own perennial challenge to live the life of God as fully as we can in the time between Christ's ascension and second coming. What we have in the meantime is liturgy and especially the Eucharist, which is both our "daily bread" and the sacrament that has us "wait in joyful hope for the coming [again] of our Savior, Jesus Christ."

In this connection, a poignant statement in Pope John Paul II's encyclical on the Eucharist is important to underscore. He asserts that a significant consequence of the eschatological tension inherent in the Eucharist is also the fact that it "spurs us on our journey through history and plants a seed of living hope in our daily commitment to the work before us" (n. 20). Thus the eschatological dimension of the Eucharist is reflected in a "both... and" theology—both a promise of what is yet to be as well as a challenge to live and work in accord with what we celebrate in the Eucharist.

There are always challenges that come from celebrating the Eucharist. But the contexts of where we live can shape what those consequences look like. For monastics, the challenge of the Eucharist can be to live the bond of charity in community that the Eucharist establishes and supports. For most parishioners, the life relation can well mean working toward a more equitable distribution of this world's goods. This may involve more than simply collecting gifts for the poor. It may require becoming better informed about the structures of our society that need changing so that the "common good" will indeed be common. This strikes at the heart of a society that may be so consumed with the "self" that the selflessness that brought us the Eucharist—Christ's obedient death leading to his resurrection—can barely be understood, let alone revered by many today.

That the celebration of the Eucharist leads to the challenge to live what we have celebrated is a theme that is found in particular in the prayers after communion. One example is:

Lord,
you have nourished us with bread from heaven.
Fill us with your Spirit,
and make us one in peace and love.
       (Second Sunday in Ordinary Time)

Because it combines ecclesiology and the challenge of eschatology,
the following is of particular theological interest:

God our Father,
you give us a share in the one bread and the one cup
and make us one in Christ.
Help us to bring your salvation and joy
to all the world.
       (Fifth Sunday in Ordinary Time)

If we were to put the ecclesiological and eschatological dimensions of the Eucharist together and ponder what these really mean, I
think there would be a revolution in terms of the way Catholics live
what they celebrate. The phrase from Pope John Paul II that "there
can be no love without justice" should challenge us to reassess our
notions of what is "just" and "right" in terms of the way we view our
corporate responsibility for sharing the resources of this world. My
own concern is that the relationship of Eucharist to social justice be
neither jettisoned nor programmed. Were it to be jettisoned then the
Eucharist would lose its eschatological edge to challenge us again and
again to live what we celebrate. And were it to be programmed, then
the celebration of the Eucharist could be perceived to be driven by
ideology—indeed "political" in a narrowly partisan sense. What is
needed is mature reflection on what we do in the Eucharist. In both
the Eucharist and in life we always need to recall that "we are not
there yet." This eschatological tension should spur us to more zealous
living of the gospel in our world.

I began this chapter with references to everyday human life and to
our impatience with getting things accomplished given the advantages (and especially the speed) of technology today. Throughout I

have tried to link experiences such as these with that part of eucharistic doctrine that deals with the Eucharist as leading to its fulfillment in the kingdom of heaven. As we pray "thy kingdom come," we are invited to reflect on the goal of every Eucharist—final and complete union with God. But the next line of the Lord's Prayer ("thy will be done on earth as it is in heaven"—is also important to ponder. Doing God's will on earth is something which even this eschatological dimension of the Eucharist should (re)commit us to. Our "both... and" rhetoric in this book is yet again borne out. The Eucharist is hope-filled yet also challenges us to live what we celebrate "in joyful hope."

## Discussion/Reflection Questions

1.  Reflect on the words of the preface for the dedication of a church[15] and evaluate how fully you appreciate the "not yet-ness" of the Eucharist.

    > Here you build your temple of living stones,
    > and bring the Church to its full stature
    > as the body of Christ throughout the world,
    > to reach its perfection at last
    > in the heavenly city of Jerusalem,
    > which is the vision of your peace.

2.  Reflect on the part of the Mass that includes the general intercessions and the collection of gifts. Ask yourself: Do I appreciate these rites as reflecting both eschatology and ecclesiology? What can I do to improve my appreciation of these realities?

## Further Reading

Read over the *Rite for the Dedication of a Church and an Altar*. It is published in various editions, including *The Rites of the Catholic Church*, vol. 2 (New York: Pueblo Publishing Co., 1983) 593–740.

## MODEL EIGHT
# Sacramental Sacrifice

*We offer to you, God of glory and majesty,*
*this holy and perfect sacrifice:*
*the bread of life*
*and the cup of eternal salvation.*[1]
—*Roman Canon*

How often do we use the word "sacrifice" to mean what we will "offer up" or "do" to benefit either ourselves or someone else? In common usage, the word has connotations of self-deprivation, inconvenience, endurance, even suffering. For example, parents willingly forego countless things so that their children may have benefits the parents themselves did not have as children. Or each of us makes financial sacrifices now in order to ensure a better financial future. During Lent we willingly forego food as a self-sacrifice so that we can share it with those who would otherwise not eat. Sometimes a sibling will undergo surgery to sacrifice a kidney so that the other sibling can live. Clearly the same word "sacrifice" conveys many meanings.

In a religious context it is clear that "sacrifice" is a very significant and often highly charged term. Literally, "sacrifice" comes from combining two Latin words meaning "to make holy" *(sacrum facere)*. Even

217

this brief, literal definition invites us to see in the term "sacrifice" a key to our appropriating the very holiness of God. In and through the Eucharist we want to share in the mystery of God's very being and from this participation both to experience for ourselves and to reflect to others the very holiness of God. But, at the same time, when used in a biblical and liturgical context "sacrifice" contains a range of meanings. Thus it is crucial that we interpret this concept as precisely as we can in terms of what the sacrifice of the Eucharist is and does. Among other things, this requires that we be faithful to the biblical background and understanding of the phenomenon of offering sacrifice. This means, for example, that the destruction of a victim and shedding blood need to be understood as evidence of other things, such as total self-dedication, obedience, and the free surrender of one's life. Why else would the signing of door posts at the exodus with blood come to mean "passing over" to life in God and being spared death? (Again, see Exodus 12, which is proclaimed as the first reading at the Evening Mass of the Lord's Supper, Holy Thursday.)

For our particular purposes in this book, our inquiry into what *sacrifice* means requires that we be as faithful as we can to the theology of what the present eucharistic prayers and rite "say" and "do" in terms of offering sacrifice. It also requires that we be faithful to what the church means when, in the theological reflection contained in the teaching of the magisterium, it refers to the sacrificial aspect of the Eucharist. Of all the issues touched on in this book, it is the real presence and the sacrificial aspect of the Eucharist that most require our paying close attention to what the magisterium has said, precisely because the church's teaching at the Council of Trent was framed by these as major concerns. Because of the polemics of the Reformation and the pressing need at the time (and since) for the Roman Catholic Church to reshape and to refocus its teachings on the Eucharist, emphasis came to be placed on how the Eucharist is understood to be sacrificial.[2]

In accord with the thesis and method followed in this book, in this model we will emphasize a liturgical theology of eucharistic sacrifice. The next model will focus on a liturgical theology of Christ's real and active presence among us through the Eucharist. Here we will be underscoring what the Eucharist does, the fact that it perpetuates the sacrifice of Christ in a sacramental way. This means that the Eucharist engages us in sacred signs and symbols that we use to perpetuate the sacrifice of Christ so that we can become holy as he is holy.

Given what we have said thus far about the polyvalence of the word "sacrifice" and our interest in a liturgical theology of this sacrament, it is important to note the way the *Catechism of the Catholic Church* asserts that "The *Holy Sacrifice* [of the Mass]...makes present the one sacrifice of Christ the Savior and includes the Church's offering. The terms *holy sacrifice of the Mass, 'sacrifice of praise,' spiritual sacrifice, pure and holy sacrifice* are also used (Heb 13:15; cf. 1 Pet 2:5; Ps 116:13, 17; Mal 1:11)" (n. 1330). This paragraph is inspired by the text of the Roman Canon which speaks of "this sacrifice of praise..." and (in the specifically "memorial" section of the Canon) of "this holy and perfect sacrifice..."

The assertion that the Eucharist is a "sacramental sacrifice" puts together two terms that had become separated in some of the decrees and canons about the Eucharist at the Council of Trent. That this separation was common and presumed in catechetical teaching and writing is evident in the contents and title of books such as *Of Sacraments and Sacrifice* by Clifford Howell,[3] which was used widely in the United States prior to Vatican II. That the *sacramental presence* of Christ was distinguished from the notion of the *eucharistic sacrifice* was presumed in a number of catechisms published after the Council of Tent. Simply put, the issues of how to describe the *presence* of Christ in the Eucharist and how to understand that the Eucharist is also a *sacrifice* were matters that understandably occupied the theological minds and pastoral hearts of those who debated the Eucharist at Trent.

In this regard it is helpful to underscore what Edward Kilmartin has argued persuasively, namely that the contemporary magisterium from Pius XII on has favored the phrase *sacramental sacrifice* when referring to the Eucharist.[4] This helpful reunification into the single phrase *sacramental sacrifice* in contemporary magisterial and liturgical documents summarizes our thesis in this chapter—namely that the Eucharist is a *sacramental sacrifice* or, alternatively, that it is a *sacrificial sacrament*. Combining these terms, "sacrifice" and "sacrament," and nuancing each of them in relation to each other and in terms of their liturgical meanings exemplifies the kind of integral theology of the Eucharist that can be derived from the church's liturgy. After all, we share in Christ's unique sacrifice of salvation through the sacrament of the Eucharist and one of the central ways in which we understand the sacrament of the Eucharist is that in it and through it a sacrifice is offered.

Clearly, Catholicism is a historical religion in the sense that it has evolved over two thousand years. In trying to understand certain terms we take for granted and repeatedly use when describing what we believe and how we phrase that belief, it is often crucial to determine the historical context that spawned such phrases and teachings. If this is true for the church's teaching in general, it is particularly true with regard to the ways in which the church has come to describe the Eucharist as a sacrifice. This is to say that an appreciation of some of the highly charged issues at stake in sixteenth-century Europe about eucharistic piety, practice, and doctrine can help us to discover why the teachings of the Council of Trent said what they said, and why in liturgical practice and in popular devotion Catholics did what they did. We will begin this chapter by examining some particulars of the historical and religious context that led the magisterium at Trent and after Trent until Vatican II to emphasize the sacrificial aspect of the Eucharist. This first section on the Reformers and the Reformation will lead to a consideration of what the church's magisterium says about the eucharistic sacrifice. Then we will discuss what the present liturgical documents and the *lex orandi* say about sacrifice and how biblical and liturgical foundations help us to understand how the Eucharist is a *sacramental sacrifice*.

## REFORMERS AND THE REFORMATION

While it is impossible to offer a complete description of the issues concerning eucharistic liturgy and the way in which the theology of the Eucharist was expressed prior to Trent, a brief consideration of Martin Luther's view of sacrifice and his revisions of the eucharistic liturgy can help us to understand why and how the fathers at Trent framed their canons and decrees the way they did.

Martin Luther began his ecclesiastical and professional church life as an Augustinian priest-professor. He popularized his theological ideas in lectures and sermons. Highly influenced by his scripture studies, he came to critique some of the then contemporary Catholic practices as being non-biblical and non-traditional. His critiques gal-

vanized a movement and spurred his followers to question a number of
issues relating to church teaching—in particular justification by faith
and the role of "good works" in a Christian's life if in fact we are justi-
fied by faith. Much of the consensus-building that has occurred since
Vatican II between Catholics and Lutherans has come about because
of dialogues between these churches on a range of issues, chiefly dialogue about justification. The signing of the Joint Declaration on Justification in 1999 by the leadership of Catholic and Lutheran church
bodies was a high point, the culmination of the hard work by theologians and church pastors on matters of clear separation at the time of
the Reformation.[5] A number of Luther's positions against the then
contemporary liturgical practice on the basis of what is stated in the
New Testament—for example, how important it is for the laity to
receive communion under two species, the significance of the proclamation of the word at Mass and preaching on the scriptures proclaimed
at the liturgy—have obviously been transcended, given the liturgical
reforms of Vatican II. However, we need to recall how divisive these
issues were in his day.

In order to do so, we need to appreciate Luther's method and the
framework for his theological teaching so that we can understand the
legitimacy of some of his demands and his concern (at least initially)
to reform Roman Catholicism and to remain within it. But, as history
has proven, some of Luther's more nuanced positions and tentative
proposals were presented in less nuanced ways by his followers. Even
Luther himself spoke in rhetorically "colorful" ways, sometimes in
terms of exclusion rather than inclusion. In a very real sense, it can be
said that he was guilty of the same kind of "either...or" binary (and
sometimes polarizing) rhetoric that is found in some areas of Catholic
church life today.

In Luther's estimation there was a clear separation between a *sacrificium*, a sacrifice which we offer to God, and a *beneficium*, that is, a
grace, blessing, or good thing we receive from God. Since it was
obvious that the Eucharist was a blessing received from God, given
Luther's "either...or" style of presentation, it was impossible that the
Eucharist could be conceived of as a "sacrifice" that we offer to God,
especially if the word "sacrifice" carried with it connotations of dero-
gating in any way from Christ's once-for-all dying on Calvary, his rising, and his ascension. In addition, his theological presuppositions

repeatedly relied on his notion of "the scriptures alone," *(sola scriptura)*, "Christ alone" *(solus Christus)*, and "only grace" *(sola gratia)*. What these pithy phrases did was eclipse other equally legitimate truths, for example truths found in the church's teachings (as well as scripture), or the power and presence of the Holy Spirit (along with the Father and the Son) in the life of the church, or the requirement that we respond to (clearly not "earn") the grace of God so freely given to us.

For Luther, if the Mass was understood to be of value ("propitiatory") for those who assemble for it, then it could be considered only as something that diminished the value of Christ's unique, once-for-all sacrifice offered for our redemption. That priests' pieties and a number of liturgical practices in Luther's day emphasized that the Mass was indeed propitiatory is both clear historically and understandable in terms of theology and piety as commonly practiced before Trent. At the same time, it was rare for the laity who attended Mass to receive communion (even under one species). Instead, the attending laity would watch the ceremony and look at the consecrated host and cup when they were elevated separately at the words of consecration. This practice has come to be called *ocular communion* (noted above in Model Six, "The Lord's Supper") meaning that seeing the species substituted for partaking in the act of eating and drinking at communion (as the priest did). So Luther's emphasis on sharing communion under both species was a clear challenge to the experience of most who attended Mass. If priests offered the eucharistic sacrifice at Mass and earned income from it, Luther argued that changes had to be made in how Christians understood the Mass. For him the choice between the two was obvious—the Mass was a benefit *(beneficium)*, not a sacrifice *(sacrificium)*.

It is important to underscore that Luther himself had little interest in liturgical forms, that he was rather "traditional" in his appreciation of the Roman Catholic (Latin) Mass, and that at least early on in his writings about the Mass he was not looking to change any of its parts—except for the sake of preaching and communion. In his (comparatively very early) treatise *The Blessed Sacrament of the Holy and True Body of Christ and the Brotherhoods* (1529) Luther taught that the Eucharist was to be understood as a "sacrament" or "sign" (as opposed to being a physical reality) and that faith was required to appreciate its full significance. These assertions were in accord with orthodox Catholic teaching. In his 1523 treatise *Concerning the Order of Public Worship,* Luther had set down basic principles for any evangelical reform of the liturgy. And this was his primary concern—an *evangelical* reform of the liturgy. The reason was that, in Luther's view, there was such great emphasis on enacting the eucharistic sacrifice that the Liturgy of the Word had been all but forgotten (or, more precisely, preaching about and from the word proclaimed had become all but unnecessary). He asserted that preaching "has been perverted by the spiritual tyrants" and the eucharistic liturgy "has been corrupted by the hypocrites" (colorful language indeed!). Thus Luther's primary intent in this treatise was to restore the Liturgy of the Word and especially preaching to a place of prominence.

In that same year he authored his first description of a revision of the Mass in his treatise entitled *Formula Missae.*[6] Here he explicitly stated his thesis that the Eucharist was a movement from God to us. Hence, the text of the Canon had to be almost completely eliminated, because for him its words turned the Mass into a sacrifice, which in turn brought about "sacerdotalism" (an emphasis on the priest as the offer-er of sacrifice) and avarice (because the priest was paid for his actions). He also removed the prayers and practices at the "offertory," that is that part of the Mass between the creed and the Canon.[7] The reason why these rites were to be removed was that they emphasized what we offer and not what God offers to us in the Mass.[8] At that part of the Mass, Luther allowed the priest to say a short version of the preface, leading directly to the words of consecration "This is my body...blood...given for you..." His rationale was that the other words of the Canon were not from the New Testament and that only biblical texts should be retained for the Mass. For the same reason, he kept the "Holy, holy, holy" (again, because it contained biblical texts, specifically Isaiah 6:3 and Matthew 21:9) and the Lord's Prayer. Communion was to be distributed to all under both forms of consecrated bread and wine. In this same treatise he insisted that there be no such thing as a "private Mass" (a solitary Mass said by the priest alone) and that hymns could be added to the Mass to allow for the participation of the people.

Three years later Luther issued his most radical adjustment to the existing Roman Mass. Entitled *Deutsche Messe,*[9] this treatise reiterated

German mass

his contention that the chief aim of any service is to preach and teach God's word. Therefore a greater exposure to and use of the scriptures was necessary. This meant replacing the (Latin) entrance verse and psalm *(Introit)* with a German hymn taken from the scriptures or a text that was a paraphrase of the Bible. The sermon was followed by a sung paraphrase of the Lord's Prayer. The words of institution followed. They were separated so that "This is my body" was followed by the distribution of the consecrated bread. Then "This is my blood..." was recited, followed by the distribution of the consecrated wine. These actions of distribution were accompanied by the singing of the "Holy, holy, holy" in German (no longer the *Sanctus* in Latin) or of another German hymn which could be used as a substitute. For Luther, the elevation of the consecrated species to the singing of the "Holy, holy, holy" functioned as a "pictorial *anamnesis*," that is, a visual reminder of how the Eucharist relates to the paschal mystery of Christ. This was important because, since he had removed almost the whole text of the Roman Canon, including the *anamnesis* (memorial) section itself, a pictorial act of remembrance was regarded as pastorally and catechetically useful.

It is frequently stated that Luther preferred the term "consubstantiation" to the prevailing orthodox Catholic term for the change in the bread and wine into the body and blood of Christ, "transubstantiation" (more on "transubstantiation" in the next chapter). However, while it is clear that Luther's disciples used "consubstantiation" and that this term is found in Lutheran catechetical books, it is very clear that Luther himself did not use the term "transubstantiation."[10] For him, both terms have to do with human language and scholastic reasoning. For him, church teaching should be biblically based and biblically infused. And, given his emphasis on *sola scriptura*, the primary magisterium is the Bible itself, not human beings crafting concepts and phrases.

This review of the main features of Luther's treatment should itself be placed in the context of Catholic eucharistic piety from the thirteenth century on. Since the Mass was not celebrated in the language of the people, the average layperson watched the Mass and was normally passive before it. Because the laity received communion so rarely, the fathers at the Fourth Lateran Council (1215) decreed that the faithful had to receive communion at least once a year during the

Easter season. Eucharistic piety was directed to the cult of worshiping the presence of Christ in the host, a practice that spawned annual Corpus Christi processions (from the thirteenth century onward, as noted above in Model Six, "The Lord's Supper"). While we can say that there was an intense cult of the real presence at the time of the Council of Trent, we can also say that there was a clear diminishment in appreciating the Mass as something to be participated in, both verbally (in terms of active participation) and sacramentally (in terms of receiving communion). Tragically, what Luther began as a reform movement within Catholicism evolved into a separatist and separating group. The Council of Trent was summoned for various reasons, among them for the purpose of dealing with errors such as those ascribed to Luther. It is no surprise that when the fathers at Trent addressed the Eucharist they found themselves debating the relative merits of describing the eucharistic presence and the sacrifice of Christ.

## TEACHING OF THE COUNCIL OF TRENT

In his directive announcing the calling of the Council of Trent (entitled *Laetare Jerusalem* issued on Nov. 19, 1544), Pope Paul III stated that the aim of the council was reform, and that its purpose was to deepen contact with the sources of belief and of cult. The council's work spanned the years from 1545 to 1563. Four of its decrees dealt with the Mass. The first, issued in 1551, dealt with the presence of Christ (to be treated in the next model). Of the remaining three, issued in 1562, one concerned "the sacrifice of the Mass." What is notable about these decrees is that they were not combined into one, and that the two burning issues at the time—real presence and sacrifice—were treated in two different decrees separated by eleven years. This suggests that the concern of the council fathers was not to provide a complete theology of the Eucharist but to deal with very specific issues of controversy (not to say church division) and these issues alone.[11]

Among those who have left us abundant insight on how to interpret the teachings of the magisterium, especially from church councils, is Piet Fransen. When discussing how one should interpret the Council of Trent, he asserts that "the assembled Fathers never intended to delineate a *complete* exposition of the doctrine of the sacraments... they aimed only at condemning the heretical positions of the Lutherans and the Calvinists, deliberately dropping whatever question, however important, was still under discussion among Catholic theologians."[12] He goes on to say that "the positive Catholic doctrine in the decrees and canons is therefore on the *necessary minimum*, in opposition and contrast to the heretical positions of that time."[13]

In addition to appreciating that the teaching of the magisterium does not contain all orthodox Catholic doctrine, it is important to realize that what is enshrined in the church's magisterial teaching is most often reactive to errors, specific in what it asserts, laconic in its use of language, and open-ended in the sense that it does not intend to say everything that can or should be said about the topic at hand. That the church's doctrines about sacraments have evolved over time is clear. We are faithful to the magisterium when we uncover the historical, theological, and cultural context in which the sacramental teachings of the magisterium were debated, sometimes because of errors, and ultimately codified. We interpret those decrees in light of this data because we understand the magisterium to be both *reactive* and *specific*. We are faithful to the magisterium when we interpret teachings precisely because we understand the magisterium to be *laconic*. We are faithful to the church's full range of sacramental teaching when we uncover it from the scriptures, the liturgy, theologians, and the teachings of the magisterium itself. We do this because we understand the magisterium to be open-ended enough to allow sacramental practices and other sources for doctrine to help to flesh out our understanding of the stated meaning of the doctrinal text. Respecting the historical evolution of rites, teachings (and teachers), and the magisterium is a prerequisite for determining as carefully and faithfully as we can the evolution of the church's sacramental doctrines. This means discovering *how* teachings evolved, by *whom* they were changed, and *what* resulted.

These methodological insights are even more pertinent when applied to the historical evolution of Trent's doctrines about the Eucharist. The fathers at Trent were understandably and necessarily concerned with sacramental presence and sacrifice. The aim of the decree on the sacrament of the Eucharist specifically was to "set out the true and ancient teaching on faith and the sacraments, and supply a remedy for all the heresies and other serious troubles by which the church is now miserably disturbed."[14]

With regard to the specific issue of the Eucharist as sacrifice, the council's teaching is laconic and focused. Clearly, but also tersely, it asserts that in the Eucharist it is "the same victim here offering himself by the ministry of his priests, who then offered himself on the cross; it is only the manner of offering that is different." Canon One asserts that "a true and proper sacrifice is...offered to God in the Mass..."[15] James McHugh points out that here Trent asserts that "in the Mass there is offered to God a true and proper sacrifice," and that the magisterium's wording is very precise.[16] The focus here is on a verb and an action; it is not on a noun which would be descriptive and objective only.

*anamnesis*

In addition to asserting that in the Mass a true and proper sacrifice is offered to God, the council fathers asserted that this sacrifice is both of praise and thanksgiving and that it is effective in that it offers benefits for the living and the dead. My own sense of this precise assertion is that it leaves open the way to develop a theology of the Eucharist that respects the dynamic, event, action character of what occurs at the Mass itself. In effect, what Trent has to say about the eucharistic sacrifice coincides with the emphasis on the liturgy of the Eucharist as the *actio* of Christ and the church. What is also significant about the discussions held at Trent about eucharistic sacrifice is that those involved in the deliberations leading to this assertion included master generals of religious orders and several theologians.[17] In fact, as the debate sharpened about exactly what a "sacrifice" was, some twenty officially appointed theologians weighed in from all over Europe for a three-week debate in December 1551. Their insights and arguments were influential on the bishops' debates and the eventual formulation in the canon.[18]

I noted above regarding the magisterium in general that it is most often reactive to errors and is specific, laconic, and open-ended. The difficulty arises when canons such as these from Trent become the axis or the sole source for subsequent understanding of the Eucharist. However, it is clear that the two main tenets of eucharistic doctrine from Trent—presence and sacrifice—came to frame and shape post-Tridentine Catholic theology. And this is quite understandable given the need to shore up the church's true teaching after the council. The apologetic nature of seminary textbooks emphasized the Eucharist as a sacrament and as a sacrifice. So did catechisms of the Catholic Church in various countries.

As I have already mentioned, it seems to me that there is no more egregious evidence of polarizing rhetoric about the Eucharist today than that which attempts to separate the Eucharist as a sacrifice from other very important aspects of the church's teaching about the Eucharist, for example that it is a sacred meal. In addition to saying that the Eucharist is obviously both sacrifice and meal, and even more than these, if we are true to the biblical and liturgical witness, we would need to say that we participate in the sacrifice of Christ through the sacramental meal that is Eucharist. When the potentially polarizing rhetoric about the Eucharist that separates out sacrament, sacrifice, and meal is dissolved and they are regarded as intrinsically interrelated, then a truly Catholic and integral theology of the Eucharist can begin to take shape.

Clearly one of the challenges inherent in understanding the eucharistic sacrifice involves examining the assumptions we bring to bear when we refer to sacrifice in general and the sacrifice of Christ in particular. Issues of atonement loom large. But here again the biblical, liturgical witness must ground the way we look at sacrifice. Our annual celebration of the Easter triduum makes us sharers in a particular way in Christ's sacrifice, part of which is obviously overturning the estrangement from God we inherited as a result of Adam's sin. The sin of Adam was disobedience; the redemption Christ accomplished was by obedience to the Father's will. If Christ learned obedience from what he suffered (Heb 5:8) and it was his redemptive suffering that brought us new life, then the sufferings we experience in life can be transformed and made redemptive through the attitude of obedience we bring to acknowledging, accepting, and, yes, even embracing them. We are "made holy" (the literal meaning of "sacrifice") by engaging in the eucharistic action and by living lives in deliberate obedience to God's will.

## CONTEMPORARY LITURGICAL DOCUMENTS

It is most significant, especially from the perspective of the theology reflected in liturgical documents, that where the GIRM 2002 lists and describes the elements that make up the eucharistic prayer, the section entitled "offering" states that "in this very memorial, the Church ... offers in the Holy Spirit the spotless Victim to the Father" (n. 79). Note how its description of offering follows the description of the *anamnesis* (memorial) section of the eucharistic prayer. The precise theological point to be made here reflects the important combination of "sacrifice" with "memorial," where what the church does in "making memory" of the paschal mystery of Christ leads to the act of offering this gift back to the Father. In other words, what we do in the act of *anamnesis* of the past, present, and future dimensions of Christ's paschal victory leads to the here-and-now offering by the church of this unique gift of redemption. What was accomplished once for all is not only made present, it is actualized and operative among us through the liturgy. And it is because the Eucharist is a liturgical memorial of Christ that we can offer to the Father all that the Son has accomplished and in so doing we experience its fullness now. This combination of terms recalls our treatment of "memorial" in Model Four, where we argued that memorial is a key to understanding what a liturgical theology of the Eucharist is all about. It is in this connection that the notion of sacrifice is rightly found.

In addition, the *Catechism* does this same thing by placing its summary of "sacrifice" after its assertion that the Mass is "the *memorial* of the Lord's Passion and Resurrection" (n. 1330). What is thus held in proper relationship is the way the liturgy marks time and the way the liturgy allows us to experience in the here and now all that Christ accomplished for us and for our salvation as we long for its fulfillment at the end of time. Is it any wonder, then, that the eucharistic sacrifice is such a central act of offering? No other sacrifice comes near to its fullness or its completeness. This is to say that what we offer is what God has accomplished through Christ and offered to us for our redemption.

It is also helpful theologically to explore the ways in which the GIRM 2002 describes the eucharistic sacrifice as related to other aspects of the enacted eucharistic liturgy. The GIRM 2002 cites the teaching of the Second Vatican Council when it asserts that "at the Last Supper our Savior instituted the Eucharistic Sacrifice of his Body and Blood, by which he would perpetuate the Sacrifice of the Cross throughout the centuries until he should come again, thus entrusting to the Church, his beloved Bride, the memorial of his death and resurrection" (n. 2).[19] Among other notable assertions here is the subtle yet clear indication that whatever we do in the liturgy, especially in the act of offering sacrifice, is done at God's initiative and accomplished through his abiding power and action. The GIRM 2002 then goes on to say in the same paragraph that "as often as the commemoration of this sacrifice is celebrated, the work of our redemption is carried out." Although they are tersely worded, these assertions contain a wealth of theological insight—principally about how the liturgy is a unique means for the church in any and every age to *experience*, not just to watch, to observe, or to reminisce about the paschal mystery. And when these texts insist that the memorial is linked to the act of offering sacrifice, they underscore what the liturgy accomplishes here and now—literally our *participation*, our "taking part in" the paschal mystery of Christ.

Have you ever noticed that the Roman liturgy rarely describes Christ's self-sacrifice and the whole of his paschal mystery without including the church in that mystery? Recall the example from the Easter preface, the last part of which is part of one of the memorial acclamations:

He is the true Lamb who took away the sins of the world.
By dying he destroyed our death;
by rising he restored our life.

The first assertion is reiterated at every Mass "Behold the Lamb of God, who takes away the sins of the world..." (at the invitation to communion). Recall that the first part, "Behold the Lamb of God," is from John 1:36. The rest of this phrase describes what is happening at the Eucharist, namely, that the Lamb of God we acclaim is active among us through the Mass to do again for us what he accomplished once for all—to take away our sins and to invite us to share in "the work of our redemption." Notice the pronouns. What Christ accomplished was and is for *our* sakes and *our* redemption. What the Mass does is allow us to share in that act of redemption through the words, actions, and sacred symbols that comprise the eucharistic liturgy. One advantage of the phrasing of the Easter preface is that it succinctly summarizes the paschal mystery in terms of the dynamic of our dying and rising through, with, and in Christ. A bit more expressive is the phrasing of Sunday Preface IV:

> By his birth we are reborn.
> In his suffering we are freed from sin.
> By his rising from the dead we rise to everlasting life.
> In his return to you in glory
> we enter into your heavenly kingdom.

In light of the title and thesis of this chapter, most notable is the assertion in the GIRM 2002 that "the Sacrifice of the Cross and its sacramental renewal in the Mass...are one and the same...[and that] ...the Mass is at once a sacrifice of praise and thanksgiving, of propitiation and satisfaction" (n. 2).

Again, what is helpful here is way the text explicitly relates "sacrifice" with "sacramental renewal." In terms of what we do in the liturgy and what God does for us through the liturgy, this text is particularly informative. What we do is to offer praise and thanks; what God does is offer us reconciliation with him through the expiation of our sins which Christ accomplished once and for all. Interestingly, the text also asserts that this is done "in the Mass which Christ instituted at the Last Supper and commanded the Apostles to do in his memory..." (n. 2). Once more the liturgy combines notions that are often separated—what we do in liturgy and what God does for us through the liturgy. These are (always) to be seen in relation to each other. In the liturgy "we commemorate" in an act of *memorial* only because of what God has accomplished for us through the paschal mystery of his Son.

With regard to the offering of eucharistic sacrifice specifically, the GIRM 2002 refers to the fact that "the Eucharistic Sacrifice is, first and foremost, the action of Christ himself..." (n.11) and that in the Mass "the sacrifice of the Cross is perpetuated" (e.g., n. 27). The importance of appreciating the integrity—liturgical and theological— of each and every sacramental renewal of Christ's sacrifice in the Mass is underscored by the protocol to be observed in consecrating sufficient bread and wine for the faithful. The rubric adds the explanation as to why we should do this—so that these signs of communion "will stand out more clearly as a participation in the sacrifice actually being celebrated" (n. 85).[20] What is emphasized here is what

is true of every Mass—that in it all who take communion literally
take part in Christ's paschal triumph by eating and drinking. This is
underscored in another place where the GIRM 2002 asserts that "at
the Last Supper Christ instituted the Paschal Sacrifice and banquet,
by which the Sacrifice of the Cross is continuously made present in
the Church..." (n. 72).

The irenic tone of such assertions is notable, as is the helpful juxtaposition of references to where the eucharistic action takes place: at
the altar/table. Recall the familiar phrase from the Roman Canon:

> Then, as we receive from this altar
> the sacred body and blood of your Son...

as well as how often the prayers after communion speak about what
we have received from the eucharistic table:

> Lord,
> you renew us at your table with the bread of life...
> (Twenty-second Sunday in Ordinary Time)

Not surprisingly the GIRM 2002 synthesizes this insight in at least
two places. Specifically in n. 73 it states that "at the beginning of the
Liturgy of the Eucharist the gifts, which will become Christ's body
and blood, are brought to the altar." And in n. 296 it states that "[t]he
altar on which the Sacrifice of the Cross is made present under sacramental signs is also the table of the Lord to which the People of God
[are] called together to participate in the Mass, as well as the center of
the thanksgiving that is accomplished through the Eucharist."

When discussing Model Four, I noted that the notion of memorial
has been a most significant category for ecumenical convergence on
the Eucharist. I would argue that one of the principal reasons for this
is that the biblical, liturgical witness about memorial is a fundamental
category for understanding the sacrificial nature of the Eucharist, and
that this witness has happily been rediscovered across denominational
lines in the Christian churches. The Reformation and post–Tridentine
rhetoric about this central yet often explosive issue, the sacramental
nature of the Eucharist, has been reevaluated in historical and ecumenical studies, often because of discussions about what the liturgies

have said and do say about the memorial sacrifice. The result is that the issue is no longer *whether* at the Eucharist a sacrifice is offered, but rather *how* what occurs in the Eucharist is legitimately regarded as a sacrifice. Again, the irenic tone of the GIRM 2002 is notable where it says: "[I]n these prayers the priest, while he performs the commemoration, turns towards God, even in the name of the whole people, renders him thanks, and offers the living and holy Sacrifice, namely, the Church's offering and the Victim by whose immolation God willed to be appeased" (n. 2, quoting Eucharistic Prayer III). It seems to me that a number of things said here in a terse manner need to be unpacked for an adequate theology of eucharistic sacrifice both within Catholicism and in any ecumenical area.

The intrinsic relationship of sacrifice and meal in the liturgy is based on the biblical background in which "memorial events" are shared at a meal. Think for example of the Passover and the telling of the story of the exodus which is experienced anew each time it is told and the Passover supper shared. Clearly this is what is going on in the Eucharist where the command "do this in memory of me" includes the sharing of the biblical word and then the taking, blessing, breaking, and giving of the Eucharist in communion. This perpetuation of the unique sacrifice of Christ implies sharing in communion in a sacred meal. Indeed, sacrifice and meal cannot be separated. Our participation in the sacrifice of Christ is made possible only by sharing in the Eucharist, a sacred meal in which the covenant is renewed, reconciliation with God is accomplished once more, and we are joined with the paschal dying and rising of Christ.

## WHO OFFERS THE SACRIFICE?

The eucharistic sacrifice is always the sacrifice of Christ, the unique mediator of our salvation, a salvation accomplished in his paschal victory. The Eucharist is the church's act of sacrifice—it is never that of an individual, even the priest, for he acts in the Eucharist (as has already been asserted) *in persona Christi capitis ecclesiae* ("in the person of Christ, the head of the church"). This is an important tenet of a Catholic theology of ordination and one that has been underscored by Pope John Paul II.

First and foremost, the priest acts in the person of Christ, meaning that his words and actions in the liturgy are always those of Christ, who himself, and himself alone, is the head of the church. This is to suggest that when the priest prays for and with the church it is almost always with the words of Christ himself. Take, for example, the institution narrative: "Take, eat, this is my body...this is the cup of my blood..." Such central texts serve as important, continual reminders that it is Christ who acts in and through the sacraments. It is the words and acts of Christ that matter. The priest acts in a specific and unique but not self-absorbed or self-concerned role. It is worth recalling here the words of the GIRM 2002 that the eucharistic sacrifice is, first and foremost, the action of Christ himself (n. 11, citing Trent). That the eucharistic sacrifice is also essentially the church's sacrifice for us and for our salvation is presumed and underscored by the words and actions of the eucharistic liturgy itself.

The issue here is to transcend any notion of the priest acting over and above the people at Mass. We must also respectfully acknowledge how a variety of ministers and ministries function in the eucharistic liturgy, with the assembly as the central locus of those ministries in any particular celebration of the Mass. Again, this is where the value of the church's *lex orandi* complements what the magisterium asserts about the unique role of the priest at Mass. The key verb of the Roman Canon, "we offer" *(offerimus)*, states this explicitly and clearly. The priest's words "we offer" indicate that he prays in the person of Christ on behalf of the whole church. It is not his personal prayer or private devotion. It is the act of the church, of which he is a part and whom he leads in the liturgy. This ecclesial emphasis in understanding eucharistic sacrifice serves such contemporary theologians as von Balthasar, whose discussion of the Roman Canon's *offerimus* underscores the relationship of priest, community, and eucharistic memorial.[21] In fact, almost all the words the priest uses to lead the liturgical prayer of the church refer to the wider church and are plural. The eucharistic prayer is unique in that it combines the plural pronouns "We come to you Father, with praise and thanksgiving..." with the words of the Lord, "This is my body which will be given up for you." When hearing these texts at Mass, one can only marvel at their ecclesiology and Christology. Is it any surprise that a liturgical theology of the ordained priesthood would uphold both the ecclesiology and the Christology we find in these prayers?[22]

Vatican II's Constitution on the Sacred Liturgy reemphasizes the importance of both ecclesiology and Christology in stating that the faithful "should be instructed by God's word, and be nourished at the table of the Lord's Body. They should give thanks to God. Offering the immaculate victim, not only through the hands of the priest but also together with him, they should learn to offer themselves " (n. 48). This latter assertion that we should offer ourselves too indicates a rich theology of communal self-transcendence and the challenge of accepting what it means to obey Christ's command to do this in memory of him.

It is significant, I think, that when discussing the notion of sacrifice at the Eucharist, Leon Dufour emphasizes how the Lord's command, "Do this in memory of me," refers not only to the enactment of the supper but more importantly to our living our lives in obedience to Christ and in imitation of his example of what it means to give our lives in self-surrender and self-sacrifice.[23] In integrating the category of sacramental sacrifice understood from a biblical-liturgical perspective, one can only hope that a major part of such an integration will involve the Pauline challenge to "offer your bodies as a sacrifice..." (Rom 12:1). Interestingly, other than the text of Hebrews referring to Christ's unique sacrifice, this is the only verse in Paul's corpus to contain a reference to "sacrifice." The issue here is to see how a cultic admonition from covenant sacrifices in the Old Law is used by Paul to refer to a far wider sense of self-offering and serving others. Here one finds more than a hint of the relationship between celebrating liturgy and living the Christian life. That the Eucharist is the sacrifice of Christ is clear; that his sacrifice should be imitated and lived out by us in lives of self-transcendence, self-sacrifice, and service should be equally clear.

One of the least remarked upon aspects of the liturgy of the Eucharist, the presentation of the gifts and the preparation of the altar, says a great deal about what we are offering. As liturgical historians often remark, when the gifts were brought forward in the Roman liturgy, it was the Roman custom to receive foodstuffs to be distributed to the poor as well as food to be consecrated at the Eucharist to be shared in communion. "Procession with the gifts" was not a token gesture, with a few people bringing up bread, wine, and monetary gifts (as is customary today). Rather, the procession would take some time. The gifts were received and some were placed on the altar for the sacrifice of the Mass. Here the notion of "sacrifice" was the act of giving from what we have planted, cultivated, and manufactured (bread and wine). It was an act of offering in the sense that these were freely given from what we possess so that others who had less could have what they needed for sustenance. No one should be in want. This liturgical rite offered a key matrix for the celebration of the liturgy and for the way the baptized offer themselves in service and charity. Even when we do not do this in the same way today, there is a theology of monetary gifts and presenting bread and wine that can be enhanced by this historical recollection. Hence the value of calling this part of the liturgy today the "presentation of the gifts."

That some of the gifts presented were then placed on the altar makes a great deal of theological sense. Hence the value of calling this part of the liturgy the "preparation of the altar." After all, the altar is the locus of where Christ's sacrifice is perpetuated. To place the gifts of human manufacture on the altar is to signify that what "we offer" in sacrifice derives from the sacrifices we make in life to prepare and to share these gifts. Similarly, today when we normally present monetary gifts, the theology behind them is that others should be cared for by the material resources we offer in the collection.

Given this brief background to these rites, is it any wonder that in its teaching on the Eucharist the *Catechism of the Catholic Church* emphasizes the ecclesial nature of what we celebrate? This is to say that when we come to Mass we come conscious of a number of things —our own sanctification, intercessory prayer for the wider church and world, and all who are in need in any way. The *Catechism* states that "the Eucharist commits us to the poor" (n. 1397). It goes on to say that "to receive in truth the Body and Blood of Christ given up for us, we must recognize Christ in the poorest, his brethren..." Can there be any more pertinent and challenging reminder of what the Eucharist is than this?

We began this chapter by referring to the many ways we use the word "sacrifice" in daily life and in the liturgy. One of the most challenging ways of understanding this term is to allow it to be a constant reminder of the total self-surrender of Jesus for us and for our salvation. He acted in humility and obedience. These are characteristic ways that we should reflect our faith in him and as celebrated in the Mass. An integral liturgical theology of the Mass as sacrifice must always be framed in a sacramental context. Similarly, a mainstay of any act of liturgy or sacrament, but especially that of the Eucharist, is that it is born from and returns us back to the one sacrifice of Christ. In effect, the celebration of the Eucharist is both a sacramental sacrifice and a sacrificial sacrament.

## Discussion/Reflection Questions

1. Read through all the eucharistic prayers of the Roman Rite, paying special attention to what they say about offering sacrifice, and specifically the kind of sacrifice offered.

2. How does the relationship of offering sacrifice to eucharistic memorial shape your understanding of how "in the Eucharist a sacrifice is offered" (quoting Trent)?

3. Read Romans 12. How do Paul's words place demands on us to offer our lives in self-sacrifice even as we offer the eucharistic sacrifice?

## Further Reading

Hans Urs Von Balthasar, "The Mass: A Sacrifice of the Church?" in *Explorations in Theology III: Creator Spirit* (San Francisco: Ignatius Press, 1993) 185–243.

MODEL NINE

# Active Presence

*Christ is really present in the very liturgical assembly gathered in his name, in the person of the minister, in his own word and indeed substantially and continuously under the eucharistic species.*
—General Instruction of the Roman Missal, *n. 27*

There is probably no more clear example of the way eucharistic doctrine and practice have merged in the history of Catholicism and influenced each other than that regarding the phrase "real presence" and the care with which "transubstantiation" was crafted and is used in the Catholic tradition. Regarding doctrine, recall the attention which the real presence received in the polls and accompanying literature cited in Part 1. Regarding the practice of revering the real presence, think about the presumption of the layout of most church buildings constructed from the Council of Trent through Vatican II.[1] Almost all parish churches were arranged so that the tabernacle was placed in the center of the main altar, where the Eucharist was celebrated. Where previously acts of reverence were made to the altar itself—such as bowing and kissing it—during the Mass, after Trent other acts of reverence to the tabernacle, namely genuflections, were added to the rubrics of the Missal. Immediately after the Vatican II reforms of the liturgy were issued, many

Catholics felt at least awkward initially if not truly ill at ease with the new protocols for Mass which did not call for any genuflections to the tabernacle. The reason was that the (former) GIRM presumed that there was no tabernacle in the sanctuary, hence no such acts of reverence were required. The new GIRM 2002 (n. 274) clarifies the situation. When a tabernacle is present in the sanctuary, the ministers of the liturgy should make a genuflection at the beginning and at the end of Mass. They do not genuflect to the tabernacle during Mass simply because the attention during the Mass is on what occurs at the ambo, chair, and altar. The theological principle here is that the *enactment* of Mass is central; acts of devotion to the tabernacle are legitimate and are to be encouraged, but not during the Eucharist. During the celebration of Mass, what is paramount is the *actio ecclesiae*, the celebration of the Eucharist.

This liturgical practice reflects a theological principle, namely that the enactment of the Eucharist is to be distinguished (but not separated) from the reservation of the eucharistic species in the tabernacle. For many Catholics raised in the pre–Vatican II church, making this distinction did not come easily. And for some post–Vatican II Catholics, the lack of reverence to the eucharistic species has been something of a scandal, or at least something they have missed and wish to insist upon. At the same time, it is also clear that the way Catholics understand how Christ is present in the Mass relates to what they understand, or do not understand, by the phrase "real presence." (Recall the data in Part 1 on "The Questions" about polls and the replies of American Catholics.) Clearly a major concern of the American bishops is that the abiding, real presence of Christ through and in the Eucharist should be emphasized. This concern is summarized in their document "The Real Presence of Jesus Christ in the Sacrament of the Eucharist: Basic Questions and Answers."[2] It is also found in the comparatively more expansive encyclical of Pope John Paul II, significantly entitled *On the Eucharist in Its Relationship to the Church*.[3] What is most interesting, not to say important, theologically is that this document immediately and consistently relates the eucharistic presence of Christ in the Eucharist with its implications for the church. It begins by asserting the traditional Catholic principle that "the Church draws her life from the Eucharist" (n. 1). It also consistently speaks about the importance of participating in the eucharistic sacrifice. In these (and other) ways one can regard the encyclical as a very complete treatment of a number of aspects of the Eucharist in general, in which real presence is legitimately emphasized.

Our concern in developing this model on *active presence* is to unpack some of the theological issues and liturgical practices that converge on the real presence of Christ in the Eucharist. The very fact that we have added the adjective *active* to *presence* underscores the premise of this book, namely, that it is in and through the celebration of the Eucharist that Christ is active among us. One way of talking about this action is the term "presence." In many ways this model is a direct complement to the previous one on sacrifice, given that both "real presence" and "sacrifice" have been the twin poles for a Catholic understanding of the Eucharist since the Council of Trent. Hence, the structure of the treatment of these models is similar.

We will begin with a historical perspective on the ways of understanding the active presence of Christ in the Eucharist that led to the decrees of Trent on eucharistic presence. This will lead to an examination of the ways in which the contemporary magisterium describes Christ's presence in the Eucharist. Parts of the post–Vatican II liturgical rites will then be explored to determine how best both to distinguish and to relate the eucharistic *actio* and eucharistic presence. Throughout, our concern will be to forge an integral understanding of what the liturgy of the Eucharist is and does. This chapter will accord with the thesis of this book in two ways. First, it will insist on the interrelationship of presence and enactment of the Eucharist. Second, it will place this cornerstone of Catholic belief and practice with regard to the Eucharist in relation to the other models for the Eucharist that have already been articulated. Throughout we will argue that a certain liturgical and theological priority should be given to the enactment of the Eucharist, from which derive a number of ways to understand what this celebration is and means.

## INSIGHTS FROM HISTORY

One needs to respect both the *context* and *content* of theological assertions, lest we force onto a document or onto an author something that was never intended. If this is true for the enterprise of engaging in theology in general, it is all the more true when we study what our forebears in the faith had to say about the Eucharist. Matters that are of great import and that need elaboration and explanation at one time in the church's life may well not have the same import in another era. And the way people worded their assertions and crafted their statements in their time and place needs to be respected so that we can learn what they wanted to say and understand why and how they said it. Once we have embarked upon this careful study of *context* and *content*, we can then apply to our own time the insights gained. In what follows, we will be concerned with some general observations about the patristic era, medieval debates, and what the magisterium has to say about Christ's presence in the Eucharist. Obviously what is presented here is only a sketch of what is an enormously important body of theological literature. Our purpose here will be to uncover something of what was said about Christ's presence at different times in the church's life. Then we shall make some applications to how "real presence" can be understood today.

*Patristic Era.*[4] A principal source for understanding the way the fathers of the church understood and spoke about the Eucharist is contained in the genre of theological literature called the mystagogic catecheses.[5] What we have retrieved today as mystagogy, an essential part of adult initiation (evangelization, catecumentate, election-initiation and finally mystagogy itself), derives largely from the way initiation was undertaken in the patristic era. After sacramental initiation (normally at the Easter Vigil), the newly baptized would return during the week after Easter to learn about what had happened to them when they participated in the ceremonies of the liturgy of sacraments for the first time. These instructions were called "mystagogy" (from the Greek term *mueo* meaning "to teach a doctrine" or "to initiate into the mysteries") because what the newly initiated learned concerned the sacred mysteries they had celebrated and experienced in and through the liturgy.[6] Mystagogic catecheses (catecheses delivered about these "mysteries") often emphasized what the sacred symbols of the liturgy meant in terms of how these material elements—water, oil, bread, and wine— were used in the liturgy so that participants could experience through them the action and power of the Triune God. Through this liturgical participation they could truly take part in the life of the Trinity revealed and enacted in the liturgy. One key to interpreting these documents, therefore, is to understand that their main concern was to help the newly initiated to appreciate what had occurred to them through the liturgical rites at the Easter Vigil. The genre of these instructions is more like a homily or a spiritual conference than a systematic treatise of a later (e.g., the medieval) era. We should not expect to find in them the same kind of finely chiseled, laconic phrases that we would find in the magisterial teachings codified in a council like Trent.

In addition, we need to be clear that we are dealing with documents from a comparatively irenic period, especially in terms of talking about the Eucharist. In the patristic era the phrase "real presence" had not yet been coined and authors explored a whole host of issues about what the Eucharist is and does, one of which certainly concerned how Christ was active and present in the liturgy. But these expositions concerned many other insights about sacraments and what they mean for leading the Christian life. This is to say that such expositions contain deep theological and spiritual insight. But respecting their *context* requires that we not impose on them the kind of "system" we can glean from other sources. Respecting their context also requires that we appreciate what words meant at that time, as distinguished from what using the same word would convey in another era. The danger here would be a "literal anachronism," where we take a word and reuse it in a different time and place and presume that its meaning is obvious. As will become clear, terms used in the patristic era that were content-rich and reality-filled would wind up being regarded as much less helpful when used in the medieval period.

In general we can say that what the great mystagogic teachers did was recall the rites and words used at the Easter Vigil and unpack their meanings so that the newly initiated could call to mind what had occurred and learn about the sacraments from that experience. These documents are rich in biblical allusions and imagery. Many (most?) of them reflect a world view in which symbols are very real. "Symbolic reality" is a phrase used by some commentators today to describe how seriously the fathers of the church in this era took the symbols used in the liturgy. And the use of symbols reflected important theological insight. For the fathers of the church, "symbol" was a supremely rich theological concept. So were words such as "copy," "image," and "likeness." These terms connoted an understanding of what was truly real, powerful, and content-rich. Compare this with the way we today customarily use the terms "copy" or "likeness." We normally tolerate a "copy" of a document, but we really prefer the original. Or, we use the copy until we can get the original text, which is all that really matters. (For example, we can fax documents in preparation for a mortgage "closing," but at the closing we have to appear in person to sign the originals, since the originals are the texts that really matter.)

Such words as "symbol," "copy," "image," and "likeness" were used by many patristic authors to describe the particular way in which the liturgy enables us to experience what we humans could not otherwise experience—namely the life, death, and resurrection of Jesus. This is to say that we were not present when Jesus lived as a Jewish man and teacher in first-century Palestine. Nor were we there when he was crucified, buried, and rose again. What the liturgy offers us here and now is the ability to share in all of those events and in fact in the fullness of who Christ was and is as well as in the power and dynamism of the Trinity experienced in and through the liturgy.

In point of fact, what we experience through the liturgy is more than any one or even all the historical events of Jesus' life. What we experience is the totality of who Christ was, what he came to accomplish, and who he is forever. In celebrating the liturgy we do not parcel out one or another aspect of his paschal mystery, e.g., suffering on Calvary, empty tomb in the garden. Liturgy is always about the whole event and experience of Christ. At the same time, liturgy is always paschal—it is always about the entirety of the paschal life mystery of Christ and by its very celebration we are incorporated into those self-same saving mysteries here and now. Therefore what the liturgy offers us is a repeated entrance into and experience of what it was impossible to experience during Christ's earthly life—the fullness of all the redemptive deeds Christ accomplished once and for all.

Think about it. The liturgy is really a unified moment in our time which encapsulates all that Christ accomplished on earth, events that lead now to his interceding on our behalf at the Father's right hand in glory. In effect, what the liturgy commemorates is far richer, fuller,

in the liturgy, we are able to experience all of Christ

and more complete than any individual aspect of the life, death, or resurrection of Christ. That fullness was impossible during Jesus' life simply because the resurrection and ascension had not yet happened. We should feel no prejudice at not having lived in the first century and not having been eyewitnesses to the earthly Jesus. We should feel privileged that through the liturgy we can share in the totality of what Christ came to accomplish—and accomplishes still for us in and through the liturgy until his second coming. The task is how to describe the way in which the liturgy does this. The challenge in every age of the church's life is to find adequate terminology that distinguishes—but does not separate—the events of the paschal mystery as they occurred once in history from the way the liturgy allows us to share in them in their fullness in succeeding generations.

For many authors in the patristic era, the words "copy," "image," and "likeness" were the terms used to describe this distinction between the original (and originating) events of the paschal mystery and what we can experience of that same paschal mystery in and through the liturgy. The paschal mystery is indeed the axis and heart of our salvation. The eucharistic enactment of the paschal mystery is indeed "the mystery of faith." In the terminology of the patristic era, the paschal mystery is the "original." What we experience in and through the liturgy is its "copy." Therefore, for them, the notion of "copy" is by no means less real than the original and perduring dying and rising of Christ. Rather, for them, the "copy" of the originating event of Christianity—the paschal mystery—is experienced in a unique way in and through the liturgy. In fact, for them, the only way contemporary Christians can experience the paschal mystery is in and through the liturgy. The value of sacramental liturgy (as noted, for example, in Model Four, "Memorial of the Paschal Mystery") is that it is a unique experience of time and place wherein what was accomplished once for all in the first century can be experienced really, fully, and as completely as possible in any succeeding century through the liturgy.

This kind of terminology offers us a way to distinguish the "original" from the "copy" by saying that the "original" was the death and resurrection of the exalted Lord and Christ. The "copy" of this unique and central act of Christ is experienced in the liturgy. Specifically for the Eucharist, such distinctions helped patristic authors to express the fullness of what participating in the Eucharist means—sharing in the Eucharist is the sacrament of the whole of Christ's life, death, resurrection, and ascension. And when one would try to describe how important sacramental liturgy is, one would use terms such as "copy," "image," and "likeness." What the liturgy does in a unique way is to make the Christ event available and real through its signs, symbols, and sacred actions.

In effect, what we can say is that when the fathers of the church dealt with the Eucharist it was in order to disclose the dynamism and the uniqueness of what the liturgy is and does, especially the eucharistic liturgy. Rather than focus only on the species of the consecrated bread and wine (an issue that was clearly part of the concern in the patristic era), the fathers offered glimpses and insights about what the whole eucharistic liturgy enacts and the riches that sacramental liturgy contain for contemporary believers. Thus their distinction between "original" and "copy" was by no means a separation between the two. In fact, for them, the "copy" was the closest to the "original" they could come this side of the kingdom of God.

Another important distinction that the fathers consistently made was between the "already" and the "not yet." This was (and is) a central assertion that underlies much of what liturgy and sacraments are all about. What the liturgy enacts is the dying and rising of Christ—his paschal mystery and our paschal mystery through, with, and in him—until the second coming. In other words, the liturgy is a central and unique experience of Christ. But it is also, and always will be, promissory, in that it looks to the fulfillment of the paschal mystery in the kingdom of heaven. A number of early and patristic liturgies ended with the acclamation *maranatha*, meaning "may the Lord come" (or "the Lord comes"). This is an explicit acclamation of what all liturgy is and does: it is a foretaste of the completion of the paschal mystery. (Recall here the discussion in Model Seven, "Food for the Journey.")

Thus, if one were to combine these two distinctions commonly found in the patristic era, one could say that the original paschal mystery is present in the Eucharist as a copy and that this copy is not yet complete. The Eucharist is a "symbolic and promissory reality" yearning for its completion. In the idiom and language of the time, these distinctions were presumed and elaborated on. The active participation of the newly baptized in the rites of initiation coupled with this kind of explanation made the "sacred mysteries" of the liturgy a central experience of the paschal mystery and a key to understanding both what the paschal mystery is and the way in which the liturgy draws us into it. Central to the patristic understanding is a view of liturgy as the dynamic, ongoing means that the church in every age has of experiencing the power and action of the Trinity among us through the paschal mystery of Christ. In the Eucharist specifically, the emphasis in the mystagogic catecheses is on what God does for us as we share in this act of eucharistic memorial and in the banquet of life by taking and eating/drinking the food of everlasting life. The presumption that those participating in the liturgy would partake in this sacred meal was clear. The mystagogic catecheses reflected how the Eucharist is our ongoing and deepening initiation into Christ by observing the command "Do this in memory of me." We "take" and "eat/drink" and in so doing partake in as complete a way as possible in the death and resurrection of Christ.

What happened in later centuries, however, for a variety of liturgical and theological reasons, was that this kind of language and these distinctions were not so readily understood, nor was this meaning so apparent. In fact, to repeat the words "symbol," " copy," and "likeness" at a later time caused confusion rather than offered clarity. Different times and places—*contexts*—require different emphases and new distinctions. Hence we now move to glimpse how later teachers in the faith would use different words and concepts to try to explore the meaning of the Eucharist.

*Medieval Period.* The period from the patristic era through the medieval era was the time when the term "transubstantiation" came to be coined as a useful way to describe the presence of Christ in the Eucharist. These centuries offer a veritable array of persons engaged in theological debates about the Eucharist. In order to offer a general overview of this period and its theological debates, we will be concerned again with both *context* and *content.* The liturgical context of the time was different from that of the patristic era. The Eucharist itself was received less frequently, the language of the Western liturgy was Latin (which not everyone understood), and the roles and ministries at the liturgy were being reduced in many circumstances to those of the priest and a server. While it is clear (and sometimes this is overlooked) that people continued to participate in the medieval Eucharist with great devotion,[7] nevertheless it is also clear that the emphasis in this period shifted toward what participants *received from* the liturgy rather than what they *participated in* at the liturgy.

With regard to the Eucharist, attention came to be focused specifically on the eucharistic species. While in the patristic era the sources for theological insight about the Eucharist came from commenting on the whole of the liturgical rites at initiation (word, water baptism, chrismation, and Eucharist), beginning in the ninth century attention came to be focused on the eucharistic species of the consecrated bread and wine and how to describe what this species contained. Debates among theologians began to refine language, especially about the presence of Christ in the Eucharist. Although the dynamism of the liturgical *actio* and the range of ways that the patristic authors used to describe the Eucharist were not contradicted or ignored in the medieval period, it is not surprising to find that, given the state of the liturgy and the needs of the time to refine theological terminology, emphasis came to be placed on Christ's presence in the sacrament.

Among others, two monks who lived in the Abbey of Corbie (in France), Paschasius and Ratramnus, left us rich insight about the Eucharist in their treatises on the Eucharist, both of which were entitled "On the Body and Blood of the Lord,"[8] titles that themselves indicate a shift of focus to the species. Their arguments reached back to the patristic era, since the origin of each of their positions is in emphases argued by St. Augustine and St. Ambrose. Augustine asserted that a sacrament is a "sign of a sacred thing." For him, language about liturgy and sacraments was about signs and symbols— in all their reality, content, and liturgical fullness of expression. His approach is sometimes termed a "sacramentalist" approach. By way of contrast, it is often asserted that Ambrose offered a more "realistic" understanding of what happens in and through the liturgy. He tended to emphasize a more specific linkage between what the liturgy accomplishes and the events of Jesus' life, including his passion and death. What Paschasius attempted to do was combine these insights and thus offer a credible way of appreciating what the

Eucharist is. However, even some of his contemporaries criticized him as being too "realistic" and insufficiently "sacramental." In fact, it was his monastic confrere Ratramnus who attempted to reclaim the Augustinian "sacramental" emphasis in his (opposing) treatise.

At least part of the problem was how to appropriate in the ninth century the important insights established in the patristic era. A major issue was terminology. Terms such as "symbol," "image," "likeness," and "copy" simply did not carry the weight and value in the ninth century that they had carried in the fourth and fifth centuries. Hence, for the orthodox faith to be transmitted, what was needed was new terminology and new expositions of what the Eucharist was and what it accomplished. One can say that, in general, throughout the medieval period the main theological issue relating to the Eucharist was the struggle to remain faithful to the orthodox faith by steering a course between "empty symbolism" and "gross realism" when it came to describing the Eucharist. By "empty symbolism" I mean to suggest that, since "symbol" had come to be regarded as less and less "real" by the ninth century, it was important to offer new terms that retained notions of sign, symbol, and sacrament but expressed the fact that such terms were rich in content and in the reality they conveyed. By "gross realism" I mean to suggest that, while the Eucharist is always utterly real and is the fullness of Christ's presence and action among us, one also needs to be careful lest one equate Eucharist with anything that is "physical" or localized or (only) "historical." This means that the term "physical presence" is too limiting to describe the Eucharist, because it refers to a localized presence of Christ on earth, when what the Eucharist is and does among us is always much more than what anyone ever saw or experienced of Jesus' earthly presence. The Eucharist is always about Christ as he existed before time, in time on this earth as he accomplished the paschal mystery, and outside of time as he now exists at the right hand of the Father interceding for us in glory. His physical, local presence on this earth during his earthly life is a snapshot of one part of the whole Christ whom we experience in the Eucharist. Thus, the ninth-century debates concerned how to make it clear that Christ's presence in the Eucharist is true and real while avoiding terms that were "physical" or "historical."

What resulted from the ninth-century theological debate between these two monks was a certain framing of positions with no established result. Their (and other) theories about the Eucharist were allowed to remain. One advantage of their work was that, despite their obvious differences, these men helped to frame the debate about theological terminology for later generations of theologians.

In the eleventh century another Frenchman, Berengarius of Tours, was to take the theological stage and attempt to describe the change that occurred in the bread and wine at Mass. While he did not coin the term, he was certainly one who emphasized *substance* as a way to try to emphasize a true, sacramental presence of Christ that was not confined to what is physical or historical. For him, the substance of Christ in the Eucharist was indeed "real." For him, (to recall patristic terminology) the Eucharist was the "copy" of Christ's paschal mystery. The "original" of the paschal mystery was remote, so much so that it was, in effect (almost) "unreal." Berengarius so emphasized the exalted and glorified body of Christ present in the Eucharist that his sacramental (dare we say "symbolic"?) approach to the Eucharist was believed to be unorthodox because in the terminology he used it seemed removed from the historical events of Jesus' life on earth, including his passion and death. Therefore it is not surprising that he was forced sign two professions of faith asserting his belief in the reality of Christ's presence in the Eucharist.[9] Unlike Paschasius and Ratramnus, who are regarded as important because they helped to frame the medieval debate about the real presence, more often than not Berengarius is regarded as a heretic for whom "real presence" was less than "real." Not surprisingly, after Berengarius theologians still had to grapple with how best to describe Christ's presence. Again the issue was adequate terminology to support proper eucharistic theology.

Later in the eleventh century another Frenchman, Lanfranc, entered the ongoing debate about eucharistic presence. If Berengarius can be viewed as having been too "sacramental" (Augustinian) in his understanding of the Eucharist, Lanfranc may be said to have set out to formulate a more realistic understanding of eucharistic presence (along the lines of Ambrose). Lanfranc argued that God's power could change what already exists into something else and that such a change in the bread and wine at Mass occurred at the consecration.

He distinguished between what was "outward" and what was "inner," between "appearance" and "hidden truth." For him, the outward appearances were bread and wine and the inner truth was Christ's body and blood.

It was another compatriot, Alan of Lille, who was to add to these ongoing debates by asserting the importance of making the distinction between the "already" and the "not yet," between the "original" and the "copy," and between "substance" and "accident." From then on in theological circles, the words "substance" and "accident" were to become key words in describing how Christ is really present in the Eucharist. Thus, by the time of Thomas Aquinas in the thirteenth century one can say that the terms "substance" and "accident" were commonly being used (likely with a variety of interpretations[10]) to describe the change from bread and wine into the body and blood of the Lord.

Aquinas treats the Eucharist in the *Summa* under the title "The Eucharistic Presence," which itself is an indication of the importance that eucharistic "presence" had in the medieval liturgical-theological imagination. While we applaud his genius, synthesis, and insight, it is also important to recall that what he offers is not a complete doctrine about the Eucharist. His attention is focused on the issue of how to describe Christ's "real" presence in the Eucharist.[11] At the same time, Thomas also makes important assertions that from our perspective draw on and complement what patristic authors and the scriptures reveal about the Eucharist. For example, when writing about the "sacramentality of the Eucharist,"[12] he asserts that the effect of the Eucharist (*res sacramenti:* literally "the thing of the sacrament") is nothing less than "the unity of the mystical body, the church." A bit later he asserts that "the gathering of the whole Church is symbolized in the bread made from many grains of wheat and wine made from many crushed grapes."[13] Thus we have reiterations of what we saw in the patristic era and what is found throughout our liturgical tradition, expressed so clearly in the *lex orandi*, that Eucharist and the building up of the church are always to be seen in relation to each other.[14] (Recall Model Two, "The Church's Eucharist.") In addition Thomas notes several names for the Eucharist and links them with parts of the paschal mystery. He refers to the past, to what Christ accomplished, and calls it "sacrifice." He refers to the present reality of the Eucharist and calls it "communion" and "*synaxis.*" And he relates the Eucharist to the future when he uses the term "viaticum" as the communion that leads us to eternal life. What Thomas does here is reiterate the emphasis he placed on the paschal mystery in his discussion of "sacraments in general."[15] In that section he asserted that sacraments are commemorative (of what happened in the past), are demonstrative (of what occurs in the present), and are prognostic (of what will be completed in the future). The centrality of liturgical memorial is evident here.

In question 75 of the *Summa*, Thomas raises the specific issue of "transubstantiation" and asserts that at Mass "the whole substance [of bread and wine is changed] into the whole substance [of Christ and this is called] transubstantiation." Here we see the key term which the Council of Trent would use to describe the presence of Christ in the Eucharist. Thus the medieval debates about what the Eucharist is and the way in which these authors strove to avoid "empty symbolism" and "crass realism" finds its culmination in the distinction between *substance* and *accident*. At the same time, however, Thomas's genius is that he also notes that the ritual of the Mass (and not just the eucharistic species) is important because in and through it "we are made sharers of the fruit of our Lord's passion" and "whenever the commemoration of this sacrifice is celebrated the work of our redemption is carried on." These words refer to the way in which the liturgy remains the unique and privileged means for participants to share in the very paschal mystery of Christ.

The point here is that we should not interpret Thomas in a way that sets up an "objective," "out there" notion of real presence. What Thomas does is assert the value of "transubstantiation" as a way of describing the eucharistic change. But he does so by referring to what this presence does and accomplishes among those who participate in it. He specifies the value of participating in the Eucharist as a way of sharing in the fullness of the redemption Christ gained for us through his paschal dying and rising. From Thomas Aquinas on, the way was clear for the Council of Trent to use "transubstantiation" as a key, central term in describing Christ's presence in the Eucharist. Since the Council of Trent, the term has been and continues to be used by the magisterium in reference to the Eucharist.

## THE COUNCIL OF TRENT

It is helpful to set the context for the teachings on eucharistic presence at Trent in relation to the preceding magisterial teaching of the church on the Eucharist in general. As Norman Tanner asserts:

> If one is to speak in general terms, [about the magisterium on the Eucharist] the early councils are mainly concerned with the people present at the eucharist; the medieval councils and Trent turned their attention towards the priest, the objects used in the eucharist and especially towards the presence of Christ; Vatican II returns to the concern of the early church for the people present, though with rather different interests in mind.[16]

This succinct and profound insight comes from an internationally renowned expert on the magisterium.[17] It capsulizes a major part of our concern in this book, namely the fact that the church reasserts its eucharistic doctrine in often new and different ways in different periods because of the needs of that particular time. Only when one gains insight into the evolution and contents of what the magisterium has decreed can one truly learn from it and do justice to it in the present. Part of the craft of understanding what the magisterium says is to put it into proper historical context and to be as precise as possible in our interpretation. (Thus we recall the assertions in the previous model about how to interpret Trent.)

Overall we recall (as argued in the previous model) that Trent did not intend to offer a complete theology of the Eucharist and that its intention was to respond to errors of the Reformers. Since the two most neuralgic issues at the Reformation concerned eucharistic sacrifice and presence, it is no wonder that there are canons on each of these topics.

When it comes to understanding magisterial assertions about sacraments, it is important to take note of the liturgical life and piety of the time.[18] Certainly from the thirteenth century on, increased emphasis was placed on the cult of the Eucharist outside of Mass. Part of the reason for this was that, as noted above, the Mass was celebrated in Latin, a language that was not understood by most of those who attended, and that people received communion very infrequently. It is no surprise that, as pointed out in the previous chapter, in 1215 a decree from the Fourth Lateran Council required that everyone had to receive communion at least once a year, during the Easter season.[19] When people no longer received the consecrated species, their attention at Mass was on the elevation of the species at the words of consecration. These gestures were added to the longstanding tradition of elevating the eucharistic species at the end of the eucharistic prayer leading to the acclamation, the great "Amen." This final doxology to the eucharistic prayer speaks about offering the Father "glory and honor"[20] through Christ. The gesture of raising the species at the end of the eucharistic prayer has often been understood as a sacrificial act of offering these gifts both to God the Father and then, in communion, to the church gathered for the Eucharist. What often happened in medieval celebrations of the Mass was that priests would prolong this gesture in order to provide the faithful with the opportunity of seeing the consecrated species for a longer period. This was done largely because people would not see the eucharistic species at communion, since they received it infrequently. The addition of the elevation at the words of institution thus provided believers with yet another opportunity to see the sacred species. Its purpose was to engage people in contemplation of the eucharistic mystery and to distinguish the elevation at the words of institution from the elevation made just prior to communion. This last gesture was indeed the invitation to communion, an invitation not commonly accepted by the faithful at the time.

In the thirteenth century Pope Urban IV (1264) established the feast of Corpus Christi as a feast for the universal church. Urban's concern was to connect the feast with the eucharistic liturgy itself. While outdoor processions with the species and benediction of the Blessed Sacrament were not envisioned as being part of the ceremony of this day, such practices spread very quickly through various parts of Europe. It would not be conjecture to say that the faithful's desire to see the Eucharist outweighed the value of the Mass on that day. People could see the consecrated host for a longer period of time and in this way have their eucharistic piety nurtured. One effect of such processions was to separate in some people's minds the ideas of real presence and communion.

In addition, there was at this time a clear shift toward emphasizing the role of the priest and his "power" to consecrate the species. While this power obviously comes from God and the words of consecration are those of Jesus ("This is my body... blood"), still the medieval emphasis was on the priest as the sole agent of eucharistic consecration at Mass. It is not surprising to find that in this period the three principal parts of the Mass were seen as the "offertory," the "consecration," and the "*priest's* communion." This terse way of describing the Eucharist placed the emphasis on what the priest did in enacting the Mass for the faithful.

Recall here that the canons of Trent on eucharistic sacrifice are preceded by explanatory chapters describing various aspects of what the phenomenon of eucharistic sacrifice comprises. Similarly, the eleven canons of Trent on eucharistic presence are preceded by eight explanatory chapters. They deal with the real presence of Christ in the eucharistic sacrament, the institution of this sacrament, the excellence of the most holy Eucharist above other sacraments, transubstantiation itself, the cult and veneration of this sacrament, taking the Eucharist to the sick, preparing oneself for receiving Eucharist, and the use of this wonderful sacrament. Obviously, for our purposes in this model, what Trent says in its chapters about real presence and transubstantiation is of central importance.[21]

Regarding presence Trent states: "After the consecration of the bread and wine, Our Lord Jesus Christ, true God and true man, is truly, really and substantially contained in the precious sacrament of the holy Eucharist under the appearance of those things which are perceptible to the senses."[22] With regard to transubstantiation specifically, the council fathers state: "By the consecration of the bread and wine, there takes place the change of the whole substance of the bread into the substance of the body of Christ our Lord, and of the whole substance of the wine into the substance of his blood"; they note that "the holy Catholic Church has suitably and properly called this change transubstantiation."[23] (The Latin word describing the term "transubstantiation" is *aptissime*. This word could also be translated "most fittingly.")

Of the eleven canons from Trent on the eucharistic presence of Christ, three are of particular import here.[24] The first asserts that in the sacrament of the Eucharist the body and blood of our Lord Jesus

Christ are contained "truly, really and substantially... together with the soul and divinity." He is not present "only as in a sign or figure ..." Clearly what is operative here is the language minted through the medieval debates about presence. The fact that the last part uses the phrase *"only* as in a sign or figure" means that these words can be used but that they must be understood to bear the weight of the value of the terms "truly, really, substantially." "Sign" and "figure" are, after all, words that were used earlier on in the church's experience. The difficulty occurs when they are used in a new context in which some of their "reality content" can be perceived to have been lost.

The second canon refers to the "substance of the bread and wine," "that marvelous and unique change of the whole substance of the bread into the body, and of the whole substance of the wine into the blood, while only the appearance of bread and wine remains," and states that this is "a change which the Catholic Church most fittingly calls transubstantiation." Clearly these words reflect the description of the eucharistic change offered in the introductory chapters that led up to these canons at Trent. The fact that the council fathers use "transubstantiation" and call it "most fitting" is significant. Obviously what they want to affirm here is the true, traditional Catholic belief in real presence. And, in the language and idiom of the time, "transubstantiation" is "most fitting." What the fathers did not (and would not) say is that this is *the only* term one should have ever used or could ever use to describe the real presence. (This becomes operative in the teaching of Pope Paul VI below.) Thus orthodox faith is to be preserved by using "transubstantiation." It is worth noting that, as Johann Auer has observed, the fact that "the doctrine of transubstantiation was an attempt to explicate the mystery of faith in no way intends to make a pronouncement concerning the physical matter of bread and wine; and just such an idea is what enters the field of discussion today as soon as the word 'substance' is spoken."[25]

A final canon that is important for our consideration is number 8, which asserts that when one consumes the Eucharist one consumes it "sacramentally and really." What is interesting here is that the text clearly emphasizes real presence and there is a concern as to whether simply using the term "sacramentally" will be sufficient to describe real presence. This is to say that a term like "sacrament," which reflects the fullness of Christ's presence and action and was used in an earlier era of the church's life, was not seen in the sixteenth century to be sufficient to describe Christ's presence in the Eucharist. Again, in accord with the thesis of this book, words convey important meanings, and we must be precise when we use them, especially theologically. In understanding the words used to describe eucharistic change and presence, it is crucial to understand when and why they were used.

The achievement of Trent was to assert and affirm the real presence of Christ in the Eucharist in an idiom and language that was true to its medieval heritage and that could convey orthodox Catholic belief at the time of the criticisms of the church and church teaching by the Reformers. While Trent expressly asserts that the Eucharist is "to be received" (ut sumitur), an assertion that implies the value of participation in the Mass and in sacramental communion, it is clear that the fathers at Trent were (legitimately) preoccupied with presence and sacrifice. Provided that we see this achievement for what it is and the decrees for what they say as a reaction to errors in language that is specific, laconic, and open ended, then we can appreciate the value of Trent as a significant building block in the edifice of Catholic teaching about the Eucharist.

## THE CONTEMPORARY MAGISTERIUM

Beginning with teaching in the Constitution on the Sacred Liturgy of Vatican II through the teachings of the GIRM 2002 it is clear that the church wanted to expand on its focus in Trent on eucharistic sacrifice and presence. That there was a much more irenic climate in church life leading to Vatican II is clear. Beginning in the late nineteenth century, there had been a revival of interest in the study of church history, of the fathers of the church, and of the scriptures, and this revival led to what is now often termed the "liturgical movement" of the twentieth century. That the liturgy should be appreciated as the central prayer of the church in which all were to participate was noted early on in that century with statements from Pope Pius X on frequent reception of communion and participation in the liturgy, especially by singing Gregorian chant. Pius XII himself offered significant endorsements to the growing movement toward reforming and reviving the liturgy by issuing the encyclicals *Mystici Corporis* on the church[26] and *Mediator Dei* on the liturgy.[27] The teachings of the papal magisterium in this century up to and including Pope John Paul II's recent encyclical on the Eucharist make clear that the liturgical movement was thoroughly ecclesiological, rooted in the nature and life of the church. Pius XII's endorsement of the biblical movement and his concern with fostering the study of the scriptures added significantly to an appreciation of why the liturgy should be revived as the key to Christian identity, spirituality, and mission. His concern with fostering active participation in the liturgy and his allowance for the use of the vernacular in some of the liturgy were also important moves toward the kind of wholesale revision undertaken at the direction of Vatican II's 1963 Constitution on the Sacred Liturgy, particularly chapter 1 of that constitution.[28]

In point of fact, the whole of chapter 1 should be seen as offering the clearest theological framework to date on the basis for revising and reviving the liturgy as the "source and summit" of the church's life. It is in this chapter that the council fathers articulate an expanded notion of the way Christ acts in the liturgy and of his manifold presence. (While some commentators refer to the listing in n. 7 of the constitution as describing the *presences* of Christ, I prefer to consider this articulation as concerning the *manifold presence* of Christ. My concern in offering this nuance is to suggest that what is being discussed is the one Christ active in and present to the church through the liturgy in a number of ways.) The paragraph begins by stating that "Christ is always present in his Church, especially in its liturgical celebrations." Note here how liturgy and ecclesiology are intrinsically linked. The text then continues:

> [H]e is present in the sacrifice of the Mass, not only in the person of his minister, "the same now offering, through the ministry of priests, who formerly offered himself on the Cross," but especially under the eucharistic species. By his power he is present in the sacraments so that when anybody baptizes it is really Christ himself who baptizes. He is present in his word since it is he himself who speaks when the holy Scriptures are read in the Church. Lastly, he is present when the Church prays and sings, for he promised: "Where two or

three are gathered together in my name, there am I in the midst of them" (Mt 18:20).

Clearly one of the aims of this assertion at Vatican II is to move beyond the Tridentine framing of the issues surrounding eucharistic presence in the species only. What is very significant from a liturgical and theological perspective is the way in which the council fathers describe presence; they do so by describing how Christ himself is *present and active* in and through the liturgy in a variety of ways. The threefold reference to Christ himself being active in and through offering the eucharistic sacrifice, in the Liturgy of the Word, and in the sacraments ("it is really Christ himself who baptizes," "it is he himself who speaks...") is also significant theologically, first because it reminds the ordained minister that he acts in the person and name of Christ—not on his own in any way—and second because it contextualizes the discussion of *presence* by linking it intrinsically to the liturgy. The point here is that presence should not be understood in any sense as passive. Christ is active when present, and when he is active in and through the liturgy we can say that he is present in a unique and special way. (Hence my purpose in using *active presence* as the title of this model.)

At about this same time, a number of theologians wanted to go beyond Trent's use of "transubstantiation" in order to articulate what Trent had affirmed in a new language and idiom that they judged would be better able to be understood in the contemporary world.[29] Such is the task of the church in any age, to present its teachings in a manner that is as understandable as possible for contemporary believers. However, by 1965 Pope Paul VI found himself in a situation where some of the "newer" approaches to describing eucharistic presence were insufficient and did not reflect the depth of orthodox Catholic belief. Hence he issued the encyclical *Mysterium Fidei* ("On The Mystery of Faith"), in which he makes a number of important theological points that reflect traditional church teachings about the liturgy and theology of the Eucharist. In the encyclical he repeats the assertions of paragraph 7 of the Constitution on the Sacred Liturgy; at the same time he adds to them and reorders them (see nn. 34–38). The first mode of Christ's presence articulated in the encyclical is how "Christ is present in his Church," which is where the constitution starts (and ends). In terms of what is added in the encyclical, what is notable is the assertion that immediately follows, namely that Christ "is present in his Church as it performs works of mercy, not only because we do to Christ whatever good we do to one of these least of his brothers and sisters, but also because it is Christ, performing these works through the Church, who continually assists by his divine charity. He is present in the pilgrim Church longing to reach the harbor of eternal life..." One could easily argue that the Holy Father here wants to assert the relationship of eucharistic worship with the living of the Christian life, especially in acts of mercy.

Then the pope goes on to describe Christ's presence as "different but most real in the church as it preaches..." What is of note here is the fact that comments on the proclamation of the word come after comments on Christ's presence in the church (whereas in the constitution comments on the proclamation of the word follow comments on the presence of Christ in the eucharistic elements). Furthermore, where the constitution speaks of Christ present "when the Holy Scriptures are read in the Church," Pope Paul specifically mentions preaching. Again, from a theological perspective one could argue that the pope places emphasis not only on proclamation but also on preaching, an insight that certainly reflects the spirit and letter of the rituals revised in the light of the Constitution on the Sacred Liturgy. "Real presence" is the last of the modes of Christ's presence in the Mass discussed by Paul VI. The pope says that this is "not to exclude the other kinds as though they were not real, but because it is real par excellence, since it is substantial in the sense that Christ whole and entire, God and man, becomes present." The language used here is that of Trent (which is cited in the footnote). What follows in the succeeding paragraphs is a quasi-summary of the way in which church documents and theologians have attested to this unique presence. The pope then goes on to reiterate the value of the term "transubstantiation" and asserts that the whole substance is changed into Christ's body and blood. But he also offers something of a more dynamic interpretation of transubstantiation when he says "after transubstantiation has taken place, the appearances of bread and wine undoubtedly take on a new meaning and a new purpose, for they no longer remain ordinary bread and ordinary drink, but become the sign of something sacred and the sign of spiritual nourishment" (n. 46).

It is significant that in this encyclical the pope has added "works of mercy" to the other modes of Christ's (sacramental) presence and that he has ordered the manifold presence of Christ in this way: church, word, mercy, and real presence in the species. That same year, in the instruction *Eucharisticum Mysterium* ("On the Eucharistic Mystery"), the Sacred Congregation of Rites repeated (in n. 9) much of what Pope Paul had asserted in *Mysterium Fidei*, although it did not include the pope's reference to "works of mercy." It also elaborated slightly on the preaching of the word (in n. 10) and showed its close connection with the celebration of the Lord's Supper (as found in the Constitution on the Sacred Liturgy, n. 56).

The GIRM (in the 1975 edition, n. 7 and in the 2002 edition, n. 27) sustains both the way the constitution names the manifold presence of Christ (n. 7) and the way Pope Paul VI orders the forms of presence in *Mysterium Fidei*. The revised GIRM 2002 states:

> (27) At Mass—that is the Lord's Supper—the People of God [are] called together, with a priest presiding and acting in the person of Christ, to celebrate the memorial of the Lord, the eucharistic sacrifice. For this reason Christ's promise applies in an outstanding way to such a local gathering of the holy Church: "Where two or three are gathered in my name, there am I in their midst" (Mt 18:20). For in the celebration of Mass, in which the Sacrifice of the Cross is perpetuated, Christ is really present in the very liturgical assembly gathered in his name, he is present in the person of the minister, in his word, and indeed substantially and continuously under the eucharistic species.

> (28) The Mass is made up as it were of two parts: the Liturgy of the Word and the Liturgy of the Eucharist. These two parts are so closely interconnected that they form but one single act of worship. For in the Mass the table both of God's word and of Christ's Body is prepared, from which the faithful may be instructed and refreshed. There are also certain rites that open and conclude the celebration.

The clear and consistent point made in both the Constitution on the Sacred Liturgy and these succeeding documents is that the Tridentine framework and emphasis on sacrifice and presence has been reconfigured so that a more adequate description of Christ's presence can be articulated. From a liturgical point of view, the emphasis on the proclamation of the word and preaching on it is an important contemporary shift. While not new (as we have seen), the emphasis on the presence of Christ in the church is particularly significant because these documents deal with the sacrament of the Eucharist, the bond of charity for the pilgrim church on earth. Where contemporary magisterial texts refer to the eucharistic species and cite it as privileged or "real presence" "par excellence," almost always the footnote references are to the teaching of Trent. What emerges from these documents, therefore, exemplifies part of the thesis of this book. When the church finds itself in new and different circumstances and experiences the need to articulate its belief about the Eucharist, it reframes its teaching to suit those new circumstances. In so doing it draws on what was articulated in previous eras (e.g., especially Trent) and repeats it and it also reemphasizes or restores elements of eucharistic belief and practice that had become atrophied over the years as well as aspects of our teaching that need to be newly emphasized. Once the liturgical and ecclesiological emphases to eucharistic presence can be restored to their rightful and central places in understanding "presence," then any static notions that might be associated with the notion of presence will be eliminated.

The eucharistic presence of Christ is part of the *actio ecclesiae* whose expression is the Mass itself. As all the post–Vatican II liturgical and magisterial texts about (the very legitimate) devotional practices of benediction and processions, etc., assert, these all derive from the celebration of the mystery of faith in the Mass. And it is in the Mass that the eucharistic presence of Christ is most clearly experienced. That Christ's presence in the Mass is manifold and that it is lasting in the eucharistic species are clear emphases today. What this active presence requires of those who celebrate the eucharistic liturgy is attentiveness and the kind of participation that hopefully will lead us to reflect and witness to the presence of Christ in our lives in manifold and untold ways.

*Discussion/Reflection Questions*

1. The church's magisterium has used the term "transubstantiation" to describe the unique presence of Christ in the eucharistic species. What words can I use today to describe this presence so that the reality of what is contained in the term "transubstantiation" can be more easily understood?

2. The contemporary magisterium describes Christ as present in the Mass in manifold ways. How well do I appreciate each of these aspects of Christ's presence?

*Further Reading*

Norman Tanner, "The Eucharist in the Ecumenical Councils," *Gregorianum* 82, 1 (2001) 37–49.

# Work of the Holy Spirit

*Let your Spirit come upon these gifts to make them holy,*
*so that they may become for us*
*the body and blood of our Lord, Jesus Christ.*
*May all of us who share in the body and blood of Christ*
*be brought together in the unity of the Holy Spirit.*
                                                    —*Eucharistic Prayer II*

When Pope Paul VI issued the document officially promulgating the Order of Mass (the "Apostolic Constitution") as it was revised after Vatican II,[1] his concern was to support this revision and to indicate some of the more significant changes that were being made to the existing Roman Mass. One of these concerned the eucharistic prayer. In fact the pope declared: "It must be acknowledged that the chief innovation in the reform concerns the eucharistic prayer."[2] He noted that the Roman rite had allowed for a variety of prefaces (the first part of the eucharistic prayer), but that from the "Holy, holy, holy" on the prayer had had a fixed form[3] which had come down to us from the fifth century. He contrasted this with the practice of some Eastern liturgies which allowed a degree of variety into the anaphoras themselves. He then noted that in the revised eucharistic liturgy a number of prefaces would be added (they now number over ninety) and that three eucharistic prayers would be added to the traditional Western eucharistic prayer, the Roman Canon. While we today take this innovation for granted, at the time this liturgical change was nothing less than an astounding revision for a number of other reasons—pastoral, catechetical, and theological. Pastorally the use of different eucharistic prayers could invite greater attention to what was prayed (as opposed to the praying of the same text daily). The catechetical advantage was that proclaiming such a variety of prayer texts could offer to eucharistic assemblies a number of images to ponder. The new eucharistic prayers and prefaces would provide various ways of exploring the meaning of what the Eucharist is and does. But theologically perhaps the single most important accomplishment in the addition of new eucharistic prayers was the inclusion of explicit prayers that invoked the power and action of the Holy Spirit in the celebration of the Eucharist. These (parts of larger) prayers are called *epicleses*, taken from the Greek term meaning "invocation."

Succinctly put, the church's *lex orandi* was immeasurably enriched by the addition of the epicletic prayers. These prayers contain and reflect a rich theology about how God acts in the liturgy and in particular what role the Holy Spirit plays in the enactment of the Eucharist. Like every other act of liturgy, the Eucharist is undertaken and accomplished at God's initiative, especially through the power and action of the Holy Spirit among us.

The purpose of this chapter is to explore the ways in which emphasizing the role of the Holy Spirit in the Eucharist can help us to appreciate what the Eucharist is, does, and means. We will also examine some of the historical background to the contents and theology of the epicletic prayer. We will then discuss what the GIRM 2002 says about the role and work of the Holy Spirit in our eucharistic liturgy and the implications for eucharistic liturgy and ministry today. This will lead to a reflection on what the present *lex orandi* in the Roman rite offers us in terms of the way the Spirit's role is described. We will conclude with some observations about implications that this emphasis on the Holy Spirit can have for a theology of liturgical participation and of liturgical ministry.

## INSIGHTS FROM HISTORY

When studying liturgical prayers within the same genre, for example the eucharistic prayer, it is important to study them in their particular historical and cultural contexts. It is clear that liturgical prayers reflect the theology and mentality of people at different times and places and therefore should be respected for the variety and pluriformity they bring to appreciating what the liturgy says and does. Hence, when doing research into the origins and development of liturgy, it is customary to review sources from both East and West in order to determine more adequately the meaning of any part or any act of liturgy. Research into the historical evolution and variety of Eastern liturgical sources has contributed significantly to the way the liturgical churches in the West (Roman Catholic, Episcopalian, Lutheran, etc.) have come to appreciate the value of that section of the eucharistic prayer called the *epiclesis*.

It is now customary to use the term *epiclesis* to refer to the explicit invocation of the Holy Spirit in the proclamation of the eucharistic prayer. Historical research has shown the important place it has had traditionally as a constitutive part of many (most?) eucharistic prayers in both East and West. It is the historical and contextual study of liturgical texts that has influenced many Christian churches in the United States and internationally to revise the texts of their eucharistic prayers and to add explicit invocations of the Holy Spirit in their revised liturgies.[4] In so doing, the churches have come to benefit from the central role that the Holy Spirit has played in Eastern and (to a lesser degree) Western liturgy and the theology derived from these liturgical traditions concerning the way God initiates, sustains, and will bring to completion what we do in and through every act of liturgy.

In what follows we will comment on four examples of eucharistic texts from both the West and East. Our purpose will be to indicate that the explicit invocation of the Holy Spirit in the eucharistic prayer has rich historical precedent and that it is this historical precedent that encouraged those responsible for the reform of the Catholic liturgy after Vatican II to incorporate *epicleses* into the three eucharistic prayers added to the Roman Missal since the Council.[5] The study of Eastern sources in particular assists in uncovering the role of the Holy Spirit in enacting the liturgy in general and more specifically in discovering what role the Spirit plays in the liturgy through these epicletic invocations.

## Hippolytus

It is commonly agreed that the earliest evidence in the West for the contents of the eucharistic prayer is found in the third-century document ascribed to Hippolytus of Rome entitled *The Apostolic Tradition*. Scholars today (legitimately) debate the precise date and origins of this prayer.[6] However, for our purposes what is important is the prayer's structure and its contents and the recognition that it reflects an important, early example of what a eucharistic prayer contains. In this regard, it is worth noting that commentators have customarily referred to this text as more of a *structured outline* rather than a word-for-word, exact text. This is because there was a custom of embellishing parts of this prayer depending on the particular liturgical season, feast, or occasion, a custom derived from the precedent for such "embellishment" in Jewish table prayers for particular feasts, such as Passover.[7]

What is particularly instructive for us in this text is the structure of the prayer as well as its specific reference to invoking the Holy Spirit. In general[8] it can be said that the eucharistic prayer in *The Apostolic Tradition* is composed of:

Introductory dialogue
> The Lord be with you, etc. [to begin such prayers with this dialogue indicates that what follows is extremely important liturgically and theologically]

Recounting of the wonderful saving works God had has wrought in salvation history culminating in the Christ event (termed the *mirabilia Dei*)

Narrative of institution
> Take, eat, this is my body, which shall be broken for you. Likewise also the cup, saying, this is my blood which is shed for you...
> When you do this you make my remembrance.

*emphasizes different things*

Memorial *(Anamnesis)*
> Remembering therefore his death and resurrection, we offer
> to you the bread and the cup...

Invocation of the Holy Spirit *(Epiclesis)*
> And we ask that you would send your Holy Spirit upon the
> offering of your holy Church; that gathering her into one,
> you would grant to all who receive the holy things [to
> receive] for the fullness of the Holy Spirit for the strengthen-
> ing of faith in truth...

Doxology
> ...through [Christ] be glory and honor to you, to the Father
> and the Son, with the Holy Spirit, in your holy Church, both
> now and to the ages of ages.

Final *Amen*[9]

There are obviously a number of structural and theological things to
note here. The assembly is explicitly invited to participate vocally by
responding to the introductory dialogue and to the concluding doxology with the "Great Amen." As yet there is no "Holy, holy, holy"
acclamation at the end of what we today call the "preface" (i.e., the
first part of the eucharistic prayer),[10] nor is there the memorial acclamation (following the present invitation, "Let us proclaim the mystery of faith"), which came into the Roman rite only as part of the
changes introduced after Vatican II. Theologically what is important
about the epicletic section of this prayer from Hippolytus is that it
specifically combines the reference to offerings (bread and wine) with
the church being gathered into one. While countless anaphoras will
extrapolate and elaborate on the invocation of the Spirit over the gifts
of bread and wine for their transformation into the body and blood of
Christ and then specify the invocation for the church's unity (separately), the terse wording in this text gives an indication of the close
relationship that should always be understood between gifts transformed and the deepened unity of the church.[11] For our purposes,
what is significant is that the offerings and the church that offers
them are noted together, which reiterates our thesis above in Model
Two, "The Church's Eucharist"—namely that more often than not
Eucharist and ecclesiology are understood together. The final doxol-

ogy itself also associates the Spirit with deepened church unity when it explicitly refers to the Holy Spirit "in your Holy Church..." Once again, one of the theological issues here is the linking of ecclesiology and the gift of the Holy Spirit as experienced through participation in the act of Eucharist.

What is very clear in Hippolytus is the move from institution narrative (the part of the text that is closely derived from the New Testament accounts of the Last Supper) to *anamnesis* and then to *epiclesis*. Notably the *anamnesis* and *epiclesis* are rich in trinitarian theology and reflect how we always rely on the invocation and power of the Trinity in all liturgical prayer, but especially in the anaphora. In classical blessing prayers of this sort (others being the prayer to bless water at baptisms or the prayer to consecrate chrism, etc.), the Father is asked to send the Spirit. (Note that the familiar hymn "Come Holy Ghost" was written by Rabanus Maurus in the ninth century and uses phrasing that reflects a different approach to "invoking" the Holy Spirit, a theology that is not reflected in liturgical prayers of blessing.) The study of classical liturgical texts reveals that it is the Father who sends the Spirit to sanctify gifts and to sanctify us. Hence the importance of appreciating the role of the Trinity in all liturgies and liturgical prayer. What we do in liturgy is always done by the power of the Trinity whom we invoke explicitly in liturgical blessing prayers. From the point of view of liturgical theology, it is impossible to appreciate the value of church unity without relying on the invocation and power of the Holy Spirit in the eucharistic prayer and eucharistic action.

### (Egyptian) Anaphora of St. Basil

We turn now to the Egyptian Anaphora of St. Basil. This prayer is one of the earliest surviving eucharistic prayers and is one of three used in the Coptic Church today. It also serves as a basis for the third eucharistic prayer in the present Roman rite and was the source for the fourth prayer in Rite II of the 1979 edition of the American Book of Common Prayer.[12] It is regarded as being one of the earliest surviving eucharistic prayers, and thus is comparable to the *Apostolic Tradition* of Hippolytus in terms of antiquity. However, unlike Hippolytus, it does contain the "Holy, holy, holy" acclamation, which commentators suggest had just recently been added to the anaphoral structure. In addition, it adds intercessions after the epicletic invocation itself. Such were not in the original anaphora from Hippolytus, although they have been added to the second eucharistic prayer now in use in the Roman rite.

The structure of the Anaphora of St. Basil is:

Introductory dialogue
The Lord be with you all...

Narration of the *mirabilia Dei*
Praise for creation

Holy, holy, holy
Continued praise for
Creation of humans in the Garden of Paradise
Fall by the serpent's cunning
Incarnation of our Lord and Savior Jesus Christ

Institution Narrative
Take and eat from this, all of you, this is my body, which is given for you and for many for forgiveness of sins. Do this for my remembrance.

Likewise also the cup after supper: Take and drink from it, all of you; this is my blood which shall be shed for you and for many for forgiveness of your sins. Do this for my remembrance...

*Anamnesis*
We therefore, remembering his holy sufferings, and his resurrection from the dead, and his ascension into heaven, and his session at the right hand of the Father, and his glorious and fearful coming to us (again), have set forth before you your own from your own gifts, this bread and this cup...

*Epiclesis*
We...pray you, our God, in adoration that in the good pleasure of your goodness your Holy Spirit may descend upon us

and upon these gifts that have been set before you, and may
sanctify them and make them holy of holies.

Make us all worthy to partake of your holy things for [the]
sanctification of soul and body, that we may become one body
and one spirit, and may have a portion with all the saints who
have been pleasing to you from eternity."

Intercessions
For the church, for church leaders and ministers, for persons
in the locale, for temperate climate, and for the deceased.
[Here the deacon reads the list of the deceased from a tablet
called the "diptychs."]

Conclusion
The Father in the Son, the Son in the Father with the Holy
Spirit, in your holy, one, catholic, and apostolic Church.

Among the important theological motifs in this prayer is the way
the *epiclesis* combines an invocation of the Spirit upon the church and
upon the bread and wine in that order ("upon us and upon these gifts
that have been set before you"). This reflects the same kind of phrasing that we saw in the text from Hippolytus. The epicletic phrase
"may become one body and one spirit..." is the basis for the petition
in the present third eucharistic prayer in the Roman rite "may be filled
with his Holy Spirit and become one body, one spirit in Christ..."
The eschatological phrase at the end of this section is also notable, not
simply because it is there but also because of the way it names the relationship between the present church gathered at prayer and all the
saints from time immemorial.

The rather elaborate intercessions must be understood within the
theological perspective provided by the Jewish prayers of blessing in
which God is named, praised for all the divine attributes (particularly
creating and redeeming us), and recounted in the *mirabilia Dei*. All this
leads to the institution narrative, the *anamnesis*, the *epiclesis*, and (only)
then to the intercessions. Clearly, such intercessory prayers reflect a
deeply felt human need for God to act on our behalf and on behalf of
those whom we bring to mind and heart at liturgy. The formative

nature of such a liturgical structure is that intercessions derive from the invocation of the Holy Spirit on the church—the *epiclesis* itself.

### Apostolic Constitutions

It is commonly agreed that *Apostolic Constitutions* dates from 380 and traces its origin to West Syria. Book 8 of this work contains what is often termed the "Liturgy of St. James," a rather elaborate eucharistic prayer. In his important study on the theology and spirituality of the eucharistic prayer, Louis Bouyer offers the bold observation that this eucharistic prayer is the "ideal" and that "nowhere else has the whole traditional content of the Christian eucharist been expressed with such fullness and in such a satisfying framework for a certain logical type of mind." He goes on to say that, "despite its loquacity, it is still one of the most beautiful eucharistic texts of antiquity and it is undoubtedly... the one which expresses as completely as possible everything that the ancient Christians could find in or put into a eucharistic prayer."[13]

For our purposes here in comparing eucharistic prayers, the structure of this prayer and the text of the *epiclesis* are most important. They are as follows:

Introductory dialogue[14]

Praise of God in himself

Praise of God in creation

Praise of God in salvation history

Holy, holy, holy acclamation

Praise of God for the work of Jesus Christ

Institution narrative

*Anamnesis*

*Epiclesis*
    Send down upon this sacrifice your Holy Spirit,
    "Witness of the sufferings of the Lord Jesus" (1 Pet 5:1)

That he may make of this bread
the body of your Christ
and this cup
the blood of your Christ.
May those who share in it
be strengthened in devotion,
obtain forgiveness of sins,
be delivered from the devil and his errors,
be filled with the Holy Spirit,
become worthy of your Christ,
enter into possession of eternal life,
and be reconciled with you, almighty God.

Litanic intercessory prayer of the bishop

Doxology
For to you, Father, Son, and Holy Spirit, is all glory, worship,
thanksgiving, honor, and adoration, now and always, and to
endless and everlasting ages upon ages!

Let the people reply: "Amen."

Litanic intercessory prayer of the deacon

This structure follows that seen above. The prayer itself, however,
is far longer and richer in theology and imagery than any of the others
we have discussed. The text of the epicletic prayer specifies quite
clearly the role of the Holy Spirit in the act of making Eucharist—
specifically in the transformation of the gifts and in the sanctification
of those who participate in the liturgy. The fact that the bread and the
cup are separated from each other is of interest. Certainly one thing
that this may well have done was to emphasize the Spirit's action in
transforming the gifts. In fact, this would be faithful to an Eastern perspective, which cites the *epiclesis* and not the institution narrative as the
particular set of phrases that form the act of consecration. (More will
be said about this below.) What is of particular note in this prayer is
that the *epiclesis* specifies the *cup* as the vessel containing the "wine
mixed with water" and "the blood of your Christ."

Again, as we noted when discussing "The Church's Eucharist,"
the reference to "cup" in the part of the eucharistic prayer termed the

"institution narrative and consecration" underscores the inherent and specified ecclesiology of the Eucharist. The fact that "cup" also appears in the *epiclesis* would seem to underscore the ecclesiological ramifications of the Eucharist. We who partake from the one bread and the one cup share in the Lord's body and blood as his pilgrim church. The remainder of the *epiclesis* goes on to flesh out aspects of what it means for the church to be fed and strengthened on the consecrated bread and cup.

What is crystal clear in this (and numerous other Eastern anaphoral texts) is that the role of the Holy Spirit is emphasized throughout the whole eucharistic rite, in particular in the anaphora, and that the text of the *epiclesis* deserves special attention for the way in which it portrays the power and work of the Holy Spirit acting in the church as a result of the church's sharing in the Eucharist.

## Roman Canon

Not unlike Hippolytus, what the Roman Canon offers is a text whose structure remains the same yet whose contents vary. Yet it is also true that its structure differs in some ways from that of the other two texts just reviewed, from Basil and from the *Apostolic Constitutions*. When we examine the Roman Canon, what we detect is a prayer with a number of sections and parts that often change with the liturgical seasons and feasts. One of the clearest examples of a part that changes daily is the first part of the Canon called the "preface."[15]

The structure of the Roman Canon is as follows:

Introductory dialogue

Preface

Holy, holy, holy acclamation

Praise (continued)

Intercessions for the living

Naming of the saints (variable part)

Prayer that the offering may be accepted (variable part)

Blessing of this offering

Vouchsafe, we beseech you, O God, to make this offering wholly blessed, approved, ratified, reasonable, and acceptable; that it may become to us the body and blood of your dearly beloved Son Jesus Christ our Lord.

Institution narrative

*Anamnesis*

Therefore also, Lord, we your servants, and also your holy people, having in remembrance the blessed Passion of your Son Christ our Lord, likewise his resurrection from the dead, and also his glorious ascension into heaven, do offer to your excellent majesty from your gifts and bounty a pure victim, a holy victim, an unspotted victim, the holy bread of eternal life and the cup of eternal salvation.

Prayer for acceptance of the offering

Prayer that the angel may take these holy things to heaven ("your altar on high")

Intercessions for the dead

Naming of (additional) saints

Doxology

What is clear in this prayer, both in its structure and its contents, is that there is no explicit invocation of the Holy Spirit, unlike the previous three examples. This reflects the high christological emphasis in the Roman Canon. At the same time, some have argued that the part of the prayer that says "may [it] become to us the body and blood of your dearly beloved Son Jesus Christ our Lord" is an indirect kind of *epiclesis*.[16] Whether or not this is the case, it is also clear that it is by no means an *explicit* invocation of the *Holy Spirit*. (This leads to our discussion below about the theological value of the epicletic invocations to all eucharistic prayers added to the Roman Missal after Vatican II.)

## Some Observations

In assessing these prayers (representative of countless others), we must reiterate what was said above, namely that we must be careful to respect differences in structure and theological content. This means recognizing texts for what they say and do in different contexts (historical and geographical) in the church's life.

On the one hand, the fact that the Roman Canon has been the single eucharistic prayer prayed in Western Catholicism since the fifth century means that it should be respected as truly revered and formative of countless generations of those who prayed it and those who followed it while it was being prayed. On the other hand, in the debates following the promulgation of the Constitution on the Sacred Liturgy at Vatican II leading to the revision of the Order of Mass, a number of questions were raised as to the theological adequacy of this text for continued use in the Western church as the only eucharistic prayer. Pros and cons centered on a number of issues. Among the positive aspects of the Roman Canon and its place in the Roman rite are the following:[17]

- the tradition of the variety of prefaces as the first part of the Roman Canon

- the emphasis in the text on the efficaciousness of the act of what the Eucharist is and does

- the invocation of saints exemplifying the theology of the communion of saints

- the emphasis on Christ highlighting the central action of Christ's paschal victory for our salvation

- the custom of varied parts within the text for feasts and seasons allowing the Canon to emphasize one or another aspect of Christ's life without surrendering emphasis in the *anamnesis* on his passion, death, resurrection, and ascension

- the emphasis on the gifts presented and offered underscoring the value of the eucharistic action as an exchange of gifts: what God has given us in bread and wine are transformed, so that we can offer them back to the Father through the same Christ,

our Lord, and share in them in sacramental communion as the
bread of life and the cup of eternal salvation

What were regarded as at least debatable issues that deserved
attention were the following:

– Did the text emphasize the priest as the only one who offered
  the gifts?

– Were the lists of saints in fact too long and too local to the city
  of Rome?

– Was there sufficient emphasis on eschatology and the second
  coming?

– Did the reiterated emphasis on the offering of sacrifice diminish emphasizing other theological motifs which the eucharistic
  action encapsulates?

– And finally, especially in light of recent research into the contents and theology of eucharistic prayers in the wider liturgical
  tradition of the church, was not the absence of an explicit invocation of the Holy Spirit a deficiency in terms of the kind of
  theology that a eucharistic prayer could (should?) contain?

In addition to these structural and theological debates, there were
questions about whether to edit and rephrase the Canon or to leave it
virtually intact. In effect, the latter course was taken—a decision that
shows the deference those responsible for the revision of the Order of
Mass judged was owed to this venerable monument of the Western
church's liturgical prayer.[18]

As we move now to a consideration of the role of the Holy Spirit
in the present Roman rite, what will become clear is that the power
and action of the Holy Spirit were always at work in the enactment of
the Eucharist. This will be seen especially in some references from
the GIRM 2002 to that power and role. What will become even
clearer is that in the revision of the Roman rite after Vatican II the
Spirit's role is much more explicit and that the theology of the enactment of the Eucharist derived from it is nothing short of a theological
revolution for Roman Catholicism as well as for those liturgical
churches whose rites have been similarly revised.

### GENERAL INSTRUCTION OF THE ROMAN MISSAL (2002)
### ON THE HOLY SPIRIT

As has been stated repeatedly throughout this book, if one wants to glean the theology that undergirds the revised eucharistic liturgy one needs to review not only the church's *lex orandi*, one must also look to the General Instruction for indications of that theology. Not surprisingly, the GIRM reflects in a number of places how the Spirit acts in the eucharistic liturgy and how what we as humans do in the Eucharist derives from that ever present and sustaining action of the third person of the Trinity. Some of the statements have been in the Instruction since 1970, others have been recently added, no doubt as a result of the revived Spirit theology that is now apparent in the revised Order of Mass.

In describing the eucharistic action in general, the GIRM 2002 indicates the centrality of the Mass for the life of Christians when it says:

> The celebration of Mass, as the action of Christ and the People of God arrayed hierarchically, is the center of the whole Christian life for the Church universal and local as well as for each of the faithful individually. In it is found the high point of the action by which God sanctifies the world in Christ, the Son of God, in the Holy Spirit. (n. 16)

While more will be said in our concluding chapter about the centrality of the Eucharist in a spirituality derived from the liturgy, what is significant in this foundational paragraph is the way that what Christians do in offering the Mass is explicitly done through the Trinity. In the most recent edition of the GIRM, the phrase "in the Holy Spirit" has been added to the former GIRM text of 1975. This in itself denotes a shift in this and other similar paragraphs toward an increased emphasis on the theological understanding of the role of the Holy Spirit in Catholic liturgy. For example, when describing the vocal participation of the assembly in the Eucharist, the GIRM 2002 notes that "the Church [is assembled] in the Holy Spirit" (n. 53). This is to say that participation in the liturgy is not something self-generated or up to ourselves to do. It is always done at the inspiration and through the power of God initiating it and acting through us as we take part in the mystery of God in the Eucharist.

When it speaks of presidential prayers, the GIRM 2002 reminds us that: "In accordance with the ancient tradition of the Church, the collect prayer is usually addressed to God the Father, through Christ *in the Holy Spirit...*" (n. 54, emphasis added). The theological point made here underscores the relationship between the church ("in the unity") and the Trinity at the Eucharist. This relationship is intrinsic and inseparable. It is underscored every time we respond to a prayer that ends with the phrase "in the unity of the Holy Spirit."[19]

In addition to commenting on spoken participation, the revised GIRM includes helpful comments about the value of silence at the Eucharist. One of the paragraphs that has been added to the new GIRM about silence notes that our engagement in silent prayer, in particular during the Liturgy of the Word, is also supported by the action of the Holy Spirit. The full text reads:

> The Liturgy of the Word is to be celebrated in such a way as to promote meditation and so any sort of haste which hinders recollection must clearly be avoided. During the Liturgy of the Word, it is appropriate to include brief periods of silence, accommodated to the gathered assembly, in which, at the prompting of the Holy Spirit, the word of God may be grasped by the heart and a response through prayer may be prepared. It may well be appropriate to observe such periods of silence, for example, before the Liturgy of the Word itself begins, after the first and second reading and lastly at the conclusion of the homily. (n. 56)

Again, the theological point made here underscores that it is God's very Spirit within us and among us that deepens our reflection on and assimilation of the word of God at worship.

Clearly among the most significant paragraphs of the GIRM 2002 are those that concern the eucharistic prayer. If in fact the *lex orandi* grounds our *lex credendi* about the Eucharist, then what this central prayer has to say is extremely important. That this prayer is central is noted at the very beginning of the section on the eucharistic prayer:

> Now the center and summit of the entire celebration begins: namely, the Eucharistic Prayer, that is, the prayer of thanksgiving and sanctification. The priest invites the people to lift up their hearts to the Lord in prayer and thanksgiving; he unites the congregation with himself in the prayer that he addresses in the name of the entire community to God the Father through Jesus Christ *in the Holy Spirit*. (n. 78, emphasis added)

That this prayer is regarded as the "center and summit" of the Eucharist is no surprise. That the GIRM asserts that it is a prayer the assembly enters into through the power and action of the Holy Spirit is also no surprise, but it is a most helpful reiteration of the theological and liturgical premise that what we do in the act of worship is really as a result of the initiating and sustaining action of the Triune God in our midst at liturgy. Particularly of note here, however, is that the phrase "in the Holy Spirit" has been added to the GIRM text in this latest edition.

What is probably the most interesting addition regarding the Holy Spirit in the revised GIRM comes in the very next paragraph, which deals with the structure of the eucharistic prayer. Two things stand out theologically in this paragraph. One is that the *epiclesis* is now regarded as a constitutive element of the eucharistic prayer. This is nothing short of revolutionary, considering the fact that the Roman Canon contained (and contains) no explicit invocation of the Holy Spirit in the form of an *epiclesis*. This part of the full section in the GIRM on the *epiclesis* as contained in the eucharistic prayer reads: "*Epiclesis*: In which by means of particular invocations, the Church implores *the power of the Holy Spirit* that the gifts offered by human hands be consecrated, that is, become Christ's body and blood, and that the victim to be received in communion be the source of salvation of those who will partake of it" (n. 79, emphasis added).

The second thing that is notable is that the phrase "the power of the Holy Spirit" has been added to this latest version of the GIRM. This was not in the former editions of the GIRM from 1969 on, nor did it appear in the first printed versions of the GIRM 2002.[20] The fact that it has been added is a most significant factor in helping Catholics to understand the meaning of the eucharistic prayer and the role of the Spirit in our praying of it. It is also obviously an important phrase that can serve ecumenical relations in terms of the role of the Spirit in enacting the Eucharist, especially in conversations with the Orthodox.

## STRUCTURE OF THE EUCHARISTIC PRAYER

The GIRM 2002 offers the following as the structure of the eucharistic prayer (n. 79):

> Thanksgiving
>
> Acclamation: "Holy, holy, holy"
>
> *Epiclesis*
>
> Institution narrative and consecration
>
> *Anamnesis*
>
> Offering
>
> Intercessions
>
> Final Doxology
>
> Amen

Clearly, for our purposes, the most significant point here both structurally and theologically is the weight given to the *epiclesis* as constitutive of the anaphora. Among other things, one can only hope that this assertion in the revised GIRM will foster deepened ecumenical respect between the Catholic and Eastern churches. While the *epiclesis* is noted to be one of the elements of the eucharistic prayer, what one discovers when comparing this outline in the GIRM with a number of eucharistic prayers from the tradition (such as the prayer of Basil and of the *Apostolic Constitutions* discussed above) is a change in the placement of the *epiclesis*. In the GIRM the *epiclesis* is listed as preceding the "institution narrative and consecration." In most other traditional texts, the *epiclesis* follows the *anamnesis*.

Theologically, this tradition underscores a unity of structure: the specific memorial prayer in the *anamnesis* is followed (more often

*purpose of HS*

than not) by the *epiclesis*. God the Father is asked to send the Spirit to transform the gifts and to draw the church into deeper unity. What the revised Roman rite does is follow some of the eucharistic prayers from Egypt which separate the *epiclesis* into two prayers—one for the transformation of the gifts and one for the transformation of the church into a deeper unity. Scholars have legitimately debated whether the Roman rite should have followed this Egyptian tradition and separated out two epicletic prayers.[21] However, it can at least be said that the present Roman rite gives due emphasis to the role of the Holy Spirit in the act of Eucharist and that it is precisely that emphasis reflected in the texts of all the eucharistic prayers now in use in the Roman rite that (re)establishes the Spirit as the person of the Trinity who initiates and sustains our being able to take part in the paschal victory of Christ through the doing of the Eucharist itself.

### *Epiclesis* Prayers in the New Eucharistic Prayers

The second eucharistic prayer in the Roman rite is a revision of that taken from Hippolytus (reviewed above), a third-century prayer that is also now used in a number of Christian churches, including the Lutheran Church in America and the American Episcopal Church.[22] The editors of the 1970 Roman Missal, however, decided that the Hippolytus prayer had to be adjusted in a few places. One such adjustment concerns the way it uses epicletic prayers in two places, both before and after the institution narrative and consecration. The *epiclesis* in Hippolytus was clearly a unified prayer and followed the *anamnesis*.

Before discussing the texts of the *epiclesis*, it is important to note the role of the priest's gestures in the eucharistic prayer. It is notable that the priest holds his hands outstretched over the gifts when he is speaking about the coming of the Holy Spirit. This is a classic liturgical gesture, present in all the eucharistic prayers of the Roman rite.[23] He makes the sign of the cross over the elements when he speaks about their becoming the body and blood of Christ. This is a change from the former Tridentine Mass when the priest made the sign of the cross as many as twenty-five times over the gifts (depending on the date of the text under examination). The reducing of this repeated gesture to one signifies a simplification, given that one of the principles of the liturgical reform was to avoid "needless repetitions."

The texts of the *epiclesis* in the second eucharistic prayer are:

> Let your Spirit come upon these gifts to make them holy,
> so that they may become for us
> the body (+) and blood of our Lord, Jesus Christ.

> May all of us who share in the body and blood of Christ
> be brought together in the unity of the Holy Spirit.

The prayers in the third eucharistic prayer are a bit more complete. The first of these texts reads:

> And so Father, we bring you these gifts.
> We ask you to make them holy by the power of your Spirit,
> that they may become the body (+) and blood
> of your Son, our Lord Jesus Christ,
> at whose command we celebrate this eucharist.

This last phrase derives from the Lord's command to "do this in memory of me." It also underscores the way all the eucharistic prayers reflect the command form of the Last Supper in the gospel of St. Matthew (26:26–27) which, in addition to the verb "take," immediately adds "eat...[and] drink..." Commentators assert that the addition of an imperative here conforms to the plan for the gospel of Matthew in fostering an attitude of obedience in the community of Jesus' "disciples." The verbal reiteration of "take...eat...take... drink" underscores this motif.

The second epicletic invocation reflects the unity of the church when it says:

> Grant that we, who are nourished by his body and blood,
> may be filled with his Holy Spirit,
> and become one body, one spirit in Christ.

That it is followed a bit later on by an explicit intercession for the church draws out this motif even further. It reads: "Strengthen in faith and love your pilgrim Church on earth..." This is clearly a helpful reference to the eschatological nature of the church. It is followed by naming the pope and diocesan bishop, thus underscoring the fact that every act of Eucharist is in a local church that also prays with and for the church throughout the world.

The fourth eucharistic prayer in the Roman rite is the most complete of these three new eucharistic prayers in terms of the theology of the Holy Spirit it articulates. Just prior to the first *epiclesis*, it refers to the Spirit by quoting St. Paul from 2 Corinthians 5:15:

> And that we might live no longer for ourselves but for him,
> he sent the Holy Spirit from you, Father,
> as his first gift to those who believe,
> to complete his work on earth
> and bring us the fullness of grace.

Then it goes on to say in the customary epicletic way:

> Father, may this Holy Spirit sanctify these offerings.
>     Let them become the body (+) and blood of Jesus Christ
>     our Lord
> as we celebrate the great mystery
> which he left us as an everlasting covenant.

Again, what is significant here is the combination of references to our reliance on the Holy Spirit for living the Christian life in charity ("no longer for ourselves...") and for the transformation of the gifts, as well as a reference to this as the covenant renewal in Jesus Christ.

The second epicletic text reads:

> Look upon this sacrifice which you have given to
>     your Church;
> and by your Holy Spirit, gather all who share this one bread
>     and one cup
> into the one body of Christ, a living sacrifice of praise.

This is an important text theologically, because it highlights the way in which the sacrifice of Christ is renewed through the Eucharist and then it refers to our living that sacrifice in our lives. The Pauline text of Romans 12:1—"offer your bodies as a living sacrifice..."—is reprised here; it is a helpful reminder of the way the sacrifice of Christ in the Eucharist is meant to be reflected in the way we live our lives.

In addition to these three eucharistic prayers that have found their way into the common liturgical practice of the Catholic Church, the other eucharistic prayers also in use (for reconciliation and for Masses with children) have motifs that are worth noting.

The first *epiclesis* in the first eucharistic prayer for Masses of Reconciliation combines the transformation of the gifts with ecclesiology. It begins and ends with specific references to the church, stating:

> Look with kindness on your people
> gathered here before you:
> send forth the power of your Spirit
> so that these gifts may become for us
> the body (+) and blood of your beloved Son, Jesus the Christ,
> in whom we have become your sons and daughters.

The association of the enactment of the eucharistic sacrifice and the deepening unity of the church is reflected in the second epicletic prayer, which states:

> Father,
> look with love
> on those you have called
> to share in the one sacrifice of Christ.
> By the power of the Holy Spirit
> make them one body,
> healed of all division.

The second eucharistic prayer for Masses of Reconciliation is most notable because of the way it emphasizes the Spirit in the entire act of both making Eucharist and living the reconciliation Christ has accomplished. A central part of the preface reads:

> Your Spirit changes our hearts:
> enemies begin to speak to one another,

> those who were estranged join hands in friendship,
> and nations seek the way of peace together.
> Your Spirit is at work
> when understanding puts an end to strife,
> when hatred is quenched by mercy,
> and vengeance gives way to forgiveness.

The first epicletic invocation in this prayer is a bit more terse than the others (save for that in the second eucharistic prayer) and is a subtle request for the transformation of the gifts:

> We ask you to sanctify these gifts
> by the power of your Spirit,
> as we now fulfill your Son's (+) command.

The Spirit is invoked after the *anamnesis*, again in rather terse phrasing:

> Fill us with his Spirit
> through our sharing in this meal.
> May he take away all that divides us.

The intercession for the church follows in the (now) customary way. That this prayer begins with a reference to the Spirt is noteworthy, again because of this prayer's emphasis on the Holy Spirit:

> May this Spirit keep us always in communion
> with N. our pope, N. our bishop,
> with all the bishops and all your people.
> Father, make your Church throughout the world
> a sign of unity and an instrument of your peace.

What is clear from this cursory review of the eucharistic prayers of the Roman rite now in use is that the assertion in the GIRM 2002 that "by means of particular invocations, the Church calls on *the power of the Holy Spirit* that the gifts offered by human hands be consecrated, that is, become Christ's Body and Blood..." (n. 79, c, emphasis added) is now very clearly asserted in the *orandi* in the present Roman rite. That this should also influence our *lex credendi* and *lex vivendi* (how we live our lives) is taken up in the last section of this chapter.

## Transformation of the Elements

When liturgical scholars began to rediscover the *epiclesis* as a constitutive element of most eucharistic prayers, they also realized that this emphasis on the role of the Holy Spirit in the eucharistic prayer had implications for how one would understand the moment of consecrating bread and wine into the body and blood of Christ. The Western tradition emphasized that, if one were to specify when the transformation occurred, it would obviously be when the priest said "This is my body... this is the cup of my blood..." These words of Jesus himself, taken from the Last Supper account, were set in large print in altar missals and the rubric indicated that the priest was to say these words clearly and distinctly. And when it became customary to genuflect before and after the (then called) elevation following these words over each species, it was clear that this was the moment in the Canon that mattered. Obviously the priest, acting *in persona Christi*, was at this point saying the very words of Christ; thus his role was confirmed and the eucharistic transformation took place.

However, when one looks to numberless eucharistic prayers in both the East and West, it becomes clear that the precise wording of many of them places the emphasis on the *epiclesis* as the moment when the gifts are transformed (e.g., "Let them become the body and blood..."). For some liturgical scholars, this has caused an impasse about when the consecration occurs at Mass. It would seem, though, that the East-West (apparent) division need not be so polarizing.[24] It appears perfectly logical that Western Christians would have emphasized the words of Jesus as central words in the Roman Canon, first because of the obvious honor due to them as the words of Jesus, and second because the text of the Canon contained no explicit *epiclesis* of the Holy Spirit. Thus, there was no other text to emphasize in its place as transformative of the gifts.

In addition, the revised rite for the concelebration of the Eucharist (published in 1968) directs all concelebrants to extend their hands and recite together the entire middle section of the eucharistic prayer containing the first *epiclesis*, the institution narrative, the *anamnesis*, and the second *epiclesis*. Each one is to extend his hands to the elements, first with both hands joined over the elements, then with his right hand pointing toward the elements for the institution narrative, and then with both hands outstretched from the acclamation through the end of the second *epiclesis*. The theological point here is that the central part of the eucharistic prayer—*epiclesis*, institution narrative, *anamnesis*, and second *epiclesis* (intercession)—is regarded as supremely important for all who concelebrate the Eucharist as indicated by their reciting these texts together and by the fact that their hand gestures accompany this part of the prayer. This rubrical and liturgical practice would seem to back up what the *Catechism* says about the transformation of the gifts— "bread and wine which, by the power of the Holy Spirit and by the words of Christ, have become the body and blood of Christ" (n. 1357). The theological point to be made now, especially in the West with the revision of the Roman Canon and the addition of new eucharistic prayers, is that we should look not only to the words of Jesus but also to the texts of the epicletic prayers to appreciate the way in which the Spirit acts in the Eucharist to effect it. The old debates need not becloud today's circumstance in which we can argue for a "both...and" appreciation of how eucharistic transformation occurs.

In addition, and this is the richer insight to be gleaned from this discussion, when we consider the words of the whole eucharistic prayer, especially its central section, we can come to appreciate the text as a lyrical, hymn-like act of praise, thanks, and blessing offered to God, and that the motivation for uttering this prayer is an acknowledgment of God's mighty deeds from the creation of the world to our re-creation in him at the second coming. It is in such a context that the *epiclesis* and words of institution find their home and are best understood.

Clearly, the restored *epiclesis* nuances the way in which priests can appreciate their role in eucharistic consecration. First, what they do is done *in persona Christi capitis*, and when they say the words of Jesus, "This is my body...blood," it is Christ himself speaking and acting among us. It is he and he alone who is the head of the church. Second, when we focus on the words and power of the epicletic prayers, we realize that everything we do in the act of liturgy is initiated and sustained by God alone, and that it is enacted always and everywhere through the power of God's Holy Spirit active here and now. One must take one's role in the liturgy very seriously. After all, the pluriformity of ministers (reader, server, cantor, eucharistic minister, deacon, priest, bishop, etc.) images the church in the variety and pluriformity of members who constitute the body of Christ on earth. But, in the end, we need to be sure that what we take most seriously is the way God acts in and through the liturgy. This means that we come to our ministry not with self-importance but with (communal) self-transcendence on our minds and in our hearts. Having such an attitude can help in enhancing our celebration of the liturgy with due reverence and with emphasis on the way the Spirit works in and through it.

If it can be said that "all liturgy is paschal," it can also be said that "all liturgy is done by the power of the Holy Spirit." The restored *epiclesis* in the eucharistic prayers makes this obvious. A careful praying over them can help allow that theological insight to take deep root in our minds and hearts. It would also put an end to any kind of "turf" battles having to do with who *does* what at Mass. The entire church participates in the act of Eucharist, each with gifts and talents from the Holy Spirit. Some of us take on particular roles and perform particular functions on behalf of the entire assembly, but the initiative does not come from us. This means that all liturgy is both the enactment of the church and the Trinity in action to make that happen.

One of the byproducts of appreciating the texts of the revised eucharistic prayers is that it supports very strongly the premise that Eucharist is always about the church. The prayers specifically speak to the reality of the wider church always needing to be drawn more fully into the unity that Christ willed for the church. In the end, the epicletic invocations about church unity demand that we seek to live lives in communion with each other, a communion initiated at baptism and sustained by eucharistic participation. Liturgy is never about *me;* it is always about *us.* The heart of liturgical ministry and liturgical participation is that we, together, make up the body of Christ and minister to the church in and through the Eucharist. But we are also challenged, every time we celebrate the Eucharist, to live what we have celebrated and to ensure that the way we live our lives is for the building up and ever deepening unity of the pilgrim church on earth.

Since every act of Eucharist is the celebration of "the mystery of faith" that deepens and renews our faith, it is a mystery that we can participate in only at the invitation and through the ever sustaining power and love of God's Holy Spirit. This means that we come to God humbly in the Eucharist and that when we celebrate the Eucharist we seek to grow in faith and in living lives of humble service. One of the values of appreciating the Eucharist as the "work of the Holy Spirit" is that it emphasizes the always self-transcending character of the Christian life, ritualized in the Eucharist and ever yet to be realized fully in our lives in the church. Until that day when we are called from this life to the next, we need the Eucharist in order to be drawn ever closer to God through Christ in the power of the Holy Spirit. Hence we need to pray from our hearts the words of the third eucharistic prayer: "Strengthen in faith and love your pilgrim church on earth." Among other things, this underscores that the Eucharist is about deepened faith and more committed service to each other and to the wider world. Gratefully we realize in and through the Eucharist that this is done by the power of the Holy Spirit.

*Reflection/Discussion Questions*

1.  How well do I appreciate the value of the whole text of the eucharistic prayer at Mass? What can help me to appreciate it more fully?

2.  The whole church is made up of people with a variety of charisms and gifts. Do I see my own charism(s) and those of others as coming from the Spirit dwelling in us? And how do I see that same Spirit working in and through the liturgy?

*Further Reading*

Edward J. Kilmartin, "The Catholic Tradition of Eucharistic Theology: Towards the Third Millennium," *Theological Studies* 55 (1994) 405–57.

III

# CONCLUSION
## A Liturgical Eucharistic Spirituality

F or some years now it has been clear that Americans have been fascinated by "spirituality." And, on the face of it, this fascination is congenial with the Christian tradition. In particular it is clear that spirituality is a deep and characteristically strong suit of Catholicism. Our tradition boasts a number of different schools of spirituality and ways (monastic, mendicant, apostolic orders, lay apostolate, etc.) of approaching the divine in prayer and service. However, for one's search for God and the transcendent to be accurately named *Christian*, one needs to be clear about what the term *spirituality* means and does not mean.

Regrettably, it seems to me that much of what passes for "spirituality" in America today is simply not what true Christian spirituality is all about. Preoccupation with "me" and the "self" which characterize much "spiritual" writing today is diametrically opposed to what Christian spirituality is and implies. A great deal of what is considered spirituality is simply a veiled (and sometimes not so veiled) narcissism. True Christian spirituality is not just about "my soul" or the "self." Spirituality that is Christian is always about taking responsibility for belonging to others, about sharing their concerns, about bearing others' burdens and washing each other's feet. There can be no Christian spirituality of any worth that does not express itself in prayer and action with and for others. The abundance of self-help manuals attests to a growing desire for self-improvement. But in Christianity real self-improvement—the real test of one's spirituality—has to do with the quality of our lives when lived among, with, and for each other.

In this chapter, our concern will be to draw out some of the implications of the models of the Eucharist delineated in this book for the concrete lived experience of Catholics who participate in the Eucharist. This last chapter is less about what we should do in terms of liturgy planning and execution than about how to prepare ourselves for and seek to live more and more fully the challenges and the consolation which the celebration of the Eucharist always implies. As has been true throughout this book, I want to avoid a self-conscious and rubrical approach to the Eucharist. I am concerned with what the Eucharist enacts and means.

I would argue that it should always be the case that the celebration of Eucharist challenges us to be ever more self-transcending and self-giving. In the words of Aidan Kavanagh, while it is true that we do liturgy, it is more true that *liturgy does us*. My focus in this conclusion is on the ways in which the Eucharist should shape how we look at life, how we evaluate life, and how we live the Christian life. As I would judge should be true for all Christian spirituality, our thesis is diametrically opposed to any sort of preoccupation with the self. Simply put, liturgy is constitutive of understanding what Christianity is all about.

In essence, our thesis is: *Eucharist is integral to and integrating of the Christian life*. This thesis is based on the relationship among *lex orandi, lex credendi,* and *lex vivendi*. In other words, the "law of prayer" enshrined in the enactment of the Eucharist has implications for the "law of belief" in terms of what we believe about the Eucharist and for the "law of living" in terms of the way we live our lives in relation to what we pray and believe. This concluding chapter is more about that last—and ever elusive—task, about the way we live our lives.

## "SOURCE AND SUMMIT" LANGUAGE

In two often quoted texts, the documents of Vatican II speak emphatically about the high priority that the liturgy is to receive in the church's life. The Constitution on the Sacred Liturgy states that "the liturgy is the summit toward which the activity of the Church is directed; at the same time it is the fount from which all the Church's power flows" (n. 10). The Constitution on the Church specifies this by stating that "[t]aking part in the eucharistic sacrifice [is] the source and summit of the Christian life" (n. 11). In what follows we will presume the truth of these assertions and base our reflections on them.

However, it is important to note that some have criticized these phrases as being too "cultic" in that they seem to place too much emphasis on the liturgy, and too "churchy" in that they place so much emphasis on an inner directed and inward focused way of looking at and experiencing the Christian life. While I can understand that these phrases when taken out of content could be thought to be "cultic" and "churchy," in point of fact I would argue that their meaning is the exact opposite. My judgment is that "source and summit" language is not meant to say that the enactment of liturgy is all that matters. I would argue that the "liturgy" and more specifically "the Eucharist" are based on the reality of the life we live before and after the celebration of the liturgy itself. Liturgy should always be understood to be the *axis and anchor* that gives the Christian life its purpose, shape, and meaning. Life lived before and after the liturgy is celebrated is really what matters. The real object of liturgy is not getting the rituals right; the real object of liturgy is that it puts our very lives into perspective.

For me, the account of the transfiguration is helpful. The disciples Peter, James, and John go up the mountain in order to come down again. While on the mountain in the presence of Christ they listen to him and experience his transfiguration. But then they come down again from the mountain to deal with the challenges of daily life. The liturgy functions in something of the same way. We enter into the world of liturgy in order to see the world in which we live from the perspective of the gospel we hear and the sacraments we celebrate. We enter into the realm of ritualized worship so that we can come again to know and experience God's realm and kingdom in at least a partial way in our daily lives until the Lord comes again in glory. This way of looking at the liturgy makes the sacred liturgy less an escape from daily, "real" life than a time to put daily life (back) into the perspective of the gospel, with all its paradoxes, challenges, comforts, and consolations.

Succinctly put, liturgy is both a means and an end. It is a means of integrating the various aspects of our lives, with all our strengths, weaknesses, successes, failures, possibilities, and limitations. We bring our real lives to the enactment of the mystery of faith so that our faith in God can guide the way we deal with all that makes life a challenge. Liturgy is also an end in the sense that it is a glimpse here and now of the eternal "day of the Lord" when God will be all in all and we will be united in the Triune God forever. Liturgy is thus a privileged but provisional experience of God. It is also a unique but not an exclusive experience of God. It is in fact the source and summit of the Christian life when we appreciate that it comes from real life and leads us back to real life. It is a focal point for the Christian spiritual life.

## LITURGY, PRAYER, AND SPIRITUALITY[1]

Some working distinctions need to be made explicit as we move to articulate the important features of what a eucharistic spirituality derived from the liturgy should look like. We can start by saying that liturgy, prayer, and spirituality are intrinsically interrelated, that they are fundamentally theological realities, and that they are at the heart of the Christian way of life. If one were to diagram how liturgy, prayer, and spirituality are interrelated, one could effectively use concentric circles. The innermost circle would be *liturgy*. To my way of thinking, its position in the center indicates that it is an essential and intrinsic part of both prayer and spirituality but that neither prayer nor spirituality is limited to the liturgy. This means that the enactment of liturgy is not coterminous with either prayer or spirituality and that liturgy has implications both for other forms of prayer and for spirituality.

The second concentric circle, larger than liturgy and smaller than spirituality, is *prayer*, understood as the direct and explicit communication with God in many and various ways. In our understanding, liturgy is a central form of prayer; but it is not the only act of prayer in which Christians should or do engage. Other kinds of Christian prayer—from *lectio divina* to meditation, from centering prayer to contemplation—are here assumed and deemed essential for both engaging in the act of liturgy and for living the Christian life. The *way* one prays is less important in this configuration than the *fact* that one prays. But, at the same time—in keeping with our argument throughout this book—the more we reflect on the texts and prayers as well as the rites and gestures of the liturgy, the better we will be at allowing the liturgy to offer us a perspective through which we can look at our lives.

The third and largest of the concentric circles is *spirituality*, understood to mean *viewing* and *living* the Christian life as profoundly and explicitly graced in Christ and continually enlivened by the Trinity. Spirituality has to do with how one views all of life from the perspective of Christian revelation and faith and how one's life values and actual daily living are shaped by that revelation as enacted in the celebration of the liturgy. Spirituality thus relies on and is nurtured by both liturgy and prayer. Liturgy and prayer are its constant nourishment. They afford the means through which the Christian receives divine revelation and the lens through which the Christian views human life as graced and redeemed in Christ, a grace and redemption now made available through the Trinity and operative and experienced in all of life.

Thus, to my way of thinking, spirituality derived from liturgy is essentially *integrative*, and the *integral* vision of the Christian life experienced in liturgy derives from and leads to continuing to experience that integration in all of life. This is to say that liturgy derives from the context of human life and daily living. It also returns participants back to daily living with their vision of the Christian life sharpened and their understanding of the challenge of living that vision enhanced. It relies on, and at times will articulate, aspects of what can be termed a "catholic," liturgical, and sacramental vision of life (understanding, of course, that this vision is not particular to Roman Catholicism). Sacramentality (recall Model One, "Cosmic Mass") derived from Christ's incarnation includes the discoverability of God in the human, based on the fact that all of creation and human life is (at least potentially) a source of revealing the divine. This integral vision of life is presumed and celebrated in liturgy. That the rest of life still needs to achieve the harmony expressed and experienced in liturgy is among the more precise tasks of spirituality. To put life in this kind of perspective presumes regular engagement in the church's liturgy, the Liturgy of the Hours and all the sacraments. But, for our purposes, here it presumes regular engagement in the Eucharist in particular. The familiar phrase of the early Christians, "Without the Eucharist we cannot exist," is also true for us in every succeeding generation of the church's life.

The words of the GIRM 2002 put the relationship between church belonging, liturgical participation, and Christian spirituality (my own term) in this way:

> The celebration of Mass, as the action of Christ and the People of God arrayed hierarchically, is the center of the whole Christian life for the Church both universal and local, as well as for each of the faithful individually. In it is found the high point both of the action by which God sanctifies the world in Christ and of the worship that the human race offers to the Father, adoring him through Christ, the Son of God, in the Holy Spirit. In it, moreover, during the course of the year, the mysteries of redemption are recalled so as in some way to be made present. Furthermore, the other sacred actions and all the activities of the Christian life are bound up with it, flow from it, and are ordered to it. (n. 16)[2]

For me, this indicates the way the theological descriptions of what occurs at the Eucharist as described in the GIRM help us to understand the "source and summit" language of the council. In what follows, I want to draw out some implications of the models of the Eucharist delineated in this book with an eye toward offering an integrated spirituality derived from the enactment of the Eucharist.

## IMPLICATIONS OF THE MODELS FOR THE SPIRITUAL LIFE

As I hope has been clear, my main intention in offering these "models of the Eucharist" has been to present an integral theology of the Eucharist as derived from the present Roman Catholic liturgy of the Eucharist. My aim has been to offer a number of mutually enriching and interconnected "models" which, when taken together and seen in relation to each other, can be understood to be a liturgical theology of the Eucharist. Much of what has been presented concerns a way to look at the Eucharist through the lens provided by the liturgical revisions in the eucharistic rite since Vatican II. Much of what I have argued has been from the rites themselves in order to draw out the theological meanings inherent in them.

In this concluding chapter I want to sketch out some of the implications that can be derived from studying these models. These implications generally involve challenges and opportunities to put the Eucharist into practice in the way we live our lives. In essence, I am concerned here with what I have termed the *lex vivendi*—the way we live our lives in relation to the centerpiece of our liturgical prayer and life—the enactment of the Eucharist. Throughout I will draw on a number of Catholicism's "strong suits." But again, this is not meant to be denominationally narrow; rather, it is a way of offering to a wider public aspects of Catholic liturgy and life for reflection and appropriation.

## 1. Cosmic Mass

The term "Mass" is probably the most common term used for the liturgy of the Eucharist. For those of us old enough to remember, the word derives from the Latin dismissal *"Ite missa est,"* presently translated as "Go in the peace of Christ," "The Mass is ended, go in peace" or "Go in peace to love and serve the Lord." In essence, the most common term we use to describe the Eucharist is really a term that relates to our sharing in the sacred mystery and living it out in service and witness. The Eucharist is always about the dynamic of gathering and being sent forth.

The less familiar term in the title of the first model may well be the notion of *cosmic* in the sense that "cosmic" is meant to underscore our relationship to creation and the way the Eucharist affirms our place in the cosmic order of things. We are part of the world in which we live. In all liturgy, things from this good earth are used for the worship of the one true God. When it comes to the Eucharist specifically, the "cosmic" connection deals with our working with the things of this earth in order to have the materials we need for the Eucharist —bread and wine. Therefore this model reminds us also of human ingenuity, productivity, and human labor. Even before we partake in the eucharistic meal—eating and drinking the Lord's body and blood—by the very fact that we present bread and wine we are making theological statements, one of which is that the work needed to bake bread and produce wine are themselves paschal processes. Baking bread and producing wine require that things "die" in nature (at least figuratively) and "rise" to a new manner of existence. These are indeed paschal processes.

What better materials to use for the Eucharist than these goods from creation manufactured through human work to signify the "work of our redemption" accomplished in Christ's paschal mystery? The process of dying and rising continues on in the church through each of our daily lives. To face into the continual challenge of dealing with "the thousand deaths" we endure in life, we are sustained by the "living bread and saving cup" that is the Eucharist. But even before our gifts become spiritual food and drink, they are just that—food and drink produced in a paschal process of dying and rising.

When we "name" God in the prayers we use at the Eucharist, especially in the preface and the rest of the eucharistic prayer, we call upon the God of creation and redemption. For most of us, I think it is clear that we know what it means to call on a God who acts—to redeem us, to save us from our sins, and to heal us of our guilt. But how many of us take the aspect of the God of *creation* seriously? What we do in every act of liturgy is to draw on the things of this earth (light-darkness, water, oil, bread and wine, etc.) and we use them in liturgy for two reasons: for the worship of God and for our sanctification. In the doing of these things we use what we have and what we know—the goods of this earth—as fitting examples of what the God of creation and redemption gives us for nourishment, sustenance, and enjoyment.

When we look at the Eucharist as a "cosmic Mass," we are faced with several challenges in terms of how we appreciate and use God's creation. The fundamental challenge is that of taking the cosmos seriously. This means that we must see what has been given to us to enjoy and yet also preserve—God's good creation—as given to the whole human family, both here and now and for generations to come. Among other ways of understanding stewardship, one concerns the wise use of human resources and the equitable distribution of the world's resources—something that is simply not the case, at least universally, in our world today. How often are we reminded in contemporary church teachings and admonitions that in fact we have enough of the world's resources to feed the entire world population? The challenge is to move to a more equitable distribution of this world's resources. For us who readily find and consume the food we need to eat and have ready access to the Eucharist to dine on, this model challenges us to look at the Eucharist in terms of what needs to be shared, in particular clean water and sufficient food for all to eat.

It is well attested in the liturgical tradition of the Roman rite that the rite of the presentation of the gifts at Mass was a collection of gifts for the poor as well as a collection of the food to be consecrated and shared as the consecrated bread and wine of the eucharistic species.[3] In the revised liturgy of Holy Thursday, the admonition is given that after the prayer of the faithful gifts may be collected for the poor. This is an ancient practice that deserves attention both liturgically and theologically. In a real sense this collection of gifts is a key to unlocking the relationship of liturgy and real life. We who come to dine at the Lord's table are also to be continually challenged to go beyond our own needs to the needs of the wider church in terms of food distribution and caring for the poor. The liturgy of the Eucharist *presumes* this interrelationship. We domesticate and tame the liturgy when the presumption is overlooked and the challenge is blunted, or worse, ignored. Part of the church's *lex orandi* is the use of bread and wine—taken, blessed, broken, and shared. Part of the *lex orandi* of the Eucharist is the collection of gifts for the poor so that others might eat the food they need both for physical sustenance and for spiritual nourishment. This presumption continues through the present GIRM 2002 which states, "it is well also that money or other gifts for the poor or for the Church, brought by the faithful or collected in the church, should be received" (n. 73). The *lex vivendi* derived from these texts and practices implies the linking of presenting gifts at the altar table and offering our monetary and other gifts for those in need.

The goods of creation are for all God's creatures. We live out our participation in the Eucharist when part of that participation means making sure that any sense of personal entitlement is transcended in favor of doing what the Eucharist presumes—sharing food with others so that they might enjoy the benefits granted us in this world by the God of creation and redemption. It is precisely in the eucharistic

liturgy that any sense of entitlement is directly challenged and overturned. What we "have" is really only what we have received from
God. To offer it freely to others is part of what celebrating Eucharist
implies. The collection of gifts and care for the poor are essential
parts of what "making Eucharist" is all about. The bread and wine
from creation are indeed transformed into our spiritual food and
drink. But they are always that—food and drink—always God's gifts
to us to share with others, especially the poor, those deprived of an
equitable share in the gifts of God to all of us on this good earth.

Especially at a time of increased ecological awareness and concern for preserving the environment for generations yet to come, one
of the contributions which Catholicism can make is to remind us that
what we do at the Eucharist articulates relationships with others and
with the world in which we live. We can learn well from the Orthodox who have made environmental stewardship a key theme of their
social justice agenda.[4] To share in the liturgy implies caring for what
God has given to us as gifts. And it means making sure that we share
those goods with others and care for the world God has created. An
adage of some liberation theologians has been "You can't celebrate
the Eucharist with stolen bread." Another adage might well be "You
can't celebrate the Eucharist and rape the earth." The earth is the
Lord's and we are its stewards.

## 2. The Church's Eucharist

By now it should be clear that the relationship of Eucharist and church
is simply axiomatic; it is at the heart of what Eucharist means. All
liturgy is always a celebration done by, with, and for the church.
What "church" means is the local assembly for Mass, the whole diocese, and the universal church throughout the world. Every celebration of the Eucharist is about building up the body of Christ on earth,
the pilgrim church on earth, until it is called to the glory of the kingdom of heaven.

A number of advantages and (often unspoken) challenges derive
from this reality. The prime advantage is that we are not alone. In the
Judaeo-Christian tradition we go to God together. We are part of a
people called into God's very life and love who then are challenged to
live that life with one another. This is clear from the biblical para-

digms of the call of Abraham and Sarah, through all the vicissitudes of God's people in the first covenant. It is equally (if not more) true of Jesus' calling disciples and followers. In the act of liturgy we discover God where two or three are gathered in his name. The biblical paradigm is based on God's call and humans' response. The dynamic of liturgy is the same. We come together for Eucharist at God's gracious invitation to share in the enactment of his word and in the enactment of this eucharistic sacrifice commemorating Christ's paschal triumph. Our act of gathering is less self-initiated than God-initiated and sustained. All that we do, even in the act of assembling, is done in the name of the Lord and at the Lord's calling us together. As the third eucharistic prayer says, "Father, hear the prayers of the family you have gathered here before you..." It is always a consolation and comfort to know that the liturgy enacts our ongoing relationship with God, with other believers in our parish or diocese, and with the church throughout the world. The "general intercessions" and the intercessory parts of the eucharistic prayer reflect this kind of communal identity and these sets of relationships. One of the advantages of the regular celebration of the Eucharist is that it enacts such relationships. The Eucharist is a particular moment in the experience of the pilgrim church when we are consoled by the presence and prayer of other believers with us.

At the same time, one of the challenges of enacting the Eucharist is that it always involves gathering with others in the local assembly, and taking their needs and concerns seriously. Our prayer at Mass is always precisely that—*our prayer*—with and for others. Again, the general intercessions and the intercessory parts of the eucharistic prayer specify those for whom we pray in a special way at a particular Eucharist. Those prayers acknowledge that we come to the Eucharist with a wide-angle lens on the needs of the larger church and of the whole world. This directly challenges the narcissism of some of what passes for spirituality in America today. Any and every intercessory prayer at liturgy is always phrased in the plural. It is never a question of "just" our individual needs and desires. Our prayers are always other-directed. They are instances of what the Eucharist should always be about—communal self-transcendence.

For Americans, this can be a particularly acute challenge, given the fact that our forebears strove for a democracy that cherishes individual freedoms. The church itself in our day has prized the dignity of each and every human being. What the Eucharist enacts is a communal identity which is the foundation for any concern for the individual.

I am sometimes struck by what seems to have been an evolution of the magazines that fascinate our popular culture in America: the magazine of the seventies was *People*, the magazine of the eighties was *Us*, and the magazine of the nineties was *Self*. And there are times when I think we continue in these early years of the new millennium to remain in that latter category—the self.

However, there is also the phenomenon of the self-help group. People attend numerous meetings to share difficult experiences (e.g., addictions) and gain benefit from that communal experience. I wonder whether that might not be a tie-in for people to come to appreciate that the essentially communal dynamic of what happens at the Eucharist is an experience of both comfort and challenge. The comfort is that we experience our relatedness to God and to each other through the enactment of the Eucharist. And precisely because we are part of each other, the challenge is that there are consequences for the way we continue to support others in daily life. There is a solidarity that we experience in and through the Eucharist. But it is a solidarity that must go beyond receiving comfort for ourselves to a communal self-transcendence. By our very blessing of the bread and wine and sharing in it as our eucharistic communion, we are challenged to bear each other's burdens as members of the body of Christ on earth.

This is to say that if the liturgy is integral and integrating of the Christian life, one aspect of that integration must be the responsibility we assume for each other by the very fact that we celebrate the Eucharist. What we celebrate is the "source and summit" of the church's life. Part of the foundation on which that central event of the church is based is our service to each other outside the liturgy. When we pray at the liturgy, I would suggest that we always be aware of the names we use for God and the pronouns we use to refer to each other. The essential key here is relatedness to God and to others. We call upon God with a number of titles—Redeemer, Savior, Lord, God, Father, Son, Spirit, etc.—and we can do that because of our (communal) baptismal identity and communal life in the church. And it is always *we* who do that. We go to God together in prayer and service.

In a real sense, then, all liturgy is pastoral in that it is always about a wider circle than the self. One of the challenges of the liturgy is that it ought to reflect the sustaining of relationships between parish leaders (ordained and lay) and their ongoing pastoral care on behalf of the others with whom we celebrate the Mass. This is one of the ways in which the celebration of liturgy and the sacraments is integral to and integrating of our spiritual lives.

## 3. Effective Word of God

One of the most dramatic advances in the revision of all liturgies since Vatican II is that they all contain the proclamation of the scriptures.[5] The scriptures proclaimed at sacraments (especially at funerals and weddings) are almost always chosen by those particularly involved from a very full set of choices contained in the Lectionary for each liturgy. At other times, in particular for daily and Sunday Mass, they are taken from the assigned readings of the day. In both cases what we hear is somewhat determined. The liturgical and spiritual principle operative here is that we do not choose what we want to hear. We hear what the church's wisdom invites us to hear, to reflect upon, and to integrate into our lives and act on. One of the advantages of having a Lectionary system is that we are not left to our own devices in determining what to proclaim and hear. In following the Lectionary, we are invited to ponder what these scriptures mean on this given day, whether feast or "ordinary time," and what they say about our lives before God as lived with each other.

Obviously one of the practices that can enrich our spiritual lives is to prepare for the Eucharist by praying over the scripture readings, the responsorial psalm and the psalms for the entrance and communion. The more we know about them and the more familiar we are with them, the richer will be our experience of them when they are proclaimed at Mass. The challenge is to determine our openness to hearing what God says and allowing that to happen. The perennial challenge is the virtue of *obedience* to the word of God as it is proclaimed at Mass. In its classical meaning, "obedience" has to do with hearing God's word and putting it into practice. Once again we can look at this aspect of a eucharistic spirituality from the perspective of comfort and challenge.

Some scripture texts challenge us to go beyond where we might wish to go in terms of the way we look at life.

The heart of our faith and the mystery of faith as celebrated at Mass is a paradox—that from suffering and death comes rising and new life. How often are the scriptures filled with such paradoxes: faith the size of a mustard seed, the last shall be first and the first last, all the laborers in the vineyard receive the same wage no matter how many hours they work, no more "eye for an eye and a tooth for a tooth," welcoming back the prodigal son, etc. These gospels overturn our expectations and challenge us to see and live from their paradoxical perspectives, which, in essence, summarize the gospel message. We are both consoled and challenged by these paradoxes. When we find ourselves among the lost, it is a real comfort to hear the parable of the shepherd leaving the ninety-nine and seeking the lost sheep. And when we judge that we do not deserve God's mercy, it is a comfort to hear the passage about all the laborers in the vineyard receiving the same wage. What "frames the debate" here is not our notions of justice but the lived reality and experience of God's justice.

At the same time, however, these same passages offer us the challenge to treat others the way God treats people. We are not to judge solely on the basis of American distributive justice. We are to evaluate life from the perspective of the gospel and what it says about the mighty, the strong, the weak, and the chosen. There is no clearer summary of so much of the gospel than the Canticle of Mary: God raises up the lowly, sends away the rich, and fills the hungry with good things. Biblical "literacy" really means a commitment to the scriptures as set before us to proclaim them at Mass. The phenomenon of biblical proclamation at liturgy is that what we hear in the proclamation *happens* when we hear it. The phrase from the transfiguration—"This is my beloved Son, listen to him"—is the real challenge. The real comfort is in knowing that what we hear at Mass will be "fulfilled in [our] hearing" (Luke 4:21).

What makes the proclamation of the scriptures such a supreme value at Mass is that when they are proclaimed and we truly hear and listen to them, then what we have heard becomes enacted by the very act of proclamation. At the end of each reading, the reader or deacon/priest ends by saying "The word of the Lord" or "The gospel of the Lord." And we respond with "Thanks be to God." What we are responding to is the act of proclamation and what that act means in terms of God's doing something among us that is unique and proper to the act of Eucharist. Our assent, our response, is not to a text; it is to an effective proclamation in which what is proclaimed shapes us and guides us as God's pilgrim church. Our response is a particular ratification of what we have heard and an expression of our willingness to let God's word become the measure of the way we evaluate and live our lives.

Our response with the phrase "Thanks be to God" really parallels our response of "Amen" at the end of the eucharistic prayer. In both instances we assent to what God is doing among us. We are committing ourselves to what God both says and does in word and sacrament. The challenge, of course, is whether, or to what extent, we are actually committing ourselves to what we have heard. Are we really committed to the last coming first, to all receiving the same wages despite the number of hours worked, to realizing that the lowly in the world's eyes are really the exalted in God's eyes? The proclamation of the word of God and our response are less about information and ideas than about our committing ourselves to the paradoxes of our faith.

When they are proclaimed at Mass, the scriptures are not only occurrences and events of salvation experienced here and now, they also lead us to their complement at the altar table. We may well be challenged by what we hear in the Liturgy of the Word. But we are not left only to our own devices to appropriate and live that word. We move from ambo to altar table, from enactment through the word to enactment through blessing and receiving the eucharistic gifts of bread and wine. We move from the enactment of the good news as an act of salvation at Mass to the enactment of God's salvation through the good gifts of bread and wine taken, blessed, broken, and shared— all at God's gracious invitation. The act of recommitting ourselves to the effective word of God occurs both in our appropriation of what we hear at Mass and in our appropriation of what we celebrate and receive at the altar in daily life. The liturgical proclamation of the word is a continual reminder that we are not alone in appropriating the word that we hear, that the Lord himself strengthens our feeble and fallible commitments through our sharing in the sacred mysteries of the Eucharist.

## 4. Memorial of the Paschal Mystery

All liturgical celebrations in the Judaeo-Christian tradition are commemorations of what God did in history, what God does in our histories here and now, and what God will accomplish at the end of time in
bringing time to an end. All liturgy is done in time and is about
time—past, present, and yet to come.

All liturgy is communal in the sense that it is always about what
God's people are and do. This means that every act of Eucharist is a
supreme example and instance of the church making memory together
in the enactment of the Eucharist. Christian liturgy is inherently
paschal, because the heart of the Christian tradition as enacted and
expressed at Mass is a memorial of Christ's dying and rising and our
dying and rising, through, with, and in him. What makes the eucharistic action particular and unique is that it is a dynamic, involving event
whereby the bonds of time and place are broken and we here and now
share in and take part in the very dying and rising of Christ. In a very
real sense, we do not "look back" in the act of liturgy to what God did
in and through Christ once in history. Rather, what God accomplished
in and through Christ happens here and now through God's gracious
action and because of a unique way of looking at time.

What God does in and through us at the Eucharist is enable us to
make memory together of (literally "commemorate") Christ's paschal
victory. It is important to notice that when the church describes what
it is doing in the act of liturgy, rather than describe what Jesus said
and did in human history, it enacts the fullness of the mystery of
Christ past, present, and future. Every Eucharist is a memorial, an
event, an action, an occurrence. It is not a mental recollection or
"looking back." Neither is it an act of imagining what the future will
be like in heaven. Liturgical memorial is a communal action which is
structured so that when we engage in it God works to draw us into
Christ's paschal victory once again here and now. It is precisely
through the enactment of the word and the enactment of the paschal
supper that we are remade in God's image and likeness and we are
restored to new life in and through him.

There is a world of difference between our individual thinking
about Christ's death and resurrection and our privileged experience of

it in the eucharistic liturgy. When we ponder it in meditation and other prayer we can savor its depth and breadth and its impact on our lives. But when we celebrate the Eucharist what occurs is that *God acts* among us through this act of memory to shape us and mold us in the image and likeness of his Son. Clearly, when we "make memory" at Mass, we give ourselves over to a structured prayer which God uses for our sanctification here and now based on what that same God accomplished through his Son's triumphant death and resurrection.

It seems so obvious, but the pause for silence between the priest's saying "Let us pray" before the opening prayer and the singing (saying) of that prayer is the moment during the liturgy for calling to mind and heart what it is precisely that we want to "bring" to this Eucharist. In terms of this model, that moment of silence is the time when we should ponder those things in our lives that need paschal clarity and paschal healing. By this I mean those areas in life that need to be set right and in proper order—such as self-deception, delusion, and self-concern—through Christ's paschal mystery. I also mean those things from which only the Lord can truly change and free us, such as our compulsions, our addictions, our deepest held hurts, and our sins. When these are brought to mind and heart at the beginning of the liturgy, then we have at least set the stage for our particular lives with all their disorder and frailty to be drawn into the prayer and worship of the whole body as the church is reborn and made new through the paschal mystery of Christ.

What God does at Mass is invite us into this marvelous mystery of faith yet one more time, so that the paradoxes of the gospel and of Christ's paschal victory might be realized for and among us in the present circumstances of our lives. This notion of "remembering God" is really about our opening ourselves to Christ's triumphant victory. The way we do it is derived from Jewish liturgical traditions—specifically word and table.

If in fact "we remember" the paschal mystery and are drawn into it at Mass, there is a way in which what God does at Mass is *remember us* through his Son's dying and rising. This is to say that God enacts the paschal mystery of his Son and our incorporation into Christ occurs because of that enactment. When we celebrate the Eucharist, we do so in accord with Christ's invitation to "do this in memory of me." But in doing so we can also say that God "remembers" us by inviting us to experience and to live the paschal paradox and paradigm of his Son's cross and resurrection.

Our appropriation of Christ's paschal triumph varies throughout our lives, and in a very real sense it depends on our willingness to lay before God our strengths and weaknesses, our good deeds and our failures, so that the paschal triumph can indeed be reproduced in us. Thus, when we come to the Eucharist we should be very conscious of the defeats, the setbacks, the sufferings, and the illnesses which we and our fellow believers are enduring. It is only from the perspective of the paschal mystery of Christ that we will be able to see beyond these limitations *in hope* to their being overcome through Christ's paschal victory. At the same time, when we come to the Eucharist we should be very aware of our successes, our triumphs, our virtues, and our accomplishments, especially our growth in the spiritual life. Again, what the paschal mystery does is remind us that any real success and accomplishment in life comes through God in Christ. And what the Eucharist as the memorial of the paschal mystery does is draw us into an experience of real triumph and victory—the paschal victory of Christ and our victories through this same paschal mystery.

We call it the "paschal mystery" for a number of reasons. One of them is because what Christ accomplished continues to be accomplished in us, in our very human lives, with all our successes as well as our shortcomings, our triumphs as well as our defeats. All of our life should be looked at from the perspective of Christ's dying and rising. And when we do that, we are both challenged and encouraged. We are challenged to see human success for what it is—always temporary and passing, at least in terms of what really matters. And we are encouraged to see human failure for what it is—an opportunity to turn again and again to God in hope because of Christ's invitation to new life through him. The enactment of the paschal mystery in the Eucharist presumes that we not only "remember" what Christ did but we identify with it.

This means that we need to shed illusions, that we need to come to the Eucharist as we truly are and as God sees us. Then, through the Eucharist, we can be transformed and bear his image and likeness more fully and richly. Just as bread and wine are transformed at Mass into Christ's body and blood, so too are we to be transformed into the more committed and the more richly graced people of God. This happens at the Eucharist through Christ's dying and rising and through our making memory of that mystery. The way it happens in the rest of our spiritual lives depends on the way we allow the paschal mystery to be the measure of our lives.

## 5. Covenant Renewal

One aspect of the liturgical revisions that resulted from the Second Vatican Council has been the emphasis now placed on the "sacraments of initiation." Formerly, baptism and confirmation were understood to be separate. And their relationship to the Eucharist was somewhat theoretical, simply because they were celebrated separately from the Mass itself. In the revised rites for these sacraments they are now understood by the general phrase "sacraments of initiation" (both for adults and for children). Sacramental initiation of adults occurs at the Eucharist, and more often than not at the Easter Vigil. Similarly, the rite for infant baptism allows for the communal celebration of baptism at Mass; in some parishes this is normative. And, unlike the prescriptions for the rite of confirmation prior to Vatican II, the revised Rite of Confirmation directs that it be celebrated at Mass, preceded by a renewal of baptismal promises. The theology behind the terminology of "initiation" and the liturgy encompassing baptism, confirmation, and Eucharist has to do with seeing these sacraments as moments of participation in God's covenant life and love.

In other words, baptism and confirmation are to be understood as sacraments that initiate us into a deep and abiding relationship with God. When seen from this perspective, the celebration of the Eucharist can be understood as the "goal" of sacramental initiation, as the sacrament that deepens and renews the relationship with God forged at the font of baptism and sealed by the anointing with chrism at confirmation. Baptism and confirmation are sacraments celebrated once and for all in a person's life. They lead to the Eucharist, the "daily bread" that renews and deepens the bond with God and each other first experienced at baptism and sealed at confirmation. This theological fact is supported by two aspects of the *lex orandi* in the liturgy of the Eucharist—the rite of blessing and sprinkling with water and the words over the cup in the eucharistic prayer.

Since Sunday is *the* day of the Lord and the day on which baptisms occur, it makes logical sense to offer an introductory rite on Sundays that links the rite of water baptism with the liturgy of the Eucharist now seen as the renewal of the baptismal covenant. Theologically we can say that baptism and confirmation lead us to the Eucharist as the ongoing sacrament of the new covenant in Christ. And the Eucharist should be appreciated as the means whereby what was once forged at baptism is deepened and renewed. The very introduction to the rite of water blessing states: "This water will be used to remind us of our baptism." And in the first blessing prayer we hear: "Give us your protection on this day which you have made your own." This first day of the week is the privileged day of the Lord on which we experience anew the re-creating and life-sustaining grace that comes from the God of the covenant. We rely on this God of relationship—on our relatedness to him and through him with each other—to renew and strengthen us as we seek to respond to his initiating and sustaining love. But the real point at issue here is not only the blessing of the water, it is our deepened renewal. Again, in the introduction to this prayer we hear the words: "Let us ask God to bless [the water] and to keep us faithful to the Spirit he has given us." And in the first blessing prayer we pray:

Renew the living spring of your life within us
and protect us in spirit and body,
that we may be free from sin
and come into your presence
to receive your gift of salvation.

Water—blessed and sprinkled—becomes the means at Sunday Mass whereby we begin to deepen our covenant relationship with God. What happens in the rest of the Eucharist is the celebration of the sacrament that accomplishes this covenant renewal. This part of the prayer also indicates that what is renewed and deepened at the Eucharist will be fulfilled only when we are called from this life to eternal life in God—when "we come into your presence" forever.

Much of this same theology is presented even more forcefully in the prayer to bless water on the Sundays of the Easter season. It begins by noting the life-giving properties of water: "fruitfulness to the fields," "refreshment," and "cleansing." These natural properties are not to be ignored. In fact, the very use of water is a theological statement about life. Water is the only element without which we cannot live. Hydration is necessary for life. Hence, to use water at baptism and its renewal at Mass is to use the very element that symbolizes what baptism is about—giving us new life in Christ. Then the prayer goes on to recount moments in salvation history when water was used as a sign of God's constant fidelity and redeeming love: the water at the Red Sea, water from the rock to slake the people's thirst, and Christ's baptism in the waters of the Jordan. The juxtaposition of water and covenant redemption is clear in salvation history.

The point here is that we not only bless water, we invoke God's power to be with us and to sustain us in our lived response to the covenant he has invited us into. This theological theme is effected in the very celebration of the Eucharist. It is reflected in the words we hear spoken over the cup in the eucharistic prayer.

> This is the cup of my blood,
> the blood of the new and everlasting covenant
> It will be shed for you and for all
> so that sins may be forgiven.

These words are finely tuned and contain a wealth of theological insight. The juxtaposition of *blood* with *covenant* immediately offers a context in which to interpret "blood." Given our Judaeo-Christian scriptural tradition, this juxtaposition means that we should look at Christ's blood in the Eucharist from the perspective of the ways in which covenants were forged in the Old Testament—by the shedding of the blood of the Passover lambs. The shedding of blood and the sprinkling of blood on doorposts at the exodus were annual rituals to renew the unbreakable bond and relationship that the chosen people had with God. What seemed to be the inducement of death—shedding the blood of the lambs—should really be looked at from the perspective that blood signified not death but *life*. The very expression "life blood" is one way of capturing this insight in common speech. We give blood so that in emergencies others may have the blood they need to live. In most biblical contexts, the shedding of blood was not for the victims' destruction; rather it was so that people might realize and ritualize their new identity as sharing in the relationship offered them by God. And this relationship in the text of the eucharistic prayers is called the covenant.

Whatever may be said about defining or describing the term "covenant," it is clear that the bondedness which this term signifies is due to God's taking the initiative to call us into a relationship that makes us

a chosen race, a royal priesthood
a holy nation, a people set apart.
(Sunday Preface I)

These terms from 1 Peter harken back to commonly used terms in the Old Testament and articulate how our very identity has come about because the God of the covenants has always taken and still takes the initiative in calling us into a people who share the very life of God.

Thus, a central way of appreciating the Eucharist is to see it as part of a life continuum and a sacramental continuum. We respond to God's invitation to a deep and abiding relationship that was offered to our first parents, to Noah and his wife and his family, to Abraham and Sarah and their family, and now to us through Christ. What we do in the eucharistic liturgy is renew and deepen the covenant God has forged with us in sacramental initiation, specifically in the sacraments of baptism and confirmation as well as in the Eucharist. The first two of these sacraments occur in our lives once and for all. But since we are weak and know our fragility, we celebrate the Eucharist as the sacrament that renews and deepens that covenant, especially because of our infidelity and lack of living up to it. The Eucharist then becomes a sacrament of ongoing and sustained initiation until we are called into God's presence for eternity. In the meantime, the sprinkling of water and our sharing in the eucharistic body and blood of Christ are the means we need to have our covenant relationship with God deepened and renewed.

With regard to what God does for us, a phrase in the fourth eucharistic prayer gives us a key: "Again and again you offered a covenant..." God never forsook the people he had invited and chosen as the elect, despite the fact that he had more than enough reason to do so. Ever since Adam and Eve's banishment from the garden, the chosen of God have lived "east of Eden" awaiting the restoration of their lost innocence. Again and again God forged new covenants, each time assuring those invited that his overarching and overwhelming covenant love would always be there for them. And the challenge of such divine initiative in covenant-making and covenant-sustaining was that the people would turn with all their minds, hearts, and wills to God. To share in God's covenant could never be understood as a partnership between equals. To share in God's covenant had to mean that the chosen would respond and strive to live up to the demands that the covenant put on them. There was no allowance for presuming God's love, nor was there any possibility that the chosen could earn God's love. It would always be a question of relying on God to initiate and to sustain the covenant relationship. On the people's part, it was always a matter of growing in a more complete and faith-filled response.

To be the elect of God carries with it a challenge. The challenge is to live according to what we have committed ourselves to in baptism, confirmation, and the Eucharist. Each in its own way can be understood as a sacrament of initiation. But each in its own way can best be appreciated as God's invitation to live the values of his kingdom in this passing world until we are called to live with him forever in glory. The ultimate covenant renewal will occur when sacraments cease and we have met the Lord in the kingdom. Until that day, our celebration of the sacraments of initiation will be seen to be just that—the means God uses to initiate us into his very life here on earth.

## 6. The Lord's Supper

Human beings need food and drink to survive. "Food groups" and "food pyramids" tell us how much of what to eat and what to avoid. Recent research indicates the value of drinking several glasses of water each day. Issues of hydration and feeding the sick are matters of concern for us as we seek to do what is right for the terminally ill.

Each time we celebrate the Eucharist we hear the words "Take this, all of you, and eat it...take this, all of you, and drink from it..." And at communion we receive the eucharistic bread and cup.

We do what we do at the Lord's command—we eat and drink in the context of a meal. Through this sacred meal we join in an ever deeper communion with God in Christ. The theological point here is that we best appreciate the eucharistic species first and foremost as food for our spiritual lives—"holy gifts" for God's "holy people," taken in common in the ritual action of a sacred meal. Hence we refer to it as *communion*—the Eucharist taken in union with each other.

The act of communion is about being fed and nurtured by the very act of assembling with others in the faith. It is about being fed on "every word that comes from the mouth of God." And it is about dining on eucharistic bread and drinking from the eucharistic cup. Fundamentally, it is about dining at the Lord's invitation and command.

But there is another, deeper, more spiritual level that the images of "dining" and "hunger and thirst" tap into. Two examples from the scriptures can help us here. One is a psalm often prayed at morning prayer, Psalm 63:1—"O God, you are my God whom I seek; / for you my flesh pines and my soul thirsts / like the earth, parched, lifeless and without water." Human thirst is something with which we can all identify. The psalmist capitalizes on this common human experience and applies it to our soul's journey to God. It is akin to St. Augustine's famous "Our hearts are restless until they rest in you." What the food and drink of the Eucharist do is offer us a remedy for our spiritual thirsting for God and the ways of God. The second text is from the Beatitudes—"Blessed are they who hunger and thirst for righteousness, / for they will be satisfied" (Matt 5:6). This reminds us that the food of the Eucharist is never for ourselves alone. It is always about our recommitting ourselves to seeing things God's way and to committing ourselves to God's will. Among other things, "righteousness," means God's plan of salvation for us all. Our partaking in the Eucharist is meant to be a re-commitment so that we can work toward that saving work for all people.

The Eucharist is always about food—food taken together. One of the challenges of our contemporary fast-paced American society is the phenomenon of fast food. Statistics show that many Americans live such busy and productive lives that we have little time for cooking or baking. Hence we consume fast food and often do it quickly in order to get to the next thing we have to do. Given that phenomenon, the

Eucharist is more like Thanksgiving Day than it is like an ordinary (fast food) meal during the week. It presumes coming together, sharing in the proclaimed word, and sharing in the eucharistic action, part of which is receiving communion. This is the privilege of the initiated who deepen their initiation through partaking in the eucharistic meal.

In the Jewish tradition (which provides a rich background for appreciating the Christian Eucharist), to share a meal with others was to share an intimate bond, like that of family. To be invited to dinner was to be privileged, honored, and served. Hence the poignancy at the Last Supper when Judas, who had been at table with Jesus and the other disciples, was the one who would betray Jesus with a kiss. These common examples of relationship and hospitality—table sharing and a kiss of recognition and affection—are completely turned around in Judas's case and are made to represent the exact opposite—denial and betrayal.

In some Eastern eucharistic liturgies to this day, the sign of peace is exchanged at the time of the presentation of gifts, in direct response to the command in Matthew 5:23–24: "If you bring your gift to the altar, and there recall that your brother has anything against you, leave your gift there at the altar, go first and be reconciled with your brother, and then come and offer your gift." That the Lord's Supper and reconciliation are to be intrinsically connected in our minds and lived out in our lives is presumed in such a ritual gesture.

In our present Missal there are numerous references in the prayers over the gifts for "unity" and for "peace" and that we might "live more fully the love we profess." Such prayers look forward to what the whole Eucharist is meant to accomplish—more unity and peace for those who participate, for the whole church, and for the world itself. Praying such texts can be regarded as the Western church's way of praying for what the Eastern gesture of peace at ths point of the liturgy ritualizes.

In addition, our Western practice of exchanging the sign of peace after the Lord's Prayer and before the Lamb of God carries a similar connotation—ever deepening unity with and in the body of Christ as we share in the eucharistic body of Christ. There is an inherent logic at work in the structure of this part of the Mass. We pray the Lord's Prayer together, we are reminded that "peace" is Christ's farewell gift, we exchange the sign of peace, we acclaim the Lamb of God who takes away the sins of the world, we break the eucharistic bread and we partake in the eucharistic communion of the body and blood of the Lord. Here we see how the Eucharist is traditionally understood to be the bond of charity that unites the church as the body of Christ on earth.

This model that has to do with food taken and shared presents us with a number of challenges regarding those who literally hunger and thirst and have no food or potable water. One of those challenges is that we who have the advantage of being able to eat sufficient food daily and the eucharistic food when we choose need to also have as part of our commitment to the Eucharist a real commitment to the poor. In the words of St. John Chrysostom, who challenges us to recognize Christ in the poor, "You have tasted the blood of the Lord, yet you do not recognize your brother... You dishonor this table when you do not judge worthy of sharing your food someone judged worthy to take part in this meal... God freed you from all your sins and invited you here, but you have not become more merciful."[6]

The taking of the eucharistic food and drink in the Christian tradition has often been termed just that, "taking communion." This signals that the Eucharist is more than the food itself: it is those with whom we dine, it is what we commit ourselves to, and it is the ramifications of that commitment for food distribution throughout the world. There are enormous implications for what sharing in the "Lord's Supper" is all about.

## 7. Food for the Journey

One of the more consoling practices of the church is that of taking communion to the sick. We have evidence that dates back as far as the time of St. Justin in the second century that deacons were sent forth after Mass to bring the eucharistic species to those who were unable to be present. This practice continues in our day and has expanded thanks to the proliferation of special ministers of the Eucharist. Some parishes send them forth at the end of Sunday Mass with a special blessing and the assurance of the prayers of those assembled for Mass. One of the pastoral advantages of the revised rite for the Pastoral Care of the Sick is the number of prayers it offers for visits with communion to the sick.

One of these prayers is the rite of viaticum. Again, this is a traditional Catholic practice. It shows the church's concern for the sick and, in this particular instance, for those near death. The term "viaticum" is taken from the Latin and means "food for the journey." The Instruction that accompanies this rite states that "the sacrament should be described as the sacred food which strengthens the Christian for the passage through death to life in [the] sure hope of the resurrection" (n. 188). When one draws near to death, this rite can provide immeasurable hope and consolation.

Yet there is a sense in which every act of celebrating the Eucharist is an act of the church partaking in viaticum. The Eucharist is always our spiritual food which strengthens us for the journey through this life to the kingdom of heaven. Every time we celebrate the Eucharist and receive the Eucharist we are professing faith in Christ present as well as in the risen Lord whom we hope to meet face-to-face in the kingdom of heaven. Viaticum is the spiritual food and drink we need here and now until we will have met the risen Lord to be with him in the kingdom forever. In the meantime, in the in-between time, we need this food as hope for the journey through life and as an expression of our hope of heaven. Indeed, we live on the daily bread of the Eucharist until one day we receive it for the last time. "Officially" the last time we share in the Eucharist it is called "viaticum." In the meantime it is, in the words of the Lord's Prayer, "our daily bread."

Especially given the theological advances at and since Vatican II concerning the church, we realize that we are always the pilgrim church on earth, that body of believers who make up the church, yet whose vocation is to share in a vocation that leads us beyond ourselves to eternity. The now deceased Cardinal Basil Hume (of London, England) entitled one of his books of pastoral reflections on the Christian life *To Be a Pilgrim*. In fact that is always who we are. We have guideposts along the way—and the primary guidepost is the Eucharist. There is great consolation in knowing that God feeds and nourishes us as we pass through the vicissitudes and difficulties of this mortal life.

At the present time the pilgrim church has experienced severe challenges to its moral authority and to its very credibility. Abuse involving inappropriate behavior of clerics—whether sexual or in their handling of immoral conduct—has left many with a sense of suspicion, if not outright cynicism, toward the church's ministers. Part of the challenge of being members of the pilgrim church, however, is to realize that we are indeed—all of us—pilgrims. We are "not there yet."

Our personal and communal sanctification has not yet been finally or fully accomplished. Our personal and communal conversion has not yet been finally or fully accomplished. Our personal and communal transformation has not yet been finally or fully accomplished. Our personal and communal purification has not yet been finally or fully accomplished. But precisely because we are pilgrims on this journey to the kingdom, we need to acknowledge that we are the imperfect church on earth. We are the church that always stands in need of reformation. We will never be the perfect church on earth.

The consoling parable from Matthew 13:24–30 comes to mind. The growing of the weeds and the wheat together in the field until harvest images the fact that the church will always have its share of sin as well as sanctity, its share of scandal as well as examples of true holiness, its share of corruption even as it dines on the bread of incorruptibility and truth.

Because we are pilgrims, we know that all will not be perfected until the Lord's second coming. But at the same time, precisely because we are the church on this earth that is fed on the Eucharist, we have the ability and the strength to face the perennial challenge of living less imperfect lives. We are the pilgrim church that needs deeper sanctification, conversion, transformation—especially through deepening purification. One of the means the Lord gives us to accept those challenges is the Eucharist. The "daily bread" of the Eucharist is the daily assurance of God's concern to have us be changed more and more fully into his divine image and likeness. To be pilgrims means that we are to surrender to God and that it is that divine plan for us that really matters. To be pilgrims means that we know our need for a leader, a guide—the Lord himself. It also means that in the Eucharist we discover him as host at this table fellowship until we are called beyond it to the eternal banquet in God's kingdom forever.

Another challenge is to acknowledge that we believe in and experience the real presence of Christ in the Eucharist and yet that we also yearn for a final and full revelation of Christ in the eternal banquet in heaven.

## 8. Sacramental Sacrifice

The privilege of participating in the Eucharist is that we literally *take part in* what we enact—the very dying and rising of Christ. The previous model—on "Food for the Journey"—reminds us of the eschatological nature of the Eucharist as we yearn in hope: "Lord Jesus, come in glory." This model helps us realize that for any of that to be accomplished we need to imitate Jesus' willingness to be sacrificed for our salvation.

What is clearly stated in the second eucharistic prayer is a crucially important spiritual insight, that Jesus went to "a death he freely accepted..." As noted earlier, there is a difference between the emphasis in the Synoptics and the gospel of John with regard to what occurred to Jesus prior to his death. The Synoptics describe Jesus' anguish, noting that at least at first he hesitated to give over his life to God his Father completely and fully. The anguish is capsulized in the cry "Let this chalice pass from me..." However, in John's gospel what is described is almost the exact opposite: Jesus willingly goes to his death so that we might experience eternal life.

One of the challenges of the Christian life is to live according to the gospel of John and surrender freely and fully to the will of God, especially when what we feel is more like what the Synoptics describe —let this cup pass. At a deeper level, however, is not the conflict that Jesus felt and his final surrender to the Father's will in the Synoptics an even more poignant and helpful example of what is operative in the Christian life? The knowledge that Jesus himself had to struggle with this choice may in fact be a great contribution the Synoptic authors have given to us. Jesus' ready acceptance of "a death he freely accepted" is a high and lofty goal. In fact, are we not more usually like the Jesus in the Synoptics, struggling to submit ourselves to God's will? The key for us here is not how Jesus died for our salvation. It is the manner in which he approached his death. An important phrase here is from the letter to the Philippians, "He humbled himself, becoming obedient to death, even death on a cross" (2:8). The challenge for us is to imitate Jesus' obedience and to obey God's will in living lives of service for others.

The kind of behavior that the Eucharist presumes is deeds of self-sacrifice reflecting obedience to the Father's will. There is a certain

logic to the rites for communion and what they offer for our reflection. The Lord's Prayer contains the words "thy will be done..."
This is followed closely by acclaiming the "Lamb of God... [who
takes] away the sin of the world..." The image of the lamb is an
image of one who is sacrificed for us. The challenge for us who
receive eucharistic communion is to see in these blessed and shared
gifts the food we need to live as obedient servants of the Father.

One of the consoling aspects of the structure of the Eucharist is
the way it places these things in order so that we can be helped to live
what we have celebrated. The taking of the eucharistic bread and cup
gives us the presence of Christ within us to do the Father's will. We
are not left on our own as we struggle with obedience. We are graced
with the Eucharist so that we can accept and live that will. And part of
receiving communion is the realization that this is what we do—share
in common union with each other—as we struggle to live the Christian gospel. This sense of community and communal sharing is always
presumed in what the Eucharist enacts and does among us. It is
therefore a supreme source of comfort to know that others are struggling to do the right thing(s) and that the Eucharist is food that nourishes us and helps us to accomplish this.

Some years ago the Jesuit theologian John Courtney Murray gave
a talk to the Jesuit community at Georgetown in Washington, DC.
His presentation was about the traditional three vows of religious:
poverty, chastity, and obedience. Succinctly put, he argued that
poverty was easy enough. Jesuits have their material needs taken care
of and they know that they should not deprive themselves for what is
needed for their apostolate and personal lives. As for chastity, he
argued that life in community is a privilege and that those living in
community have a responsibility to support each other in living a
chaste life. He reminded them that chastity is not simply a negative
deprivation from sexual union; rather, it is meant to be life-giving in
that not having a single partner should enable them to share their lives
with others in community. But when he came to obedience, he said
that this was really the chief challenge always and everywhere, for to
live obediently means to imitate Christ's knowing and accepting his
Father's will and doing it. It requires imitating all the characteristics
listed in Philippians 2, especially emptying oneself and allowing the

word and will of another to be the measure of success and fulfillment in life. Obedience is clearly not meant to be the imposition of unreasonable burdens by authority figures for the sake of efficiency or expediency. Rather, it is the virtue that captures hearing and doing the will of God as revealed in the scriptures and as discerned in light of the community's needs and an individual's talents.

In terms of sacrifice, it is clear that one of the central tenets of a Catholic doctrine of the Eucharist is that the Mass is the unbloody sacrifice of Christ. It is the perpetuation of this sacrifice that strengthens us to live the unbloody sacrifices which the Christian life often requires of us. The key to appreciating and living this aspect of the Eucharist is found in fostering the proper attitude we should bring to its celebration—an attitude of being willing to live lives of self-sacrifice in imitation of the self-offering of Christ on the cross of Calvary.

But lest self-sacrifice seem to refer only to one's personal relationship with God, we need only recall the words of the Cistercian monk who wrote about the challenge of community living. He asked the rhetorical and perennially challenging question: If we in community can act as though we live in isolation, then...

Whose feet will we wash?
Whose burdens will we help carry?
Whose hunger will we feed?
Whose thirst will we slake?
Whose wounds will we bind up?

In fact, the self-sacrifice of Jesus enacted at the Eucharist is about his following the Father's will for him and his offering his life for the salvation of all believers through the ages. Our participation in the Eucharist once again is about "both...and" in that it is both the doing of God's will for us and the living of that will of God in the community of a servant church. We come to the Eucharist with others. We are to live the sacrifice we commemorate with and among others. To "do this in memory of me" is to enact a ritual and to commit ourselves to living life in imitation of Christ, the servant of the Father's will and the savior of the world.

### 9. Active Presence

How often do we long to hear the phrase "I will be there for you?" We long to hear it when we are (sometimes painfully) aware of our weakness, of whatever kind. At moments of transition in life we long for the presence of others to be with us to support us, to help see us through a crisis, like facing a terminal illness or dealing with death. Sometimes we yearn for the presence of others in the longer term to help us deal with deep-rooted problems in life, like addiction to alcohol, food or drugs, gambling, work, or the Internet. Twelve-step programs can be extremely helpful in providing support and challenge from individuals who know similar kinds of human weakness. In all kinds of circumstances, we need to know that there are people who are "there" for us.

In terms of eucharistic presence, it is clear that church teaching would have us affirm as explicitly and clearly as we can the many ways in which Christ is present to us in and through the celebration of the Eucharist. Today we have the advantage of appreciating the presence of Christ in the church gathered for worship, in the proclamation of the word, in the person of the minister acting in the person of Christ, and in a unique, enduring way in the eucharistic species. To know that Christ is "there for us" as the pilgrim church yearning for the kingdom of God and the fulfillment of this life is an enormous consolation and privilege.

This emphasis on presence is, among other things, a clear and continual reminder that the Eucharist is not of our own making. One advantage of the present post–Vatican II reform of the liturgy is that it places due emphasis on active participation in the enactment of the Eucharist. But our theology of eucharistic presence reminds us that what we do in liturgy is always a response to God's initiating and sustaining power. We legitimately emphasize active participation only when and if we also emphasize how what God does for us is the source of anything we can claim to be and do. The classic prayer of the Roman liturgy now used on the Thursday after Ash Wednesday is clear:

> Direct, O Lord, all our actions
> and carry them on with your gracious assistance

so that our every prayer and work may begin in you
and through you be brought to a blessed conclusion.[7]

There is no room for any sort of Pelagianism here. We "earn" nothing in liturgy or in the Christian life. What we do and have is the result of God's initiating and sustaining presence.

However, in keeping with the purpose of this chapter, we also need to look at the way Christ's presence in the Eucharist challenges us to be "present" to the Eucharist and to the needs of others. Throughout this book we have emphasized the dynamism of the eucharistic action. One of the important nuances of that dynamism is the realization that Christ is present *and active* among us through the Eucharist. It is this emphasis on dynamism and action that invites us to respond actively and fully to the enactment of the liturgy and thereby realize the dynamic way in which Christ is present in the Eucharist. What a liturgical theology of the Eucharist does is underscore that celebration of the Mass and any act of eucharistic adoration outside of Mass is never to be regarded as something that is passive or that does not require a response from us. If in fact Christ is active among us through the Eucharist, then one of the required responses is that we be engaged in acting on this gift by the way we are present to others in the community with which we celebrate the Eucharist.

In addition to avoiding any sort of Pelagianism regarding the Eucharist (or in fact the whole spiritual life in general), we also need to avoid any kind of undue self-concern. This is to say that we cannot ever regard the presence of Christ in the Eucharist to be only for me and my sake. It is there and active for *us* and for *our* sakes. And it is there so that we can be challenged by it to be "there" for others the way Christ is truly "there" for us in the Eucharist.

The question we always need to ask ourselves is: How do we relate our eucharistic belief and practice with the living of the Christian gospel in our lives? Regarding "presence" language, one of the issues concerns our being present to others, especially at times of tragedy or sorrow. Is it not the case that it is in those moments that we are most aware that we cannot take away the pain, or remove the illness, or restore the life of the deceased? At such life-changing moments we realize that perhaps the most important thing we can offer to others is simply to be there for them. Being present should mean being supportive in the sense of personal presence and liturgical prayer with others. Being present should also mean that, when necessary, we challenge others on conduct and behavior that is destructive—for themselves or for others. This is an aspect of active presence to and with the other that requires wisdom and a true loving heart.

When the Eucharist is seen to be the center of the Christian life, then it can be seen as the supreme act of the Christian in terms of experiencing the dying and rising of Christ. It should be a continual reminder of the perennial challenge to be "present" to each other. The real presence of Christ in the Eucharist consoles us. The real presence of Christ should also be a challenge, reminding us to be present to others as fellow pilgrims on the journey of life to complete union with God forever.

## 10. Work of the Spirit

There is more than a "word match" when it comes to this aspect of a eucharisitic spirituality as the "work of the Spirit" and that very reality —*spirit*uality. Obviously, "spirituality" concerns living the converted Christian life. What should be equally obvious is that we can do this only by the power and presence of the Holy Spirit among us. If in fact the Eucharist is regarded as the "work of the Holy Spirit," it is so largely because all of the Christian life is lived under the guidance and through the inspiration of the Holy Spirit. As we have repeatedly asserted throughout this book, it is a false presumption that we "do" anything by ourselves at the Eucharist. The Eucharist is always enacted only through the power and action of the Holy Spirit. At base it is always about what God does for us.

When we assemble for worship, it is at the Spirit's prompting and through the Spirit's action among us. This is part of the background to the traditional response to the greeting "The Lord be with you"— "and with your spirit." Whatever can be made of the Latin here, *et cum spiritu tuo*, part of what is asserted is that the Spirit of God resides in the church composed of many members, all of whom have talents, often termed charisms. Any charism we have and any charismatic actions we perform rely on the powerful presence of the Holy Spirit acting in and among us in the church. The assembly's response to the priest (or bishop) "and with your spirit" is an acknowledgment that he is ordained for the service of the church for a number of things, including presiding at the Eucharist. The response "and also with you" seems flat when compared with "and with your spirit," simply because "spirit" places the emphasis on God's grace acting through the priest (and obviously in the whole church) and this response names the power and presence of the Holy Spirit acting here and now among us.

That charisms are constitutive of the life of the church is clearly stated in New Testament passages such as Romans 12, 1 Corinthians 12, and Ephesians 4. Reflecting on these passages invites us to realize once more that any gift, talent, or charism we have is from God's Spirit. What the eucharistic liturgy does is enact those charisms and invite us to marvel at the manifold gifts and talents that God has given to us through the Holy Spirit. The dynamism of the Eucharist implies a living experience of charisms shared in and for the church. These come from and always rely on the power of God's Holy Spirit in enacting them.

The scripture scholar David Stanley has offered an interesting interpretation of the death of Jesus in John's gospel (specifically John 19:30). Relying on patristic exegesis, he asserts that the text about Jesus giving over "his spirit" implies that the spirit of God that resided in him and enabled him to accomplish the paschal victory was, at the moment of Jesus' death, given over to the church, and that what the church does and is always relies on the action of God's Spirit in us. He then applies this to the charisms whose diversity always should be seen and experienced as building up the body of Christ.

I think it is not inappropriate to see liturgical ministries as extensions of the gifts of the Spirit through different charisms in all the members of the church. This is to say that whatever individuals "do" in performing liturgical ministries should always be seen as extensions and examples of the work of the Holy Spirit among us. Again, the issue is liturgical *ministry*, not liturgical *ministers*. In a culture of the "self" and "self-promotion," it is especially important to realize that what is at stake in liturgical ministry is *ministering*, not drawing attention to oneself. Always and everywhere it is God's Holy Spirit who makes the Eucharist "work." If the liturgy is indeed the "public work" of the church, then it is the Holy Spirit who makes this public *work* possible. While this has always been the case theologically, what is especially helpful about the restoration of liturgical ministries in the revised liturgy today is that we can see the church's charisms and ministries enacted in and through the Eucharistic liturgy.

In addition to realizing this in general, we have the privilege of reflecting on the revised liturgy and the poignant emphasis the eucharistic prayers place on the *epiclesis*. And what is it that we pray for? We ask the Holy Spirit to bless the gifts and to bless the church that offers them. Note again the clear relationship of consecrating the eucharistic gifts and the church. It is impossible to appreciate the eucharistic liturgy without appreciating that it is about ecclesiology. And it is impossible to envision any true Catholic understanding of ecclesiology without seeing the church as essentially eucharistic. Again, while these are traditional and classical aspects of a Catholic doctrine of the Eucharist, the restoration of the *epiclesis* to a privileged position in the eucharistic prayer offers us the opportunity to have this centrally important notion reiterated again and again as we celebrate the Eucharist.

And it is the conclusion to the eucharistic prayer that in a sense completes what that prayer has been about. The assertion that we pray "in the unity of the Holy Spirit" reminds us that we always pray in the name of the Trinity and relying on the Trinity to enact the Eucharist. The fact that the phrase "in the unity of..." refers both to the Spirit and to the church again underscores the crucial role that the Spirit plays in establishing and fostering church unity. At the same time, the fact that we conclude the eucharistic prayer with this doxology is itself a statement that the most important doxology we offer to God is the Eucharist itself. What we offer is returned to us as transformed eucharistic gifts, to strengthen us to live in the power of God's Spirit.

The consolation in all of this is that what we do is really done through the power of God's Spirit. And the challenge is that we realize that our charisms and gifts are just that—gifts from God to be used in his service. The Eucharist is indeed the "work of the Spirit." And any "work" that we do in the Spirit is for the building up of the church.

The spiritual life is precisely about that—*life*—not merely prayer and liturgy, as crucially important as these are in constituting the Christian spiritual life. What really matters is the way we allow God to shape and form us, to grace and guide us, as we live and share the charisms and talents he has given us as God's pilgrim church on earth. The spiritual works we do as essential aspects of the spiritual life are always done because of the dynamic action and work of God's Spirit in us.

My aim in writing this book has been to explore how the liturgy can offer us insight into the theology and spirituality of what the Eucharist is and does. The Eucharist is always about a larger world than that which we experience each day. It is always about the whole cosmos in which we live. The celebration of the Eucharist in particular local churches is always about something larger and more all encompassing than we can ever understand. What we do in celebrating the Eucharist is to gather with each other in local churches to be built up as the body of Christ—the pilgrim church on earth. One of the purposes of the Eucharist is to build up the church in such a way that each of us leads a less and less imperfect spiritual life. We "gather" for the Eucharist to "disperse" and to live what we celebrate. In light of this perspective, we need the repeated celebrations of the Eucharist until the pilgrim church on earth becomes the community of the fully redeemed in the kingdom of God forever. In the meantime, we are well served if we see the Eucharist as integral to the Christian life and as integrating of the Christian life. Reflection on what we pray and do in the Eucharist is for our own sake and for the sake of the church in the world. In our day and age one of the most consoling aspects of the Eucharist is that it offers us hope in a world whose messages are often less than hope-filled. Often enough what we need so desperately in life—hope to continue to live the Christian life—is granted to us again and again in the Eucharist. It is any wonder that it is the jewel in the crown of Catholicism?

To "do this in memory of me" is to engage in a privileged set of actions whereby all that Christ has accomplished for our salvation is made available and acts among us through the liturgy. The challenge lies in being honest and humble about what it is in our own lives that needs changing, forgiving, reassessing, revitalizing. The key is to appreciate how the unique and privileged experience of the paschal mystery in the Eucharist is meant to renew us—our very real and human lives—through Christ's paschal victory and our paschal victory through, with, and in him.

This concluding chapter began with the council's assertions that the liturgy, and the Eucharist in particular, are the "source and summit" of the church's life. They are not identical with that life. Rather, the liturgy of the Eucharist is the source from which we receive the powerful and always amazing grace of God to lead us to deeper union with him and communion with each other. The spiritual life is not a privatized part of life or time out of our usual lives. It is nothing short of living the life of God in the Spirit in all of life.

In the end, one of the ultimate purposes of the Eucharist is not about the eucharistic action itself but about the entire Christian life itself. In the end, one of the ultimate purposes of the Eucharist is not to get the ritual right, but to get *life* right. Or—at least until the kingdom comes—to get life less wrong.

# NOTES

## The Questions: Eucharistic Polls, Practices, Polarization

1. See the summary in James D. Davidson, "Yes, Jesus Is Really There. Most Catholics Agree," *Commonweal* 128 (October 12, 2001) 14–16.

2. The "traditional" phrasing for this occurs in the General Instruction to "Holy Communion and the Worship of the Eucharist Outside of Mass," *The Rites of the Catholic Church as Revised by the Second Vatican Ecumenical Council* (New York: Pueblo Publishing Co., 1983) 476, at n. 5, which states that "the primary and original reason for reservation of the eucharist outside Mass is the administration of viaticum. The secondary reasons are for the giving of communion and the adoration of our Lord Jesus Christ who is present in the sacrament."

3. See "Holy Communion and the Worship of the Eucharist Outside of Mass."

4. At this writing, the Bishops' Committee on the Liturgy is evaluating the adequacy of this rite and its title. The Canadian title, *Sunday Celebration of the Word and Hours*, is clearly more descriptive of what is contained in this rite.

5. Subtitled "Apologists, Evangelists, and Theologians in a Divided Church" (Collegeville: The Liturgical Press, 2000).

6. *The New York Times*, June 1, 1994, B 8.

7. *The New York Times*, June 18, 1994, A 20.

8. Trent affirmed (and subsequent magisterial documents have repeated and adapted the teaching) that Christ is present "truly, really and

substantially" (Denzinger-Schönmetzer [DS] 1651) and that "the whole substance of bread and wine is changed into Christ's body and blood" (DS 1651). No mention is made of *physical* body. A fuller explanation will follow under the various models delineated below in Part 2, especially Model Eight, "Sacramental Sacrifice," and Model Nine, "Active Presence."

9. *Young Adult Catholics* is subtitled "Religion in the Culture of Choice." Ed. Dean Hoge, William Dinges, Mary Johnson, Juan Gonzales (Notre Dame: University of Notre Dame Press, 2001) 160–62. The way this survey was conducted and the way some of its results were summarized have been the subject of debate. See, for example, the correspondence between Andrew Greeley (negative assessment) and Peter Steinfels (positive assessment) in *Commonweal* 128 (December 21, 2001) 2.

10. A highly debatable presentation of survey results, based on a perfunctory understanding of the meaning of terms, is found in Peter Stravinskas's, "Christ's Body and Blood—Well Maybe," in *National Catholic Register*, March 15, 1992. He asserts that only 30 percent of those polled responded with orthodox Catholic teaching on the Eucharist. However, what he terms "orthodox" teaching is itself worth scrutinizing. Then he laments that this decline in belief in the "real presence" is due to practices that have been adopted and approved by the church's hierarchy: standing for communion, taking communion in the hand, reduction of the eucharistic fast, and allowing laypeople to distribute communion.

11. Davidson, "Yes, Jesus Is Really There," 16.

12. See, "Holy Communion and the Worship of the Eucharist Outside of Mass," *The Rites*, 469–532.

13. See, "Rite of Eucharistic Exposition and Benediction," n. 93. It is notable, however, that the next paragraph (n. 94) states: "[I]n the case of more solemn and lengthy exposition, the host should be consecrated in the Mass which precedes the exposition and after Communion should be placed in the monstrance on the altar."

14. See, General Introduction to the ritual for "Holy Communion and the Worship of the Eucharist Outside of Mass," n. 2. This quotation is taken from the 1967 document issued by the Congregation of Rites entitled *Eucharisticum Mysterium*, n. 3e.

15. For some very helpful insights about the relationship between liturgy and devotions, see *Directory on Popular Piety and the Liturgy*. Congregation for Divine Worship and the Discipline of the Sacraments, especially nn. 1–75 about the priority of liturgy and historical perspective on the way the liturgy was central to Catholic spirituality (available

on the Vatican website: www.vatican.va) and *Popular Devotional Practices, Basic Questions and Answers*, from the United States Catholic Conference of Bishops, Committee on Doctrine (available on the USCCB website: www.usccb.org).

16. In point of fact, the journal entitled *The Latin Mass: A Journal of Catholic Culture* is really misnamed. The editors of this journal advocate the Tridentine Mass, not the Latin Mass.

17. Entitled *Quattuor Abhinc Annos*, October 3, 1984.

18. Translation from *Origins* August 4, 1988, 151–52. Original date for the document is July 2, 1988.

19. The reference to the 1962 rite is interesting. In fact, the Tridentine Mass was approved for use throughout the church in 1570. But from the sixteenth century to the twentieth the rite did not remain exactly the same. The latest, pre–Vatican II edition of this Missal was 1962, reflecting changes made to that date.

20. See *Catechism of the Catholic Church*, nn. 1328–1332.

21. See my "The Development of Sacramental Doctrine in the Church: Theory and Practice," in the collected essays, *Rediscovering the Riches of Anointing*, ed. Jennifer Glen (Collegeville: The Liturgical Press, 2002) 59–81.


## A Proposal: Principles for a Liturgical Theology of the Eucharist

1. See my article on "Sacramental Theology," in *New Catholic Encyclopedia*, 2nd ed., vol. 12 (Washington, DC: The Catholic University of America Press, 2003 / New York: Thompson Glade, 2003) 465–79.

2. Another issue concerns the ongoing reform of the liturgy in terms of cultural adaptation of even the reformed liturgy. This is called for by the Constitution on the Sacred Liturgy (nn. 37–40) and is discussed in greater detail in the Fourth Instruction on the Proper Implementation of the Liturgy, *Varietates Legitimae* and (especially for our purposes in this book) chapter 9 of the revised *General Instruction of the Roman Missal*.

3. A summary of a number of representative approaches to liturgical theology is found in my *Liturgical Theology: A Primer* (Collegeville: The Liturgical Press, 1990) and *Context and Text: Method in Liturgical Theology* (Collegeville: The Liturgical Press, 1994). Among others, see also Aidan Kavanagh, *On Liturgical Theology* (New York: Pueblo, 1984) and Geoffrey

Wainwright, *Doxology: The Praise of God in Worship, Doctrine and Life* (New York: Oxford University Press, 1980).

4. Henceforth this important document will be referred to as the GIRM. In most instances I will cite the latest edition as revised to accompany the publication of the "third typical edition" of the *Missale Romanum* (Vatican City: Polyglot Press, 2002). The translation used here is the officially approved text found in *General Instruction of the Roman Missal*, Liturgy Documentary Series 2 (Washington, DC: United States Catholic Conference of Bishops [USCCB], 2003) from the translation done by the International Commission on English in the Liturgy in 2002. What is also contained in this edition of the GIRM are adaptations that the American bishops have made to certain sections and prescriptions of the GIRM for use in the dioceses of the United States. Thus, those from other English language countries may find here slight variations on some details of pastoral implementation based not on the GIRM itself but on these American adaptations. Where helpful, comparisons will be made with the former GIRM of 1975.

5. See Prayer for Blessing of Water, Easter Vigil, in the *Sacramentary for Mass* (New York: Catholic Book Publishing Co., 1985) 201–202. This prayer is also found in the Order for Christian Initiation of Adults and the Rite for the Baptism of Children.

6. There are a number of contemporary explanations of the meaning of this phase, both when it was first enunciated and how it can be appropriated today. Among others, see my *Context and Text*, chapter 1. Also see my article entitled "Liturgical Theology," in *The New Dictionary of Sacramental Worship*, ed. Peter Fink (Collegeville: The Liturgical Press, 1990) 721–33. For some very insightful reflections on the question of relating liturgy and theology see the articles by Jeremy Driscoll, "Liturgy and Fundamental Theology: Frameworks for a Dialogue," *Ecclesia Orans* 11 (1994) 69–99; "The Eucharist and Fundamental Theology," *Ecclesia Orans* 13 (1996) 407–34; "Deepening the Theological Dimension of Liturgical Studies," *Communio* 23 (1996) 508–23; and "Anamnesis, Epiclesis and Fundamental Theology," *Ecclesia Orans* 15 (1998) 211–38.

7. It is notable that Pope John Paul II's encyclical on the Eucharist contains a number of references to liturgical texts and rites.

8. These are of varying length. The Latin term for them is *Praenotanda, Proemium,* or *Institutio Generalis.*

9. More on this below under Model Eight, "Sacramental Sacrifice," and Model Nine, "Active Presence," largely because these models deal with issues of great controversy during the Reformation.

10. See my *Context and Text*, chapter 2.

11. Louis Bouyer, *Eucharist: Theology and Spirituality of the Eucharistic Prayer*, trans. Charles U. Quinn (Notre Dame: University of Notre Dame, 1968).

12. See the very helpful summary of the magisterium about the Eucharist in Norman Tanner, "The Eucharist in the Ecumenical Councils," *Gregorianum* 82, 1 (2001) 37–49.

13. *Models of the Church*, expanded ed. (New York: Doubleday Image, 1986) 12. In addition, Pope John Paul II devoted several weekly audience addresses to the Eucharist. See *L'Osservatore Romano* Weekly English Edition, N. 40 (October 4, 2001) "Eucharist is a celebration of divine glory," p. 11; N. 41 (October 11, 2001) "Eucharist: 'memorial' of God's mighty works," p. 11; N. 42, (October 18, 2001) "Eucharist is a perfect sacrifice of praise," p. 11; N. 43, (October 25, 2001) "Eucharist, banquet of communion with God," p. 11; N. 44, (November 1, 2001) "The Eucharist, 'a taste of eternity in time,'" p. 11; N. 46 (November 15, 2001) "Eucharist is a sacrament of the Church's unity," p. 11; N. 47 (November 22, 2001) "Word, Eucharist and divided Christians," p. 11.

14. Dulles, *Models of the Church*, 32, from *Images of the Church in the New Testament* (Philadelphia: Westminster Press, 1960) 253.

## Model One: Cosmic Mass

1. My purpose is not to disparage such treatments that emphasize, for example, salvation history or the scriptural word proclaimed in the liturgy, or the use of human speech and gestures in the liturgy, which at times can come across as diminishing the value of ideas related to sacramentality. It is rather to offer a wider lens within which to view them, which "lens" I would argue, is more traditional and foundational for understanding the theology of the liturgy.

2. *RB80. The Rule of St. Benedict*, in Latin and English with notes, ed. Timothy Fry et al. (Collegeville: The Liturgical Press, 1981) Chapter 31:10, 229.

3. See *On Liturgical Theology* (New York: Pueblo Publishing Co., 1984) p. 23, and the whole chapter on "The World," 23–38.

4. See Michael Kunzler, *The Church's Liturgy*, trans. Placid Murray et al. (London, New York: Continuum, 2001) 23–31.

5. See Joseph Ratzinger, *The Spirit of the Liturgy*, trans. John Saward (San Francisco: Ignatius Press, 2000) 24, from the chapter entitled "Liturgy—Cosmos—History." Recall that the title of this book is the same as the "classic" pre–Vatican II work by Romano Guardini.

6. See my *Context and Text*, chapter 8.

7. For an overview of the evolution of sacramental teaching and practice in Catholicism, see my "Sacramental Theology," in *New Catholic Encyclopedia*, revised and updated edition.

8. Among the clearest English language summaries of these insights as fundamental to sacramental theology, see Kenan B. Osborne, *Sacramental Theology: A General Introduction* (New York/Mahwah, NJ: Paulist Press, 1988) 69–99.

9. *Lumen Gentium* 1: "Cum autem Ecclesia sit in Christo veluti sacramentum seu signum et instrumentum intimae cum Deo unionis totiusque generis humani unitatis…"

10. See Kenan B. Osborne, *Christian Sacraments in a Postmodern World: A Theology for the Third Millennium* (New York/Mahwah, NJ: Paulist Press, 1999) 62.

11. See, for example, "A Modern Approach to the Word of God and Sacraments of Christ: Perspectives and Principles," in Francis A. Eigo, *The Sacraments: God's Love and Mercy Actualized* (Villanova: University of Villanova Press, 1979) 59–109, esp. 68–93 and "Theology of the Sacraments: Toward a New Understanding of the Chief Rites of the Church of Jesus Christ," in *Alternative Futures For Worship*, vol. 1, General Introduction, ed. Regis A. Duffy (Collegeville: The Liturgical Press, 1987) 123–75.

12. *Symbol and Sacrament: A Sacramental Reinterpretation of Christian Existence*, trans. Patrick Madigan and Madeline Beaumont (Collegeville: The Liturgical Press, 1995). Translation of *Symbole et sacrement: Une relecture sacramentelle de l'existence chretienne* (Paris: Les Editions du Cerf, 1987). See also his more recent, shorter work, *The Sacraments: The Word of God and the Mercy of the Body* (Collegeville: The Liturgical Press, 2001) first published as *Les sacrements: Parole de Dieu au risque du corps* (Paris: Les Editions de L'Atelier, 1997).

13. *Christian Sacraments in a Postmodern World*, especially chapters 4 and 5, "Jesus and Primordiality" and "The Church as Foundational Sacrament," 84–136.

14. Phrase adapted from Kenan Osborne's in *Christian Sacraments in a Postmodern World*, p. 65 and *passim*.

15. Definition from *The HarperCollins Encyclopedia of Catholicism* (San

Francisco: HarperCollins, 1995) 1148. For brief treatments of saramental-
ity, see Michael Schmaus, *The Church as Sacrament*, Dogma 5 (Westminster:
Christian Classics, 1988) chapter 1, pp. 3–19, and Herbert Vorgrimler,
*Sacramental Theology*, trans. Linda M. Maloney (Collegeville: The Liturgical
Press, 1992) chapter 1, "Theological Preconditions for Sacramental Theol-
ogy," esp. pp. 12–15.

16. Notice, however, the precise phrase about "all reality" in the above
definition, specifically that it "is potentially or in fact the bearer of God's
presence and the instrument of God's saving activity." The caution evident
in the phrase "is potentially" is important and much needed, lest an overly
optimistic view of creation and created reality be presumed. This is where
the helpful cautions of Kenan Osborne are important and welcome. In his
most recent book, *Christian Sacraments in a Postmodern World*, Osborne cites
Louis Marie Chauvet's assertion that the world and history are recognized
as "the *possible* place of sacred history." See Osborne, *Christian Sacraments*,
67–68.

17. Kilmartin, "Theology of the Sacraments," 158.

18. See Louis Marie Chauvet, "Place et fonction de l'histoire dans une
theologie des sacrements," *Revue de l'Institute Catholique* 24 (1987) 49–65.

19. See *Catechism of the Catholic Church*, nn. 1077–1112.

20. It is not coincidental, I think, that among American authors it is
the priest sociologists Philip Murnion and Andrew Greeley who emphasize
that "sacramentality" is truly a Catholic principle the loss of which imperils
Catholic identity.

21. Taken from David N. Power, *Unsearchable Riches* (New York:
Pueblo Publishing Co., 1984) 96.

22. "The Contemporary Person and the Church," *America* 185:3 (July
30–August 6, 2001) 7.

23. *Journal of Gastronomy* 7 (Winter/Spring, 1993) 35–45.

24. Exceptions are penance and marriage.

25. The fact that these phrases replicate the genre of the blessing
prayers of the eucharistic prayers makes them somewhat problematic.
However, for our purposes here, we can see reflected in these phrases the
theology of things from this earth, human productivity, and sacramentality.

26. Similarly, the precedent of consecrating chrism at the end of the
Roman Canon on Holy Thursday and of blessing milk and honey on Pentecost at this same point in the liturgy is attested to in the text of the Roman
Canon in R. C. D. Jasper and G. J. Cuming, *Prayers of the Eucharist: Early
and Reformed*, 3rd ed. (New York: Pueblo Publishing Co., 1987) 166.

27. Throughout this book we will use the translation of prayers from the *Sacramentary for Mass* (New York: Catholic Book Publishing Co., 1985), understanding that they are presently being retranslated, and that a principle for this revision is the use of inclusive language where possible. The use of square brackets is meant to note where gender specific language referring to "men" should be understood to refer to men and women. On occasion the Latin texts will be offered in footnotes and explanations made about how a particular translated word or phrase might be better rendered.

28. Taken from *Christ in Sacred Speech: The Meaning of Liturgical Language* (Philadelphia: Fortress Press, 1986) 30.

29. See the listing and summary in Thaddaus A. Schnitker and Wolfgang A. Slaby, *Concordantia Verbalia Missalis Romani* (Munster: Aschendorff, 1982) cols. 313–14.

30. See, among others, prayer over the gifts, Fifth Day in the Octave of Christmas.

31. Translation from Jasper and Cuming, *Prayers of the Eucharist*, 23. What is notable in this connection is the fact that this text from the *Didache* was proposed as one of the choices that the committee charged with revising the Order of Mass after Vatican II debated using at the presentation of the gifts. One can only wonder what kind of impression repeated use of this text might have made on those who said or heard it daily at the Eucharist.

## Model Two: The Church's Eucharist

1. This text, *opus nostrae redemptionis exercitur,* is also found in the prayer over the gifts for the Second Sunday of the Year. In the previous Missal it was found as the secret prayer on the Ninth Sunday after Pentecost. See the classic essay by Odo Casel "Beitrage zu romischen Messbuch," *Jahrbuch fur Liturgiewissenschaft* 11 (1931) 35–37; also see his classic *The Mystery of Christian Worship* (New York: Crossroad, 1999, originally printed in 1962).

2. See Josef Jungmann, "Constitution on the Sacred Liturgy," in *Commentary on the Documents of Vatican II*, vol. 1 (New York: Herder and Herder, 1966) 15.

3. For an excellent overview of the debates and issues inherent in the final drafting of this teaching, see Michael Witczak, "The Manifold Pres-

ence of Christ in the Liturgy," *Theological Studies* 59 (December 1998) 680–702. That these aspects of the one presence of Christ are ordered differently is to be noted (see, for example, *Eucharistic Mysterium* and the revised GIRM [2000]). What is of concern here is that the focus on assembly has been explicitly restored to our consciousness by the contemporary magisterium.

4. *Dies Domini*, chapter 3, esp. nn. 32–34.

5. Ibid., n. 36. The footnote reference here is to St. Cyprian, as well as to two documents of Vatican II, the Constitution on Church, *Lumen Gentium*, n. 4, and the Constitution on the Sacred Liturgy, *Sacrosanctum Concilium*, n. 26. It is at least intriguing that the reference to the church as the "sacrament of unity" which was in the first drafts of the revised GIRM 2000 (n. 91) was deleted in the final version published in 2002.

6. The Latin phrase is *Votis huius familiae, quam tibi astare voluisti, adesto propitius*. In passing we should note that *adesto propitius* would seem to require a stronger petition than "Father, hear the prayers…" But that is not our main concern here. That God initiates and sustains any act of assembling is the heart of *quam tibi astare voluisti*.

7. The GIRM 2002 states:

> The Eucharistic celebration is an action of Christ and the Church, namely, a holy people united and ordered under the Bishop. It therefore pertains to the whole Body of the Church, manifests it and has its effect on it. It also affects the individual members of the Church in different ways, according to their different orders, offices and actual participation. In this way, the Christian people, "a chosen race, a royal priesthood, a holy nation, a people of his own," demonstrates its cohesion and its hierarchical ordering. All, therefore, whether they are ordained ministers or Christian faithful, in fulfilling their office or their duty, should carry out solely but completely that which pertains to them. (n. 91)

8. For a fine overall treatment of the evolution of Christian worship with special attention to the influences on the Roman rite from other places, especially Gaul, see Herman Wegman, *Christian Worship in East and West: A Study Guide to Liturgical History*, trans. Gordon Lathrop (New York: Pueblo, 1985).

9. The whole of the Fourth Instruction on the Proper Implementation of the Liturgy *(Varietates Legitimae)* deals with inculturation.

10. See above, Part 1, "A Proposal" p. 26.

11. See Model One, note 31, p. 338. See also Maurizio Barba, *La riforma conciliare dell'<<Ordo Missae>> Il percorso storico-redazionale dei riti d'ingresso, di offertorio e di comunione* (Rome: Edizioni Liturgiche, 2002) 201–15.

12. For helpful background on this practice, see Nathan Mitchell, *Cult and Controversy: The Worship of the Eucharist Outside of Mass* (New York: Pueblo Publishing Co., 1982) 35–36, 57–58, 60–62.

13. See his doctoral thesis, *The Eucharist Makes the Church: Henri de Lubac and John Zizioulas in Dialogue* (Edinburgh: T. & T. Clark, 1993) and *Sacrament of Salvation* (Edinburgh: T. & T. Clark, 1995). The latter explores the topic at once more broadly and more briefly.

14. See also John Zizioulas, *Being as Communion* (Crestwood: St. Vladimir's Seminary Press, 1985).

15. See Paul McPartlan, "The Eucharist as the Basis for Ecclesiology," *Antiphon* 6:2 (2001) 15.

16. Ibid.

17. Ibid.

18. From Frank Senn, "Liturgical Reconnaissance 2000," *Liturgy*, Journal of the Liturgical Conference, *What's New About the Past?* 16:1 (Summer, 2000) 4–5.

19. I use "active" participation to underscore the role of the whole church assembly in being consciously engaged in the rites and prayers of the liturgy. That there was liturgical participation in the Middle Ages is clear. That it was more passive in terms of watching what was occurring is also clear. See the insightful writings of John Bossy in such articles as "The Mass As Social Institution 1200–1700," *Past and Present* 100 (1983) and *Christianity in the West 1400–1700* (New York: Oxford University Press, 1985).

20. See Hans Urs Von Balthasar, "The Mass: A Sacrifice of the Church?" in *Explorations in Theology III: Creator Spirit* (San Francisco: Ignatius Press, 1993) 185–243.

21. Herve Legrand, "The Presidency of the Eucharist According to Ancient Tradition," in *Living Bread, Saving Cup*, ed. R. Kevin Seasoltz (Collegeville: The Liturgical Press, 1987, 1982) 196–221.

22. A classic reference today for *in persona Christi* is B.-D. Marliangeas, *Cles pour une theologie du ministere: In persona Christi, In persona Ecclesias* (Paris: Beauchesne, 1978). There is abundant literature about the traditional understandings of *in persona Christi* and about its contemporary form *in per-*

*sona Christi capitis* among American authors such as Sarah Butler and Dennis Michael Ferrara. See, among others, the "dialogue" between them in Dennis M. Ferrara, "Representation or Self-Effacement? The Axiom *In persona Christi* in St. Thomas and the Magisterium," *Theological Studies* 55:2 (1994) 195–224; Sara Butler, "A Response to Dennis M. Ferrara," *Theological Studies* 56:1 (1995) 61–80; Dennis M. Ferrara, "*In Persona Christi*: A Reply to Sara Butler," *Theological Studies* 56:1 (1995) 81–91; and *In Persona Christi*: Towards a Second Naivete," *Theological Studies* 57:1 (1996) 65–88.

23. Among the more complete sets of instructions and the rationale for them, see *Special Circumstances for the Admission of Other Christians to Communion at Catholic Church Celebrations of the Eucharist*, Diocese of Rockville Center, pp. 1–9, Q and A pp. 1–3; Companion Guide, pp. 1–3. Available from www.drvc.org.norms

24. *Directory for Ecumenism*, n. 31. Full text in *Origins* 23 (July 29, 1993) 129–60.

25. See *One Bread, One Body*, A Teaching Document on the Eucharist in the Life of the Church, and the Establishment of General Norms on Sacramental Sharing (London: Catholic Truth Society, 1998) 19–44.

26. Full text available from www.usccb.org/liturgy/current/intercom.shtml

27. See the helpful essay by Frederick R. McManus, "Pastoral Ecumenism: The Common Lectionary," in Gerard Austin et al., *Eucharist: Toward the Third Millennium* (Chicago: Liturgy Training Publications, 1997) 103–18.

## Model Three: The Effective Word of God

1. Constitution on the Sacred Liturgy, *Sacrosanctum Concilium*, n. 51; Constitution on Divine Revelation, *Dei Verbum*, n. 21; Decree on the Ministry and Life of Priests, *Presbyterorum Ordinis*, n. 4.

2. Both of these texts are taken in turn from *Sacrosanctum Concilium*, n. 33 and n. 7.

3. I am deliberately using the term "altar table" to be sure to include an emphasis on both the sacrificial nature of the Eucharist and the fact that from it we are also offered the gifts of consecrated bread and wine to "take and eat/drink."

4. *Ordo Lectionum Missae* (Rome: Libreria Editrice Vaticana, 1969). The present edition is the third revised edition, 1981.

5. See Frederick R. McManus, "Pastoral Ecumenism: The Common Lectionary," 103–18.

6. See my "The Good News of Repentance and Conversion," in *Repentance and Reconciliation in the Church* (Collegeville: The Liturgical Press, 1887) 32–56.

7. Introduction, *Lectionary for Mass,* Second Typical Edition. Liturgy Documentary Series 1 (Washington, DC: USCCB, 1998) n. 3.

8. More precisely, it is proclaimed both on Wednesday of the first week of the year, Year II, and on the Second Sunday in Ordinary Time, Year B.

9. See 1 Samuel, chapter 3.

10. It is well understood that these antiphons are not always sung as proposed in the *Missale Romanum* and the *Graduale Romanum.* However, the theological point I want to make here is that, because they have been chosen to be sung, these texts deserve to be probed for their theological, liturgical, and spiritual meaning. In addition they can be useful as guides for what might be sung at this part of the liturgy.

11. "The Contemporary Person and the Church," *America* 185:3 (July 30–August 6, 2001) 7.

12. Paul VI, apostolic constitution *Missale Romanum,* in *Documents on the Liturgy,* nn. 1361–1362, p. 459.

13. Introduction, *Lectionary for Mass,* n. 3.

14. Ibid., n. 10, citing *Presbyterorum Ordinis,* n. 4.

15. See Jeremy Driscoll, "The Fathers and Liturgical Preaching," *Antiphon* 5:3 (2000) 29–38.


## Model Four: Memorial of the Paschal Mystery

1. The Latin title for this preface is *Praefatio Paschalis I,* thus a more literal translation would read "paschal," whose meaning includes Easter but goes far beyond it. The deliberate multivalence of liturgical terminology is again an important issue to recall here.

2. Maria Boulding, *The Coming of God* (London: SPCK, 1982).

3. See, among others, Fritz Chenderlin, *"Do This As My Memorial":* *The Semantic and Conceptual Background and Value of* anamnesis *in* *1 Corinthians 11:24–25* (Rome: Biblical Institute Press, 1982).

4. Thomas Cahill, *The Gifts of the Jews* (New York: Simon and Schuster, 1998).

5. The footnote cites the following documents from Vatican II: Constitution on the Sacred Liturgy, *Sacrosanctum Concilium*, December 4, 1963, art. 47; see Vatican Council II, Dogmatic Constitution on the Church, *Lumen Gentium*, November 21, 1964, nos. 3, 28; see Vatican Council II, Decree on the Ministry and Life of Priests, *Presbyterorum Ordinis*, December 7, 1965, nos. 2, 4, 5.

6. Among others, see Anscar J. Chupungco, *Liturgies of the Future* (New York/Mahwah, NJ: Paulist Press, 1989). Many of Chupungco's writings on inculturation derive from his doctoral thesis entitled *Toward a Filipino Liturgy* (Rome: Studia Anselmiana, 1974). The last chapter of the thesis contains a helpful set of criteria for evaluating what should (not) occur in any attempts at liturgical inculturation.

7. Joachim Jeremias, *The Eucharistic Words of Jesus* (New York: Scribners, 1966) 237–55.

8. See, Frederick R. McManus, *Liturgical Participation: An Ongoing Assessment* (Collegeville: The Liturgical Press, 1986).

9. See the comments throughout Joseph Ratzinger's *The Spirit of the Liturgy*. It is enormously helpful to read this book in light of the perspective gained from the "classic" by Romano Guardini, *The Church, the Catholic and the Spirit of the Liturgy*, trans. Ada Lane (New York: Sheed and Ward, 1940).

10. The Latin reads: "[N]unc centrum et culmen totius celebrationis initium habet." Obviously this statement has enormous ramifications for Catholic theology and practice, some of which are noted in the next section of this chapter.

11. From *Sacrosanctum Concilium*, n. 56.

12. The Latin reads: "Unde et memores, Domine, nos servi tui, sed et plebs tua sancta..." The present translation is rather "flat" and could be improved by reinserting a word or two to underscore that God's people is a "holy people."

13. This assertion is not meant to pronounce upon or even take a position on the contemporary debate about the authorship of this prayer. For discussion of the debate, see, among others, *The Apostolic Tradition*, ed. Paul F. Bradshaw, Maxwell E. Johnson, and L. Edward Phillips (Philadelphia: Fortress Press, 2002) 1–18.

14. Note that I did not say "improvise," since that word carries connotations of making something up. The eucharistic prayer in general and that text specifically are not meant to serve as the bases for improvisations. The second eucharistic prayer presents a formula that can be adapted but not restructured.

15. For a useful summary of the debates about its authorship and the fact that it is more inspired by other traditional texts than an ancient text itself reproduced, see Enrico Mazza, *The Eucharistic Prayers of the Roman Rite*, trans. Matthew O'Connell (New York: Pueblo Publishing Co., 1986) 123–25.

16. The Latin reads: "Unde et nos, Domine, redemptionis nostrae memoriale nunc celebrantes..."

17. A clear exposition of this precise issue can be found in Cipriano Vagaggini's *The Canon of the Mass and Liturgical Reform*, trans. Peter Coughlan (Staten Island, NY: Alba House, 1969).

18. See Bryan D. Spinks, *The Sanctus in the Eucharistic Prayer* (Cambridge: Cambridge University Press, 1991).

19. The Latin reads: "Quotiescumque manducamus panem hunc et calicem bibimus, mortem tuam annuntiamus, Domine, donec venias."

20. "Salvator mundi, salva nos, qui per crucem et resurrectionem tuam liberasti nos."

21. See, among his other works, Max Thurian, *The Eucharistic Memorial*, Part 1 and Part 2, trans., J. G. Davies (Richmond: John Knox Press, 1960) and *The One Bread*, trans. Theodore DuBois (New York: Sheed and Ward, 1969). It is significant that it was after his research into memorial and his participation in ecumenical dialogues about the Eucharist that Thurian became a Roman Catholic and was ordained a priest.

22. See, among others, the text of the so-called "Lima document" on *Baptism, Eucharist and Ministry* from the Faith and Order Commission of the World Council of Churches.

## Model Five: Covenant Renewal

1. From *Covenants: A Cycle of Plays Covering Significant Events from the "Creation of Everything" to "The Nativity,"* adapted from the medieval mystery plays of the northern English towns of York, Wakefield, Chester, and Digby, edited and produced by Roland Reed, Drama Department, The Catholic University of America. Quoted in Stephen Happel, "The Interaction of Two Genres: Roland Reed's *Covenants* and the Drama of the Eucharist," in Gerard Austin et al., *Eucharist: Toward the Third Millennium* (Chicago: Liturgy Training Publications, 1997) 2.

2. See below, pp. 153–154 in this chapter under the discussion of Genesis 22.

3. We will be primarily concerned in this section (and chapter) with the model of Abraham. However, the reference to Abel here should not be lost. That it is reiterated in the prayer over the gifts on the Sixteenth Sunday in Ordinary Time as a parallel to Christ's sacrifice, sacramentally perpetuated in the Eucharist, should not be forgotten:

> Accept the perfect sacrifice you have given us,
> Bless it as you blessed the gifts of Abel.

4. As discussed in Model Three in the section entitled "The Importance of a Lectionary."

5. For more on this kind of "liturgical hermeneutic" see my *Context and Text*, chapter 3, "Word."

6. More on this below under "life blood."

7. One of the contemporary authors whom the pope quotes in this letter is Abraham Heschel in *The Sabbath* (New York: Farrar, Strauss and Giroux, 1951). The fact that in 1988 this book was in its twenty-seventh printing attests to the contribution it continues to make to how believers "tell time."

8. As specified both in the GIRM 2002 nn. 281–286 and in the American elaboration on occasions for receiving communion under both kinds in *Norms for the Distribution and Reception of Holy Communion Under Both Kinds in the Dioceses of the United States of America*, nn. 27–54.

9. See *Built of Living Stones*, Guidelines of the National Conference of Catholic Bishops (Washington: USCCB, 2000) nn. 66, 69.

## Model Six: The Lord's Supper

1. This translation was proposed for ICEL revision of the translation of the *Sacramentary for Mass*. It is used here to underscore the differences between saying "This is the Lamb" as at present and a translation that captures the sense from John 1:29, "*Ecce Agnus Dei...*" In addition, it captures more fully the sense of the text from Revelation 19:9 about the "banquet of the Lamb" (presently translated as "his supper").

2. According to the GIRM (both present and former) the Latin ending of this prayer is "Per Dominum nostrum Iesum Christum Filium tuum, qui tecum vivit et regnat in unitate Spiritus Sanci, Deus, per omnia saecula saeculorum..."

3. This argument refers to the majority of occasions when the conclusion to this prayer is explicitly trinitarian. With regard to other cases, the GIRM 2000 requires the following:

> If it is directed to the Father, but the Son is mentioned at the end: *Who lives and reigns with you in the unity of the Holy Spirit, God for ever and ever;*
>
> if it is directed to the Son: *You live and reign with the Father in the unity of the Holy Spirit, God for ever and ever.*

> Si dirigitur ad Patrem, sed in fine ipsius fit mentio Filii: Qui tecum vivit et regnat in unitáte Spíritus Sancti, Deus, per ómnia sáecula saeculórum;
>
> si dirigitur ad Filium: Qui vivis et regnas cum Deo Patre in unitáte Spíritus Sancti, Deus, per ómnia sáecula saeculórum.

4. In practice we also (often) hear "we ask this in the name of Jesus the Lord." However the Latin in the GIRM (both previous and present) is explicit when it states that the prayer ends "per Christum Dóminum nostrum."

5. The Latin text from the GIRM reads:

> si dirigitur ad Patrem: Per Christum Dóminum nostrum.

> When the prayer is directed to the Father, but the Son is mentioned at the end [the text says]: *Who lives and reigns for ever and ever;* and
>
> if it is directed to the Son [it reads]: *You who live and reign for ever and ever;*

> Si dirigitur ad Patrem, sed in fine ipsarum fit mentio Filii: Qui vivit et regnat in sáecula saeculórum;
>
> si dirigitur ad Filium: Qui vivis et regnas in sáecula saeculórum.

6. Not surprisingly, because some of these connotations can signify domination of one over another, in particular of a husband over a wife, some theologians shy away from using "Lord," at least without self-criticism and a clear understanding of respect for persons.

7. The "O" antiphon for December 18th reads: "O Adonai and leader of Israel. You appeared to Moses in a burning bush and you gave him the Law on Sinai. O come and save us by your mighty power."

8. The Latin is: "Celebratio Passionis Domini."

9. Suffice it to say here that I am concerned with the depth and breadth of symbolic engagement and interaction involving whole persons on many levels. In particular I am concerned with the aspects of symbol that refer to joining together, to combining our present experience with the unique paschal mystery. We do this liturgically through (real!) signs and symbols.

10. Sacred Congregation of Rites, *Instruction on the Correct Use of the Restored "Ordo" of Holy Week*, November 16, 1955 (Washington, DC: National Catholic Welfare Conference Publications Office, 1955) 6.

11. Understanding that in liturgical tradition the Chrism Mass was celebrated at the diocesan cathedral on Holy Thursday morning and that other practices, such as a Mass for the Reconciliation of Penitents, was also celebrated on this day. Our focus is precisely on the Evening Mass as it begins the triduum. These other liturgies were part of Lent, not the Easter triduum.

12. The full text (taken from the Bishops' Committee on the Liturgy, *Newsletter* 23, February 1987, 5–6) reads:

> Because the gospel of the mandatum read on Holy Thursday also depicts Jesus as the "Teacher and Lord" who humbly serves his disciples by performing this extraordinary gesture which goes beyond the laws of hospitality, the element of humble service has accentuated the celebration of the foot washing rite in the United States over the last decade or more. In this regard, it has become customary in many places to invite both men and women to be participants in this rite in recognition of the service that should be given by all the faithful to the Church and to the world. Thus, in the United States, a variation in the rite developed in which not only charity is signified but also humble service.
>
> While this variation may differ from the rubric of the Sacramentary which mentions only men ("viri selecti"), it may nevertheless be said that the intention to emphasize service along with charity in the celebration of the rite is an understandable way of accentuating the evangelical command of the Lord, "who came to serve and not to be served," that all members of the Church must serve one another in love.
>
> The liturgy is always an act of ecclesial unity and Christian charity, of which the Holy Thursday foot washing rite is an

eminent sign. All should obey the Lord's new commandment to love one another with an abundance of love, especially at this most sacred time of the liturgical year when the Lord's passion, death, and resurrection are remembered and celebrated in the powerful rites of the Triduum.

13. The Latin is "Simili modo, postquam cenatum est..."

14. The Latin is "et cenantibus illis..."

15. It is not our intention to take a position on whether Jesus' last meal was the Passover. This debate has exercised commentators for generations. Suffice it to say that there is clearly a paschal context to this last supper and that Passover overtones are evident in the way the gospels recount it and the way in which the liturgy enacts the Lord's Supper as influenced by the Passover meal structure.

16. See Francis J. Moloney, *A Body Broken for a Broken People: Eucharist in the New Testament*, rev. ed. (Peabody, MA: Hendrickson Publishers, 1997; orig. pub. Victoria: Collins Dove, 1990, 1997).

17. See *Luke: Artist and Theologian: Luke's Passion Account as Literature*. (New York/Mahwah, NJ: Paulist Press, 1985).

18. The complete title is *Norms for the Distribution and Reception of Holy Communion Under Both Kinds in the Dioceses of the United States of America*. Approved by the United States Conference of Catholic Bishops on June 14, 2001. Final document approved by the Congregation for Divine Worship on March 22, 2002.

19. As noted under Model One, again see Philippe Rouillard, "From Human Meal to Christian Eucharist," in *Living Bread, Saving Cup*, ed. R. Kevin Seasoltz (Collegeville: The Liturgical Press, 1987).

20. The use of the verb form here—"is offered"—should be noted; our thesis in Model Nine is that this is central to Trent's assertions and is normative for our theology today.

21. The *Norms* cite both *Eucharisticum Mysterium*, n. 31 about eucharistic communion from the "sacrifice actually being celebrated..." and the GIRM 2002, n. 284b that remains of the eucharistic species are consumed at the altar by the eucharistic ministers.

22. Again, see Herve Legrand, "The Presidency of the Eucharist According to Ancient Tradition," in *Living Bread, Saving Cup*.

23. Such as *Inaestimabile Donum* of 1980.

24. The balance of this paragraph reflects the tension between "ordinary" and "extraordinary" ministers, noting that we should not blur the distinction between the two, when it says:

When recourse is had to Extraordinary Minister[s] of Holy Communion, especially in the distribution of Holy Communion under both kinds, their number should not be increased beyond what is required for the orderly and reverent distribution of the Body and Blood of the Lord. In all matters such Extraordinary Ministers of Holy Communion should follow the guidance of the diocesan bishop.

25. *Summa Theologiae*, IIIa, Par, Q. 60, on "What is a Sacrament."

26. See, GIRM 2002, n. 283.

27. For what can only be regarded as the English language classic study of the doctrine of concomitance, see James Megivern, *Concomitance and Communion: A Study in Eucharistic Doctrine and Practice* (Friburg: University Press, 1963).

28. At the same time, the *Norms* say the following about intinction:

Holy Communion may be distributed by intinction in the following manner: "the communicant, while holding the paten under the chin, approaches the priest who holds the chalice and at whose side stands the minister holding the vessel with the hosts. The priest takes the host, intincts the particle into the chalice and, showing it, says: 'The Body and Blood of Christ.' The communicant responds, 'Amen,' and receives the Sacrament on the tongue from the priest. Afterwards, the communicant returns to his or her place." (n. 49)

29. See Miri Rubin, *Corpus Christi: The Eucharist in Late Medieval Culture* (New York/Cambridge: Cambridge University Press, 1991).

30. For short, helpful explanations of these and other liturgical gestures, signs, and symbols, see Antonio Donghi, *Actions and Words: Symbolic Language and the Liturgy*, trans. Wm. McDonough and Dominic Serra (Collegeville: The Liturgical Press, 1997).

## Model Seven: Food for the Journey

1. The translation can also be the indicative "The Lord comes." Again, the deliberate multivalence of liturgical language should not be diminished. However, in this instance, the urgency of the imperative suits the eschatological orientation of this chapter.

2. This is not to say that this is the only way to describe saving history, much less the only way to interpret the Hebrew Scriptures.

3. Isaiah 58:1–9 is read on Friday after Ash Wednesday and 58:9–14 is read on Saturday. Both texts are combined, however, and are read at the first reading at the Office of Readings for Ash Wednesday. This repetition is a liturgical way of underscoring the importance of these texts.

4. The book is subtitled *The Phenomenon of Christian Worship* (New York: Seabury, 1969).

5. See the helpful summaries in Alexander Gerken, *Teologia dell' eucaristia*, trans. from the German original, *Theologie der Eucharistie* (Roma: Edizione Paoline, 1977) 65–104 and in "Historical Background of the New Direction in Eucharistic Doctrine," *Theology Digest* 21 (1973) 46–53.

6. The translation used here is from *The Rites of the Catholic Church*.

7. The Rite speaks about the relationship of celebrating the sacrament of the sick as a communal Eucharist in nn. 108–9 and 132–34.

8. See Chapter 8 of the *Rite for the Pastoral Care of the Sick*.

9. The Latin reads: Altare exstruatur a pariete seiunctum, ut facile circumiri et in eo celebratio versus populum preagi possit, quod expedit ubicumque possibile sit.

10. At the same time, the other assertion in this text, namely that there can be only one altar for the Eucharist, should not be ignored. As a result, the architecture of some older buildings may require a reexamination of the placing of a second altar.

11. See Nathan Mitchell, *Cult and Controversy: The Worship of the Eucharist Outside of Mass*, 35–36, 57, 60–62 for his illuminating discussion of the *fermentum* and *sancta* customs.

12. This is the translation for the proposed (second edition) of the *Sacramentary for Mass*. This classic Christmas text is from Leo the Great. The Latin reads:

> Deus, qui humanae substantiae dignitatem
> et mirabiliter condidisti, et mirabilius reformasti,
> da, quaesumus, nobis eius divinitatis esse consortes,
> qui humanitatis nostrae fieri dignatus est participes.

13. Here you build your temple of living stones,
and bring the Church to its full stature
as the body of Christ throughout the world,
to reach its perfection at last

in the heavenly city of Jerusalem,
which is the vision of your peace.
—Preface for the Dedication of a Church

14. San Francisco: Harper and Row, 1982.
15. The Latin reads:

Hic enim est templum illud quod nos sumus aedificas,
Et Ecclesiam per orbem diffusam
in dominici compagem corporis facis augeri,
In pacis visione complendam, caelesti civitate Ierusalem...

## Model Eight: Sacramental Sacrifice

1. The Latin reads:

Offerimus praeclare maiestati tuae
de tuis donis ac datis
hostiam puram,
hostiam sanctam,
hostiam immaculatam,
Panem sanctum vitae aeternae
et Calicem salutis perpetuae.

Clearly the stylistic emphasis in the Latin on *hostiam* is not emphasized in this (present) translation.

2. Recall the comments made in Part 1 on "The Questions" about the church's task of "reinventing" its sacramental doctrines in light of contemporary doctrinal and catechetical challenges.

3. Clifford Howell, *Of Sacraments and Sacrifice* (Collegeville: The Liturgical Press, 1966).

4. See Edward Kilmartin, *The Eucharist in the West: History and Theology*, ed. Robert Daly (Collegeville: The Liturgical Press, 1998) 187.

5. See "Catholic-Lutheran Joint Declaration on the Doctrine of Justification," *Origins* 28 (July 16, 1998) 120–27.

6. For a translation of and brief commentary on the *Formula Missae*, see Jasper and Cuming, *Prayers of the Eucharist*, 191–94.

7. It is noteworthy that in the GIRM (both 1975, n. 40 and 2002, n. 73) the terms for this part of the eucharistic rite are "presentation of the gifts" and "preparation" of the altar—not the "offertory."

8. Especially for those not familiar with the Roman Rite for the Mass celebrated after Trent, it would be a useful exercise to review the prayers and gestures that were used prior to the Missal of Pope Paul VI to accompany the presentation of the bread and wine. In many ways, these texts and gestures replicated what was to occur during the Canon. Hence, if the Canon had to be "purged" (as Luther did indeed do) then it was no surprise that these rites had to be eliminated.

9. Again, for translation of and brief commentary on the *Deutsche Messe*, see Jasper and Cuming, *Prayers of the Eucharist*, 195–99.

10. A detailed summary and assessment of these issues is in James McCue, "Luther and Roman Catholicism on the Mass as Sacrifice," in *The Eucharist as Sacrifice* (New York/Washington, DC: National Committee of the Lutheran World Federation, 1967) 45–74.

11. For Trent on the Eucharist as sacrament, see DS 1651–1661 and on sacrifice see DS 1751–1759.

12. "Sacraments, Signs of Faith," in Piet Fansen, *Hermeneutics of the Councils*, collected by H. E. Mertens and F. De Graeve (Leuven: University Press, 1985) 418.

13. Ibid.

14. "Decree on the Most Holy Sacrament of the Eucharist," Session 13, October, 1551. Translation from *Decrees of the Ecumenical Councils*, ed. Norman P. Tanner (Washington, DC: Georgetown University Press, 1990) II:693.

15. The text reads "in missa...offerri Deo verum et proprium sacrificium" (DS 1751).

16. James F. McHugh, "The Sacrifice of the Mass at the Council of Trent," in Stephen W. Sykes, ed., *Sacrifice and Redemption*, Durham Essays in Theology (Cambridge/New York: Cambridge University Press, 1991) 157.

17. Ibid. 157–81.

18. The outline of the Tridentine "Teaching and Canons on the Most Holy Sacrifice of the Mass" are as follows:

DS 1738: Introduction
1739–1742: Chap. 1 On the Institution of the Mass as Sacrifice
1743: Chap. 2 The Visible Sacrifice Is Propitiatory for the Living and the Dead

1744: Chap. 3 On Masses in Honor of the Saints
1745: Chap. 4 On the Canon of the Mass
1746: Chap. 5 On Solemn Ceremonies of the Mass
1747: Chap. 6 On a Mass at which Only the Priest Communicates
1748: Chap. 7 On the Water Mixed with Wine
1749: Chap. 8 On Not Celebrating Mass in Various Tongues
1750: Chap. 9 Prologue to the Following Canons

Canons on the Mass as Sacrifice
1751–1759: Canons One to Nine

19. Cites the Constitution on the Sacred Liturgy, *Sacrosanctum Concilium*, n. 47.

20. Recall the discussion in Model Six regarding consecrating bread at each Mass for the faithful, as asserted from Benedict XIV on.

21. See Hans Urs Von Balthasar, "The Mass: A Sacrifice of the Church?" in *Explorations in Theology III: Creator Spirit* (San Francisco: Ignatius Press, 1993) 185–243.

22. See Susan Wood, *Sacramental Orders* (Collegeville: The Liturgical Press, 2001) and Avery Dulles, *The Priestly Office* (New York/Mahwah, NJ: Paulist Press, 1997).

23. Xavier Leon-Dufour, *Sharing the Eucharistic Bread: The Witness of the New Testament*, trans. Matthew O'Connell (New York/Mahwah, NJ: Paulist Press, 1987).

**Model Nine: Active Presence**

1. I say "most" here because some very important churches, for example cathedrals and basilicas (e.g., St. Peter's in Rome) did not have tabernacles placed on the main altar but rather in side chapels or on side altars. Of course, the phenomenon of having more than one altar in a church building is itself an anomaly. Clearly "required" for the celebration of the Eucharist privately, such a proliferation of altars in churches is no longer needed. As stated clearly in *Built of Living Stones*, "in new churches there is to be only one altar so that it 'may be a sign of the one Christ and the one Eucharist of the Church'" (n. 56, citing the GIRM, n. 303). (Where *Built of Living Stones* used the former GIRM translation, we have supplied the final, approved translation here.)

2. See USCCB website, http://nccbuscc.org/dpp/realpresence.htm

3. See *On the Eucharist in Its Relationship to the Church*, n. 15, where the pope states that regarding real presence the Tridentine decree asserts that the church "has fittingly and properly called this change transubstantiation." He goes on to quote Pope Paul VI "that in objective reality, independently of our mind, the bread and wine have ceased to exist after the consecration, so that the adorable body and blood of the Lord Jesus from that moment on are really before us under the sacramental species of bread and wine."

4. Much of what follows is based on Alexander Gerken's *Teologia dell' eucaristia*, 65–104.

5. Among other convenient sources for a commentary on the major mystagogic catecheses of the fourth century (from Sts. Cyril of Jerusalem, John Chrysostom, Ambrose, and Theodore of Mopsuestia, see High Riley, *Christian Initiation: A Comparative Study of the Interpretation of Baptismal Liturgy*, Studies in Christian Antiquity, n. 17 (Washington, DC: The Catholic University of America Press, 1974) and Edward Yarnold, *The Awe-Inspiring Rites of Initiation: Baptismal Homilies of the Fourth Century* (St. Paul: Slough, 1972).

6. See, Enrico Mazza, *Mystagogy: A Theology of Liturgy in the Patristic Era*, trans. Matthew O'Connell (New York: Pueblo Publishing Co., 1989) 1.

7. As already cited in Model Two, "The Church's Eucharist," see the writings of John Bossy, "The Mass as Social Institution 1200–1700," *Past and Present* 100 (1983) 29–61 and *Christianity in the West 1400–1700* (New York: Oxford University Press, 1985).

8. The titles for the treatises by Paschasius Radbertus and Ratramnus are the same: *De Corpore et Sanguine Domini*.

9. See Nathan Mitchell, *Cult and Controversy: The Worship of the Eucharist Outside of Mass*, 73–86.

10. Ibid., for a consideration and summary of various ways that the term "substance" was understood in this period, 137–42.

11. In the "Introduction" to the Blackfriars edition of the *Summa*, the editor astutely observes that Aquinas's "treatise does not offer a complete eucharistic theology. The Church has existed for a mere two thousand years and it is unlikely that a complete theology—in any field of dogma—will ever be achieved. There are many approaches to the great dogmas of the faith and no one generation and no one mind can hope to combine them all." See *Summa Theologiae*, vol. 58, *The Sacrament of the Eucharist* (London: Blackfriars/New York: McGraw Hill, 1975) xix.

12. *Summa Theologiae*, Third Part, q. 73, article 2.

13. *Summa Theologiae*, Third Part, q. 74, article 1.

14. Hence the importance of the way in which Pope John Paul II's letter on the Eucharist is structured: chapter 1 on the mystery of the Eucharist, chapter 2 on how the Eucharist builds the church, chapter 3 the Eucharist and ecclesial communion, and chapter 4 on the apostolicity of the Eucharist and the church.

15. *Summa Theologiae*, Third Part, q. 60–65.

16. Norman Tanner, "The Eucharist in the Ecumenical Councils," *Gregorianum* 82, 1 (2001) 37–49, at 38.

17. See the enormously important work edited by Tanner, *Decrees of the Ecumenical Councils*, 2 vols. (Washington, DC: Georgetown University Press, 1990).

18. Among others, see, Andre Duval, "Le culte eucharistique" in *Les sacrements au concile du Trente* (Paris: Les Editions du Cerf, 1985) 11–151.

19. This is what came to be called the "Easter duty."

20. Recall that these terms are from the cluster of terms derived from the *berakah* tradition, that is, they were the customary ways of ending Jewish prayers of blessing, and thus the eucharistic prayer(s) that evolved from them.

21. The outline of the contents of the decrees of Trent on the Eucharist as Sacrament are:

> DS 1635—Introduction
> 1636–1637: Chap. 1 On the Real Presence of Christ in the Eucharistic Sacrament
> 1638: Chap. 2 On the Institution of This Sacrament
> 1639–1641: Chap. 3 On the Excellence of the Most Holy Eucharist Above Other Sacraments
> 1642: Chap. 4 On Transubstantiation
> 1643–1644: Chap. 5 On the Cult and Veneration of This Sacrament
> 1645: Chap. 6 On Taking the Eucharist to the Sick
> 1646–1647: Chap. 7 On Preparing Oneself for Receiving Eucharist
> 1648–1650: Chap. 8 On the Use of This Wonderful Sacrament

The *Canons* from Trent on the Most Holy Sacrament of the Eucharist are found in DS 1651–1661, Canons 1 to 11.

22. Tanner, Trent, p. 693.

23. Ibid., p. 695. The Latin text for the last sentence reads: "Quae conversio convenienter et proprie a sancta catholica ecclesia transsubstantiatio est appellata."

24. When it comes to summarizing the canons of the council of Trent, it is important to recall that they are most often framed in negatives, ending with "let them be condemned." In what follows I will offer the teachings in a positive set of assertions.

25. Johann Auer, *A General Doctrine of the Sacraments and the Mystery of the Eucharist*, trans. Erasmo Leiva-Merikakis and ed. Hugh Riley (Washington, DC: The Catholic University of America Press, 1995; German original 1971 and 1980) 231.

26. As I noted when discussing Model Two, "The Church's Eucharist," that the Eucharist was traditionally referred to as the "mystical body of Christ" and that the church was "the body of Christ" are argued carefully and persuasively by Paul McPartland in *The Eucharist Makes the Church: Henri de Lubac and John Zizioulas in Dialogue* and *Sacrament of Salvation*. But the point I wish to make here is that the liturgical movement was both thoroughly scriptural and thoroughly ecclesiological. *Mystici Corporis* was published in 1943.

27. *Mediator Dei* was published in 1947. See helpful insights on this document as leading to the Vatican II and post–Vatican II explications of Christ's presence, in Michael Witczak, "The Manifold Presence of Christ in the Liturgy," 680–702.

28. Among the more important documents was the 1958 decree from the (then) Congregation for Rites on allowing laypersons to be engaged in parts of the liturgy. For more on these statements and the progress toward the common use of the vernacular in the liturgy, see Keith F. Pecklers, *Dynamic Equivalence: The Living Language of Christian Worship* (Collegeville: The Liturgical Press, 2003) chapters 3 and 5.

29. A convenient summary is found in Edward Schillebeeckx, "Transubstantiation, Transfinalization, Transignification," in *Living Bread, Saving Cup*, ed. R. Kevin Seasoltz (Collegeville: The Liturgical Press, 1987, 1982) 175–189.


## Model Ten: Work of the Holy Spirit

1. This apostolic constitution was entitled *Missale Romanum* and was dated April 3, 1969, which was Holy Thursday that year.

2. Translation from *Sacramentary for Mass*, 9*.

3. This is not to say that the text in its entirety was fixed. As we will note, certain sections were changed depending on a particular feast or season.

4. This is kind of investigation has led to the revision of a number of liturgies across denominational lines. Among them are the 1978 *Lutheran Book of Worship* and the 1979 *American Episcopal Book of Common Prayer.*

5. Our discussion in this chapter will emphasize the three prayers added to the Roman rite when it was revised in 1969. However, what is said here can well apply to the eucharistic prayers added since then, e.g., three for Masses with Children, two for Masses of Reconciliation (one of which will be cited) and the more recent "Eucharistic Prayer for Various Needs and Occasions."

6. Among others, see Paul Bradshaw, *Search for the Origins of Christian Worship*, 2nd ed. (New York: Oxford, 2002).

7. This is an enormously rich field of inquiry, because it deals with a number of issues including the extent to which early liturgical texts were "normative" and what, in effect, "normative" meant. See, among other references, the brief discussion of this Jewish practice in Jerome Kodell, *The Eucharist in the New Testament*, and the comments by R. C. D. Jasper and G. J. Cuming in their introductory remarks on Jewish prayers and the *Didache* in their collection of eucharistic prayers, *Prayers of the Eucharist: Early and Reformed*, 7–24.

8. The use of "in general" is meant to signal that there are various manuscript traditions for this text and to respect the ongoing scholarly debates about the exact contents of this prayer.

9. The translation is from Jasper and Cuming, *Prayers of the Eucharist*, 31–38.

10. For a thorough treatment of the meaning of this hymn and its entrance into the eucharistic anaphora, see Bryan D. Spinks, *The Sanctus in the Eucharistic Prayer*.

11. In fact, scholars debate whether the text refers explicitly to the Spirit's being invoked to transform the bread and wine into Christ's body and blood.

12. Commentary from Jasper and Cuming, *Prayers of the Eucharist*, 67.

13. Louis Bouyer, *Eucharist: Theology and Spirituality of the Eucharistic Prayer*, 245–46.

14. It is notable that the greeting is adapted from 2 Corinthians 13:13 and states: "The grace of almighty God, the love of our Lord Jesus Christ..." as opposed to the scriptural text "The grace of our Lord Jesus Christ..." Certainly this is an instance where the *lex orandi* was adjusted to suit the author's concern for a carefully articulated trinitarian theology.

15. The translation below is taken from Jasper and Cuming, *Prayers of the Eucharist*, 163–67.

16. See, among others, Cipriano Vagaggini, *The Canon of the Mass and Liturgical Reform*, trans., Peter Coughlan (Staten Island, NY: Alba House, 1967).

17. See the very helpful comments in Dominic E. Serra, "The Roman Canon: The Theological Significance of Its Structure and Syntax," *Ecclesia Orans* 20 (2003) 99–128.

18. More recently, some authors have so emphasized the antiquity and tradition of this prayer that they have called into question the orthodoxy and suitability of the prayers added to the Roman rite after Vatican II. This controversy reached such a level of importance that Bishop David Foley of Birmingham, Alabama, asked the Congregation for Divine Worship and the Discipline of the Sacraments to clarify the value of these prayers. Needless to say, the Congregation indicated that all approved eucharistic prayers were equally valid and useful. See, "Documentation," *Antiphon* 5:1 (2000) 47–48.

19. One of the more useful adjustments that has been proposed for recent English language vernacular translations to come from ICEL is that presidential prayers that ended with the phrase "we ask this...who lives and reigns with you and the Holy Spirit" will now become "in the unity of the Holy Spirit," which is both a more accurate translation and a more adequate reflection of the whole theology of liturgical participation.

20. The phrase was not found in the first editions of the revised GIRM but it was added to the final version and is now part of the official revised GIRM. See the discussion of the various editions of what eventually became GIRM 2002 in my article "Overview of GIRM," *Liturgical Ministry* 12 (Summer 2003) 121–32.

21. Among those who fiercely oppose splitting up the prayer into sections is Aidan Kavanagh.

22. See the 1978 *Lutheran Book of Worship* and the 1979 *American Episcopal Book of Common Prayer* for the Hippolytus text.

23. The gesture was also present in the Roman Canon at the words beginning with "Vouchsafe..." which is why some interpreted this to be an implicit *epiclesis* of the Holy Spirit.

24. It is most interesting that St. Cyril of Jerusalem places emphasis on both the *epiclesis* and the words of institution in his *Mystagogic Catecheses*.

Taken from *Mystagogic Catechesis III:*
On the Holy Chrism

But beware of supposing this to be plain ointment. For as the Bread of the Eucharist, after the invocation of the Holy

Ghost, is mere bread no longer, but the Body of Christ, so also this holy ointment is no more simply ointment, nor (so to say) common, after the invocation, but the gift of Christ; and by the presence of His Godhead, it causes in us the Holy Ghost. It is symbolically applied to thy forehead and thy other senses; and while thy body is anointed with visible ointment, thy soul is sanctified by the Holy and life-giving spirit.

From *Mystagogic Catechesis IV:*
On the Eucharistic Food

This teaching of the Blessed Paul is alone sufficient to give you a full assurance concerning those Divine Mysteries, which when ye are vouchsafed, ye are of *the same body* and blood with Christ. For he has just distinctly said, *That our Lord Jesus Christ the same night in which he was betrayed, took bread, and when he had given thanks He brake it, and said, Take, eat, this is My Body: and having taken the cup and given thanks, He said, Take, drink, this is My Blood.* Since then He Himself has declared and said of the Bread, *This is My Body*, who shall dare to doubt any longer? And since He has affirmed and said, *This is My Blood*, who shall ever hesitate, saying that it is not His blood?

Translation from F. L. Cross (ed. and trans.), *St. Cyril of Jerusalem's Lectures on the Christian Sacraments* (London: SPCK, 1966) 65, 67–68.

## Conclusion: A Liturgical Eucharistic Spirituality

1. This is the title of a book I authored some years ago about the relationship among these terms. I reprise the main distinctions I made in that book and which I have subsequently refined. See *Liturgy, Prayer and Spirituality* (New York/Mahwah, NJ: Paulist Press, 1984) and *Context and Text: Method in Liturgical Theology*, chapter 8.

2. Much of this text is taken from the Constitution on the Sacred Liturgy, *Sacrosanctum Concilium*, specifically n. 10 and n. 102, as well as from the Decree on the Ministry and Life of Priests, *Presbyterorum Ordinis*, n. 5.

3. See Edward Kilmartin's essay on the presentation of the gifts entitled "The Sacrifice of Thanksgiving and Social Justice," in *Liturgy and*

*Social Justice*, ed. Mark Searle (Collegeville: The Liturgical Press, 1980) 53–71.

4. See, for example, the 1989 statement by Patriarch Dimitrios, *Orthodoxy and the Ecological Crisis* (Gland, Switzerland: World Conservation Center, 1989) and *So That God's Creation Might Live: The Orthodox Church Responds to the Ecological Crisis*, Proceedings of the Inter-Orthodox Conference on Environmental Protection, The Orthodox Academy of Crete, 1991 (Constantinople: Ecumenical Patriarchate, 1992).

5. Admittedly, sometimes this proclamation is rather brief and attenuated, as, for example, in the celebration of the rite for individual penance.

6. Quoted in *The Catechism of the Catholic Church*, n. 1397.

7. Note that this is not the translation from the *Sacramentary for Mass*.

# INDEX